World Ordering

Drawing on evolutionary epistemology, process ontology, and a social-cognition approach, this book suggests "cognitive evolution," an evolutionary-constructivist social and normative theory of change and stability of international social orders. It argues that practices and their background knowledge survive preferentially; communities of practice serve as their vehicle; and social orders evolve. As an evolutionary theory of world ordering, which does not borrow from the natural sciences, it explains why certain configurations of practices organize and govern social orders epistemically and normatively, and why and how these configurations evolve from one social order to another. Suggesting a multiple and overlapping international social orders approach, the book uses three running cases of contested orders – Europe's contemporary social order, the cyberspace order, and the corporate order – to illustrate the theory. Based on the concepts of "common humanity" and "epistemological security," the author also submits a normative theory of "better" practices and of bounded progress.

EMANUEL ADLER is the Andrea and Charles Bronfman Chair of Israeli Studies and Professor of Political Science at the University of Toronto, and Honorary Professor at the University of Copenhagen. He is also a Fellow of the Royal Society of Canada and of the European Academy of Sciences. His publications include *Security Communities* (co-edited with Michael Barnett, Cambridge University Press, 1998) and *International Practices* (co-edited with Vincent Pouliot, Cambridge University Press, 2011).

Cambridge Studies in International Relations: 150

Global Norms with a Local Face

Cambridge Studies in International Relations is a joint initiative of Cambridge University Press and the British International Studies Association (BISA). The series aims to publish the best new scholarship in international studies, irrespective of subject matter, methodological approach or theoretical perspective. The series seeks to bring the latest theoretical work in International Relations to bear on the most important problems and issues in global politics.

Cambridge Studies in International Relations

149 *Brian C. Rathbun reasoning of state* Realists and romantics in international relations

148 *Silviya Lechner and Mervyn Frost Practice theory and international relations*

147 *Bentley Allan Scientific cosmology and international orders*

146 *Peter J. Katzenstein and Lucia A. Seybert (eds.) Protean power* Exploring the uncertain and unexpected in world Politics

145 *Catherine Lu justice and reconciliation in world politics*

144 *Ayşe Zarakol (ed.) Hierarchies in world politics*

143 *Lisbeth Zimmermann Global norms with a local face* Rule-of-law promotion and norm-translation

142 *Alexandre Debs and Nuno P. Monteiro Nuclear Politics* The Strategic Causes of Proliferation

141 *Mathias Albert A theory of world politics*

140 *Emma Hutchison Affective communities in world politics* Collective emotions after trauma

139 *Patricia Owens Economy of force* Counterinsurgency and the historical rise of the social

138 *Ronald R. Krebs Narrative and the making of US national security*

137 *Andrew Phillips and J. C. Sharman International order in diversity* War, trade and rule in the Indian Ocean

136 *Ole Jacob Sending, Vincent Pouliot and Iver B. Neumann (eds.) Diplomacy and the making of world politics*

135 *Barry Buzan and George Lawson The global transformation* History, modernity and the making of international relations

134 *Heather Elko McKibben State strategies in international bargaining* Play by the rules or change them?

133 *Janina Dill Legitimate targets?* Social construction, international law, and US bombing

Series list continues after index

World Ordering

A Social Theory of Cognitive Evolution

Emanuel Adler

University of Toronto

CAMBRIDGE
UNIVERSITY PRESS

University Printing House, Cambridge CB2 8BS, United Kingdom

One Liberty Plaza, 20th Floor, New York, NY 10006, USA

477 Williamstown Road, Port Melbourne, VIC 3207, Australia

314–321, 3rd Floor, Plot 3, Splendor Forum, Jasola District Centre, New Delhi – 110025, India

79 Anson Road, #06–04/06, Singapore 079906

Cambridge University Press is part of the University of Cambridge.

It furthers the University's mission by disseminating knowledge in the pursuit of education, learning, and research at the highest international levels of excellence.

www.cambridge.org
Information on this title: www.cambridge.org/9781108419956
DOI: 10.1017/9781108325615

First published 2019

Printed and bound in Great Britain by Clays Ltd, Elcograf S.p.A.

A catalogue record for this publication is available from the British Library.

Library of Congress Cataloging-in-Publication Data
Names: Adler, Emanuel, author.
Title: World ordering : a social theory of cognitive evolution / Emanuel Adler.
Description: Cambridge : Cambridge University Press, 2019. |
Series: Cambridge studies in international relations
Identifiers: LCCN 2018034221 | ISBN 9781108419956 (hardback) |
ISBN 9781108412674 (paperback)
Subjects: LCSH: International relations–Sociological aspects. | International relations–Philosophy. | Social constructionism. | BISAC: POLITICAL SCIENCE / International Relations / General.
Classification: LCC JZ1251 .A26 2019 | DDC 306.2–dc23
LC record available at https://lccn.loc.gov/2018034221

ISBN 978-1-108-41995-6 Hardback
ISBN 978-1-108-41267-4 Paperback

Contents

Acknowledgments *page* vi

Prologue: The Crux of the Matter 1

Part I Social Constructivism as Cognitive Evolution 11

1 Samurai Crabs and International Social Orders 13

2 Evolutionary Ontology: From Being to Becoming 45

3 Evolutionary Epistemology 77

4 Practices, Background Knowledge, Communities of Practice, Social Orders 109

Part II Cognitive Evolution Theory and International Social Orders 135

5 International Social Orders 137

6 Cognitive Evolution Theory: Social Mechanisms and Processes 165

7 Agential Social Mechanisms 198

8 Creative Variation 219

9 Selective Retention 234

10 Better Practices and Bounded Progress 265

Epilogue: World Ordering 295

References 304

Index 364

Acknowledgments

Because this book is about how thinking involves relationships – how relationships are about practices and their evolution – it is not surprising that my own thinking and academic practice evolved with and because of relationships. I first began conceiving of cognitive evolution in graduate school forty years ago in close interaction with Ernst Haas, without whom this book would never have happened. I trace my intellectual origins to him. The ideas themselves evolved through universities I worked at, projects I was involved with, articles and books I wrote, conferences I attended, and most important, interactions with colleagues around the world and with my graduate students. Throughout all this time, I've had the good luck to accumulate numerous debts. If, because of the book's long gestation, or for reasons of mere distraction, I forgot to mention individuals and institutions who deserve acknowledgment, I apologize.

I thank my graduate students who made this long journey much more meaningful, helping me to bring the book to fruition from a love for teaching and learning. In particular, Gustavo Carvalho, Steven Loleski, Craig Smith, and Simon Pratt, four of my research assistants, played a major role in putting together the book's empirical illustrations. I am immensely indebted to their knowledge, research, large amounts of material, lengthy discussions, and positive dispositions. My editor and friend Jacqueline Larson made the book much more readable by eliminating the many traces of Spanish and Hebrew in my use of the English language. Two reviewers gave me excellent suggestions for revision, most of which I followed. The book improved because of them. I am grateful to John Haslam, who, as always, provided encouragement and guidance. Robert Dreesen read a messy first draft and pointed out its flaws. He and Patrick McCartan encouraged me to write the book.

This journey would have been different, duller, and probably would have headed in a different direction had it not been for Janice Stein and Michael Barnett, two of my best friends and colleagues, whose intellectual inspiration and continuous encouragement were essential for me to write this book. Janice was instrumental for my move to the University of Toronto almost twenty years ago, which opened a new scholarly world and access to excellent students and colleagues who knowingly or unknowingly contributed to this book. Charles Bronfman established the Bronfman Chair of Israeli Studies and therefore made writing this book possible. I also owe a huge intellectual debt to my good friend Chris Reus-Smit, who was my "compass." He read all the drafts and consistently provided feedback and advice that always pointed in the right direction. In 2015, Chris organized a book workshop at Queensland University in Brisbane, Australia, where I received excellent comments that forced me back to the drawing board to revise the manuscript one more time. In particular, I thank Robyn Eckersley, Colin Wight, Toni Erskine, Jason Sharman, Ian Hall, and Renee Jeffrey, who discussed different chapters. Among many of the workshop's participants whose comments were useful, I thank Tim Dunne, Andy Hurrell, Richard Devetak, Andrew Philipps, Heather Rae, Richard Shapcott, and Martin Weber.

Vincent Pouliot read all the drafts and has been providing invaluable feedback and advice since we first met more than a decade ago. Vincent, together with Markus Kornprobst and Piki Ish Shalom, all former students and currently colleagues and friends, appointed themselves as a "junta" that organized a festschrift conference in 2017. With many former and current students, as well as colleagues and friends all in one room, the feedback I received on the book was invaluable. In addition to the members of the "junta," I especially want to highlight Chris Reus-Smit (again), Stefano Guzzini, Michael Barnett, Janice Stein, Peter Katzenstein, Peter Haas, and Alena Drieschova, who wrote papers and provided excellent feedback and advice that sent me to revise the manuscript still once more. Their comments, along with Chuck Beitz's, were important for conceiving Chapter 10, where I suggest a normative theory to supplement cognitive evolution's analytical theory.

Of the many colleagues and friends at the University of Toronto, I will single out David Cameron, Rob Vipond, Pekka Sinervo, and Louis Pauly. Lou was also my pal as co-editor of *International Organization*, which become another milestone in the book's journey because it taught me a lot about the field of international relations. I am also very grateful to Stephen Toope, who, as former director of the Munk School of Global Affairs and Public Policy, provided intellectual guidance and financial support, and to Steven Bernstein, Matt Hoffmann, Lilach Gilady, Seva Gunitsky, Teresa Kramarz, Wendy Wong, Bob Brym, Jutta Brunnée, and John Lindsay. I thank my former students Alena Drieschova, Corneliu Bjola, Ruben Zaiotti, Nisha Shaw, Alanna Krolikowski, Joelle Dumouchel,

Patricia Greve, and David Polanski, as well as my current students Maika Sondarjee, Michael Faubert, Steven Loleski, Michael Faubert, and Ryder McKeown. Through their work and our exchanges, they have contributed to my own thinking on cognitive evolution and practice theory.

My graduate students at the International Relations Department of the Hebrew University were among the first to be exposed to the idea of cognitive evolution. I learned from them and am particularly grateful to Piki Ish Shalom, Tal Dingott, Raffaella Del Sarto, Amir Lupovici, Emily Landau, Tal Sadeh, Tommy Steiner, Arie Kacowicz, and Orit Gazit. I am also grateful to the late Yaacov Bar Siman Tov, Yaacov Vertzberger, Moshe Hirsch, and Alfred Tovias. I especially want to mention Yaron Ezrahi, whose brilliant mind I mined.

While still a student in Berkeley and then throughout my career, I received support and advice and learned a lot from my good friend Beverly Crawford. She and I first conceived of minimalist progress in IR. I developed many of my ideas on progress and humanist realism together with her – she was my harshest critc but also my greatest enthusiast. I thank colleagues who contributed to Bev's and my edited book on progress in IR, particularly Jack Donnelly, Peter Haas, John Ruggie, and Ben Schiff, for inspiring my ideas on progress. John Ruggie, and his lifetime work on "what makes the world hang together," was one of the main inspiration sources for this book. In the late 1980s I spent two years as a fellow of the Center of Science and International Affairs (CSIA) at Harvard University, where I first published on cognitive evolution. I am especially grateful to Joe Nye and Thomas Schelling for intellectual inspiration. Tom was one of my mentors then, and I am sure that he was surprised when, in an International Studies Association (ISA) panel in his honor years later, I claimed that deep down he was a constructivist. My ideas on cognitive evolution kept evolving as a consequence of my cooperation with Peter Haas in putting together a special issue of *International Organization* on epistemic communities in 1992, and then my cooperation with Michael Barnett on an edited book on security communities, which we published in 1998.

My many conversations with Karl Deutsch deeply enriched me and my understanding of security communities and cognitive evolution. In 1998–99, I started to conceive the book in its present form while taking a sabbatical year at the Weatherhead Center for International Affairs (WCFIA), Harvard University. I still remember when I discovered by chance the concept of communities of practice, and how I could not sleep that night because of my excitement at the implications. The concept helped organize many of my loose thoughts on cognitive evolution. I am grateful to the then-director of WCFIA, Jorge Dominguez, and to Herbert Kelman, from whom I learned much.

In 2011, I first presented some rough ideas on the book at an inaugural lecture for an honorary professorship I received from the Political Science Department at Copenhagen University. I am very grateful to Lene Hansen, Rebecca Adler-Nissen, Stefano Guzzini, Trine Flockhart, and James Der Derian for their critical but extremely useful feedback and suggestions.

Two sabbatical years gave me the opportunity to write the first draft. In 2012–13, I was a Senior Braudel Fellow at the European University Institute (EUI). I am grateful to Laszo Brust for the opportunity to become a Braudel Fellow and for his comments on my work. I also thank Fritz Kratochwil, Nikolas Rajkovic, Philippe Schmitter, Sven Steinmo, Raffaella Del Sarto, Federica Bicchi, Hanspeter Kriesi, Ulrich Krotz, and Gerald McDermott, with whom I enjoyed useful conversations on my book plans. Gabriella Unger, Maureen Lechleitner, and Filipa de Sousa provided useful staff support. In 2014–15, I spent another year, this time in the Kolleg-Forschergruppe, the Transformative Power of Europe (KFG) program at Freie Universitat, directed by Thomas Risse and Tanja Börzel. There, I wrote most of the first draft. I am immensely grateful to Thomas and Tanja for giving me this opportunity and also for their useful feedback on my project, which I presented when it still was in a preliminary stage. KFG fellows, too many to mention, also provided good advice. I thank Hans Joas, Michael Zürn, Andrea Ribeiro Hoffmann, Tobias Berger, Wolfram Kaiser, and Gil Murciano, who offered useful comments. Astrid Roos, Anne Morgestern, and Torsten Spickhofen provided wonderful administrative support.

I thank the Centre for International and Policy Affairs at the University of Ottawa, particularly Michael Williams; the Institut Barcelona D'estudis Internacionals (IBEI); Universitat Pompeu-Fabra, Barcelona, particularly Esther Barbe; the Hebrew University and the Halbert Program, particularly Moshe Hirsch and Jutta Brunnée; and the Centre for International Governance Innovation, University of Waterloo, particularly Ambassador Jorge Heine for inviting me to give talks on cognitive evolution theory.

In 2017, I gave two talks on cognitive evolution and democracy, one of them by invitation at the Conference of the Association of Latin American Political Scientists (ALACIP), in Montevideo, Uruguay. I am immensely grateful to my friend Adolfo Garcé, with whom I have been speaking about cognitive evolution ever since, for inviting me and for his invaluable feedback. I gave the other lecture at the Conference of the Society of Argentinian Political Scientists (SAAP) in Buenos Aires. Special thanks go to Emanuel Porcelli and Daniela Perrotta for their kind invitation and for extensive feedback on the talk. I profusely thank

Nicolas Saldias, who offered invaluable research assistance in preparing my talks. I am happy to have helped establish a bridge to these countries with cognitive evolution and practice theory ideas, and hope that my book will be published in Spanish, not only for the sake of knowedge diffusion but also because "a mucha honra soy Uruguayo."

I am grateful to Alex Wendt, Fritz Kratochwil (again), Christian Büger, Anna Leander, Jeff Checkel, Alexandra Gheciu, Yosef Lapid, Jennifer Mitzen, Antje Wiener, William Thompson, Charles Kupchan, Jean-Marc Coicaud, Huen Fung-Khong, Barry Buzan, Ole Weaver, Janice Bially Mattern, Iver Neumann, Ole Jacob Sending, Michael Williams (again), Raymond Duvall, Daniel Levine, Nicholas Bremberg, and Magnus Ekengren for their comments and advice at different stages of this project.

I thank the Charles Bronfman Foundation; the Center for Science and International Affairs at the Kennedy School of Government, and the Weatherhead Center for International Affairs (both at Harvard University); the Munk School of Global Affairs and Public Policy at the University of Toronto; the European University Institute; and the Kolleg-Forschergruppe, the Transformative Power of Europe at Freie Universitat for financial support.

In my eclectic and synthetic approach, I stand on the shoulders of giants without whom I would not have been able to develop cognitive evolution theory. The particular giants are Ernst B. Haas, Ilia Prigogine, Karl Deutsch, Kenneth Boulding, Ludwik Fleck, Karl Popper, Thomas Schelling, John Searle, Stephen Toulmin, and Etienne Wenger. Because of Robert Pirsig's *Zen and the Art of Motorcycle Maintenance*, which I read back in 1976, I had my first "aha" moment on the construction of social reality (a.k.a. the motorcycle).

Finally, my deepest gratitude goes to my family. Sylvia, my wife, stoically endured my struggle to write this book and accompanied me on the wild ride. Shirli, my daughter, Nadav and Jonathan, my sons, and Daniel, Elisha, Nina, and Lily, my delightful grandchildren, patiently waited for the moment that I'd be finished writing this book. Without their love, support, and understanding this work would have never seen the light of day. I dedicate it to them, and to my students, whom I also consider part of a larger family.

Prologue
The Crux of the Matter

We usually identify international orders with stability and established arrangements of units and institutionalization. But international orders also constantly change and sometimes evolve into new orders. When international relations (IR) scholars focus on international order transformation (e.g., Cox and Sinclair 1996; Nexon 2009; Phillips 2011), with a few exceptions (Pouliot 2016; Reus-Smit 2013a), they study either stability *or* transformation, but not how both occur simultaneously. Some scholars understand stability as the opposite of change (Ringmar 2014) and consider change to be either the transition between orders (Ikenberry 2001) or their opposite: "disorder" (Bull 1977). I aim to remedy the relative lack of focus on both change and stability with an approach that considers "order through fluctuations" (Prigogine 1980). I focus mainly on a range of spatially, temporally, and functionally overlapping international social orders that cut across domestic, international, transnational, and supranational boundaries.

This book aims to explain change and stability in international social orders as a subset of change and stability in social orders more generally. I suggest an *evolutionary constructivist* social theory and its metaphysical foundations, which I apply to the evolution of international social orders. We may even be able to apply this theory to the evolution of any kind of social order, for example, domestic political orders such as democracy, or to art, health, law, and economics. The IR discipline has been reluctant to engage in social theory.[1] But explicitly engaging with social theory (Wendt 2015) can enhance our understanding of world politics and, particularly, international social orders' change and stability.

Drawing on a general model of evolutionary change associated with "evolutionary epistemology" and on a processual and interactive ontology, as well as on practice social theory (e.g., Schatzki 2002; Schatzki et al. 2001), I develop an evolutionary theory of change and stability of

[1] For exceptions, see Kratochwil 1989; Wendt 1999; Wight 2006.

international social orders. Because I build on the notion that cognition is social (Fleck 1979; Tomasello et al. 2005; Vygotsky 1978),[2] I call this theory "cognitive evolution" (Campbell 1974b). Social orders originate, derive from, and are constituted constantly by practices, the background knowledge bound with them, and the communities of practice that serve as their vehicles. While American pragmatists (e.g., Dewey 1922) taught us that we know through action and practice, Etienne Wenger (1998a), who together with Jean Lave (1991) developed the concept of "communities of practice," added that we practice in communities. Hans Joas (1996) showed how – because creativity is a socially emergent collective process – self-organizing collectivities, such as communities of practice, creatively learn. *Cognitive evolution thus aims to explain where social orders, and particularly international social orders, come from; how and why the world is organized and governed around certain configurations* (Elias 2000) *of practices rather than others; how, when, and why these configurations evolve from one kind to another; and how all this is related to collective learning.* Cognitive evolution is primarily a constitutive evolutionary social theory of international social ordering – a way to think through the conditions of their possibility – and an explanatory evolutionary social theory of why some social orders evolve instead of others.

It is, however, also a plausibility probe into normative theorizing. I use analytical social theory, namely cognitive evolution, to derive a normative theoretical framework on the propensity for *better practices* to evolve, when enacted, for *bounded progress* (Chapter 10). I therefore couple my (1997) argument about constructivism's analytical "middle ground" with a new evolutionary constructivist argument for a second, normative, middle ground.[3]

[2] My approach to cognition as a social condition does not focus on the individual mind, which is what important theories in cognitive psychology, widely known as "social cognition" (Fiske and Taylor 2013) and "social cognitive theory" (Bandura 2001), do. Instead, I focus on the embodied and participatory aspects of social understanding, namely, on social cognition as constituted by social interaction (Dewey 1922; Fleck 1979; Goffman 1963; Nicolini 2012; Vygotsky 1978), particularly within communities (Lave and Wenger 1991). "An important shift is taking place in social cognition research, away from a focus on the individual mind and toward embodied and participatory aspects of social understanding. Empirical results already imply that social cognition is not reducible to the workings of individual cognitive mechanisms" (De Jaegher et al. 2010, 441. See Tomasello 2009; Tomasello et al. 1993, 2005). Engel, Maye, Kurthen, and König claim that in "cognitive science, we are currently witnessing a 'pragmatic turn,' away from the traditional representation-centered framework towards a paradigm that focuses on understanding cognition as 'enactive,' as skillful activity that involves ongoing interaction with the external world" (2013, 202). See also Bandura 2001; Krueger 2011; Lave 1991; Lemke 1997; Resnick 1991; Wenger 1998a.

[3] I thank Chris Reus-Smit for the invaluable insight that, by following this road, I am "seizing" a second, normative, middle ground.

Cognitive evolution theory claims that practices and the background knowledge bound with them are the structural "stuff" that is passed on in replication in the sociocultural world, that communities of practice are their vehicle, and that practices account for both the consecutive *and* simultaneous change and metastability of social orders in general, and of international social orders in particular. I understand metastability as practices' continuity in a stable state of flow below a sociocognitive threshold. Fluctuations, such as practice learning, negotiation, and contestation, keep social orders in a metastable state.[4] Near thresholds (the fall of the Berlin Wall comes to mind) – a single fluctuation or a combination of them – can become so powerful by positive feedback that an order tips, thus shattering the preexisting field of practices or social order, and leading to its evolution. A new order takes the place of the old one. Liminal states that have changes of flows or trajectories near thresholds, as well as resilience[5] processes, create propensities for either social orders' metastability or evolution. Change and flows occur continuously, even and especially when a social order is presumed to be stable. However, social order evolution is infrequent.

According to cognitive evolution theory, social orders develop, spread, and remain metastable when communities of practice establish themselves, when their background knowledge diffuses and becomes selectively retained, and when their members' expectations and dispositions preferentially survive. The master mechanism for understanding cognitive evolution, and particularly selective retention processes, is *epistemic practical authority*. This authority is made up of deontic power – the structural and agential establishment of status functions, such as rights, obligations, duties requirements, and other entitlements (Searle 1995, 2010). It also involves "performative power" – the capacity "to present a dramatic and credible performance on the world stage" (Alexander 2011, 8), thus bringing epistemic practical recognition to a variety of audiences and stakeholders. Both types of social power refer to capacities and propensities to constitute social reality (Guzzini, personal communication). Together, they explicate *practical meaning fixation*: the structural and agential authoritative ascription of practical meaning to material and social reality, which promotes

4 For an excellent theory of norm contestation, see Wiener 2014, 2018.
5 Resilience is the measure of a social order's ability to absorb change and remain metastable (Adler 2005; Holling 1976; Schoon 2006). I define and refer to resilience in more detail in Chapter 6's last section, and apply the concept in Chapter 9's last section.

practices' horizontal and vertical spread, for instance, the practical meaning fixation of monetary value to a piece of paper.

Three sociostructural mechanisms and four agential social mechanisms play an important role in constituting social ordering and explaining the creative variation and selective retention of social practices, as well as of the background knowledge bound with them. These are, respectively:

1. endogenous collective learning within, competition among, and innovation of practices in communities of practice
2. practice-driven changes and stability in dispositions and expectations
3. transactions, negotiation, contestation, and identification-shaping processes
4. socially generated agents' reflection and judgment
5. practitioners' capacity to affect material and cultural-social environments in desired ways.

Technology, in turn, can exogenously affect all these mechanisms.

The mechanisms listed are part of two key processes associated with cognitive evolution or, more generally, with evolutionary epistemology (Campbell 1960): *creative variation* and *selective retention*. Creative variation from a cognitive-evolutionary perspective means social creation, which can be intentional, but it also derives from the uncertainty and contingency of social life (Katzenstein and Seybert 2018). Thus, epistemic and practice innovation are propensities rather than determinants of change. Agents' creation and innovation becomes social innovation via practice within collective processes that communities of practice help create. Selective retention's main mechanism – the alternative to natural selection in biological evolution – is epistemic practical authority, the legitimate power to rule on the adoption of practices and their meanings. Retention involves the mainly "horizontal" spread of practices across space, for example, across state boundaries, and time – and, as newcomers learn the communities' practices, also the "vertical" spread of practices within communities of practice.

Cognitive evolution theory claims that all practices are normative. Society sets normative standards in and through practice and practitioners' acquired performative knowledge. Norms enter practices, among other ways, through ascription of function, status, and value. They become part of practices' background knowledge and are related to standards of competence and virtue (as in practicing well) and to justification processes (Boltanski and Thévenot 2006). In contrast to views that normative change relates to reason attached to transcendental values, or to values particular to national communities, I make the case that normative standards reside in practices that diffuse by means of communities of practice. While all practices are normative, however, *not all practices are ethical.* This argument opens a space for considering better practices and social orders, as well as bounded progress.

The concepts of better practices and bounded progress transcend unhelpful dichotomies, such as practice approaches and normative approaches. I also mean cosmopolitanism (Beitz 1979; Rawls 1971) and communitarianism (MacIntyre 1981; Taylor 1985; Walzer 1990), transcendental and immanent values, the Enlightenment idea of progress and normative relativism, practice and discourse, interconnectedness and disassociation, and realism and idealism, the latter of which is why I call my approach "humanist realism." My emphasis on better practices is consistent with what I consider to be humanist values beginning with the value of life, which in my view is based on the acknowledgment (Markell 2003) of our "common humanity" (Stuurman 2017). This acknowledgment suggests a reinterpretation of the "golden rule" as *value other human beings' lives as you value your own.* At a minimum, this is what accounts for our common humanity. Equality, liberty, fraternity, and mutual self-respect follow from this golden rule, albeit as a propensity rather than a determinist and teleological process. Bounded progress, however, is also realist because it takes progress as being based on the evolution *away from* humanist values' antithesis, namely, less domination, poverty, and war, and because better practices are not necessarily related to creating a global community.

A bounded idea of progress based on a common humanity ethical value is partial, nonteleological and indeterminist, reversible and contingent, and rests on a practice principle, namely, on practices and interactive learning and contestation in and among communities of practice. Moreover, better practices and bounded progress are more likely to be associated with interconnectedness and horizontal systems of rule rather than with disassociation and vertical systems of rule.[6] While interconnectedness – for example, regional integration and democratic social orders – is a double-edged sword, meaning that it can lead to both bounded progress and regress (Linkater 2011), it is, however, associated primarily, but not exclusively, with informal horizontal systems of rule, in which epistemic practical authority and

6 This view is consistent with Darwin's little-known moral theory of evolution (see Chapter 3, note 11), and more recent findings (Henrich 2016) that explain how the main reason for *Homo sapiens*' success is humans' ability to collectively interconnect and learn from one another.

accountability are distributed horizontally, and the politics associated with them.[7] Disassociation, on the other hand – die-hard, ethnic, religious, and populist nationalism and power politics – is primarily, but not exclusively, associated with vertical/hierarchical systems of rule and the politics associated with them. Horizontal systems of rule, therefore, have the propensity for enhancing human well-being within and across national borders, if, and when, the negative effects of interconnectedness are controlled. Vertical systems of rule and their disassociation practices, on the other hand, tend to underscore a lack of freedom and equality, suffering, and violent coercion. Systems of rule in IR are usually a hybrid of both along a continuum.

Democracy, for example, is mainly about the horizontal distribution, rather than vertical concentration, of power (Bernstein 2018) and epistemic practical authority, which is why, comparatively speaking, it has the propensity of promoting better practices. Moreover, what sustains democratic institutions are knowledge and identity, and primarily practices (Dewey 1916), not all of which are discursive (Habermas 1996). Seen this way, one of the largest threats to a democratic social order is what I call *epistemological insecurity.* Without epistemological security, namely collective trust in a common-sense reality, the distribution of rule becomes precarious; thus, liberal democratic social order may erode.

Cognitive evolution theory suggests a concept of multiple international social orders, which for now I define briefly as configurations of practices that organize social life. Even before, but primarily since the advent of nationalism and liberal internationalism in human history, international social orders have distinctly spanned a spectrum between nationalist and liberal-internationalist practices and communities of practice.[8] My

[7] I thank Stefano Guzzini for the argument that horizontal power and accountability, as much as vertical domination, amount to a system of rule, albeit informal. See Arendt 1965, 174; 1970, 44.

[8] Nationalism and liberal internationalism are individual and collective categories of identification that become institutionalized in the practices of international entities. Namely, national communities (Brubaker 1996, 21) and supranational communities (e.g., the European Union) are dynamic processes of, and entities constituted by, practices. But whereas classical nationalism takes the world as being classified, categorized, and divided exclusively by nations, many of which consider themselves "exceptional," and emphasize practices of disassociation from other nations, liberal internationalism puts a premium on practices of interconnectedness between nations and other entities. International social orders, for the last couple of centuries, have been characterized and constituted by a dialectical relationship between classic-nationalist and liberal-internationalist practices. However, international social orders can be, and at least in the case of the European Union have been, characterized by a mixture between liberal-nationalist and communitarian-internationalist (some call the latter communitarian cosmopolitan) practices (McCormick 2010).

understanding of multilevel (regional and functional) international orders is thus more dynamic and comprehensive than the one suggested by the concepts of "international regimes" (Krasner 1982) or multilevel global governance (Enderlein et al. 2010; Hurrell 2007a).[9] This is the case particularly as communities of practice participate in the joint performance of institutions and organizations that help prevent regional and global chaos (Linklater 2010, 2011).

For example, when observed beyond its reified institutions, the postwar European social order amounts to novel practices of interconnectedness or integration – such as economic, security, citizenship, and human rights – which, in spite of their contested political nature, became selectively retained in communities of practice, their practices, and their normative and practical epistemic intersubjective understandings bound with them. To understand postwar European order, and its bounded progress in preventing interstate war (Adler and Barnett 1998), we therefore have to identify the practices, background knowledge, and communities of practice that made postwar European social order possible: those currently associated with its metastable, albeit increasingly contested condition as well as the practices that are currently challenging Europe's social order.

From a cognitive evolution perspective, the collective learning that helped constitute a European social order based on interconnectedness after World War II is being seriously challenged by alternative practices of disassociation and nationalism, their background knowledge, and the communities of practice that serve as their vehicle. Fluctuations of practices (particularly contestation of the present social order) may be approaching a sociocognitive threshold. If it gets crossed, Europe's social order could tip and evolve. Whether the European social order will evolve or not depends largely on the resilience of interconnectedness practices. Understanding why and when social orders evolve requires us to also identify the alternative set of practices, the background knowledge bound with them, the communities of practice that carry them, and the mechanisms and processes through which they may become dominant.

In a similar way, the corporate social order became possible by the coalescence of a community of practice around a set of core or "anchoring" (Swidler 2001) practices such as the corporation's legal personality. The idea of a company's identity confers on a corporation:

[9] The concept of multiple and overlapping international social orders, while different from the concept of multilevel governance (Zürn 2010), can contribute to better understanding this concept.

(1) a separate legal personality from that of its owners, with its own rights and obligations; (2) the limited liability of its shareholders (who are not liable to compensate creditors with their own assets in case the corporation defaults on its debts); and (3) the separation between the corporation's ownership and management, that is, the delegation of management to a group of agents other than the shareholders. These practices' content was interpreted, contested, and reinterpreted, eventually spreading from within the original geographical area in which they emerged – Great Britain, the United States, and some Western European countries such as France and the Netherlands – to other areas. This is not to say that the spread was uncontested or inevitable. Grasping what the corporate order means today, including the partial change of its ethical practices (a bounded progress of sorts), requires us to identify the core practices and background knowledge that informs corporate order, as well as how they spread and were historically contested or reinforced by actors within and outside corporate communities of practice.

Cognitive evolution theory, while eclectic and building on a variety of sociological, philosophical, political theory, and IR theory-established traditions, suggests a novel way of thinking about social and cultural evolution. By highlighting sociocultural evolution as carried in and by communities of practice, it also suggests a novel way of thinking about social order, change, and metastability, and the role of practices in constructing the social world. Because the concept of communities of practice transcends our understanding of social reality as organized in levels (Onuf 1995), it enables a better understanding of agency and structure. A dynamic cognitive evolutionary social theory adopts a processual or "becoming" ontology, and evolutionary epistemology that, beefed up with complexity-theory concepts, does not rely by analogy, homology, or metaphor (Ma 2016) on natural evolution mechanisms and processes.

A social theory of cognitive evolution can be particularly important and useful to IR theory because the theory's notion of social order remains stuck in a dated debate between materialist and/or utilitarian theories, on the one hand, and holistic normative theories, on the other. Its understanding of change is undertheorized and usually studied as derivative of theoretical agendas that aim to explain something else. Until the recent "practice turn" in IR (Adler and Pouliot 2011a, 2011b; Büger and Gadinger 2015; Neumann 2002), practices were taken as mostly exclusively material outcomes of other factors and were seldom understood as what orders social life or, as Ruggie notably said, as what "makes the world hang together" (1998b).

I wrote this book neither to participate in (let alone to settle) a particular debate now raging in IR nor to replace a particular theory. The book adopts practice social theory (Schatzki et al. 2001) and the "practice turn" in IR (Adler and Pouliot 2011a; Büger and Gadinger 2015; Neumann 2002) – a relational approach (Jackson and Nexon 2009; McCourt 2016) and an evolutionary approach that does not borrow from natural evolution's processes and mechanisms. Cognitive evolution theory, as a specific account of evolutionary constructivism, is distinct from mainstream IR evolutionary approaches (e.g., among others, Axelrod 1984; Cederman 1997; Florini 1996; Gat 2009; Modelski 1990; Spruyt 1994; Sterling-Folker 2001; Tang 2013; Thayer 2004; Thompson 2001) and improves on past constructivist perspectives that invoked cultural evolution (e.g., Wendt 1999).

I recognize that cognitive evolution theory is (1) large-scale in scope; (2) systemic, without hardly invoking the concept of systems; (3) dynamic, trying to explain simultaneously change and stability; (4) general, as applicable to a multitude of social orders across space and time; (5) synthetic in tying together existing knowledge in new ways; (6) novel as a social-science evolutionary theory; and (7) ambitious in attempting to understand the social world and social change. While I would not call cognitive evolution a "grand theory," but rather a theory of world ordering, I nevertheless believe that, though they are rare, grand theories should not be objectionable. Although past IR grand theories (e.g., Bull 1977; Deutsch 1963; Haas 1964; Morgenthau 1949; Waltz 1979; Wendt 1999) did not settle outstanding issues in international politics, they did open new ways of framing IR. They suggested new research programs, elicited new debates, and showed the way to theorize at the middle-range level (Rosenau 1968). I will be pleased if I can achieve some very small portion of this, especially generating criticism and other scholars' attempts to improve and expand the theory.

Although this book has an abundant number of empirical examples, it is primarily theoretical. For reasons of space and expediency, incorporating detailed case studies here was not an option. My aim and hope are that the book will open a space for original empirical work that revises or contests cognitive evolution theory.

I derived cognitive evolution social theory and normative ideas related to it from IR theory, rather than the other way around. Throughout my career, my work has been driven by a desire to develop dynamic theories of change, collective meanings (such as ideology, identity, and scientific knowledge), international relations' epistemic foundations, international practices, and progress in international relations. So while this book is to some extent a synthesis of my past work, it suggests a new theory and looks ahead to new vistas for theoretical reasoning and empirical work.

Finally, but not less important, the book is unusual because it approaches international relations from the perspective of neither states, their interests, resources, and ideologies nor of nonstate actors and international organizations, such as the United Nations. These perspectives are, to use a computer metaphor, international relations' "hardware." Practices, background knowledge, and communities of practice, as well as the social orders they constitute, are international relations' "software." The main purpose of cognitive evolution theory and my use of the concepts of communities of practice, practices, background knowledge, and social order is inspecting what lies behind the computer screen, the 010101, the "ghost in the machine." The computer needs both hardware and software to run. Unlike most studies in IR, cognitive evolution theory uncovers international relations' mostly hidden epistemic and practice instructions, and shows how international social orders remain dynamically metastable or, alternatively, evolve.

Part I

Social Constructivism as Cognitive Evolution

1 Samurai Crabs and International Social Orders

> Thoughts survive if they work, if they propagate, if they find an appropriate milieu, a welcoming territory ... They will only maintain their appeal if they can form some kind of alliance with what we do. (Thrift 1999, 31)

> [Practitioners] draw upon the body of knowledge that is being sustained in and as the local culture; for in the tribe across the river, or the laboratory down the road, or the other social science department along the corridor, a different body of collectively sustained knowledge may be drawn upon by individuals with similarly various eyeballs assisted by equally diverse artifacts. (Barnes 1995, 96)

Carl Sagan (1985) tells the story of an old Japanese legend about an emperor who was also the nominal leader of the Heike clan of samurai. He drowned during a naval battle in 1185. Fishermen descended from the Heike clan still commemorate the battle each year. Whenever they catch a crab with samurai-like markings on its back, they throw it back, believing that the emperor still wanders the bottom of the sea. Sagan explains the curious markings on the crabs as the result of natural selection. Suppose that one crab just happened to acquire this trait and reproduced. The fishermen threw its descendants back into the sea because of the chance resemblance between their backs and the face of a samurai who drowned there. Other crabs were eaten but "samurai crabs" survived preferentially, even though their "wants" had nothing to do with it.

One is tempted to argue that the Heike clan's legend promoted the survival of the samurai crab. The crab had a symbolic meaning and benefit for the Heike, but it flourished as an unintended consequence of their beliefs about the long-dead emperor. The Heike did not have a clue about the causal relationship that favors the crab's survival. More crucial is the notion that, to cause the outcome, the legend must motivate individuals to do what they do, thus keeping the legend alive.

We would be hard pressed to explain the survival of the samurai crab on the basis of some hidden function or need of the Heike clan. Even if it was true that their legend contributed to the attainment of a latent function or need, such as social integration, it cannot explain the unintended consequence of throwing the samurai crab back into the sea, namely, the preferential survival of the species, unless, as Jon Elster (1983) argued, it invokes human intention. On the other hand, a rational-choice explanation would be too thin: even if the samurai crabs had been smaller than regular crabs, the Heikes' behavior was not motivated by food needs or economic reward but by the myth.

Enter cognitive evolution. At one level, there is the case of *natural* (thus physical, though artificial) *selection*, according to which a human myth actually *caused* the selective survival and inheritance of samurai crab *genes*. The crabs were in interaction with an environment that included humans who threw the crabs back into the sea. The unintended consequence was the survival of samurai crab genes. Without the myth there would be fewer or no samurai crabs.

At another level, however, there is *cognitive evolution*, the selective retention of the myth, not only in the minds of individuals (if the myth existed only there it would die together with those individuals), but also in the recurrent practice of throwing samurai crabs back into the sea. The practice survived, not because it fulfilled some social function for the Heike people, as naïve functionalism would presuppose, or to achieve some gain, as rational choice would assume, but for three other reasons. First, the Heike attached symbolic meaning to a species of crab they perceived to resemble the drowned emperor. Second, when they threw the samurai crab into the sea, the Heike acted intentionally and with knowledge. They did what they did because they drew on the myth for their intentional acts. Third, the act of throwing the crab into the sea perpetuated the myth and bequeathed it to future members of the community. Without the crab's markings on its back there would be no myth.

The illustration shows not only how and why a particular type of crab species preferentially survived. It also shows how a particular kind of social order, symbolically represented by the drowning of a Japanese emperor, evolved and was sustained across time by a community of practice whose members, because of what they knew and who they were, threw samurai crabs back into the sea.

Think now about Europe's post–World War II social order, particularly since the creation of the European Union (EU). Europe's social order cognitively evolved; Europe reinvented itself after World War II with an entirely new set of practices. These practices – for example, European multilateralism, citizenship, borders, peacekeeping, enlargement, partnerships, single-market economic practices, human-rights practices, and much more – while currently under evolutionary pressure from competing practices, nevertheless still constitute European order to this day. Of the various social-order alternatives post–World War II Europe could have evolved toward, Europeans adopted an original and unique social order based on a compromise between liberal nationalism and internationalist communitarianism.

An evolved European social order followed the catastrophe of World War II, the Holocaust, and European colonization in the past. But rather than resulting merely from a change of "ideas," for example, the centuries-old "idea of Europe," the social order's evolution meant innovation of *practices*. The innovations had begun before World War II but were applied in practice after it. These practices, which were not copied from other lands and did not diffuse to the European continent from different places or times, accounted for variation – as it were, the creative emergence of a European "samurai crab." But cognitive evolution also meant the preferential selective survival of these practices across time. It required a collective learning process, according to which, in and through practice, integrationist communities of practice established themselves preferentially.

This meant that selected European practices and background knowledge became naturalized and legitimate to a growing number of practitioners across geographic and institutional divides. And they still continue to be adopted by new practitioners. European integrationist background knowledge, however, does not "float freely" (Risse 1994) but, rather, is both bound with the practices themselves and grounded in practitioners' dispositions and expectations. Integrationist background knowledge is institutionalized in organizations (the Council, the Commission, the European Parliament, the European courts, etc.) and in halls of government of Europe's member states. Background knowledge also survives as discourse, legal codes, public policies, plans, books, and other material artifacts like European passports.

Like the Heike people, who have now ceased throwing "Heike crabs" back into the sea, Europe's post–World War II social order may come to an end – it may, but it need not necessarily, evolve again. In other words, because of the contestation within its community of practice, it could evolve in the future toward a dissociation-type social order. This is a result of the European Union's worst crisis of its existence – its institutional faults, the "Euro economic crisis," resurgent populist nationalism, lack of solidarity at the people's level, the vast influx of refugees to Europe, and, therefore, the delegitimization of European integrationist practices. However, the European Union has proven to be resilient to the crisis. Because of the changes that occurred in the United States with the election of President Donald Trump, the EU, with some of its members' exceptions, such as Hungary and Poland, is supporting liberal and multilateral institutions and practices.

The active spread of practices by individual practitioners, and by the organizations that find an institutional "home" within and between communities of practice, promotes the selection of the practices and background knowledge, and the dynamic stabilization of new subjectivities. The selection and inheritance of Europe's novel practices mean that expectations and dispositions survive in practitioners' minds where they become the reasons that European practitioners keep the practices and background knowledge institutionalized, and why the European social order, while struggling, is still in place. By facilitating both the innovation and stabilization of practices, Europe's recently constituted communities of practice structure consciousness and intention, constitute agency, and encourage the evolution and spread of social structure. Cognitive evolution is also facilitated by communities' acquisition of new material and organizational capabilities, or "mobilization" in Bruno Latour's (1999) sense – creating alliances, competing for and mobilizing resources and allegiances, and devising interpretations that align interests with negotiated identities – and by negotiability about, and the reification of, the background knowledge on which Europe's practices were based (Wenger 1998a).

The gradual expansion of computer networking among technical communities as well as the more dramatic expansion of the Internet in the 1990s illustrates the growth of what we know as cyberspace – another example of an evolving social order. The innovative concept of packet switching that breaks data into packets and simultaneously transmits them across available network channels means that communications are more reliable, efficient, and scalable. Packet switching was the foundation for computer networking, and the Advanced Research Projects Agency Network (ARPANET) was among the first networks to put this concept into practice. In the early 1970s, the next step beyond developing an interactive computing network was to think about how to connect different packet-switching networks like those in Europe (Britain's National Physical Laboratory and France's Cyclades) along with ARPA's. Different computer networks needed standard communication protocols to connect to each other and a number of different designs were in use. In June 1973, Vinton Cerf (later recognized as one of the founders of the Internet), organized a conference at Stanford to discuss an emerging consensus in the computer science community around the future Internet, and its universal host protocol called the Transmission Control Protocol (TCP) was selectively retained because of its reliability and scalability (Abbate 1999, 127). Important network design issues had broadened the community of practice to computer engineers outside ARPA, Europeans, and corporate researchers in Xerox PARC. It ultimately took the US Department of Defense in the form of the Defense Communications Agency to impose unified TCP standards once it regained control of the ARPANET in 1975 and reoriented the network to more immediate military operational concerns (ibid., 136). This again broadened the background knowledge of computer networking and sharing files. Military dispositions concerning command and control contested this background knowledge.

At the same time, the first personal computer, the Altair 8800, was introduced. With a growing "hacker" culture making more user-friendly updates, by the late 1970s there was an increasing demand for personal computing (Abbate 1999; Castells 2002). The spread of networking PCs encouraged the growth of a "grassroots tradition of computer networking" with large open-source communities innovating bulletin board systems (BBS), e-mail, UNIX, and then later LINUX operating systems (Castells 2002, 12–14). At the same time, the "spread of computer expertise to a much wider segment of the population" heightened the risk of malicious hackers (Abbate 1999, 138) as depicted by the 1983 film *WarGames* portraying a teen computer whiz hacking into NORAD and nearly triggering World War III. The film captured US President Ronald Reagan's imagination and led him to ask the chairman of the Joint Chiefs of Staff, "Could something like this really happen?" "Mr. President," came the reply, "the problem is much worse than you think" (Kaplan 2016, 2). Ultimately, Reagan signed a presidential directive, NSDD-145, on a "National Policy on Telecommunications and Automated Information Systems Security." National security communities began to contest the emerging open and global Internet by addressing the challenges this consensus presents to national security and law enforcement. Information controls have continued apace to spread globally from basic content filtering or geoblocking to legal/regulatory codes to next-generation targeted information denial (Deibert and Crete-Nishihata 2012; Deibert et al. 2010).

Ultimately, the World Wide Web and later user-friendly browsers like MOSAIC and Netscape coupled with increasingly capable personal computers and operating systems developed by open-source communities were responsible for the dramatic global spread of cyberspace (Abbate 1999; Castells 2002). Multiple competing communities and their expansion continue to define and contest an increasingly securitized, global cyber order.

In contrast to the cyberspace social order, the evolution of the corporate social order happened more gradually. It started with the reinvention of the business organization and its relationship with political communities, where it was entrenched. It also involved reinterpretation of existing practices and background knowledge both inside and outside corporate communities of practice. For instance, the corporation followed other forms of organization in attaining legal personality. We can trace the core practice of limited liability back to organizational types developed in the Italian city-states during the late medieval and early modern eras.

The corporation was a novel form of conducting business and production. From its origins, it not only spread geographically from Western Europe and, later, the United States to other regions, but it eventually came to dominate economic production and social life in the modern world, affecting areas as different as finance, education, social welfare, and even war making. The corporate social order shows that a theory of cognitive evolution can account not only for the selection of the practices that constitute new social orders but also for the way in which communities of practice build over previous background knowledge and practices. Building on previous practices, they translate them to different social and geographical environments, transforming older social orders or making them more resilient to change. As in the story of the Heike clan's selection of the samurai crab, a theory of cognitive evolution aims to explain not only the emergence of social orders, but also how they keep metastable through time.

Practices, Background Knowledge, and Social Orders

Cognitive evolution theory makes seven moves.

1. It substitutes Pierre Bourdieu's (1977, 1990) concept of "habitus," and pragmatism's concept of "habit," with the concept of *practice*.
2. Building partly on John Searle's (1995) concept of the "background," and to a lesser degree on Bourdieu's concept of habitus, it takes *background knowledge* as bound up with the execution of practices.
3. It substitutes Bourdieu's concept of "field," which refers primarily to arenas of power stratification and hierarchy, with Etienne Wenger's (1998a) concept of "*community of practice.*"[1]
4. Following Jeffrey Alexander (2011), it stresses contingency by referring to practices/background knowledge as performative, where agents act out and interpret social texts and display "*performative*

[1] Barab and Duffy 2000 first suggested this move. See also Dumouchel 2016.

power" – the capacity to present a dramatic and credible performance on the world stage (ibid., 8).[2]

5. It takes *cognition as social*, which means that it is not reducible to the human mind, but arises from social interaction.
6. It focuses on a multiplicity of social orders, including international social orders, rather than one specific historical or contemporary order, including *the* international or global order.
7. It uses the concepts of practice, background knowledge, communities of practice, and performative power not merely to show that "practice matters" or to introduce yet another communitarian-advocacy group of people who "do things," but because these concepts are the building blocks of cognitive evolution social theory.

Practices are socially meaningful patterned actions that, performed more or less competently, simultaneously embody, act out, and possibly reify background knowledge and discourse in and on the material world (Adler and Pouliot 2011a, 6).[3] Practices, such as environmental, legal, medical, financial, arms-control, and human-right practices, are embedded in particular organized contexts. As such, they are articulated into specific types of action and socially developed through learning and training. Action is always a constitutive part of any practice, yet the reverse is not necessarily true. Action is specific and located in time; practices are general classes of action that, although situated in a social context, are not limited to any specific enacting (ibid.). Practices are dispositional; if we adopt a practice, we do not necessarily need to act on it all the time (Hodgson and Knudsen 2010, 79), but practices are also creative. Practitioners, through understanding, interpretation, imagination, and experimentation (Taylor 1985, 26–27), reflexively learn and change their practices. Understanding how implicit practices become reflexively explicit requires social theory (e.g., Foucault 1977; Schatzki 1996).

Practices have an epistemological dimension – they are bound with background knowledge and context (Cook and Wagenaar 2012). "Background knowledge" is collective and intersubjective, yet at the same time it is also distributed in practitioners' dispositions and expectations. Norms and rules, for example, are not "just in the minds of the actors but are out there in the practices themselves" (Taylor 1971, 27). In other words, background knowledge is a Janus-faced social structure.

[2] I refer to "performative power" in more detail when I discuss social power in later chapters.

[3] For recent critiques of Adler and Pouliot 2011a, see Büger and Gadinger 2014, 2015; Frost and Lechner 2016a, 2016b; Kustermans 2016; Ringmar 2014.

In addition to being intersubjective knowledge embedded in practices, it also includes the subjective representations of intersubjectivity – mainly dispositions and expectations – that make intentional states possible. Individuals and groups act, interact, reason, plan, and judge and have expectations of the future within a dominant interpretive backdrop that sets the terms of interaction, defines a horizon of possibility, and provides the background knowledge of expectations, dispositions, skills, techniques, and rituals that are the basis for constituting practices and their boundaries. We should understand background knowledge as the conditions of possibility or propensities (Popper 1990) for practices to emerge, remain metastable, and evolve. Said otherwise, background knowledge is emergent – it is only through action and social transactions (Dewey 1922) that background knowledge "collapses" (Wendt 2015) as practices and institutional facts (Searle 1995), and why certain practices become more likely.

According to Etienne Wenger (1998a), a community of practice is a configuration of a *domain of knowledge* that constitutes like-mindedness. It is a *community of people* that "creates the social fabric of learning," and a *shared practice* that embodies "the knowledge the community develops, shares, and maintains" (Wenger et al. 2002, 27, 29). The knowledge domain endows practitioners with a sense of *joint enterprise* that "brings the community together through the collective development of a shared practice" that is constantly being renegotiated by its members. People function as a community through relationships of *mutual engagement* that bind "members together into a social entity" (Wenger 1998b, 2). Shared practices, in turn, are sustained by a *repertoire of communal resources*, such as routines, sensibilities, and discourse.

While communities of practice are analytical constructs, they are also real (Wenger 1998a) in the sense that, constituted by practices, practitioners possess collective intentionality (Searle 1995; see also Mitzen 2013) and collective agency, so have real consequences. As social structure and agents, communities of practice are emergent propensities that become (intersubjectively) "objective" by practices (Schäfer 2014, 2; Wendt 2015).[4] Communities of practice organize differences, *rather than generate uniformity*, and often change endogenously. This is not only because there are differences of performance across practitioners, and

[4] Social structures and human agency become tangible only through practices and action. While I refer to social structural and agential mechanisms and processes, they are part of the same reality – processes, doings, and sayings (Schatzki 2002), namely practices. It follows, also, that when I occasionally refer to "macro," "micro," and "meso" "levels" I do this for descriptive rather than for epistemological and ontological purposes (see Wendt 2015, 264).

because of learning and contestation within communities of practice, but also because at every repetition of practice there may be a difference: "every repetition occurs under already altered circumstances" (Shäfer 2014, 2). Diplomats, for example, not only differ in how they use social media effectively, but their competence may increase or decrease as an international situation unfolds. Because we cannot reduce practice communities' properties to those of their individual and corporate practitioners (Hodgson and Knusden 2010, 171), practitioners' interaction gives rise to emergent properties.

Social orders are fields, configurations or "landscapes"[5] (Wenger-Trayner et al. 2015) of practices and communities of practice, whose *epistemic practical authority* assigns functions and status (Searle 1995) thus organizing, stabilizing, and managing social life (Schatzki 1996, 2001a, 2002). Social orders ontologically exist, as both human action and transactions in and between communities of practice (Wendt 2015). They are not social representations of people's values and norms but rest on practices, the intersubjective background knowledge that sustains them, and the material resources that nurture them. At the agential level, social order rests on individuals' dispositions and expectations, which keep practices organized and metastable. But social orders are neither exclusively material nor mental phenomena, and because social structure and agency are ontologically indivisible, I refer to them separately for epistemological and heuristic purposes only.

Social orders are profoundly associated with politics. Politics is a constellation of practices through which agents govern societies; manage and resolve conflict; organize, guide, and control interconnectedness and dissociation processes; and strive either to keep social orders metastable or to bring about their evolution. Politics enters social orders' change and stability by shaping what competence means and is (Pouliot 2016), by constituting the conditions of possibility for certain social orders to exist, and in contingently and nondeterministically affecting practices' preferential selection. Politics also enters in how practices and communities of practice constitute the institutions and organizations of multilevel global governance and how they steer and manage social orders.

Perhaps more importantly, different kinds of politics are related to interconnectedness and disassociation practices, the forms of rule associated with them, and practices' normative dimension, including

[5] By "landscapes of practices," Wenger-Trayner and colleagues refer to "complex systems of communities of practices and the boundaries between them" (2015).

"better" practices.[6] We should expect, for example, a very different kind of politics in a Deweyian-type democracy (1922), for example, Uruguay, which embraces liberal-negotiation practices, than in an authoritarian order, for example, Venezuela, which involves illiberal populist practices. Similarly, we should expect different kinds of politics in international social orders, characterized by liberal-internationalist economic and institutional practices, than in international social orders characterized by mercantilist and power politics' nationalist practices.

There are no ideal types of interconnectedness and disassociation practices in international relations that constitute social orders. Regional integration, multilateral diplomacy, and international law, for example, are closest to the pole of interconnectedness. Mercantilism and immigration bans, on the other hand, are closest to the pole of disassociation. The majority of international and regional social orders are a hybrid and so not necessarily contradictory. Thus, we should understand international interconnectedness less as a rejection of national communities than as practical measures to adapt national communities to global reality and to a strategy to contain the threat of authoritarian-populist nationalism to democracy.

Power and rule, of course, permeate politics. In contrast to classic meanings of social order that focus exclusively on the vertical distribution of material power (Ikenberry 2011) and on hierarchical relations that involve practical interaction (Adler-Nissen 2014a; Adler-Nissen and Pouliot 2014; Bourdieu 1977; Pouliot 2010, 2016), I highlight horizontal systems of power and accountability of informal rule. Horizontal systems of rule span a spectrum between interconnectedness and disassociation. The closer social orders are to the interconnectedness pole of the spectrum, for example, regional integration and democracy, the more politics will highlight epistemic practical authority, mainly deontic power and performative power. As social orders get closer to the disassociation pole, for example, ethnic and/or populist nationalism, vertical hierarchies will begin dominating politics. We should expect "better" practices and bounded progress with interconnectedness-type politics and more control of its negative effects than with disassociation-type politics. Interconnectedness, as in postwar Europe, contingently enables the

[6] When engaging the world with their practices, practitioners carry rules, normative dispositions, and expectations embedded in practices about what is good and what is better. A notion of social orders as configurations of practices, therefore, understood not only as regularities, but also as being endowed with normative meanings, underscores that social orders result not from rule following but from rule enactment, and that "actors share a practice if their actions are appropriately regarded as answerable to norms of correct and incorrect practices" (Rouse 2001, 190–91).

creation of security communities where states cannot imagine armed conflicts among them (Adler and Barnett 1998). It fosters propensities for a global cyber social order and creates incentives for corporations to adopt economic ethical responsibility for their transactions.

As I show in more detail in Part II of the book, vertical forms of power also come into play in selective retention processes, although to a lesser extent. Note that power here refers not to a determinant "variable" but to processes and relations characterized by propensity and contingency. These come into play as practitioners transact within and between communities of practice and thus emerge as authoritative through practical action (Foucault 1984, 92–93; for this notion applied to communities of practice, see Fox 2000, 7).

International social orders are configurations or "landscapes" (Wenger-Trayner et al. 2015) of practices and communities of practice that straddle a spectrum between interconnectedness and disassociation. Their *epistemic practical authority* assigns functions and status (Searle 1995) thus organizing, stabilizing, and managing social life (Schatzki 1996, 2001a, 2002). In contrast to most IR studies that focus on either *a* or *the* historical or contemporary international or world order, cognitive evolution theory focuses on a plurality of international social orders. We can conceive of international social orders as overlapping in space and time. Thus, for example, we can identify a post–World War II European social order, but also social orders within the European space (e.g., the EU economic social order). We can also refer to the transnational corporate social order, in general, and to multiple corporate orders, in particular. The same is true of the contested cyberspace social order and derivative international social orders. Existing and emerging international social orders can be superimposed for extended periods of time when the existing order has not yet evolved but the emerging order has still not taken hold.

All this means that international social orders might exhibit a dynamic "balance of practices"[7] in a single space and time, where two or more communities of practice compete for the kind of doings and sayings that ought to keep a social order together but that end up undermining it, thus bringing about its evolution. The EU's response to the recent Syrian refugee crisis, for instance, illustrates how two distinctive communities of practice, one inclined to integrate as many refugees as possible, and the other inclined to leave them outside Europe, have been clashing. This

[7] I am not invoking the concept of equilibrium but rather the notion that there may be clashing ways of doings things that coexist simultaneously in space and time.

contestation between communities of practice[8] may lead to the evolution of the European refugees' social order without entirely undermining Europe's other political and economic social orders, for example, its governance social orders.

Similarly, groups inside the corporate community of practice held different views on whether businesses had a responsibility to remedy the negative impact of their activities – ultimately consolidated under the set of practices known as corporate social responsibility (CSR). These differences led to contestation but also eventually contributed to the stability of the corporate social order in the long term. Practitioners initially pushed back against the idea that corporations had any social responsibilities (Carroll 2015, 87, 91; Carroll and Shabana 2010, 87; Shleifer and Vishny 1997, 751). Milton Friedman famously argued that the only responsibility of management was increasing the profits of its shareholders (Carroll and Shabana 2010, 88). However, arguing that consumers would reward corporations for adopting socially and environmentally responsible practices (Carroll 2015, 89), such contestations led practitioners from the 1990s to attempt to reconcile CSR with profitability.[9]

At the same time, from a spatial perspective, traditional concepts of "international order" (see, most promintently, Ikenberry 2011) have never covered the entire globe and have always been a matter of perspective and context. The interpretation of international order since World War II has been different, for example, in the United States than in the Soviet Union, later Russia, and in most of the Middle East. Functionally, the cyberspace and corporate practices and communities of practice that organize international social orders have markedly differed, especially when it comes to their interconnectedness and disassociation features. All of these examples illustrate the benefits of understanding the concepts of international and global order as a plurality of international social orders that can overlap in space and time, and change and remain metastable at the same time.

Cognitive Evolution Theory

Cognitive evolution refers to an evolutionary collective-learning process that takes place within and between communities of practice and through their action in their broader material and social environments. Based on

[8] Rather than referring to the contestation of norms, as most of the extant IR literature does (e.g., Wiener 2014, 2018), I refer to contestation of communities of practices, thus, also, of practices, and the background knowledge bound with them. Norms, however, as I explain in later chapters, are an intrinsic part of background knowledge.

[9] See also Carroll and Shabana 2010, 86, 88, 92; Esty and Porter 1998, 36; Eweje 2006, 28; Jeppesen and Hansen 2004, 265; Lindgreen and Swaen 2010, 3; and Reinhardt 1999.

the idea that cognition is social – that it depends on social interaction – cognitive evolution theory argues that social orders originate, derive from, and consist of practices, the background knowledge (such as the myth) bound with them, and communities of practice (like the Heike) that contain them and serve as their vehicles. Social orders' institutions and organizations (the hardware) cannot function without practices/ background knowledge (software). What binds societies together, the "cement of society" (Elster 1989c), is therefore epistemic: practices and the background knowledge bound with them.

Cognitive evolution is a constructivist evolutionary theory of social ordering, particularly of world social ordering. It explains the conditions of possibility for social orders to become the way they are, although they could be otherwise. It addresses, therefore, the contingent effects of open processes and social mechanisms that dispose social orders to evolve in one direction, for example, a democratic social order, rather than another direction, for example, an authoritarian social order.

At the same time, cognitive evolution is an explanatory theory of how and why open, indeterminate, and nonteleological evolutionary processes, particularly practices, the background knowledge bound with them, and the communities of practice that serve as their vehicle, end up organizing world politics. The theory also explains how communities of practice establish themselves preferentially, how their practices and background knowledge spread and become selectively retained institutionally through practitioners' transactions with stakeholders outside the communities, how their members' expectations and dispositions survive in people's minds, and, therefore, how social orders evolve or are kept in a metastable state of flow. In other words, cognitive evolution theory explains the creative variation and selective retention of social orders. Cognitive evolution "differs from both 'mere' description and 'law-like' explanations . . . [It] combines 'how' questions, understanding, descriptive inference and constitutive analysis on the one hand, with 'why' questions, explanation, causal inference and causal analysis on the other" (Seybert and Katzenstein 2018, 20). As such, cognitive evolution theory is about neither efficient causes nor probabilities (Guzzini 2016) but about *propensities* (Popper 1990; see also Chapter 2) of social order to occur, and whether social orders remain metastable or evolve.

In accordance with its process-oriented ontology and evolutionary epistemology, cognitive evolution theory is not predictive but retrospective. This should not be surprising. It is in the nature of all evolutionary explanations to not be able to predict the evolution of a species or, for that matter, a social order, through time (Hull 1988, 430). But evolutionary theories provide explanations of processes through which the propensities for evolution come into play (Guzzini 2016). Cognitive evolution is also in the nature of explanations of complex nonlinear, emergent social phenomena. According to complexity theory (Waldrop 1992), stability requires permanent fluctuations, and even small changes can drive a social order over an intersubjective cognitive threshold and tip into a new social order.

Cognitive evolution's main concepts, to which I will return in more detail in Chapter 6, are as follows: *practices*, and the *background knowledge* that sustain them, are the *structural makeup that is passed on in replication.* They are inherited by future generations of practitioners and are diffused across geographical and institutional boundaries, thus becoming selectively retained. While practices are performances, they are also ontological "entities" whose trajectories can be followed (and studied) over time (Shove et al. 2012; see also Schäfer 2014).[10] Background knowledge is simultaneously intersubjective knowledge embedded in practices and practitioners' subjective dispositions and expectations.

Communities of practice are practices' "*vehicles*" that, interacting with the environment, make selection and replication differential. At the same time, they are the spatial field where practititoners' transactions take place. *Institutions* are emergent yet persistent social structures that manifest materially and meaningfully as a collection of practices. Incorporating prevalent anchoring practices (Swidler 2001) and constitutive rules as part of background knowledge, institutions can remain metastable by epistemic and normative public recognition and by gaining legitimacy and competence (Douglas 1986; Hodgson 2006; Searle 2010). Institutions help promote metastability, manage relationships among practitioners, and disseminate practices/background knowledge, including constitutive rules, in time and space. *Organizations*, and more broadly, *polities*, are *corporate practitioners* that incorporate communities of practice and populate social orders. The *environment* consists of cognitive evolution's *sociocultural and material contexts.* This includes other practices and their background knowledge, as embedded in communities of practice, individual and corporate practitioners, and material and institutional resources, audiences or stakeholders, and exogenous shocks or crises. Communities of practice create their own environments by selectively becoming sensitive and attentive to contexts (Gronow 2011, 121) and by collectively and purposefully acting to engage with them. *Social orders evolve over time.*

[10] Because intersubjective and subjective background knowledge collapses into practices, we should look for explanations of social change in the practices themselves, rather than solely in subjectivity and social structures (Schäfer 2014).

By way of introduction, these concepts theoretically relate in the following way (keep in mind the tale of the Heike): novel or transformed practices and background knowledge's selection and institutionalization explain the survival of expectations and dispositions in practitioners' minds. These subjectivities then become the reasons for the actions of practitioners who keep the practices and background knowledge institutionalized. Because communities of practice consist of practices and collective background knowledge as well as agents who practice what they know, the active spread of practices by the institutions, organizations, and polities within which communities of practice become embedded promotes the selective retention of new subjectivities. Social structures are therefore mirrored in human subjectivity, and simultaneously reflected back as practices (Wendt 2015, 269).

As I mentioned in the prologue, the master mechanism for understanding cognitive evolution, and particularly selective retention processes, is *epistemic practical authority*, the capacity for *practical meaning fixation* or the structural and agential authoritative ascription of practical meaning to material and social reality, to "stick," or be authoritatively selected and retained. It connotes the structural and agential ability to reorganize social life, break new social ground, and offer previously unavailable modes of consciousness and discourse (Adler 2008, 203; Wuthnow 1989, 3). Epistemic practical authority results primarily from the enactment of socially recognized functions, status, or rights that practitioners are normatively entitled to as practitioners. The sense of practitioners' entitlement I refer to, and of knowledge and practices' authority, therefore relies on deontic power (Searle 1995, 2010; see also Hall 2008, 9) that the community of practice confers on practices and their background knowledge. It then also depends on performative power (Alexander 2011), which brings in audiences that affect the practices' eventual capacity to be selectively retained. Performative power can enhance practitioners' competence status and functions, or because of malperformance it can weaken the meanings of practitioners who others may see as incompetent. As such, performative power affects the trajectories that practices and background knowledge take within and between communities of practice. Performative power is contingent; it constantly changes, dependent on whether audiences accept practitioners' performances.

So epistemic practical authority is the combined result of both types of social power and itself is a cause of practices' selection and social orders' evolution. Practices' epistemic authority is emergent and "earned" in practice. It results from processes of epistemic authority contestation between different claims. Competing claims can take place both within and between communities of practice. Regular changes in practice performance and competence, practices' combination and recombination, their spread across communities of practice – which sometimes results in constellations of communities of practice (Wenger 1998a) – play a role in settling competing practices' epistemic authority claims. Both deontic power and performative power, and epistemic practical authority more generally, constitute propensities, albeit not certainties, for fixing practical meaning. By this I mean the endowment of meanings with deontic (epistemic and practical) authority and naturalness that come only with practice. I cannot think of a stronger kind of power than the processual informal capacity to fix the meanings on which practices are based.

Social orders cognitively evolve according to three sociostructural processual mechanisms.[11] First, they evolve when, as an effect of endogenous learning processes involving negotiation, contestation, and identification within communities of practice, there is a transformation of background knowledge and of new configuartions of practices and their constitutive effects. Second, social orders also evolve when communities of practice establish themselves preferentially vis-à-vis competing communities of practice and their selected practices and background knowledge are inherited by future practitioners. When social orders evolve, existing practices lose their authoritative attraction and pull. They and their practitioners lose their epistemic practical authority and communities of practice lose their legitimacy, naturalness, and access to material and institutional resources while the practices and background knowledge of competing communities preferentially survive.

Finally, international social orders evolve because of the invention of new social actors and/or the effects that the replacement of one type of political entity and institution by another may have on background knowledge and practices, on the negotiability processes within communities of practice, and on the selection processes between different communities. The invention of the modern corporation in the nineteenth century led to the development of myriad corporate practices and communities of practice that make up current corporate orders. These practices, in turn, led to the development of new institutions, such as the multinational corporation, that affected myriad corporate orders. Similarly, the invention of packet switching networks spurred the development of computer science and fundamentally altered and displaced other established communications actors like telephone network operators (Abbate 1999, 40; Russell 2014). Novel integrative practices, which as

11 On structural change, see Sewell 2005.

part of their background knowledge consisted of pooled sovereignty principles and new conceptions of territoriality, constituted the postwar European social order (Adler 2010). Increasingly embodied in European institutions, they became more robust through iterated treaty negotiations from the 1957 Treaty of Rome to the 2009 Lisbon Treaty. Each iteration reflected the high ideals of the European project through both sociocultural and agential social mechanisms of creative variation and selective retention. The contestation of treaty negotiations, though sometimes politically fraught, illustrates the order's metastability. In turn, the EU's treaties and institutions conditioned the selective retention of practices.

Four agential processual social mechanisms are involved in the evolution of social order and their subsequent maintenance in a metastable state of flow. But practices constitute agents or practitioners. We are teachers because there is the practice of teaching. Others are legislators because there is the practice of legislation. The first social mechanism refers to agents' dispositions and expectations' resilience, as well as propensities for change, for instance, inventing new terms and redefining and abandoning old ones, creating and breaking routines, and changes in perceptual and linguistic interpretations (Wenger 1998a, 96). Emotional attachment to particular objects and subjects and agents' foresight faculties may also help generate dispositions and expectations and create propensities for their metastability or their change. The differential selection in and among communities of practice is at the same time the differential extinction or perpetuation of individuals' dispositions and expectations. The opposite is also true: stability or change in dispositions and expectations help sustain stability or change in and among communities of practice.

The second social mechanism refers to agents' transactions within communities of practice – most important, learning and negotiations over meanings – that help constitute social cognition. Because any one practitioner's cognition in a community of practice, which embodies her/his experiences and consciousness (Wendt 2015), is intrinsically bound to those of other practitioners' cognitions, together with their experiences and consciousness, transactions give rise to intersubjective background knowledge or what Ludwik Fleck called (1979) "thought collective." Communities of practice are therefore where practices' social-cognition dimensions – dispositions and expectations that embody both experiences and imaginings of the future – emerge, become metastable, and eventually evolve further.

The third social mechanism refers to agents' reflexivity, judgment, and justification (Boltanski and Thévenot 2006; Kornprobst 2014), which contribute to learning processes within and between communities of practice, and thus to the evolution of social orders. Practitioners reflect on their practices and background knowledge, not only, as Dewey (1922) suggested, because of environmental challenges but also because of endogenous processes affecting practitioners' relationships. Practitioners make value judgments about their performance and its outcomes, and if disenchanted, intentionally act differently from before. Individuals' ability to imagine the future allows them to take actions that can change the future in and by practice. Through self-fulfilling phrophecy-type processes (Feather 1982), agents' foresight turns individuals into active members of communities of practice. Agents are the "constructors" of communities of practices' identities; they think through and define what competence means in particular contexts (Pouliot 2016).

The fourth agential social mechanism refers to the agential material and socially contingent and indeterminate capacity to affect material and cultural-social environments in desired ways. As a result of the politics of competence, normative constitution, and communities' contestation, practitioners, including corporate practitioners like states, for example, exercise deontic and performative power to intentionally change their communities of practice's contexts.[12] In doing so, practices and practitioners organize social life; manage social, political, and economic processes and flows; and thus also informally and sometimes formally through organizations govern such processes and flows. Affecting selective-retention processes through attempts to change environments will depend on what practitioners consider relevant to action processes and to solving problems (Gronow 2011, 24; Mead 1967, 251), and on what they reciprocally do. They depend on learning of, and negotiating and contesting, meanings about what goes on in communities of practice.

These mechanisms are mainly a synchronic way of understanding cognitive evolution. From a diachronic perspective, cognitive evolution, like all evolutionary theories and evolutionary epistemology (Campbell 1960), consists of creative variation and selective retention processes.

Social interaction within and between communities of practice generates new continuities and discontinuities. Perhaps the most important discontinuity in cognitive evolution is *creative variation*: the innovation processes leading to the generation of new background knowledge and practices and/or their transformation, for example, through practices' recombination (Runciman 1989; Schatzki 2002) and translation (Callon

[12] Searle 1995 calls this capacity and competence "world-to-mind" relation of fit.

1986; Latour 1993). Consistent with my argument about social cognition, innovation, recombination, and translation are collective processes and thus socially emergent processes rather than individuals' property. Variation can take place as a result of nascent forms of awareness, experimentation, improvisation, learning, differences in interpretation, and in the way practices apply in diverse contexts or environments (among other things).

Selective retention of innovations refers to processes by which the differential extinction and proliferation of communities of practice mean also the differential demise or, alternatively, the perpetuation of practices and the background knowledge that sustains them. The selective retention of practices and background knowledge takes place thanks to epistemic practical authority (discussed earlier), and horizontal and vertical forms of practice communities' spread or expansion. *Horizontal* replication involves their expansion across geographical space and institutions. *Vertical* replication is the inheritance of practices and background knowledge by new generations of practitioners.

The horizontal expansion of communities of practice across physical and/or cyberspace and their endurance in time promote the selection of practices and the background knowledge bound with them. Practices and background knowledge spread because communities of practice enable practitioners to learn together by sharing how to do things. Spread occurs by embedding background knowledge and practices in routines, in the knowledge flows that run within and between communities of practice, and in polities' public policies, law, and regulations and, simultaneously, in individuals' dispositions and expectations. The expansion of cyberspace, for instance, became possible by the development of user-friendly platforms, such as the World Wide Web, that more readily allowed new users to share and participate in cyberspace (Abbate 1999; Castells 2002). Likewise, the EU's post–Cold War enlargement into Central and Eastern Europe expanded the European social order's territorial extension through practices and background knowledge embedded in technocratic and bureaucratic sociolegal processes of candidacy and accession, which some Europeans described as a grand historical and normative process of "returning to Europe" (Wallace 2002).

Vertical replication is how "newcomer" practitioners become "old timer" practitioners in communities of practice (Wenger 1998a). Through transactions with practitioners, "rookies" learn a practice, the competence that is required to practice well, what competence means, and the identity that identifies a particular community of practice. Vertical replication can also occur because of explicit instruction, not only through formal teaching, but also by informal tips about practical competence.

Cognitive evolution theory benefits from complexity theory's concepts (Waldrop 1992) that explain the simultaneous change and stability of social worlds. Complexity theory, which is associated with nonlinear dynamics and the concepts of emergence and self-organization, deals with systems that exhibit complex, self-organizing behavior. Against the received notion of equilibrium in sociology, economics, political science, and IR (but see, for example, Connolly 2011; Lewis and Steinmo 2012; Steinmo 2010; Tang 2013), social orders are in a permanent state of nonequilibrium. Paradoxically, it is fluctuations, such as practice learning and contestation, that help keep social order in a spatially and temporally metastable state, whereas changes occur below epistemic and intersubjective thresholds, or phase transitions. When fluctuations associated with endogenous changes in and competition between communities of practice (and with the invention of new polities and other corporate actors) reach thresholds or liminal conditions, a single fluctuation, or their combination, can become so powerful by positive feedback that it shatters the old order, which then tips and evolves, and a new social order replaces it (Prigogine 1980).

Evolutionary Constructivism

Social constructivism and evolutionary epistemology *are* compatible and evolutionary constructivism makes sense. Social constructivism is a combination of ontological and epistemological assumptions, social theory, and IR theory that, unlike materialism, rational choice, and functionalism, explain social reality, including its material foundations, as constructed by social practices and socially constituted knowledge (Adler 2002, 2013; Guzzini 2000).

We can best understand social constructivism as the unfolding of evolutionary social processes in space and time. Unlike positivism and materialism, which take the world as it is, evolutionary constructivism sees the world as a project under construction or "becoming." Unlike idealism, which takes the world only as we can imagine it or talk about it, evolutionary constructivism argues that not all practices have the same epistemic value and authority and that they are socially and culturally selected. Evolution, as both description and explanation, enters into the process-based constitution of intersubjectivity and social context, and the equally process-based construction of social facts by practices, background knowledge, and language; the relational co-constitution of agent and structure as instantiated in practices; and the emergence and evolution of practice and rule-governed international society. Evolution is therefore useful for understanding the contexts that make social reality possible, and the mechanisms involved in explaining change and the stability of social orders.

Evolutionary theoretical understandings of world politics are not uncommon.[13] In some cases, evolutionary theories in IR were associated with complexity concepts, such as "emergence."[14] Realist evolutionary theories mainly take a Darwinian approach based on power and natural selection analogies (e.g., Modelski 1990; Tang 2010, 2013; Thayer 2004; Thompson 2001). Liberal evolutionary theories (e.g., Spruyt 1994) mainly look at how humans shape their own environments, especially drawn by efficiency motives with the help of institutions. Based primarily on analogies to natural evolution, some evolutionary-minded IR scholars took a constructivist approach (e.g., Barnett 2010; Blyth 2011; Cederman 1997; Florini 1996). Even fewer scholars, most strikingly Ernst Haas (1990, 1992), Peter Haas (1992a), Peter Haas and Ernst Haas (2002), and Alexander Wendt (1999; see also Pouliot and Thérien 2015), developed constructivist cultural and social evolutionary theories of change that do not borrow from natural evolution's mechanisms and processes.

In his later years, Ernst Haas, with his son Peter (2002), suggested an approach they called "pragmatic constructivism," a combination of constructivism, pragmatism, and "evolutionary epistemology." According to pragmatic constructivism, "institutions may, at times, be willful actors on their own, but are also the venue in which reflexive new practices and policies develop" (Haas and Haas 2002, 573). Initially, Ernst Haas (1982, 1990), later Peter Haas (1989, 1992a), and then both of them together assumed a consensus theory of truth (Haas and Haas 2002; Ruggie et al., 2005) where changes in shared meanings based on rationalized and scientific understandings lead states and groups of states, mainly via international institutions, to rationalize and coordinate their interests.

Haas and Haas's (2002) pragmatist interpretation of evolutionary epistemology focused on provisional and interim notions of truths that "epistemic communities" arrive at according to truth tests by their

[13] See, for example, Axelrod 1984; Barnett 2010; Blyth 2011; Cederman, 1997; Cederman and Gleditsch 2004; Florini 1996; Gat 2009; Gilady and Hoffmann 2013; Modelski 1990; Shelef 2010; Spruyt 1994, 2001; Sterling-Folker 2001; Tang 2010, 2013; Thayer 2004; and Thompson 2001. In comparative politics, see Lewis and Steinmo 2012; Lustick 2011; Steinmo 2010; Thelen 2004.

[14] Robert Axelrod's evolutionary game theoretical models that explain cooperation (Axelrod 1984) and Lars-Erik Cederman's 1997 work on complex adaptive systems models are some of the most valuable texts on evolutionary IR, and emergent properties, respectively.

members.[15] Ernst Haas (1997, 2000) also developed a liberal evolutionary theory of progress that I discuss in Chapter 10. Although Ernst Haas, to whom this book is deeply indebted, focused on the pragmatist concept of truth, he did not acknowledge enough the larger message of American pragmatists and philosophers of science about the inseparable relationship between practice and knowledge. Haas and Haas's (2002) epistemic agential approach to epistemic communities, for example, placed practices as an outcome, rather than as the driver of consensual knowledge.

Wendt's systemic theory of global cultures' evolution (1999), based on Herbert Mead's (1934) concept of interactive learning, focused on how self and other learn to adopt shared identities, and showed that cultural rather than natural selection is at work in the evolution of global cultures. However, the evolutionary part of Wendt's grand constructivist theory was partly underdeveloped, particularly the mechanisms of change that explain the transition from identities at the individual level to global cultures and their directionality, and the relationship between changes at the interaction level and at the global-cultural level. Attempting to sustain the argument that the international system is moving in a teleological way toward a global state, Wendt (2003) did not explicitly suggest the mechanisms and processes that take us from here to there.

Cognitive evolution theory, which builds on evolutionary constructivism, is more in line with Wendt's latest book (2015) (without the quantum subject), according to which the dualities between change and stability, and material and ideational existence, are overcome and social structures and agents are conceived as emergent potentials that become actualized in practice.[16] Cognitive evolution theory best characterizes constructivist-evolutionary theory by placing practices and the background knowledge bound with them in the driver's seat, thus coming to grips with the structure/agency, material/meaning, and change/stability duality dilemmas. It avoids conceiving of constructivist theory from the top down (Finnemore 1996; Guzzini 2000; Katzenstein 1996; Kratochwil 1989;

[15] Ernst Haas introduced to IR (1982) and Peter Haas (1989, 1992b) and I (Adler 1987, 1991, 1992) further developed this concept, which Ernst Haas defined as making up professionals "who shared a commitment to a common causal model and a common set of political values" (1990, 41). For Peter Haas's definition, see Peter Haas 1992a.

[16] As Wendt (2015) argues, the relationship between agents and social structures is not one of "levels" but of social structures distributed locally in agents' experiences, understood in synchronic ways. In addition to his singularly synchronic theory, however, cognitive evolution theory also highlights diachronic processes – trajectories, paths that are taken, and others that could have been but were not taken (Suteanu 2005). Suteanu cites Bohm's argument that "when searching for meaning, one should not concentrate on separate system states, but rather on the transformations taking place, on the change, on the so-called 'becoming'" (2005, 122).

Onuf 1989; Reus-Smit 1999; Wendt 1999; and to some extent Wight 2006) or bottom up (Checkel 2001; Keck and Sikkink 1998; Peter Haas 1989, 1992; Risse-Kappen 1997) perspectives. It therefore explains not only change but also systemic change, as in the evolution of international social orders, and it makes systemic theory itself more dynamic.[17]

With a few exceptions (Modelski 1990; Spruyt 1994), evolutionary-minded IR scholars have not explicitly focused on the evolution of international orders.[18] Modelski argues in his theory of evolutionary international order that "the basic principle of world politics is evolutionary learning (rather than, for example, anarchy); it shapes the political process and gives it meaning, organizes its past, and generates its future" (1990, 24). Through the "long cycle," evolutionary learning determines the direction of change in international order: increasing complexity of the role that global leadership assumes, increasing democratization, and the decline of war in macro decision-making. The results of these factors are increasing international community, specialization, and vertical political differentiation. Spruyt (1994) framed his domestic theory of social-order change with an evolutionary framework, according to which the international order transforms with the selection of one type of polity among a variety of others. While Modelski's theory of international order change typifies the shortcomings of a structural-functionalist approach – "systems learn" – in Spruyt's case, individuals "choose" how orders will evolve. Evolutionary constructivism, building on an evolutionary ontology and evolutionary epistemology, can reach further. Cognitive evolution theory is simultaneously structural and agential, and while it explains both change and systemic change, it is also more dynamic.

There are many reasons that an evolutionary approach to social cognition and practices, on one hand, and constructivism, on the other, are compatible.[19] First, constructivism is not only about "ideas" and "norms," but it also blends material and corporal reality and collective and subjective meanings, as congealed in human action and practices. Constructivists should therefore not be concerned about taking an evolutionary approach because of evolution's association with materiality.

[17] I thank one of the reviewers for helping make this point more forcefully.

[18] Sterling-Folker (2001) is correct in arguing that realist and liberal IR theories build on *implicit* evolutionary understandings of international order. See, for example, Tang 2010, 2013. In comparative politics, see Sven Steinmo 2010.

[19] Several scholars recently attempted to bridge social constructivism and evolutionary psychology (Mallon and Stich 2000; Wilson 2005). As I discuss in more detail in Chapter 3, evolutionary psychology, because of its naturalistic approach to evolutionary epistemology, is inappropriate for my study. David Wilson (2005) used the concept of evolutionary social constructivism.

Second, constructivists take culture as a social construction. The growing evidence that cultural and natural evolution (Boyd and Richerson 1985) coevolve should thus stimulate constructivists' imaginations on how social constructions themselves evolve.

Third, as I show in detail in Chapter 2, when based on process and relational ontology, constructivism is by definition evolutionary. This does not mean that "everything changes" but that the construction of social reality depends on the creative – read emergent – variation of alternatives and their selection and retention. In other words, the way things are could have been different. Evolutionary constructivism need not necessarily rely on either "scientific realism" or exclusively on subjective perspectives of social reality. Instead, as I show in Chapter 2, it can rest on an ontology based on pragmatism that simultaneously takes reality as a condition of intelligibility (Searle 1995) and understands propensities as objective processes (Popper 1990).

Fourth, constructivism need not rely, either directly or by analogy and metaphor, on natural processes and mechanisms. While studies on the coevolution of nature and culture (Boyd and Richerson 1985; Henrich 2016) have yielded important insights on the interaction between nature and culture, when we explain the evolution of social order, practices, habits, institutions, and social facts, a general epistemological principle of evolutionary change makes it unnecessary to study evolutionary processes based on natural processes and mechanisms.

Fifth, both constructivism and evolutionary theory are "historical." This means that they involve duration, trajectories – some argue also path-dependent trajectories (Thelen 2004) – and branching points, which in indeterminist (Popper 1982b) ways sway trajectories' direction. Because IR constructivism historically traces the origins, development, and institutionalization of norms, practices, and language, constructivism is amenable to concepts of evolutionary variation and selective-retention processes (Adler 1991; Finnemore and Sikkink 1998).

Sixth, contrary to past interpretations of constructivism as being agnostic about change (Hopf 1998),[20] and others that see change and stability being mutually exclusive (Ringmar 2014), change is ubiquitous and may be taken as a necessary condition of metastability. Both constructivism and evolution conceptualize change as the historical branching out of possibilities and propensities rather than as the teleological

[20] Recently, Hopf (2018) developed an excellent theoretical argument on tacit and reflective change in practices. Although I place more emphasis on reflective change and evolutionary change, and highlight different change mechanisms, than he does, our conceptions of change in practices are to some extent compatible.

development toward increasing complexity (this notion was not Darwin's, but Herbert Spencer's; see Padgett 2014) or "nirvana" (de Chardin 1959).

Seventh, adaptation and learning processes have played a major role in conceptualizing changes in both constructivism and evolution. IR constructivists theorized about learning as an important mechanism of social reality construction and social change (Adler 1991; Checkel 2001; Haas 1990; Haas and Haas 2002; Wendt 1999). Likewise, beyond Lamarckian evolutionary theory, which has been associated with constructivist theories of adaptation and learning in IR (Gilady and Hoffmann 2013), recent developments in mainstream evolutionary biology (Henrich 2016) show that the main reason for *Homo sapiens*' success is humans' ability to collectively interconnect and learn from one another. Recent evolutionary analyses from a network perspective point in the same direction. As John Padgett recently argued, "fixed mountains of optimality dissolve into locally malleable adaptive landscapes that change with movement upon them. Genes and species don't defeat each other so much as learn (through relative reproduction as well as other mechanisms) how to fit together in mutually consistent ... ways" (2014, 6).

Eighth, power, although differently understood, plays a key role in explaining social evolution's selection processes (Tang 2013; Thayer 2004) and the construction of social reality (Barnett and Duvall 2005; Searle, 1995, 2010).

Ninth, social cognition, intersubjective understandings, and interactive understanding of social reality are some of IR constructivism's most important concepts. Social cognition is involved in practices' development and in the evolution of social skills and competences. Embedded in practices, social cognition helps us understand both how the past may affect the future in path-dependent ways, the so-called ratchet effect (Axelrod 1984; Pouliot and Thérien 2015), and how collective imaginaries and expectations of the future pull social structures and agents toward that future (Phillips 2011; Taylor 2004). According to Herrmann and colleagues (2007), social cognition plays an equally important role in the natural evolution of skills, especially in exchanging knowledge in cooperative groups and communities.

Finally, from both epistemological and methodological perspectives, the nomological-deductive or "normal" model of science, which relies on law-like statements and predictions, applies neither to evolutionary epistemology nor to the social construction of reality. In both cases, explanations are retroductive, rather than predictive – they ask how the past contingently affected the present. In other words, both constructivist and evolutionary explanations are contingent and sensitive to initial conditions, to context (constructivism), or to boundary conditions (evolution) in which they arise.

The compatibility of constructivism and evolution rests on evolutionary epistemology and evolutionary ontology. As a subset of evolutionary constructivism, rather than building by analogy on biological evolution, cognitive evolution theory assumes a general model of evolutionary change, associated with one strand of "evolutionary epistemology." Going back to American pragmatists, such as Charles Peirce (1965a), William James (1890), John Dewey (1922), and George Herbert Mead (1967), philosophers of science like Karl Popper (1959) and Stephen Toulmin (1972), and psychologist Donald Campbell (1974a), it suggests a unique social explanation of social orders' evolution. Complexity theory concepts such as nonlinear change, emergence, and "order through fluctuations" strengthen evolutionary epistemology (Prigogine 1980; Urry 2005). My interpretation of evolutionary epistemology buys into Donald Campbell's (1965) notion that there exists a general model of evolutionary change of which organic evolution is only one instance. This means that the power of cognitive evolution theory need not depend on a strict analogy of natural evolutionary theory. Cognitive evolution theory's mechanisms and processes thus differ from natural evolution's mechanisms and processes.

Cognitive evolution theory eschews a strict separation between cognitive and social phenomena. It embraces Ludwik Fleck's assertion that cognition is a collective activity "since it is only possible on the basis of a certain body of knowledge acquired from other people" (1979, 38). It espouses Jon Elster's (1983) argument that for an evolutionary principle to make sense in the social sciences it must adopt a feedback loop through human cognition, experience, and consciousness. One can establish the feedback loop less by "deciphering" psychologically what is *in* the human mind than by following a relational sociological approach that examines intersubjective and subjective (mainly dispositions and expectations) background knowledge, which, embodied in practices, emerges from, and is maintained by, mutual engagement in communities of practice (Rouse 2007; Taylor 1992).

Cognitive evolution theory suggests an ontological move from "being" (as proposed by Parmenides), which emphasizes substances or entities and takes everything as being static – even what changes – to "becoming" (as suggested by Heraclitus), which highlights processes and relationships and takes everything as changing – even what appears to be stable (Prigogine 1980; Rescher 1996; Whitehead 1929). However, a "becoming" ontological perspective does not reject the existence of substances but takes them as instantiations of processes (Abbott 2001, 87–72;

Wendt 2015). From this perspective, practices are "performances and entities at the same time" (Schäfer 2014, 1).

As a corollary of my epistemological and ontological assumptions, I suggest "pragmatic realism," whose designation I liberally borrow from Hilary Putnam (1990). It is a concept that combines both pragmatist and realist-ontological assumptions with pragmatist-epistemological assumptions. A pragmatic-realist approach underscores how the propensity of social facts to emerge is related to material and social objects' collective meanings. It also emphasizes the practical and creative quality of knowledge (Joas 1996), including scientific knowledge, contingency, the socially constructed nature of knowledge by communities, and the effects of social reality's construction on knowledge.

Contributions

As a theory of simultaneous change and stability, cognitive evolution suggests an alternative to theories that explain exclusively either change (Holsti et al. 1980) *or* stability (Keohane 1984), and to arguments that deny that change and stability might be part of the same ontology (Ringmar 2014). It also transcends IR theories that analyze change in the position of "things," particularly rational choice theories (Lake 2011), and material-based structural-functionalist theories (Gilpin 1981; Wallerstein 2004; Waltz 1979).[21]

In contrast to Wendt's (1999) social theory of international politics, but in partial accord with his process-oriented ontology (Wendt 2015), cognitive evolution theory rejects dualism, suggests practice-based mechanisms of cultural evolution (not only individual-based), and shows what and whose ideas become cultures, though not necessarily global cultures. Wendt and I now agree that the social world is emergent and contingent, that thinking depends on social relations (ibid., 254), that agency is always in a state of becoming (ibid., 207), and that social reality is a set of processes and relationships that practices congeal into entities. While not subscribing to Wendt's social quantum theory, I agree with his argument that "agents and structures are both emergent effects of practices" (ibid., 33). However, my theory has more practical and empirical applications than his, particularly for IR theory, and opens a space for researching empirically the evolution of social orders.

[21] For theories in comparative politics that also look at simultaneous stability or reproduction of institutions and their change, see Thelen 2004; Lewis and Steinmo 2012.

Cognitive evolution theory also departs from classic constructivism by suggesting evolutionary constructivism to explain the adoption of practices less by imitation, internalization, and socialization than by the very nature of practicing and joining communities of practice. By moving away from the notion that social order results from following rules, rather than enacting rules, cognitive evolution theory improves on constructivism's "logic of appropriateness" (March and Olsen 1998). Rules are part of practices' background knowledge but they become "real" and constitutively efficient only when practices enact them (Dewey 1922). Norms are processes and relationships that cannot be sustained over time without recurrent practices (Hofferberth and Weber 2015). Cognitive evolution theory, while acknowledging the relevance of discursive practices, departs from postmodern and poststructural theories that conceptualize "the order of things" (Foucault 1970; in IR see Walker 1993) as only discourse.[22]

Cognitive evolution theory suggests an alternative to current theories of international order in IR, including material power–based theories (Waltz 1979), normative and institutional theories (Reus-Smit 2013a), or both (Ikenberry 2011). It also improves on, adds more dynamism to, and provides a more general explanation of multiple and overlapping social orders' change and stability than recent theories that highlight practices from a Bourdieu-based perspective (Adler-Nissen 2014a; Pouliot 2016).

Cognitive evolution theory derives a set of normative theoretical claims about better practices, social orders, and limited, reversible, contingent, nonteleological, and nondeterministic progress from the analytical theoretical claims. More specifically, I argue that, first, normative claims and actions rest in practices that spread through communities of practice, and that while values and normative practices may *become* universal they *are* not a priori universal. Second, I argue that while all practices are normative, *not all practices are ethical.* This opens a space for considering better practices and bounded progress, which I claim that, at a minimum, are grounded in the acknowledgment (Markell 2003) of a "common humanity" (Stuurman 2017). Third, I argue that better practices and bounded progress are more likely to be associated with horizontal systems of rule, which are anchored in interconnectedness (Arendt 1965). Fourth, after Dewey (1916), I suggest that democracy rests on a practice principle, namely on community, knowledge, and practices, not all of which are

[22] Foucault "rehabilitated the subject by assuming that actors appropriate and incorporate these practices, using them to engage with the world ... Practices are now not only restricted to discursive processes, but may also ... be physical phenomena" (Rasche and Chia 2009, 717).

discursive (Habermas 1996). Seen this way, one of the biggest threats to a democratic social order, and to the current liberal international order, is *epistemological insecurity*, the loss of our collective trust in a common-sense reality that comes with practices of post-truth.

Equipped with cognitive evolution theory, IR scholars will be able to study the simultaneous evolution and stability of multiple and overlapping international and social orders more dynamically and describe them more socially "thickly" than was possible when relying on the international regimes and multilevel governance literatures. Regarding governance, cognitive evolution highlights not only institutions, international organizations, and norms, but primarily global governance practices and the communities of practice that are behind international social order management. Change helps prevent stagnation with new practices of management and organization. Metastability, at the same time, endows social order with permanence and duration and guards against the breakup of social arrangements. Without change there is stagnation but without stability society cannot sustain itself.

Cognitive evolution theory allows us to understand why certain international security, economic, legal, human rights, and environmental practices become prevalent, while others do not. It suggests understanding IR through the lenses of not only states and individuals, but mainly of communities of practice, which cut across structure and agency.

Most substantively, cognitive evolution theory is a learning theory whose sociostructural manifestation is the sociocognitive selection of collective consciousness and meanings that become institutionalized in human practices and held subjectively as dispositions and expectations. Cognitive evolution theory is thus an alternative to social psychological and sociological theories that exclusively interpret learning as a change of "beliefs" or "ideas" *in* peoples' minds (Levy 1994) or as ideas that "jump" from mind to mind (Checkel 2005).

As social theory, cognitive evolution transcends both positivism and relativism. It proposes a dynamic social-evolutionary alternative to rational choice, functionalist theories, and institutional and norm-based constructivist theories. Highlighting practices and communities of practice, cognitive evolution theory builds on pragmatism's theory of action where knowledge and practice are inseparable, practices are creative, and knowledge develops and evolves in communities. Communities of practice are a spatial-organizational platform where practitioners interact, learn, and end up creating and diffusing practices and promoting their adoption by future practitioners. It suggests a complement to, and perhaps a different way of understanding, the oft-used concept of networks (Emirbayer 1997; Jackson and Nexon 1999a) and fields (Bourdieu

1977; Fligstein and McAdam 2011). By arguing that agents and structures not only recursively reproduce each other but also move in time historically, and that practices must be made ontologically primitive, cognitive evolution theory adds dynamism to Giddens's (1984) structuration theory.

Building on evolutionary epistemology, cognitive evolution theory breaks ranks with evolutionary works in the social sciences that rely mostly on natural-science analogies, and adopts an evolutionary ontology, according to which "being" or substances exist as instantiations of "becoming," or processes and social relations.

Empirical Illustrations

The book's theoretical chapters are enriched by three main examples and minor examples, as I see fit, all of which I borrow from international politics. The main examples illustrate my concept of multiple international social orders, the workings of one or more of the sociostructural mechanisms, and of the four agential mechanisms, which I develop in Chapters 6 and 7, as well as the creative variation and selective retention processes, which I explore in Chapters 8 and 9. The evolution of European order after World War II and the current countervailing pressures against it, which may bring about the evolution of a new order, make up the three sociostructural mechanisms: the invention of a new type of polity, practice communities' endogenous changes, and selection between competing communities of practice. The evolution of the cyberspace social order, which is my second example, pits two competing constellations of communities of practice in a struggle to determine the web's social order. As shorthand, we can call these constellations "NSA" and "Snowden." Think of cyberspace metaphorically as a "universe" whose "big bang" origins occurred only forty years ago. Since then, its newly created practices have been expanding in different directions and forming colliding communities of practice. Finally, the invention of the corporation is a case of cognitive evolution where economic and social innovation in the nineteenth century led to the modern corporation – a business whose "owner" can live forever. In turn, a multitude of corporate practices developed, constituting the social and economic corporate orders that now construct us in myriad forms of social life.

Plan of the Book

Chapter 2 anchors this study in an evolutionary ontology of "becoming," which in turn, I base on a "pragmatic-realist" (Putnam 1990) approach.

This chapter and the next on evolutionary epistemology are not "metatheory" in the sense usually encountered in the IR literature, but are an integral part of evolutionary constructivism, in general, and social-cognitive evolution theory, in particular. As I wrote in my chapter on constructivist theory in the *Handbook of International Relations* (2002, 2013), social constructivism is made of three layers: metaphysics, social theory, and IR theory. So, for instance, without grounding evolutionary constructivism in process ontology, we may not be able to understand properly the theory of cognitive evolution, which I develop in Chapters 6 through 9.

Chapter 3 explains and defends the concept of evolutionary epistemology and suggests a short history of its development since the nineteenth century. Chapter 4, after discussing pragmatist-based practice theory, makes seven moves on practices, background knowledge, communities of practice, and social power that set the foundations for cognitive evolution theory as I apply it to IR in Part II of the book. In this chapter I also define social order and highlight practices' and social orders' normative qualities. As I mentioned before, I adopt an approach to practices that it is different from Bourdieu's (in IR, for example, from Adler-Nissen 2014a, 2014b or Pouliot 2010, 2016), and while I am closer to pragmatism, I do not adopt a standard pragmatist approach either. I also revise my own work on practices (Adler 2005, 2008; Adler and Pouliot 2011a, 2011b). Because I develop my own eclectic approach to practices, change, and orders, and my own terminology, this chapter is necessary for understanding cognitive evolution theory and its application to IR in subsequent chapters.

Chapter 5 defines the concept of international social order(s), discusses how it can more dynamically and effectively explain social order than the international-regime literature, and supplements the global governance literature. It also explores how my approach to a multiplicity of international social orders improves on existing approaches to international order and global order's stability and transformation.

In Chapters 6 through 9, I discuss cognitive evolution theory in detail. Chapter 6 defines the theory's main concepts, uses complexity theory concepts to theorize the simultaneous change and metastability of international social orders, and describes cognitive evolution's sociostructural mechanisms. Chapter 7 describes cognitive evolution's main agential mechanisms and processes. It ends by briefly comparing cognitive evolution theory with Elster's (1983) and Giddens's (1984) efforts to overcome functionalism, Elster by means of rational-choice theory, and Giddens by means of structuration theory. Chapter 8 analyzes creative variation's processual mechanisms, while Chapter 9 discusses processual mechanisms of epistemic and practice selection, as well as processual mechanisms of retention and institutionalization. Combined, Chapters 8 and 9 suggest new ways of understanding variation, diffusion, selection, retention, and institutionalization processes. I end Chapter 9 by comparing my approach to diffusion and institutionalization processes as conceived by institutionalist sociology and comparative politics.

Chapter 10 purports to develop a preliminary normative theoretical framework on better practices and bounded progress that rests on the analytical features of cognitive evolution theory. In other words, cognitive evolution theory suggests the mechanisms and processes by which the selective retention and institutionalization of ethical practices take place. My plausibility probe into normative theorizing is particularly relevant to our contemporary time in history when interconnectedness, or liberal internationalist practices, seem to be losing ground to disassociation, or populist and authoritarian nationalist practices, including the "post-truth" phenomenon.

I conclude the book with a short epilogue in which I characterize cognitive evolution theory as an exemplar of theories of world ordering and suggest that world-ordering theories should take center stage in IR theory and social theory. I also suggest an agenda for future research.

Some IR readers might be tempted to skip Part I and go straight to Part II. But by choosing "the highway" (say from Florence to Siena) rather than "the scenic route" (the same direction but through the Chianti region), the reader will miss the often-unspoken ontological and epistemological assumptions that theories are based on, as well as the description of my own approach on practices, background knowledge, communities of practice, and social order. This should be of interest not only to scholars who follow the so-called practice turn in IR theory but also to IR theorists more generally with an interest in learning about evolutionary constructivism and world ordering, and to social theorists. What may be lost in speed may be a net gain in depth. I'd hate for anyone to miss the pleasures of those glasses of wine in the Chianti region.

2 Evolutionary Ontology

From Being to Becoming

Arguing that reality – even what appears stable – is flux, Heraclitus, a pre-Socratic Greek philosopher, first suggested a "becoming" ontology. Opposed to this notion, there is a "being" ontology. First identified with Parmenides, another pre-Socratic Greek philosopher, it refers to fixed essences and substances. According to Parmenides, the everyday perception of reality as changing is a mirage, so reality is unchanging. "Being" can be identified with both "external realism" (Aristotle 1984; Putnam 1981, 1983) and "idealism" (Berkeley 1975; Kant 1998). "Becoming," on the other hand, can be identified with process philosophy (e.g., Emirbayer 1997; Rescher 1996; Whitehead 1978), some forms of pragmatism (Dewey 1983, 1988, 2008; James 1907; Peirce 1965a, 1965c), Popper's propensity theory (1990; see also Naraniecki 2014), social constructivism (Berger and Luckman 1966; in IR, see Adler 1997; Wendt 1999), and complexity theory (Prigogine 1980).

The becoming ontology I am interested in here assumes that what is real are processes – including practices, communities of practice, social structures such as institutions, and social orders – material entities, and individuals. Social entities are, as Searle calls them, "placeholders for pattern of activities" (1995, 57). A "becoming" ontological perspective does not reject the existence of substances, but social substances are instantiations of processes (Abbott 1988a, 87–72; 2005; Wendt 2015). Practices, for instance, are processes or propensities that congeal into enduring thingness. From this perspective, practices are "performances and entities at the same time" (Schäfer 2014, 1) Background knowledge is intersubjective, but at the same time distributed in practitioners' dispositions and expectations.[1] Norms and rules, for example, are not

[1] Wendt 2015 refers to reality as processes distributed in individuals' consciousness and experience. Dispositions, pushed by, or "coming from some past," comprise both consciousness and experience. Expectations, in turn, add the purposeful dimension of actions, which, in Heidegger's tradition, are pulled toward imagined futures (Nicolini 2012, 162; Schatzki 1996).

"just in the minds of the actors but are out there in the practices themselves" (Taylor 1971, 27). Communities of practice are analytical constructs but are also real (Wenger et al. 2002),[2] in the sense that, constituted by practices, practitioners, and materials, they possess collective intentionality and collective agency[3] (Elsenbroich and Gilbert 2014; Searle 1995; Tuomela 2007), and thus have real consequences. Again, the "samurai crab" legend comes to mind. Agents, and social structures such as institutions, are emergent propensities that become concrete by practices (Schäfer 2014, 2; Wendt 2015). Social orders are emergent processes through action, even when they are stable.

More specifically, practices evolve together with the practical knowledge bound with them, and result from transactions between practitioners and between them and their environment. In Sami Pihlström's words, it "is in our activities and practices themselves that our ontological construals of the way(s) the world is are to be formed" (2008, 52). Practices are real because they consist of material bodies and other material objects. And through practices agents and social structures have a real impact on the physical and social worlds. (Recall the "samurai crab" story.) But practices are in a constant state of flux as a result of creative, reproductive, and transformation processes. Practices are dispositional yet also creative (Joas 1996). Institutions, organizations, and polities, which usually are associated with essences and a "being" ontology, actually become as a result of practices' processes, background knowledge, and transactions between practitioners and between them and the wider world or environments. Background knowledge, including social norms, rules, and values, is how the world makes sense to us in and through practices (Schatzki 2002). Like all other social structures, background knowledge, which is both intersubjective and distributed across practitioners' dispositions and expectations, consists of propensities that have ontological effects in and through practice. According to Popper's "propensity theory," which I discuss later in this chapter, every possibility holds propensities of becoming real that are not inherent in an object, but in a situation and performances (Popper 1990).

[2] "You can go into the world and actually see communities of practice at work. Moreover, these communities are not beyond the awareness of those who belong to them, even though participants may not use this language to describe their experience" (Wenger 2002, 2340). Gherardi, Nicolini, and Odella contest this point. They warn of a danger in reifying communities of practice (1998, 279).

[3] "The intentional states that accompany agents' practices are not fully separable from the collective intentions which make them possible, since the latter define the context in which agents are acting" (Wendt 2015, 265).

While they embody individuals and a myriad of materials related to the practices that they hold, communities of practice – as conduits of, and sites for, the emergence, reproduction, and transformation of practices – are neither substances nor independent variables that cause social order in any naïve sense, but mostly processes. Learning and contestation within communities of practice, which are at the core of practices' production and reproduction, can not only keep social orders in a state of metastability, or stable flow, but also create propensities for their transformation and replacement, thus bringing about change in social orders.

Social orders are also processes rather than "things." Practices, "by conferring upon entities interrelated meanings," arrange and organize entities (Schatzki 1996, 115), thus constituting social orders. Practices and intersubjective background knowledge, which constitute social orders' organization and metastability, can constantly be the subject of redefinition, reconceptualization, learning, and contestation. So are individuals' dispositions and expectations, which is how individuals experience practices and background knowledge. Institutions and organizations, as well as strategic interaction between agents, emerge from fluctuating knowledge and practices, which is why we should start social analysis from practices and knowledge, rather than with their reified "substances." Practices, background knowledge, communities of practice, and social orders are in a constant state of nonequilibrium.

I find it essential to devote a chapter to "becoming" ontology because cognitive evolution does not mean just change from here to there, a change in the position of things or substances, a mere development and transformation of ideas and practices, and the development of social institutions and organizations. Instead, we should understand cognitive evolution as (1) *processes* and *relations* by which entities become what they actually are (Whitehead 1929, 28), and which therefore precede the agents and organizations that we deal with in the social world. This means that change is ubiquitous not only when social orders evolve but also when they are metastable, thus maintaining the appearance of stability of our institutions and organizations. In other words, cognitive evolution gives ontological primacy to practices and communities of practice and to individuals' subjective experiences and expectations. Cognitive evolution also highlights (2) *time* and *duration* (Bergson 1910) – the open-ended creative emergence of reality and the emergence of consciousness and its effect on the constitution of reality. It emphasizes (3) *the construction of social facts* (Searle 1995), (4) *propensities* for something to become rather than the determination of something that *is* (Popper 1990), and (5) *immanence*, or the preservation of the past in the present (Chia 1999, 220).

I do not look to uncover reality's foundations or fundamentals (Chernoff 2009), but I am doing what most theorists do, usually implicitly. I am setting the theory's ontological and epistemological grounds before its full exposition (Cox 1996, 144; Jackson 2010). I put the theory's ontology "on the table," not for its own sake but because the theory I advocate deals with simultaneous transformation and stability, and with an ontology that only recently has begun making inroads in IR (Albert and Kratochwil 2001; Jackson and Nexon 1999b; Lapid 2001; Wendt 2015). Engaging in metaphysics, as Karl Popper argued, is important because it can lead to good ideas for testable theories. It can also play a "pervasive role in shaping and selecting our problems, the way we formulate them and the way we evaluate our tentative solutions" (Simkin 1993, 16–17). We should evaluate the following ontological arguments, asking whether they take us further toward understanding change and stability in the social world. I am therefore open to critique of both cognitive evolution theory and its ontological and epistemological assumptions.

From Being to Becoming

For Heraclitus, "reality is at the bottom not a constellation of things at all but . . . processes" (Rescher 1996, 10). He argued that "all observable changes result from a 'strife' of opposing forces to overcome each other, thus creating transformative power as the ruling condition of existence" (Seibt 2017, n.p.). Heraclitus thought that "reality is both one *and* many – a singular unifying implicit reality with multiple explicit manifestations. Only wisdom achieved through critical reflection allows us to comprehend the one in the many" (Chia 1996, 34). One of the most crucial aspects of Heraclitus's ontology is how things come to be (ibid., 46). Most strikingly, "Heraclitus assigned to process or dynamicity the role of explanatory feature, not only of a feature of nature to be explained . . . [H]e suggested that processes form organizational units and occur in a quantitatively measurable and ordered fashion [and] contrasted dynamic transitions or alterations with dynamic permanence, and thus for the first time identifies, and differentiates between, two basic 'Gestalts' or forms of dynamicity" (Seibt 2017, n.p.).

Parmenides responded to Heraclitus that there is only one true world, "which is *unitary, already constituted*, and *unchanging*. Observed changes in the world are not just apparent but false, since reason shows that what is one cannot also be many" (Chia 1996, 35). "Being" means unchangeable reality. Substance metaphysics recasts this intuition as the claim that the primary units of reality (called "substances") must be static – they must be what they are at any instance of time (Seibt 2017). To accommodate the possibility of change, Democritus, among others, subsequently modified Parmenides's views. Thus, "we end up today with a modified . . . world view, in which it is acknowledged that reality is actually made up of discrete, atomic entities which are capable of entering into a variety of combinations – forming and reforming into different configurational structures . . . change is absorbed and incorporated as a secondary feature or epiphenomenon of reality" (Chia 1999, 216).

Plato portrayed "being" as the view of "that which always is and has no becoming" and "becoming" as "that which is always becoming and never is" (Bolton 1975, 67 citing Plato's middle dialogues). Whether Plato, who embraced "universal forms" metaphysics, also followed Heraclitus's processual views is controversial (ibid.). Rescher argues that Plato understood the world "as processual, unable to provide a stable, orderly foothold required for rational apprehension, description, and explanation" (1996, 10).[4]

However, one should be careful not to take the dichotomy between "being" and "becoming" as fundamental and mutually exclusive. I agree with Yosef Lapid, who said that "despite their insistence on process and change, process philosophers in no way deny the reality of substances and nouns; they merely re-conceptualize them as temporarily stabilized moments in the implicate movement of flux and transformation" (2001, 19). The same can be said about philosophers who adopted a "being" ontology but who, at the same time, had "becoming" leanings. For example, while Aristotle referred to reality as substance, he also considered that substances exist because they have *potential* to become.

According to Aristotelian metaphysics, "'being' of a natural substance is always in transition involved in the dynamism of change." The "cosmos manifested stability only at its outer limits with the fixed stars and . . . all else is pervaded by change" (Rescher 1996, 11). Thus, Aristotle's middle position between "being" and "becoming" is "substances-in-process" (ibid.). Kostman (1987) interpreted Aristotle's definition of change, mainly through his concept of "interlecheia," as a process of actualizing rather than change's outcomes or the state of being actual. Pragmatism adopted Aristotle's process-oriented approach by emphasizing his concepts of *praxis* and practical judgment ("*phronesis*") (Bernstein 1971). Karl Popper (1982b, 1990) relied on Aristotle's concept of potential to develop "propensity theory." Heidegger (1962

[4] Bolton (1975) associated this view with Plato's early writings (*The Republic* and *Phaedro*).

[1927]) also tried to have it both ways: while emphasizing "being" as "Dasein" ("being-in-the-world"), he also stressed modes in which being-in-the-world occurs and, most important, knowing in practice, "a form of mindless *non-thematic* everyday practical coping skills over mental representation" (Chia and MacKay 2007, 232). While the world is dynamic and processual, change and metastability cannot exist without each other. Transformation constitutes metastable orders whose state of flux breeds more transformation.

Galileo Galilei, René Descartes, and Isaac Newton embraced a naturalistic approach based on substances where entities exist before their interaction. Accordingly, "space and time were absolute, in the sense of existing objectively and of being completely independent of any physical content. Matter, to be sure, occupied space, and moved in space, but space itself remained . . . always similar and immovable" (Baumer 1977, 59). Gottfried W. Leibniz, by contrast, adopted a processual understanding of nature, arguing that the world consisted of process forms, called "monads," that he took to be "bundles of activity" (Rescher 1996, 12).

Later, "becoming" ontological notions became part of philosophical debates between Johann Fichte, Georg Hegel, and Friedrich Schelling, who were trying to counter Immanuel Kant's "transcendental idealism." This debate, which "deeply influenced the further development of 'continental' philosophy from Nietzsche to Heidegger to Derrida . . . can be viewed as ensuing from the assumption that cognitions are productions of sorts" (Seibt 2017, n.p.). Hegel was among the most important philosophers to embrace a "becoming" ontology. For him, "being" is devoid of content because it is the undetermined condition of possibility for things. "Becoming," on the other hand, is the process by which the endless possibility of being is narrowed down or determined. It is "an unsteady unrest which sinks together into a restful result [that] falls together through its inner contradictions into a unity in which Being and Nothing are superseded" (Hegel qtd. in Findlay 2013, 158). "Becoming," in other words, means that whatever exists is a process constantly being reshaped "in an ongoing development proceeding through the operation of a dialectic that continually blends conflicting opposites into a unitary but inherently unstable fusion" (Rescher 1996, 13).

Among German idealists, Nietzsche also stands out as a follower of a "becoming" ontology. "Heraclitus," Nietzsche argued, "will eternally have it right, that being is an empty fiction. The apparent world is the only one: the 'true' world is merely lied into it" (Nietzche qtd. in Richardson 2006, 221). Nietzsche's concept of "will" is fundamentally related to "becoming." As Richardson explains, "we must think of Nietzschean will not as a persistent thing, but as a feature of doing or activity" (ibid., 216). The intention that animates action is in this case creation (*macht*), and it stretches into the future in an oriented function (Nietzsche 1968, 353). Nietzsche's "becoming" ontology takes mind and the world as evolving together in "the social practices in which people . . . engage as they live their life and go about their business" (Jackson 2010, 126).

A "becoming" ontology received a big boost with Charles Darwin's evolutionary theory (see Chapter 3) and the formulation of quantum theory by Max Planck and the theory of relativity by Albert Einstein (Popper 1982a, b). Quantum theory, for instance, brought about "the dematerialization of physical matter." "Instead of very small *things* (atoms) combining to produce standard processes (avalanches, snowstorms) physics envisions very small processes (quantum phenomena) combining to produce standard things (ordinary macro objects)" (Seibt 2017, n.p.).[5] Time and irreversibility, in turn, acquired new urgency because of relativity theory (Prigogine and Stengers 1984, 231).

By adding a dynamic dimension to our understanding of evolution, which enables the development of theories to simultaneously explain change and stability, complexity theory's concepts, such as "self-organization," "emergence," and "order through fluctuations" (Prigogine 1980; in IR, see Connolly 2011), recently support a "becoming" ontology. Most strikingly are Nobel Prize-winning Ilya Prigogine's theories of nonequilibrium thermodynamics about the self-organization of evolving systems in the face of permanent instabilities and fluctuations. "Classical or quantum physics describes the world as reversible, as static. In this description there is no evolution, neither to order nor to disorder" (Prigogine and Stengers 1984, xxiv). Instead, a theory of nonequilibrium and "order through fluctuations" maintains that under nonequilibrium conditions, fluctuations can lead to order and organization (Prigogine and Stengers 1984, 231).

Twentieth-century philosophers and sociologists were aware of quantum theory and of relativity theory's implications and how they fundamentally changed the understanding of nature's order from substances to fluctuations. Lloyd Morgan (1923) even anticipated complexity theory's concept of emergence. American pragmatists like Charles S. Peirce, John Dewey, William James, and G. H. Mead came to terms with the implications of evolutionary theory, as developed by Darwin, Lamarck, and others. They thus assumed a world made of processes and their theories became an important source of "becoming" ontological understandings.

[5] For an excellent analysis of "process ontology" based on the notion that quantum theory applies not only to the physical world but also to the social world, see Wendt 2015.

Evolutionary theory, as I show in Chapter 3, provided "a template for understanding how novelty and innovation come into both the human world and the world of nature" and called for "a new metaphysics, which would articulate the pervasive role of process and of the passage of time" (Seibt 2017).

American pragmatists and their followers came to terms with evolutionary theories by making a simple argument about the evolution of knowledge, beliefs, and habits. They also developed a conception of the world as action, knowledge as practice (Dewey 1922), and acting as preceding knowing (Kilpinen 2008, 7). The pragmatists' process-related world is inherently creative (Dewey 1922; Joas 1996), emergent (Morgan 1923), and spontaneous (Peirce 1965a); it is about processes based on the projection of human experience into the future (James [1909] 1977), the evolution of the social world through human transactions (Dewey 1922), and the evolution of consciousness as emerging from processes of social engagement (Mead 1913).

More specifically, while Peirce was committed to realism (Hausman 1993), he embedded his realism in process metaphysics. While for Peirce "laws came into existence as reality evolves from chance to determinacy" (Peirce 1965b), in contrast to conventional causal determinism, he argued that any present is determined by a past that has undergone a process of evolution toward an ever-decreasing range of potentiality. Peirce's notion of life's spontaneity is overtly processual (Hausman 1993, 160). Finally, objects are dynamic because they change in nature, and also because of what people infer them to be changes of (Hausman 2002). James, in turn, argued that human experience "prevents the imposition of conceptual fixities for giving an adequate account of reality . . . the ongoing innovations launched by intelligent life characterize the tendency of an ongoing processual reality to break the rules that have grown too restrictively narrow" (Rescher 1996, 16).

Dewey held that meaning is an aspect of cooperative behavior that arises in people's "transactions." While "interaction" assumes internal essences and a separate existence of physical entities, "transaction" means that as people come into contact "'the components themselves are subject to change. Their character affects and is affected by the transaction'" (Elkjaer and Simpson 2006, 9). As Dewey and Bentley (1949, 108) argued, "transactions deal with aspects and phases of action, without final attribution to 'elements' or other presumptively detachable or independent 'entities,' or 'realities' and without isolation of presumptively detachable 'relations' from such detachable 'elements.'" Rescher claims it is precisely because he "saw human existence in terms of an emplacement with an environment of unstable flux that Dewey dismissed the prospect of governing life with rules and fixities, and saw the need of a flexible approach geared pragmatically to the changing demands of changing situations" (1996, 20). Dewey thought individual development requires individual capacities that are actualized in real time (ibid., 19). These capacities refer not to Aristotelian potentialities but to genuine novelty and creativity. Dewey understood social reality as habits that usually are associated with stability. But for him habits are part of a *chain of becoming* (my wording), whereas the world continually forces individuals to create new forms of action. Emergent evolution is not change from one thing to another but the appearance of something genuinely new: when not only the world but also consciousness evolves, both of which evoke a turning point (Morgan 1923, 5) when events express "some new kind of relatedness among pre-existing events" (ibid., 6).[6]

Mead (2015), who developed a processual perspective that Herbert Blumer (1986) later called "symbolic interactionism," took a view of actor and world as dynamic processes rather than static structures (Ritzer 2010, 351). Heavily influenced by Dewey, Mead understood cognition and action as evolving together. The capacity to engage in complex social interaction enables an actor to take the role of the other; human consciousness therefore emerges from creative social action and communication. Perhaps more than any other early American pragmatist, Mead developed a pragmatist emergent perspective and argued that past experience never completely determines events, even if they are rationalized to be conditioned by the past (Mead 1932, 46).

At approximately the same time as early American pragmatists suggested processual theories, Henri Bergson highlighted the importance of time and duration (*durée*) in the interaction between agents and world (Seibt 2017). Reality, for Bergson, is not static (as usually perceived) but movement. Static reality is but a picture of reality in people's minds (Rescher 1996, 17). In Bergson's own words, "continuity of change, preservation of the past in the present, real duration – the living being seems, then to share these attributes with consciousness. Can we go further and say that life, like conscious activity, is increasing invention?" (Bergson 1998, 23).

Alfred North Whitehead, who became one of the twentieth century's leading process philosophers, identified the privileging of "things and entities rather than relations as the proper units of analysis" as "the fallacy of misplaced concreteness" (Stripple 2007, 3). In various

[6] According to El-Hani and Pihlström (n.d.), "emergent properties are not metaphysically real independently of our practices of inquiry but gain their ontological status from the practice-laden ontological commitments we make."

landmark books, but especially *Process and Reality* (1978), Whitehead abandoned the notion that "matter and hence causal mechanisms are assumed to be simply locatable at specific coordinate points in space-time" (Chia 1999, 214).[7] Instead, he described the world as dynamic processes in which the "concrescence" of any one actual entity involves the other entities among its components (Whitehead 1978, 7, 28). "In the becoming of an actual entity," Whitehead said, "the potential unity of many entities in disjunctive diversity – actual and non-actual – acquires the real unity of the one actual entity" (ibid., 22). This implies "that 'becoming' is a creative advance into novelty . . . it belongs to the nature of a 'being' that it is a potential for every 'becoming' . . . how an actual entity becomes constitutes what that actual entity is . . . It is constituted by its 'becoming'" (ibid., 23, 28). In other words, what we experience as reality is a diverse and stratified web of monadic entities engaged in a continual process of creation that consists of the actualization of one of many potential arrangements into which they could fall.[8]

According to Elizabeth Krauss, Whitehead thought "that being and becoming, permanence and change must claim coequal footing in any metaphysical interpretation of the real, because both are equally insistent aspects of experience" (1998, 1). She quotes Whitehead on this: "In the inescapable flux, there is something that abides; in the overwhelming permanence, there is an element that escapes into flux. Permanence can be snatched only out of flux; and the passing moment can find its adequate intensity only by its submission to permanence" (Whitehead 1978, 338). As Krauss explains, what distinguishes the modality of the actual is the realization of one potential to the exhaustion of all others. Whitehead's view of being and becoming can be summarized as reality consisting of continually shifting arrangements of monadic quantum entities that contain all possible such arrangements within them as a potentiality, and are perceived as substantive, but which do not actually have substance at the macro-physical level, and therefore cannot be treated as static entities with properties.

The recent revival of process philosophy is indebted to Nicholas Rescher, who argues, particularly in the book *Process Metaphysics* (1996), that the central themes of process metaphysics are "becoming and change – the origination, flourishing and passing of the old and the

[7] This notion, according to Whitehead, allowed Newton to formulate his "Laws of Motion," whereas the "state of 'rest' is considered normal, whilst movement is regarded as an essentially transitory phase from one stable state to another" (1978, 215).

[8] Note the similarity between Whitehead's arguments on social reality and quantum theory. See Wendt 2015.

innovating emergence of ever-new existence" (Rescher 1996, 28). Process metaphysics "holds that physical existence is at bottom processual; that processes rather than things best represent the phenomena that we encounter in the natural world about us" (ibid., 2). For Rescher, "process metaphysics privileges change over persistence, activity over substance, process over product and novelty over continuity" (ibid., 31; Chia 1999, 217). Rescher defines process as "a coordinated group of changes in the complexion of reality, an organized family of occurrences that are systematically linked to one another either causally or functionally. It is emphatically not necessarily a change in or of an individual thing ... Contrary to 'substantive metaphysics,' processes without substantial entities are perfectly feasible in the conceptual order of things, but substances without processes are effectively inconceivable" (Rescher 1996, 38, 46). Process metaphysics therefore "replaces the troublesome ontological dualism of *thing* and *activity*, with a monism of activities of different and differently organized sorts" (ibid., 49).

Rescher devotes considerable attention to the forms and causal properties that processes take. He identifies an affinity between disposition and the nature of process: "On the one hand, processes are dispositionally structured modes of development ... On the other hand, dispositions are processual – that is, are generally dispositions to activate or continue certain processes" (ibid., 46–47). The activation of a disposition appears fundamental to Rescher's notion of "becoming." Accordingly, "if coming-into-being is itself actually to be a process, then there has to be a period or interval of transition – of reification or concrescence – during which it can neither be said truly that the thing at issue actually exists nor on the other hand that it does not exist at all" (ibid., 66). Also significant to Rescher's theory of process forms, which places him close to Peirce's pragmatic-realist views, is that "any actually occurrent process is at once concrete (context-specific) and universal (type-instantiating)" (ibid., 74).

For Rescher, evolutionary theory is essential to process metaphysics. "Darwin's discovery holds *not just in biology but everywhere*: The fundamental novelty at issue with creativity and the innovation of new kinds of species is pervasive ... The theory of evolution powerfully encouraged the view of the universe as a processual manifold rather than as assemblage of fixed and unchanging essences that perdure unaltered over the course of time" (ibid., 81, emphasis added). He goes on to say that "the evolutionary process has provided process philosophy with one of its main models for how large-scale collective processes (on the order of organic development at large) can inhere in and result from the operation of numerous small-scale individual processes (on the order of individual lives), thus accounting for innovation and creativity also on a macro level scale" (ibid., 100). Echoing "evolutionary epistemology," which I discuss in Chapter 3, Rescher argues that "the novelty that arises with the emergence of new cognitive processes is crucial both to the nature and to the availability of our ideas . . . Knowledge is not a thing, let alone a commodity of a fixed and stable make-up; it is irremediably processual in nature" (ibid., 134).

Several sociologists, in particular, Pierre Bourdieu, Erving Goffman, Norbert Elias, Mustafa Emirbayer, and Andrew Abbott, contributed to the development of a relational sociology that relies on a "becoming" ontology. Bourdieu, according to Emirbayer and Johnson, made "perhaps the most important of all recent contributors to the project of a relational sociology" (2008, 2). Because I review Bourdieu's contributions to practice theory in Chapter 4, I focus here almost exclusively on his relational sociology. While Bourdieu was clear about trying to overcome the notion of substances and actors, and that, as he said, "the real is the relational" (Bourdieu and Wacquant 1992, 97), he did not entirely shed his emphasis on social positioning over social performance and becoming. Bourdieu was thus a relational sociologist straddling "being" and "becoming."

Bourdieu's ontology affirms the primacy of relations. In his view, such dualistic alternatives as "structure *or* agent, system *or* actor, the collective *or* the individual," which he rejects, reflect "a commonsensical perception of social reality . . . which is 'better suited to express things rather than relations, states than processes'" (Bourdieu and Wacquant 1992, 15). "What exist in the social world," Bourdieu said, "are relations – not interactions between agents or intersubjective ties between individuals, but objective relations, which exist independently of individual consciousness and will" (ibid., 97). To characterize a social reality as relational, Bourdieu breaks ranks with structuralism, though never abandons it, by portraying each element of his theory, such as "field" and "habitus," as relations rather than substances, and by typifying their mutual relationships as mutually constituted (ibid., 16). Habitus and field, therefore, "are relational in the additional sense that they function *fully only in relation to one another*" (Bourdieu and Wacquant 1992, 19).

From a relational perspective, a "field" is first "a network, or a configuration, of objective relations between positions" (ibid., 97). Second, as "in the manner of a magnetic field" it is "*a relational configuration endowed with a specific gravity* which it imposes on all the objects and agents which enter in it" (ibid., 17). Third, a field "'presents itself as a structure of probabilities – of rewards, gains, profits or sanctions – but always implies a measure of indeterminacy'" (ibid., 18). Finally, fields are about social positions "which guarantee their occupants a quantum of social force, or of capital, such that they are able to enter into the struggles over the monopoly of power" (ibid., 229–30).

Bourdieu's habitus is the social world operating from within agents (ibid., 20), "the socially objective dimension of subjectivity" (Marcoulatos 2003, 76). While not being fully individual or determinative, habitus is "a system of lasting and transposable dispositions, which integrating past experiences, functions at every moment as a matrix of perceptions, appreciations and actions" (ibid., 18). It therefore "portrays social action as being historically contingent and always embedded in a particular social context" (Rasche and Chia 2009, 718). It is "creative, inventive, but within the limits of its structures, which are embodied sedimentation of the social structures which produced it" (Bourdieu and Wacquant 1992, 19). Practices, in turn, result from an "encounter between habitus and field, or between dispositions and positions" (Pouliot and Mérand 2013, 29). They are not individually induced but "are relational, collectivized, driven by a practical sense, which encompasses relations to others and past situations" (Bigo 2013, 124). In other words, "practices have historical trajectories," and following these trajectories "allows understanding of their deployment" (ibid.).

As we can see, Bourdieu suggested a sophisticated relational-sociological perspective of social reality. In Bourdieu's world, social reality *is* relational, but only habitus *becomes*, and only partly so. Because Max Weber's concept of order influenced Bourdieu, who saw fields as arenas of action in which actors and their social positions are located (Fligstein and McAdam 2011, 212), change means movement in the position of things, rather than the becoming and evolution of social reality. Bourdieu's theory is dynamic, but his interest in explaining power stratification and social domination led him to highlight how things are more than how they become. For example, historical contingency and practices' trajectories relate to the position of fields' occupants as they struggle for power. In contrast to communities of practice – where practices emerge and are transformed (even when social orders are kept metastable), and where boundaries are determined by the practices themselves – Bourdieu's fields are only vaguely generative and their limits are unclear. Bourdieu explained how a change in practical sense affects power distribution within fields, but his conception of field is insufficient for knowing where practices come from. Bourdieu's concept of intersubjectivity, which is crucial for explaining how structure is kept metastable, is weak, perhaps because he ontologically prioritized the material conditions of existence (Pouliot and Mérand 2013, 40) over background knowledge itself.

Goffman's microsociology, though it does not feature the evolutionary and historical views of process that are characteristic of "becoming" theorists, introduces a view of interaction orders that rests on dynamic processes of exchange in a context of "co-presence." Goffman is not alone in refusing to wholeheartedly embrace Heraclitus's philosophy. He takes, therefore, "being" and "becoming" as complementary rather than as entirely incompatible. Goffman's (1983) concept of interaction orders refers to the micro-orders that emerge from the temporal and bodily immediacy of individuals' activity in face-to-face communication. One of Goffman's main contributions to "becoming" ontology lies in his notion of ritual, ratifying, and participatory practices that establish and sustain the interaction order. He says, "persons come together into a small physical circle as ratified participants in a consciously shared, clearly interdependent undertaking, the period of participation itself bracketed with rituals of some kind, or easily susceptible to their invocation" (ibid., 7). Goffman also expressed processual and relational ideas when discussing informal institutions. "Informality is constituted out of interactional materials (as is formality), and the social circles that draw on this resource merely share some affinities ... what one finds, in modern societies at least, is a nonexclusive linkage – a 'loose coupling' – between interactional practices and social structures" (ibid., 11).

Elias's historical evolutionary approach added important insights to "becoming" ontology. To quote from one recent volume devoted to exploring the implications of his work:

> I can summarize Elias's legacy in terms of a series of deceptively simple propositions. (i) Human beings are born into relationships of interdependency. The social figurations that they form with each other engender emergent dynamics, which cannot be reduced to individual actions or motivations. Such emergent dynamics fundamentally shape individual processes of growth and development, and the trajectory of individual lives. (ii) These figurations are in a state of constant flux and transformation, with interweaving processes of change occurring over different but interlocking time-frames. (iii) Long-term transformations of human social figurations have been, and continue to be, largely unplanned and unforeseen. (iv) The development of human knowledge (including sociological knowledge) takes place within such figurations and forms one aspect of their overall development: hence the inextricable link between Elias's theory of knowledge and the sociology of knowledge processes. (Quilley and Loyal 2004, 5)

We can better understand Elias's process-based legacy by examining a number of his key concepts. Starting with figuration, "for Elias, the structure and dynamics of social life could only be understood if human beings were conceptualized as interdependent rather than autonomous, comprising what he called figurations rather than social systems or structures, and as characterized by socially and historically specific forms of habitus, or personality-structure" (van Krieken 1998, 52–53; see also Elias 2000). The "study of processes of social development and transformation – what Elias called sociogenesis – is necessarily linked to the analysis of psychogenesis – processes of psychological development and transformation, the changes in personality structures or habitus which accompany and underlie social changes" (van Krieken 1998, 6). Finally, Elias's use of the "habitus" concept is different from Bourdieu's (1977, 1990). For Elias, habitus "forms . . . the soil from which grow the personal characteristics through which an individual differs from other members of his society" (Elias 1991, 182). Elias's interpretation of habitus evokes a becoming ontology because it takes as axiomatic the "immanent impetus towards change as an integral moment of every social structure and their temporary stability as the expression of an impediment to social change" (Elias qtd. in van Krieken 1998, 63).

In *The Civilizing Process*, Elias claims that the transition from feudal to centralized states required a new sort of power-holding elite: rural warlords needed to become courtly gentlemen, so the process of state development was accompanied by a process of psychological change, of the rise of a new habitus. During the transition of elites from courtly to bourgeois, the mode of rationality again transformed. Along with it, manners and personal habits became increasingly sophisticated and restrained (Elias 2000, 369). In other words, the modern "civilized" subject was engaged in a process of becoming that has spanned many centuries. We can understand only with reference to that subject's relationship to broader macro-structural developments, within which individuals feature in their dynamic "figurations."[9]

Building on Elias, Emirbayer developed a "relational sociology," which, contrary to the notion that one can think about pregiven units as the ontological assumption of sociological analysis, considers configurations of ties "between social aggregates of various sorts and their component parts as the building blocks of social analysis" (Emirbayer 1997; Jackson and Nexon 1999b, 291–92). As Yosef Lapid argued, while Emirbayer's relational sociology is intimately connected to process philosophy, on a "closer examination one realizes an important difference. Whereas processists emphasize the priority of process, relationists emphasize 'the anteriority of radical relationality'" (2001, 4). Together, however, relations and processes are the two sides of the same "becoming" ontological coin. Chia (1995–1997, 2002) applied a relational

9 There are strong parallels between Elias's arguments and the English school's interest in the evolution of international societies, international order, and process sociology. For a recent exposition of these similarities, see Linklater 2010, 2011, 2017.

approach to organizational analysis and Jackson and Nexon (1999b) and Nexon (2010) built on Emirbayer to suggest a relational approach of world politics.

Similar to Whitehead, Emirbayer criticizes social sciences' "'structural' approaches, which conceive of the social world as constituted by 'self-subsistent entities,' which come 'preformed,' and only then enter the dynamic flows in which they subsequently involve themselves" (Emirbayer 1997, 283). In opposition to structuralism, he suggests transactionalism, which should be familiar from my previous discussion of Dewey. Emirbayer calls his transaction approach "relational." In this approach "the very terms or units involved in a transaction derive their meaning, significance, and identity from the (changing) functional roles they play within that transaction. The latter, seen as a dynamic, unfolding process, becomes the primary unit of analysis rather than the constituent elements themselves" (ibid., 287). Emirbayer quotes Ernst Cassirer: "[Things] are not assumed as independent existences present anterior to any relation, but … gain their whole being … first in and with the relations which are predicated of them. Such 'things' are terms of relations, and as such can never be 'given' in isolation but only in ideal community with each other" (qtd. in Emirbayer 1997, 287). Marshaling a range of sociologists from Karl Marx and Georg Simmel to Andrew Abbott, Emirbayer finds a unity of agreement in terms of what is distinctive about a relational approach: "it sees relations between terms or units as pre-eminently dynamic in nature, as unfolding, ongoing processes rather than as static ties among inert substances" (ibid., 289). As he goes on to explain, this recasting of things in terms of relations, bonds, and transactions has implications for the study of power, equality, freedom, and the linkages between the "micro" and the "macro" levels.

Emirbayer applied his dynamic approach to agency "as a temporally embedded process of social engagement, informed by the past (in its 'iterational' or habitual aspect) but also oriented towards the future … and the present … The agentic dimension of social action can only be captured in its full complexity, we argue, if it is analytically situated within the flow of time" (Emirbayer and Mische 1998, 962–63).

Like other scholars I mentioned, Andrew Abbott calls for greater attention to time and process. He suggests taking reality as constituted by "fluctuating entities" and emphasizes "the transformation of attributes into events," with the causal influence of events being determined by their "location in a story" (Abbott 1988b, 182). He also proposes treating boundaries as preceding entities. As he wrote, "we should start with boundaries and investigate how people create entities by linking those boundaries into units" (1995b, 857). Abbott called "yoking" the process of connecting two proto-boundaries "such that one side of each becomes defined as 'inside' the same entity." Creating an entity, however, also requires rationalizing the connections, so the entity may persist in time (Abbott 1995b; Jackson and Nexon 1999b). In his 2004 presidential address to the Social Science History Association annual meeting, entitled "The Historicality of Individuals," Abbott urged scholars to return "individuals" to history – not in the "great men and women" sense (2005, 1–13) – but in the sense that individuals should be treated as continually emerging and changing in the same way that any other historical structures are.

A review of becoming ontology would not be complete without mentioning "action-network theory" (ANT). Associated with Bruno Latour's (2005) work in the sociology of science, ANT offered a relational and processual view of action, agency, and the constitution of social reality. ANT is an excellent example of a "becoming" approach that still highlights material reality and substances (Lapid 2001, 19). As John Law, another seminal ANT theorist, writes, "the metaphor of heterogeneous network . . . lies at the heart of actor-network theory, and is a way of suggesting that society, organizations, agents, and machines are all effects generated in patterned networks of diverse (not simply human) materials" (Law 1992, 380). ANT refocuses attention away from stabilizing features of organization and toward "the complex and heterogeneous micro-organizational processes involved in the ongoing enactment of social reality" (Chia 1996, 59). Directed at the production of scientific knowledge, ANT treats science as "a process of 'heterogeneous engineering' in which bits and pieces from the social, the technical, the conceptual, and the textual are fitted together." Directed at society in general, ANT suggests that "the social is nothing other than patterned networks of heterogeneous materials" (Law 1992, 381). ANT's relational approach does not trace activities back to preconstituted individuals within an objective environment of constraints or resources, but to an assemblage of people and things, operating together, with agency as the emergent outcome.

I end this review with a few words on Georg Simmel, Niklas Luhmann, Michel Foucault, Jürgen Habermas, and Charles Tilly, all of whom followed a relational approach without quite adopting a discernible "becoming" perspective. Although Simmel is clearly a relational theorist, he was more interested in exploring the dynamics of different relational configurations than in change over time. He was not a theorist of "becoming," even if he was a theorist of process – he is what George Ritzer has called a "methodological relationist" (Ritzer 2010, 162). As Simmel put it, "We are dealing . . . with microscopic-molecular processes within human material, so to speak. These processes are the actual occurrences that are concatenated or hypostatized into those macrocosmic, solid units and systems" (qtd. in Ritzer 2010, 166). Donald Levine, a prominent analyst of Simmel's work, explains that Simmel's "method is to select some bounded, finite phenomenon from the world of flux; to examine the multiplicity of elements which compose it; and to ascertain the cause of their coherence by disclosing its form" (1971, xxxi). It is through process that substance gains its presence and its properties, in Simmel's view.

Luhmann's functionalist systems theory made a significant contribution to process sociology. But Luhmann is also not a theorist of "becoming," and he focuses on synchronic or integrative processes. Luhmann makes a strong ontological claim about the nature of the social world: "the concept of system refers to something that is in reality a system" (Luhmann 1995, 12). The units that constitute social systems are, in his explicit view, processes all the way down. As Joas and Knöbl explain, for Luhmann, "acts of communication are the elementary units of social systems; it is through such acts that meaning is produced and reference to meaning is constantly made" (2009, 275). In this view, actions themselves are "constituted by processes of attribution. They come about only if, for whatever reasons, in whatever contexts, and with the help of whatever semantics ('intention,' 'motive,' 'interest'), selections can be attributed to systems" (Luhmann in ibid., 276). Although a significant amount of his work is taken up with processes of growing systems differentiation within the context of modernity, what is missing is the assumption of continual transformation and flux, and hence of "becoming" as an essential metaphysical condition.

While Foucault's early work was grounded "in the tradition of Lévi-Strauss' structuralism by assuming that discursive practices were autonomous (and their reproduction detached from the subject), the 'late' Foucault rehabilitates the subject by assuming that actors appropriate and incorporate these practices, using them to engage with the world . . . Practices are now not only restricted to discursive processes but may also . . . be physical phenomena" (Rasche and Chia 2009, 717). Foucault did not entirely depart from structuralism. While his influence on practice theory is substantial, he did not fully adopt a "becoming" ontology.

Habermas's (1984, 1987) work is largely processual. His account of communicative action as an essential source of normative constitution and replenishment necessarily involves processes of ongoing discursive exchange. And his account of the public sphere's transformation is certainly an account of evolution. But Habermas does not assume flux, in contrast to entities and substances, and he seems to underwrite a normative interest in recreating something like the public sphere, rather than treating it as a fleeting historical moment constituted from a never-ending process of growth and change.

Tilly's work is exemplary of a theorist straddling "being" and "becoming." In his later years, Tilly focused on what he termed "relational realism": "the doctrine that transactions, interactions, social ties, and conversations constitute the central stuff of social life . . . Relational realism concentrates on connections that concatenate, aggregate, and disaggregate readily, forming organizational structures at the same time as they shape individual behavior. Relational analysts follow flows of communication, patron-client chains, employment networks, conversational connections, and power relations from the small scale to the large and back" (Tilly and Goodin 2006, 11).

Ways of Becoming

John Searle's theory of social reality's construction (1995, 2010), and Karl Popper's (1982b, 1983, 1990) propensity theory and theory of mind ("World 3") consider ways of becoming. I chose these theories to illustrate a becoming ontology first because they illustrate evolutionary constructivism's becoming ontological concepts, such as processes, a relational understanding of reality, emergence, immanence, and time. Second, as we will see in subsequent chapters, these concepts are "building blocks" of cognitive evolution theory. My interpretation of Searle and Popper's ontological arguments here is unconventional, and in Popper's propensity theory case, it reflects a side of his work that IR scholars seldom discuss.

Constructivism

A social-constructivist approach in IR builds, at least partially, on a "becoming" ontology. Stressing the reciprocal relationship between nature and human knowledge, constructivism describes the dynamic, contingent, and culturally based condition of the social world. The idea of a constructed social world does not deny the ontological status of material reality, but instead suggests that "material resources only acquire meaning for human action through the structure of shared knowledge in which they are embedded" (Wendt 1995, 73). "Becoming" appears in ontological assumptions about the process-based constitution of intersubjectivity and social context, and the equally process-based construction of social facts by intersubjective knowledge, practices, and language; the relational nature of the co-constitution of agent and structure; and the emergence and evolution of rule-governed international society. So rather than using history as a descriptive method, constructivism has history "built in" as part of its theories. Historicity therefore shows up as part of the contexts that make possible social reality, the processes involving changes in social structures and agents, and the mechanisms involved in the explanation of change. There is no perfect correlation between objects "out there" and our classifications of nature. And social facts, which are the objects constructivists study, emerge from the interaction between knowledge and the material world, both of which are in a constant state of flux.

Constructivism takes change less as the alteration in the positions of material things than as the emergence of new constitutive rules (Ruggie 1998a), the evolution and transformation of social structures (Dessler 1989; Wendt 1999), and the agent-related origins of social processes (Adler and Haas 1992; Goddard 2009; Haas 1992; Keck and Sikkink 1998). Constructivism's work on the mechanisms of change straddles "being" and "becoming." Some constructivists, for instance, Jeffrey Legro (2000), focus on structural mechanisms of change, suggesting that preexisting ideational structures affect the external shocks that are most likely to lead to changes in collective beliefs and affect those actors who are most likely to implement new ideas successfully. Other constructivists, however, are closer to a "becoming" ontological perspective, emphasizing epistemic change (Ruggie 1993), the "life cycles of norms" (Finnemore and Sikkink 1998), and the continuous negotiation of norms that produce regional orders (Barnett 1998). Friedrich Kratochwil (1989) and Nicholas Onuf (1989) uncover the processes by which language and rules construct social facts. They are interested in explaining how social rules and what John Austin (1962) and John Searle (1995) have called "speech acts" "make the process by which people and society constitute each other continuous and reciprocal" (Onuf 1989, 59). Other constructivists, such as Neta Crawford (2002), Ted Hopf (2002), Karen Litfin (1994), Christian Reus-Smit (1999), and Jutta Weldes (1999), conduct historical and interpretive research aimed at understanding the emergence of social reality. Critical constructivists (Cox 1986), in turn, study social structures as they change through history.

The recent shift in IR to social practices emphasizes the processual production of the entities involved in social construction, rather than the entities themselves (including ideas).[10] It thus reinforces constructivism's

[10] See Adler 2005, 2008; Adler and Pouliot 2011a, 2011b; Adler-Nissen 2014; Büger and Gadinger 2014; Jackson and Nexon 1999b; Kratochwil 1989; Neumann 2002; Onuf 1989, 2013; Pouliot 2007, 2010, 2016.

dynamic dimension and more firmly grounds it in a "becoming" ontology. To a large extent, cognitive evolution theory is an effort to highlight how practices and collective knowledge enter into the constitution of social orders and, more generally, the construction of social reality, through action. As I show in subsequent chapters, from a practice perspective the classic agent/structure dichotomy highlights action and processes rather than entities and considers agents and social structures as propensities that become actual only in and through practice. It thus identifies practices as the source of international change (Adler and Pouliot 2011a, 2011b).

Searle's Construction of Social Reality

John Searle's (1995, 1998, 2010) work on the construction of social reality, which IR scholars have increasingly used to theorize constructivism (Adler 1997, 2005; Hall 2008, 2017; Kessler and Kratochwil 2012; Ruggie 1998a), provides a clear example of a becoming ontology.[11] But given Searle's (1995, 155, 195) commitment to external realism,[12] I am not sure that he would agree with me. I have more to say about Searle's ontological commitments later. Here, I mention only his social and institutional ontology, which is emergent, maintained by processes, relations, language, and practices, and existing only to the extent that people have *confidence* over time in the status and functions they assign to material and social objects. In my view, Searle's "becoming" ontology encompasses his external realism assumptions.

According to Searle, social facts and institutions, such as money, marriage, and property, do not exist until people collectively intentionally attach meaning, mainly status and functions (Y), to material and social entities (X) in context (C).[13] Thus, social reality *emerges*[14] from the attachment of status functions to physical objects (Searle 1995), as well as to social objects, such as a corporation (Searle 2010). Social reality

[11] Material substances, of course, are part of Searle's ontology, but when it comes to social entities, he understands them as proxies for patterns of activities.

[12] The notion that there is a physical reality outside our mental representations. Searle (1995) did not take external realism as a theory of truth but as a "background" presupposition, a requirement of intelligibility, a publicly accessed reality that allows people to make accessible claims. He conceived the notion of the background to prevent an infinite regress in the interpretation of representations, such as rules, and defined it as a set of nonintentional or preintentional capacities that enable intentional states. Intentional states function only given a set of background capacities that do not themselves consist in intentional phenomena (ibid., 129, 141, 143).

[13] Searle (2010) recently argued that to have collective intentions people need to have beliefs about each other's intentions.

[14] On social emergence, see Sawyer 2005. On collective intentions as an emergent phenomenon, see Gibbs 2001; Jansen 2005.

does not *exist* until people collectively take these objects as having a certain status and exercising a function. Shared conventions and practices, in turn, determine which objects perform a particular function, thus constituting social reality (ibid., 49). The imposition of status functions is itself a *practice*; only when the practice becomes regular does it turn into a constitutive rule as in "X stands as Y in C." People need not be conscious of rules, nor "follow" rules; in most cases, people are born into a world where social facts are taken for granted. In other words, people need not be aware of collective intentionality, other than perhaps at the point of origin – when a piece of paper first became money.

Searle argues that the main move from physical objects to cultural objects or social facts relates to language, or what he calls "declarations": speech acts that "change the world by declaring that a state of affairs exists and thus bringing that state of affairs to existence" (Searle 2010, 12). Language can only describe practices or conventions that represent certain status functions (ibid.):

> The word "money" marks one mode in the whole network of practices, the practices of owing, buying, selling, earning, paying for services, paying off debts, etc. As long as the object is regarded as having that role in the practices, we do not actually need the word "money" in the definition of money, so there is no circularity or infinite regress. The word "money" functions as a placeholder for the linguistic articulation of all these practices. (Searle 1995, 52)

Once a status function is imposed on a physical or social entity, "it now symbolizes something else . . . this move can exist only if it is collectively represented as existing. The collective representation is public and conventional, and it requires some vehicle" (Searle 1995, 74–75). For example, when we say that "such and such bits of paper count as money, we genuinely have a constitutive rule, because . . . such and such bits of paper [are insufficient to consider them as money, nor do they] specify causal features that would be sufficient to enable the stuff to function as money without human agreement" (ibid., 44). In other words,

> the very definition of the word "money" is self-referential, because in order that a type of thing should satisfy the definition, in order that it should fall under the concept of money, it must be believed to be, or used as, or regarded as, etc., satisfying the definition. For these sorts of facts, it seems to be almost a logical truth that you cannot fool all the people at one time. If everybody always thinks that this sort of thing is money, and they use it as money and treat it as money, then it is money. (ibid., 32)

Searle quite clearly portrays a "becoming" world – that "what we think of as social *objects*, such as governments, money and universities, are in fact placeholders for patterns of *activities* . . . the whole operation of agentive functions and collective intentionality is a matter of ongoing activities and the creation of the possibility of more ongoing activities" (ibid., 57). He goes on to say that

> since the function is imposed on a phenomenon that does not perform that function solely in virtue of its physical construction, but in terms of the collective intentionality of the users, each use of the institution is a *renewed expression* of the commitment of the users to the institutions. Individual dollar bills wear out. But the institution of paper currency is reinforced by its continued use. (ibid., emphasis added)

Like Heraclitus's river that is not the same when we cross it twice, social reality is in a constant state of flux. "Social objects are always … constituted by social acts; and, in a sense, the object is just the continuous possibility of the activity. A twenty-dollar bill, for example, is a standing possibility of paying for something" (ibid., 36). A collectivity of people's continuous acceptance of the status function that makes a piece of paper be money entails duration and process in a world made of relationships rather than things.

Status functions, for example, the fact that Angela Merkel is Germany's chancellor, carry "deontic powers," namely rights, duties, obligations, entitlements, etc. (Searle 2010, 7–8; see also Hall 2017).[15] Deontic power emerges from the construction of social reality. Former President Barack Obama's ability to request that American troops be sent to a faraway place, which creates reasons for action that are independent of what the troops may be inclined to do (ibid., 70), rests on the imposition of status functions on Obama's persona as US president. Deontic power is not only "relational" – as in resting on the relationship between actors (Baldwin 2013) – but is also processual. It depends on the duration of and ongoing and constant recognition of the status functions that make it become, on and on, what it is. The constitution of social ontologies is thus an ongoing process. For example, the police's or the military's coercive power rests on both the power of the gun and the continuing collective agreement that people belonging to these institutions can carry guns and kill on behalf of the state. Searle is not merely saying, as in the Weberian notion of the legitimate use of coercive power, that these institutions possess authority – obviously they do. But their authority relies on deontic power; it rests on the collective creation and recognition of, and confidence in, these institutions' status and functions over time.

[15] "Deontic powers … once recognized … provide us with reasons for acting that are independent of our inclinations and desires" (Searle 2010, 8).

Once the collective intentionality and confidence keeping social facts intact stops – as in the case of the fall of the Soviet Union and South African apartheid – political and coercive power evaporates into thin air, and so do the institutions that rely on such powers. We therefore need to recognize three "becoming" processes regarding the construction of social reality: first, creation processes; second, processes involved in its continued existence, for instance, its public representation and recognition; and, finally, processes in which the collective intentionality and confidence on which the status functions rely weaken or disappear. In my own words, Searle's (1995, 2010) social facts evolve, but even when they are kept metastable, they depend on constant processes of collective recognition and acceptance of their existence.

Karl Popper's "Propensity Theory" and "World 3"

While Karl Popper's (1959, 1963, 1979) philosophy of science is usually typified as positivist (he embraced empirical falsification), very few recent philosophers have been as forceful as he was in presenting the view that we live in an indeterminate world, a notion that he did not consider incompatible with moderate realism. This is not the place, nor do I have the credentials, to engage in a thorough discussion of Popper's philosophy. But I will make the case that Popper embraced a "becoming" ontology (Caygill 1999, 1) that vividly came through in his "propensity theory" (to be found in Popper's *Postscript to the Logic of Scientific Discovery* [1956/1982]) and in his philosophy of mind about the world of objective knowledge and institutions, or "World 3."

According to the received view of quantum theory (the so-called Copenhagen Interpretation), probabilities have to do with our state of mind, a subjectivist theory of probabilities. But Popper argued that the world would be just as indeterminate even if there were no observing subjects to experiment with or interfere with it (Prigogine 1980, 132).[16] Quite apart from the fact that "we do not *know* the future," Popper (1990, 19) said, "the future is *objectively* not fixed. The future is open: objectively open" (1990, 17–18). In accordance with his indeterminism assumption, he suggested a theory of objective indeterminacies or propensity theory, where there "exist weighted possibilities which are more than mere possibilities, but tendencies or propensities … to realize themselves which are inherent in all possibilities" (Popper 1990, 12).

[16] In a seminal study, Humphreys (1985) explained why propensities are different from probabilities and why we should consider them as dispositions.

While Max Born, Werner Heisenberg, and Erwin Schrödinger influenced Popper in developing propensity theory (Caygill 1999), he probably owed the most to pragmatist Charles S. Peirce, whom Popper claimed to have been his intellectual hero (Hutcheon 1995, 2). Long before Popper, Peirce developed a dispositional theory of probabilities based on the concept of habit, which he took as "what would happen under certain circumstances" (Peirce qtd. in Miller 1975, 125).[17]

In proposing propensity theory, Popper eschewed a Platonic metaphysics of universals, but he followed Aristotle in embracing the notion of potential. As he put it, "To be is both to be the actualization . . . and to be a propensity to become" (1982c, 205). Unlike Aristotle, however, and consistent with a becoming ontology, Popper highlighted processes, relations, and dispositions, rather than substances:

> Like all dispositional properties, propensities exhibit a certain similarity to Aristotelian potentialities. But there is an important difference: they cannot, as Aristotle thought, be inherent in the individual *things*. They are not properties inherent in the die, or in the penny, but in something a little more abstract, even though physically real: they are relational properties of the experimental arrangement of the conditions we intend to keep constant during repetition. Here again they resemble forces, or fields of forces . . . Force, like propensity, is a relational concept. (1959, 37–38)

Popper understood propensities as *objective processes*; they are unrelated to our lack of knowledge although the evolution of knowledge may be an important part of a changing situation. "The world is no longer a causal machine – it can now be seen as . . . an unfolding process of realizing possibilities and of unfolding new possibilities" (Popper 1990, 18–19; see also Popper 1982c).[18] Thus, while propensities are not properties inherent in an object and are not mere possibilities or even statistical probabilities, they are "real properties of the whole physical situation" (Popper 1990, 17). They are also inherent in social situations, *in what people do or practice*, therefore, in the particular ways in which situations change: "our world of propensities is creative" (ibid., 17, 20). Faithful to a becoming ontology, Popper considered that in "our real changing world, the situation and, with it the possibilities, and thus the propensities, change all the time. They certainly may change if we . . . *prefer* one possibility to another; or if we *discover* a possibility where we have not seen one before" (ibid., 17).

[17] According to Miller, Peirce and Popper disagreed quite substantively on propensity theory, but they concurred on the view that "probabilities are physically real relational properties" (1975, 125). See also Haack and Kolenda 1977.

[18] "Causation is just a special case of propensity: the case of a propensity equal to 1, a determining demand, or force, for realization" (Popper 1990, 21).

The implications of Popper's approach are startling. First, a world of propensities means that "our very understanding of the world changes the conditions of the changing world; and so do our wishes, our preferences, our motivations, our hopes, our dreams, our phantasies, our hypotheses, our theories. Even our erroneous theories change the world, although our correct theories may ... have a more lasting influence" (ibid., 17). Second, the future is not determined entirely by the past, whether physical or subjective. "Past situations, whether physical or psychological or mixed, do not determine the future situation. Rather, they determine changing propensities that influence future situations without determining them in a unique way ... It is not the kicks from the back, from the past, that *impel* us but the attraction, the lure of the future and its competing possibilities, that attract us, that entice us. This is what keeps life – and, indeed, the world – unfolding" (ibid., 17–18, 21). For Popper, the future evolves by means of *expectations* or the human capacity of foresight. Through foresight, "one can look ahead to the future consequences of current actions, without actually committing oneself to those actions" (Holland 1992, 25), thus changing, "rearranging," or "engineering" the future.

Popper's theory of "World 3" also anchors in a becoming ontology. In most discussions about Popper's "World 3," scholars usually aim to show Popper's placement of knowledge *not only* in human minds but *also* in the world of cultural facts. My aim here is also to point out that grasping what knowledge is requires understanding the dynamic processes and relationships between Popper's three worlds. In a nutshell, Popper divided the world into "World 1," "World 2," and "World 3." "World 1 is the world of all physical bodies and forces and fields of forces; also of organisms, of our bodies and their parts." World 2 is the subjective world "of conscious experiences, our thoughts, our feelings of elation or depression, our aims, our plans of action." "World 3" is the cultural world, or the world of the products of the human mind, "and especially the world of our languages; of our stories, our myths, our explanatory theories ... of our technologies ... of architecture and of music" (Popper 1982a, 53–54). "World 3" acquires its ontological reality because "a thought once it is formulated in language, becomes an *object* outside ourselves. Such an object can then be inter-subjectively *criticized* – criticized by others as well as by ourselves" (Popper 1982b, 118). Once the objects in "World 3" are collectively generated, their reality is also predicated on the fact that they can have real consequences – intended and not.[19]

[19] While both Bourdieu (1990) and Searle (1995) conceive "habitus" and "background knowledge" respectively as the aggregate of individuals' dispositions and preintentional

The reality of Popper's three worlds is both relational, that is, consisting of processes between the "three worlds," and emergent. Nuclear-deterrence theory, for example, was first a set of abstract ideas in theoreticians' minds (World 2), recorded in books, articles, and governmental memos (World 1). In time, deterrence theory became a practice, an institutional fact (World 3) that was independent from the intellectuals' subjectivities, which conceived the theory (World 2), and whose effects went far beyond the paper on which the theory was recorded (World 1). As practice, deterrence had all kinds of intended and unintended physical and political consequences during the Cold War, including international crises, the practice of arms control, and eventually the end of the Cold War (World 3). Deterrence practice also affected and gave meaning and purpose to materials, such as bombs, bombers, and missiles (World 1). Recall the "Samurai crab" story. A myth in people's minds (World 2) became the practice/background knowledge (World 3) of the Heike people, who, in throwing the "Samurai crab" back into the sea, not only perpetuated the myth as a practice but also affected the course of a crab species' natural evolution, thus changing the physical world (World 1).

"Pragmatic Realism"

The studies I reviewed support the view that some of the differences between pragmatism and realism (in IR, see Kratochwil 2007; Wight 2006) can be bridged by a "pragmatic realist" approach, a concept that I liberally borrow from Hilary Putnam (1990, 1995) but to which I provide a partially different meaning. In Putnam's pragmatic realism,[20] while the world may be causally independent of the mind, "reality is

beliefs, Peirce and Popper concur that ideas exist objectively, beyond the individuals' minds. According to Haack and Kolenda (1977), while Popper (1978) thought that World 3 was causally related to World 1 and therefore separate from it, Peirce took material objects to be inseparable from the thoughts they contain. "Popper's doctrine of the Three Worlds ... is rather an interesting instance of overcoming dualism's problem of strict separation of minds and bodies with the aid of contemporary developments in the natural and formal sciences" (Naraniecki 2014, 146). Because I consider material objects and objective thoughts outside the mind (World 3) as ontologically inseparable, I therefore consider Popper's conception of World 1, World 2, and World 3 useful for understanding intersubjectivity and social facts (Searle 1995). The main difference between Popper and Searle on this point is that World 3 exists in the collectivity of individual minds but is also exosomatic: it exists institutionalized in practices. My view is closer to Popper's.

[20] Putnam repeatedly revised his ontological-epistemological claims. After a phase in which he adopted external or metaphysical realism, he later adopted pragmatic realism or internal realism. More recently, he moved onto what he called "natural or direct realism," the view that "we have direct access to the world – we perceive objects ... without the help of any intervening epistemological entities" (Żegleń 2002, 93).

internal to one's perspective" (Sosa 1993, 607), so the world ontologically depends on the human mind. Like Putnam, I adopt a monist and nonrepresentational view of reality (see also Jackson 2010). I also take a pragmatist and constructivist perspective on knowledge. But like Searle, I assume an external reality as a condition of intelligibility, adopt Popper's perspective on the autonomy of institutional facts, and, like Dewey (1960 [1929], 136–37), do not deny the ontological status of unobservable theoretical entities (Pihlström 2008, 42). I share with Putnam the angst one feels when caught in the "twilight zone" between external realism and conceptual relativism, and despite the fact that I am not a philosopher, I will try my nonexpert hand at squaring the circle.

Pragmatic realism combines pragmatist and realist-ontological assumptions with pragmatist epistemological assumptions; it accords primacy to movement and change by grounding pragmatic realism on practices. As Patrick Jackson said, "Nietzche's dissolution of Cartesian dualism involved detaching knowledge from the two alternative bases posed by mind-world dualism – mind, or world – and placing it somewhere quite distinct: in the social practices in which people ... engage as they live their lives and go about their business" (2010, 126). The literature on becoming I reviewed amply supports this contention.

I ground pragmatic realism on six ontological arguments. (1) Like Searle (1995), I take external reality only as a condition of intelligibility, which helps us, in Dewey's sense, to "transact," make claims, and share common practices. However, I dispense with Searle's representational understanding of reality.[21] (2) The material world enters through our knowledgeable selves – our bodies, but also through the materiality of practices and communities of practice (Latour 1993, 2005; Nicolini 2013, 168–69). (3) I adopt Popper's (1990) notion that the propensity for things to become the way they are results from how real situations evolve in practice – pragmatic realism highlights how indeterminate real propensities may be fulfilled in practice. (4) I take background knowledge as intersubjective but also as "subjective," consisting of socially generated and normatively based individual dispositions and expectations that are not just in the minds of individuals but also in the practices themselves (Taylor 1971, 27). Thus, they are "objective," in Popper's World 3 sense.

[21] Searle (1995, 154) argued that as long as we are not referring to notions of "truth," it is possible to hold a realist perspective and deny a correspondence theory. However, he held both realism *and* a correspondence theory.

(5) I agree with Gilbert (1992, 2014) that groups (such as communities of practice), have ontological status and share a "we feeling" arising from their joint actions. I also agree with her normative (but not necessarily moral) approach to collective intentionality that requires a joint commitment.[22] The collective intentionality of communities of practice requires a joint commitment toward (a) the practice that constitutes them, (b) performing competently, (c) the constitutive rules and norms that are intertwined with anchoring practices, and (d) mutual accountability and suitable justification among community members (Boltanski and Thévenot 2006; Rouse 1999, 2001, 2007). As I will argue in Chapter 10, communities of practice may also sometimes have a joint commitment to practices and knowledge's "common humanity." Because Europeans' joint commitment to a united Europe may be declining, integration practices are challenged and Europe has increasingly questioned its "we" collective intentionality.

(6) This normative approach is not the only reason that, with Searle (1995, 2010), I take background knowledge as a set of collectively shared dispositions and expectations embedded in practices. I disagree with him that the background is only preintentional. In this sense, I am closer to Bourdieu's concept of "habitus," which is endowed with meaning and significance. Except I disagree with Bourdieu's notion that the habitus is only phenomenological and embodied (see Bourdieu and Wacquant 1992, 14–16).[23] More specifically, in tune with Hume (1988), Nietzsche (1969), and Wittgenstein (1953), I take background knowledge as *intersubjective collective understandings* bound with practices. Individuals' dispositions and expectations are the subjective side of intersubjectivity, which is why background knowledge is not necessarily preintentional. I therefore agree with Goffman's (1974) and Taylor's (1985) interpretative notions that background knowledge, as embedded in material social practices, is a precondition for the constitution of the actor (Rasche and Chia 2009). "The background understanding that enables practices ... is bound to the performed practices and creates a framework that is used by actors within the practices to interpret the world and themselves" (ibid., 720).

It is important to articulate why I take background dispositions and expectations as nonrepresentational. Like Dewey, I consider that the

[22] Both Searle (1995, 2010) and Tuomela (2007) take individuals as ontological primitives without granting the community an ontological status. So while they have a nonreductive approach to intentionality, they have a reductive approach to individuals.

[23] For a very useful comparison between Searle's "background" and Bourdieu's "habitus," see Marcoulatos 2003.

"business of thought is not to conform to or reproduce the characters already possessed by objects but to judge them as potentialities of what they become through an indicated operation" (1960 [1929], 135–37; see also Pihlström 2008, 33). As I suggested in Chapter 1,[24] I take cognitions as being social. Forms of thinking are attributes of communities. Fleck (1979) expressed this argument with the concept of a "thought collective," which resonates with my interpretation of communities of practice. Thus, "members of that collective not only adopt certain ways of perceiving and thinking, but they also continually transform it – and this transformation does occur not so much 'in their heads' as in their interpersonal space" (Sady 2016, n.p.). The communitarian approach to dispositions and expectations I suggest is consistent with Schatzki's (2002, 2005) "site" ontology. In my case the "site" is communities of practice that "steer a path between individualism and societism" (Schatzki 2005, 469) ontologies. Communities of practice possess propensities for social orders' change and stability. Therefore, they are not merely a heuristic instrument for theorizing about social-order evolution. To paraphrase Karl Popper, communities of practice are real: "if kicked, they kick back" (1982a, 116).

Background knowledge is also "objective" in Popper's World 3 sense. It both embodies and is an intrinsic part of practices' material reality, like books, plans, maps, constitutions, etc. Like deterrence theory and the "samurai crab" myth, background knowledge as autonomous reality can have real intended and unintended consequences in the material and subjective worlds. I agree with Patrick Jackson that intersubjective background knowledge, bound with social practices, occupies "a public space external to the individual minds of the participants but not therefore independent of all minds in general" (2010, 129).

So far, I have referred to pragmatic-realist ontology. But pragmatic realism rejects epistemological realism. Because social reality, such as practices and social orders, is meaningful, and also because "reality is ever-changing and hence resistant to description in terms of fixed categories" (Chia 1999, 210), I adopt a pragmatist and constructivist epistemology that avoids the Cartesian trap of epistemologically separating ideas and the material world (Jackson 2010). Pragmatic realism adopts the pragmatist view that knowledge depends on the practices, procedures, and habits that acquire epistemic authority among communities of

[24] See also Clark and Chalmers 1998; De Jaegher et al. 2010; Hutchins 1995; Theiner, Allen, and Goldstone 2010; Tomasello 2009; Walter 2014; and Wilson 2001 for perspectives that suggest that "cognition takes place not just in the head but also outside in transactions with the world" (Wendt 2015, 275).

knowers. Pragmatists ground understanding on scientific consensus, after knowledge has passed many "reality checks." Knowledge is fallible (Peirce qtd. in Miller 1975) and subject to revision and replacement. Pragmatic realism also emphasizes contingency and the effects of the construction of social reality on knowledge. It also highlights how, in practice, indeterminate real propensities can be fulfilled, and that the best-up-to-date accounts of the world depend on intersubjective understandings and practical knowledge, which are socially constructed (Fish 2010). Knowledge and practice, as Dewey (1988) argued, are two sides of the same coin.

Underscoring that knowledge of the natural and social worlds is always from a point of view, the propensity of social facts to emerge is related to the collective meaning that material and social entities carry as social facts. It follows that *the intersubjective background knowledge with which communities' practices are bound, and the related dispositions and expectations of practitioners that evoke reasons for action – all of which are part of a pragmatist interpretation of social reality – may also be interpreted as being part of the social mechanisms that scientific realists* (Wight 2006)[25] *believe help causally and constitutively explain social reality*. But these mechanisms do not exist outside social practices.

Like James and Dewey, pragmatists can acknowledge scientific practices, according to which unobservable theoretical entities are postulated, while agreeing with them that theories are fallible and "above all, instruments for coping with the world" (Pihlström 2008, 37, 43). Rescher, a major exponent of process philosophy, articulated a similar approach: "Theory is ... subordinated to practice, a circumstance that speaks loud and clear on behalf of a realistic pragmatism – a position whose orientation is at once realistic and pragmatic because successful praxis is, in the end, the best index of reality that is at our effective disposal" (Rescher 2005, 79).

Pragmatic realism, as applied to cognitive evolution, has consequeces for social explanation. It requires a process-oriented, rather than a variance-type, explanation:

There is, as Geels and Schot put it, a fundamental difference between theories of variance, which explain "outcomes as the product of independent variables acting on dependent variables" and theories of process, which ... explain outcomes by tracing the stream of events through which a process unfolds. The more emergent concept of process allows that the unit of analysis "may

[25] "Scientific realism in its strongest form stands committed to the thesis that the world is as science holds it to be: that the theories of science state the literal truth about reality as it actually is" (Rescher 2005, 76).

undergo metamorphosis over time and change meaning. By contrast theories of variance necessarily suppose that "the world is made up of fixed entities that maintain a unitary identity through time." (Shove et al. 2012, 144; see also Geels and Schot 2010, 79)

Subsequent chapters will build on a "becoming" and pragmatic-realist approach. One of its payoffs will be showing that, unlike Wendt's (1999) past constructivist work, but in line with his latest ontological work (2015), we should not separate material and ideational social reality and agency and structure. We also should not treat causation and constitution as part of different epistemologies.

3 Evolutionary Epistemology

> It would probably be an understatement to say that evolution has not had a particularly good press within the social sciences; it has not done so for the better part of a century. (Dunbar 2007, 29)

Evolutionary epistemology[1] serves as the basis for the concepts of evolutionary constructivism and cognitive evolution theory. I follow a sociocultural, mainly epistemic, rather than a naturalist, evolutionary epistemology track, both of which developed almost in parallel during the twentieth century.[2] There is a straight philosophical and sociological line between evolutionary epistemology – especially as developed by early pragmatists[3] and by philosophers of science[4] – and a cognitive evolution theory of social orders. I include a short history of evolutionary epistemology here to document some of the sources of cognitive evolution theory. Against the backdrop of a plurality of interpretations of, and disagreements about, the concept of evolutionary epistemology, and the problem of how to explain sociocultural evolution, in the tradition of analytical political theory I *analyze* concepts as solutions to problems (List and Valentini 2016, n.p.).[5]

Evolutionary theories are experiencing a revival in the social sciences. But because of the wide array of interpretations of evolutionary theory,

[1] "Epistemology is a theoretical, practical, and moral enterprise that cannot be confined to the methods or forms of knowledge of any single field" (Stokes 1989, 505)

[2] My categorization departs from evolutionary epistemology's conventional classification into the "evolution of epistemic mechanisms" (EEM) and the "epistemic evolution of theories" (EET). EEM, focusing on the development of cognitive mechanisms in animals and humans (Bradie and Harms 2012), aims to study, among other things, the capacity of our evolved sensory systems to disclose truth. The EEM concept is consistent with what I mean by "naturalist" evolutionary epistemology. The EET concept, which refers to how theories or bodies of knowledge transform or are selectively retained, while closer and intimately related to what I call sociocultural evolutionary epistemology, can also be modeled after natural processes and mechanisms.

[3] Such as James M. Baldwin (1895), John Dewey (1922), William James (1890), George Herbert Mead (2015), and Charles Sanders Peirce (1965a).

[4] Such as Thomas Kuhn (1970) and Stephen Toulmin (1972).

[5] For the methodology of analytical political theory, see List and Valentini 2016.

and because for substantive and ideological reasons, social and cultural evolutionary theories have been controversial, I find it imperative to make some preliminary clarification. Basing my theory on a reading of evolutionary epistemology, according to which organic evolution is only one instance of a broader epistemological pattern of evolutionary change and metastability, I break ranks with evolutionary works in the social sciences that rest on natural science analogies. So I stay away from the concept of "generalized Darwinism" (Aldrich et al. 2008; Hodgson and Knudsen 2006b, 2010), according to which Darwinian mechanisms are highly relevant for the study of human societies and culture. I also repudiate old and new "social Darwinist" ideas (Haeckel 1905; Morgan 1903; Spencer 1904) and do not subscribe to a reduction of the social sciences to the natural sciences (Gat 2009; Lopez et al. 2011; Wilson 1975).

I do not lose any sleep worrying whether evolutionary analogies match Charles Darwin's (Hodgson and Knudsen 2006b) or Jean-Baptiste Lamarck's theories (Gilady and Hoffman 2013). While I do not attribute a predetermined direction (Wendt 2003) or claim of perfectibility (Parsons 1977) to cognitive evolution, I admit that "better" social orders may be possible, for example, practices that cultivate the value of common humanity, thus respect life, unrelatedly to particularistic identities, and reduce human suffering from war and poverty. Finally, evolutionary epistemology is interdisciplinary. While its study requires expert knowledge, it also requires epistemic humility and an open mind about the use of theories outside one's own discipline for heuristic reasons. Had Darwin abstained from using economist T. R. Malthus's theory as an insight for his natural-selection theory, perhaps Lamarck's evolutionary theory would be dominant today.

Evolutionary Epistemology

Evolutionary Theory

Charles Darwin explained evolution by natural selection as resulting from two processes: blind variation or random mutations (chance) and selective retention (necessity).[6] The first process involves the random variation in the organism's interactive traits. In the second process, only those organisms that developed some interactive trait that makes them fit to survive the competitive nature (constant struggle for finite resources)

[6] While Darwin got most of the credit for early evolutionary theory, Alfred R. Wallace developed a very similar theory at roughly the same time that Darwin did.

of their environment (resources and other organisms) will pass these advantages on to their offspring, thus outproducing, and eventually leading to the demise of, their related species. If by chance, as the popular example goes, some giraffes happened to acquire longer necks, those giraffes that could more easily reach the abundance of leaves in tall trees (given environmental pressures) preferentially survived, whereas shorter-necked giraffes eventually disappeared. Evolutionary theory therefore "tells a story about the relative rates of survival of variants within a population." In other words, the environment "chooses." It shapes "the selection pressures experienced by these preexisting variants and thus influences the relative chances of success or failure" (Shelef 2010, 16).

Several generations after Darwin, partly because of Gregor Mendel's work on the laws of inheritance, and later the development of evolutionary genetics by, among others, Theodosius Dobzhansky (1955, 1962), Julian Huxley (1942), and Ernst Mayr (1963), a "modern evolutionary synthesis" emerged. In general, it rests on three basic assumptions: natural selection, random genetic mutations and recombination as the cause of variation, and geographic isolation (Levit et al. 2011, 553). While natural selection continues to be one of the key evolutionary mechanisms at the macro level, the major agent of evolutionary change is the gene. In 1966, G. C. Williams defined a gene as "any hereditary information for which there is a favorable or unfavorable selection bias equal to several or many times its rate of endogenous change" (Hull 1988, 405).[7] Genetic mechanisms like mutation, flow, and drift amount to the micro-foundations that sustain changes at the macro level. Neo-Lamarckian approaches, emphasizing complex adaptive structures, directed evolution or orthogenesis. Molecular and other constraints determine major transitions and "saltationism" (Bateson 1894), more recently refined by Gould and Eldredge (1977) as "punctuated equilibrium" theory – became alternatives to the modern synthesis. Punctuated equilibrium theory argues that most species will not gradually transform into another species and therefore not exhibit much change for most of

[7] Later, R. Lewontin added three basic principles to our contemporary understanding of natural selection: "1. *Phenotypic variation* – different individuals in a population have different morphologies, physiologies, and behaviors. 2. *Differential fitness* – different phenotypes have different rates of survival and reproduction in different environments. 3. *Fitness is hereditable* – there is a correlation between parents and offspring in the contribution of each to future generations" (Hull 1988, 403). The genotype refers to the genetic material that the organism inherits and passes along to its offspring. The phenotype refers to the actual appearance of an organism, its parts, organs, etc.

their evolutionary history. But they may exhibit sudden change from rapid and sudden speciation.[8]

Following Williams, Richard Dawkins (1976) described "selfish" genes as "*replicators*," blueprints, or structures – anything copies are made of. They are characterized by longevity, fecundity, and fidelity. The key notion here is that replicators are structures. Even when the material organism is destroyed at replication, the structure survives and remains intact. Replicators, however, need "*vehicles*" that, according to Dawkins, are the organisms interacting with their environment. Vehicles fight for "economic" resources in the environment on behalf of their genes; they make their genes safe for the future.

Building on Dawkins, David Hull described the entire set of concepts that group together natural selection's macro and micro dimensions. He described a "*replicator*" as "an entity that passes on its structure largely intact in successive replications. [An] *interactor* [as] an entity that interacts as a cohesive whole with its environment in such a way that this interaction *causes* replication to be differential . . . *Selection* [as] a process in which the differential extinction and proliferation of interactors *cause* the differential perpetuation of the relevant replicators. *Lineage* [as] an entity that persists indefinitely through time either in the same or an altered state as a result of replication" (Hull 1988, 408–9).[9]

Darwin's natural selection theory and the "modern synthesis" put a lid on Jean-Baptiste Lamarck's (1815–22) early evolutionary theory, according to which organisms' changes in one generation may be inherited by future generations. In this view, the environment "instructs" species to develop traits that are essential to survive. Thus, for example, our oft-mentioned giraffe will develop a long neck *in order to* reach leaves on top of the trees. A genetic Lamarckian explanation would say that organisms pass through the genes the result of their "learning" onto later generations. Lamarck also argued that species evolved continually and inexorably from one form to another "along a continuum of increasing complexity" (Dunbar 2007, 30).[10] The Lamarckian concept of acquired characteristics' inheritance was discredited, but as part of a view that evolution occurs through multiple mechanisms, it recently made a

[8] Somit and Peterson (1992) criticized this approach. Gould (2002) later concluded that both punctuated equilibrium and gradual change are important. This conclusion fits with recent accounts of the issue (Levit et al. 2011, 554). In IR, see Krasner 1984; Spruyt 1998.

[9] Nelson and Winter (2002) contest the use of this terminology in the social sciences. See Hodgson and Knudsen 2010, 86.

[10] Darwin showed that evolution was not directional and that an organism's complexity has nothing to do with its age (Dunbar 2007, 31).

comeback (Nowacki et al. 2008). Natural selection theory and the modern synthesis are not universally accepted. Some people reject them because of religious convictions.

Since before Darwin, natural and cultural evolutionary theories have been reciprocally affected by what scholars regarded as significant aspects of mental factors, such as instincts, habits, intelligence, and moral norms (Baldwin 1902; see Richards 1987, 22). Darwin theorized the evolution of ethics (Richards 1987).[11] While the role that instincts and habits play in natural selection processes is a matter for those concerned with natural evolution and does not directly concern us here, as we will see, evolutionary epistemology became deeply concerned with sociocultural concepts. Habits, customs, routines, and practices were interpreted to be replicating units that are selected and inherited in the social world (Hodgson and Knudsen 2010). Cognitive evolution theory, which takes practices and background knowledge as the structural units that are passed on in replication, therefore has fertile intellectual roots.

Sociocultural Rather than Natural Evolution

Evolutionary epistemology comes in two versions, naturalist and sociocultural. A naturalist conception of evolutionary epistemology suggests that natural selection and organic evolution are relevant for the cognitive processes and human senses and are thus an intrinsic part of epistemology (Edelman 1987; Gontier 2006). Sometimes this version of evolutionary epistemology transcends the neural and brain level and, for example, discusses cultural learning as a higher level of evolution (Tomasello 2009). It is nevertheless strongly naturalistic. It extends biological evolution to explain intelligence, cognitive abilities, and notions of truth – whether it makes sense to think that our senses produce "accurate" representations of the world. According to this version, evolutionary epistemology and cognitive evolution are natural: evolution from a single cell to Albert Einstein. I do not follow this evolutionary-epistemological version.

[11] "Darwin himself recognized the potential significance of his core ideas, proposing that natural selection operates upon the elements of language and that natural selection favoured tribal groups with moral and other propensities that served the common good" (Aldrich et al. 2008, 578). Darwin's moral theory – it may be surprising to some that he held a moral theory – said that "habits satisfying peculiar individual desires would wash out over generations, and only those remaining practices conducive to the common good would become deeply entrenched instincts. The latter would constitute the moral motives characteristic of a society" (Richards 1987, 121).

The sociocultural version maintains that the evolution of practices, thoughts, ideas, conceptual understandings, scientific knowledge, norms, more generally culture, and, as I argue, social orders may best be characterized as following an evolutionary pattern.[12] *Although humans act within the limits of natural constraints, and the social constraints they jointly create, social change and metastability result from practices and knowledge's twin processes of creative variation and selective retention.* Rather than rely, via identity, homology, analogy, and metaphor (Cohen 1993, 1994; Ma 2016), on evolutionary processes and mechanisms drawn from the natural sciences, I buy into what W. H. Durham has called "Campbell's rule." This is the evolutionary epistemology I adopt.

According to Campbell's rule, there exists *a general model of evolutionary change*, of which organic evolution is only one instance (Blackmore 1999; Campbell 1965; Durham 1991; Ridley 2015).[13] This means that, while biological evolution and knowledge evolution belong to the same "family" of explanations, they need not necessarily be isomorphic and, therefore, that the power of one theory need not depend on a strict analogy of the other. In other words, natural evolution and cognitive evolution are two subsets of a much more general mechanism of transformation and metastability. This general mechanism suggests that theories of change based on evolutionary epistemology can offer a better explanation than, for instance, rational choice and structural-functionalist explanations, without having to reduce the social sciences and the humanities to the natural sciences.

The epistemic version of evolutionary epistemology I adopt is pragmatist for I eschew a strict separation between cognitive and social phenomena (Dewey 1922). On one hand, I embrace Ludwik Fleck's (1979) assertion that cognition is a collective activity, "since it is only possible on the basis of a certain body of knowledge acquired from other people" (Sady 2016). On the other hand, I also espouse Jon Elster's (1983) argument that for an evolutionary principle to make sense in the social sciences it must adopt a feedback loop through human cognition. Even if changes in an institution X, which are explained by a function Y, are unrecognized by actors Z, Y maintains X by a causal loop passing

[12] Scholars can study the evolution of individual knowledge (ontogeny) as well as the evolution of knowledge across time (phylogeny). For a critique of the second version of evolutionary epistemology, see Renzi and Napolitano 2011.

[13] According to Dennett, this general model is algorithmic. Its causal power depends less on the material used than on the algorithm's mindless and foolproof logical structure and procedure (Dennett 1995; see also Dawkins 1983; Lewis and Steinmo 2012). However, this claim is not necessary to uphold Campbell's argument about a general evolutionary model.

through Z, namely, through human cognition. Cognitive evolution theory, akin to artificial natural selection (e.g., the "samurai crab"), requires individual and collective cognition. One may establish collective cognition less by trying to "decipher" psychologically what is *in* the human mind than by following a relational sociological approach that examines intersubjective and subjective (dispositions and expectations) background knowledge. Such knowledge is bound with practices and emerges from, and is maintained by, mutual engagement in communities of practice.

My approach to evolutionary epistemology relies on the notion that there are critical differences between natural selection and sociocultural selection. For example, (1) sociocultural evolution occurs more rapidly than natural evolution. (2) The units of selection in social and cultural selection are not as clearly defined as in natural evolution (Hull 1988, 440). (3) "Cross-lineage borrowing" is much more frequent in sociocultural evolution than in natural evolution (Campbell 1987). (4) Cultural innovations are "pre-selected, in the sense that they have to fit into what a particular [scientific] investigator already believes" (Hull 1988, 456; Toulmin 1972). (5) Sociocultural evolution to some extent involves human intentions, while Darwinian natural evolution does not (Hull 1988, 440). (6) And then, of course, there is the role of human intelligence, judgment, interpretation, and creativity in the social world. (7) Finally, as Gronow argued, "learning is always based on relevance ... this means that we are more sensitive to pick out certain habits than others" (2011, 51).

Some evolutionary epistemologists take the differences between natural and sociocultural evolution to mean that sociocultural is "Lamarckian" (Hayek 1989; Toulmin 1972). They see variation as directed either toward problem solving ("instructionism") or toward anticipating the selection processes, or both, or they take selection as resulting from endogenous, rather than contingent exogenous, processes (Wilkins 1995, 45). Donald Campbell (1987) and David Hull (1988), among others, have disputed the view that sociocultural evolution is Lamarckian.[14] Forcing evolutionary epistemology to choose between "Lamarckian" evolutionary processes (which imply intentional adaptation to survive selection pressures) and "Darwinian" evolutionary processes

[14] Campbell (1987; see also Nelson and Winter 2002) argued that although individuals are purposeful actors, they approach the physical world with incomplete knowledge and so genuine innovations, while guided by the mind, are at least partially blind. Learning and intentional behavior can be consistent with Darwinian selection processes (Hull 1988, 452, 458).

(which do not imply intention) is impractical.[15] First, we can understand individuals as purposeful actors who nevertheless approach the physical world with expectations, which means that knowledge is incomplete, indeterminate, going beyond experience. Second, although people act intentionally, they may arrive at unintended outcomes. Third, although individuals' purposes play a role in the evolution of the social world, nonpurposeful and preintentional intersubjective social structures also partly sustain them (Bourdieu 1977; Dewey 1922; Searle 1995). Finally, as Boyd and Richerson argued (cited in Lewis and Steinmo 2012, 322), a system that responds to both natural selection and adaptive decision-making forces will be able to adapt to varying environments more quickly than organisms that adapt by genes and nontransmitted learning.

A Short History of Evolutionary Epistemology

The theory of evolution was first applied to the social realm around 1860 and for many years was synonymous with theories of organic growth and progress. Sociology, a "nascent" field during the end of the nineteenth century, was drawn to organic analogies of societal evolution. Particularly important was the concept of "organic growth" in the sense of expansion, complexity, and differentiation, which in many cases was strongly progressive (e.g., Comte [1853] 2009; see also Sztompka 1993, 101). Whereas Darwin's natural selection theory emphasized randomness and contingency, sociological theories of organic growth emphasized the deterministic yet gradual and incremental unfolding of potentialities that would inexorably impel particular societies (rather than populations, as in natural selection) in a teleological direction toward "nirvana." A reconstruction of the evolutionary path of human societies, from primitivism to civilization, would thus enable sociologists to explain past history and predict the future (Sztompka 1993).

One of the earliest notable evolutionary sociologists was Herbert Spencer, who believed that civilizations progressed toward more complex, as well as structurally and functionally differentiated, societies. According to Spencer's evolutionary mechanism, when something upset an organism, and thus drove it away from equilibrium, the organism would then

[15] Darwin himself held some Lamarckian notions because he lacked a convincing mechanism of inheritance. The problem was not resolved until Mendel's mechanism of inheritance came to light. Evolutionary biologists adopted the so-called Weizmann Doctrine, according to which genes influence the body but not the other way around (Dunbar 2007, 31–32, 46).

reestablish equilibrium at a higher level of complexity.[16] The evolutionary mechanism Spencer proposed had societies evolving in stages from simple societies, through complex societies, to civilizations (Spencer 1904; Sztompka 1993, 102). He thought that "habitual psychological successions entail some heredity tendency to such successions, which under persistent conditions, will become cumulative in generation after generation" (Spencer 1855, 579).

Similarly, C. L. Morgan speculated about evolution in three stages: savagery, barbarism, and civilization. He also hypothesized that "human thought could exist and become modified only through the agency of other thought ... learning by experience was the analogue of natural selection in the biological world [and] true ideas – true for the individual – would be those that survived the selective process" (Richards 1987, 396–97). Arnold Toynbee, the well-known historian, also studied civilization from an evolutionary perspective (Blackmore 1999, 24), and Emile Durkheim exhibited strong functionalist evolutionist tendencies: "The main direction of evolution is seen in the growing division of labor, differentiation of tasks, duties, and occupational roles, as society moves forward in time" (Sztompka 1993, 105).

At the same time that sociologists and historians were using Darwin to articulate progressive evolutionary theories, a more sinister ideological interpretation began taking hold in the late nineteenth century. It identified evolutionary theory, and particularly Darwin's mechanism of natural selection, with the imperative of the "survival of the fittest," a term coined by Spencer (Dunbar 2007, 31). In a straightforward fashion, it became fashionable in political and military circles to believe that the competitive struggle between races and nations was the key to the survival of some cultures and the extinction of others, that is, the key for "social evolution" and "progress." This approach, known as "social Darwinism," was later instrumental in the development of Fascist and Nazi ideologies, and one of the main reasons for its demise.

Ideas of finality, determinism, and unidirectional evolution were, and are still, characteristic of Marxist thinking, according to which societies evolve because the ownership of the means of production changes hands from one class to another. Marx (1867) and his followers saw this evolution as leading to the triumph of the proletariat and later the classless

[16] Spencer's evolutionary mechanism consisted in "the internalization of external relations and ... this mechanism progressively drove anatomical forms and conjoint mental structures from more generalized adaptive states to more definite correspondences with the environment, from simpler, more homogeneous patterns to more complex and heterogeneous configurations" (Richards 1987, 424).

society. Teilhard de Chardin (1959), Kenneth Boulding (1978), and Erich Jantsch (1981) attempted to unite natural – physical, biological, and social realms – into all-embracing theories of evolution where the processes evolve in an interconnected way toward some final stage: God for de Chardin, ethics for Boulding, and self-transcendence for Jantsch. A large portion of the "Limits to Growth" literature (Meadows et al. 1972) deterministically interpreted the growing depletion of natural resources and the disruption of the physical global environment as evolutionary decadence toward entropy and decay.

Theories of social and cultural evolution flourished in the twentieth century in the fields of sociology and anthropology without the survival-of-the-fittest argument. However, the difficulty of determining what really evolves, as well as the fact that in most cases evolution was considered a teleological concept, hindered these approaches. Talcott Parsons (1971), for example, starting from very different axioms than Marxists did, developed a structural-functional theory of societal evolution characterized by integrative and control processes that have compensatory effects – they restore equilibrium after disturbances (ibid.; Sztompka 1993, 120). Structural changes, in turn, may be progressive in terms of societies' complexity and differentiation. According to Parsons (1971; Sztompka 1993, 121), evolution followed four stages: primitive, advanced primitive, intermediate, and modern.

The evolutionary epistemology I draw from can be traced more directly back to Peirce (1965a), Dewey (1922), Mead (2015), James (1890), and other pragmatist fellow travelers, like James M. Baldwin (1895),[17] who were strongly influenced by the Darwinian revolution (Gronow 2011, 26).[18] Peirce came to evolutionary epistemology as part of his concept of truth.[19] While he was ambivalent about evolutionary epistemology (Campbell 1987, 438–39), Peirce believed that "nature is not a static world of unswerving law but rather a dynamic and dicey world of evolved and continually evolving habits that directly exhibit considerable spontaneity" (Burch 2014, n.p.). Alluding to a relationship between

[17] See Browning 1980; Kuklick 1977; Wiener 1949.

[18] The pragmatists I survey, particularly Baldwin and Dewey, understood epistemic evolution to be part of the transformation of the organism itself. While their views do not adhere strictly to a distinction between sociocultural epistemic and natural evolution, they made a crucial contribution to thinking about the evolution of knowledge and beliefs, and of sociocultural forms, such as habits, practices, institutions, and orders.

[19] Peirce, Dewey, and James "regarded a belief as a kind of bet in a probabilistic universe, and successful beliefs . . . as habits." They "rejected the theory that the mind is a mirror of an external reality. There was no way to hook up ideas with things, Peirce thought, because ideas – mental representations – do not refer to things; they refer to other mental representations" (Menand 2001, 363).

theory formation and successful practices, Peirce thought that the spontaneous development of belief continually creates new habitual beliefs. Habits allow things, from molecules to philosophers, to persist in their condition of sameness (Menand 2001, 365). Belief "is partly determined by old beliefs and partly by new experience . . . if a given habit, considered as determining an inference, is of such a sort as to tend toward the final result, it is correct; otherwise, not. Thus, inferences become divisible into the valid and the invalid; and thus logic takes its reason of existence" (Peirce 1933, 106). Peirce viewed inquiry as a communal activity – the fixation of belief results from a limited local convergence by a particular community at a particular time (Hausman 1993, 216). This communal view, rather than political theory's communitarianism (Walzer 1983), would later resonate with how some scholars conceived the evolution of knowledge and practices (Adler 1991, 2005).

John Dewey, another pragmatist philosopher, who Darwin heavily influenced, adopted a view that a theory of knowledge must begin with how humans respond to environments with the aim of restructuring them (Dewey 1983, 1988; see also Hildebrand 2008). Dewey believed that mental representations are conditioned and selected through interaction between the organism and the environment; he rejected a strict separation between them and thought that mind resulted from their fusion. While Dewey did not explicitly use variation-and-selective-retention epistemology (Campbell 1987, 75), he left an indelible mark on evolutionary epistemology.

First, Dewey understood knowledge as inseparable from doing. On one hand, knowledge is a by-product of activity (Menand 2001, 322); on the other hand, it is an instrument of successful action (Dewey 1988, 16; see also Menand 2001, 361). According to Dewey, maintaining the continuity of knowing requires "an activity which purposefully modifies the environment . . . knowledge in its strict sense of something possessed consists of our intellectual resources – of all the habits that render our action intelligent. Only that which has been organized into our disposition so as to enable us to adapt the environment to our needs and to adapt our aims and desires to the situation in which we live is really knowledge" (Dewey 1916, 388–401).

Second, habits are crucial to understanding Dewey's evolutionary epistemology. According to Dewey, habits are basic human dispositions that, by incorporating experience and the demands of the environment, structure social action and are instrumental for coping with the environment (Dewey 1922; 1983, 32). While habits refer to dispositional modes of thought and action, because humans engage in conscious reflexive deliberation, people can modify them creatively to respond to events, solve problems, and facilitate practical performance (Dewey 1983, 179). Habits are therefore not merely adaptations to a changing external world, and are not simply repetitive, but are the source of the human mind (Dewey 1983, 32). They reflect the human capacity to reconstruct the environment (Alexander 1987, 142). "The environment of action and habits, thus, are mutually constitutive" (Gronow 2011, 94).

Third, like Peirce, Dewey held a social and communitarian view of change and stability. In Dewey's view, individual and collective habits and customs interact. Conduct is always social, but it affects individual minds (Dewey 1922, 63). Dewey's communitarian perspective, in turn, sees that "sociability does not crush individuality," and individuals acquire a sense of self through communities (Gronow 2011, 68). Fourth, in contrast to Baldwin, Dewey rejected imitation as the mechanism for habits' proliferation. Instead, he saw similarity across organisms as the product of a common set of impulses interacting with a common environment. Finally, Dewey identified conflict between habits as a mechanism that promotes reflection and negotiation (ibid.). His pragmatism is to some extent an evolutionary theory of change and stability. While humans create a variety of habits, the environment continually generates the interruption of habits, and thus the need to revise them by means of creative thought and action (Joas 1996, 141–44).

George Mead's contribution to evolutionary epistemology (see Joas 1985, 1996) "lies in the elaboration of a practical theory of social psychology that is concerned with the emergence of human consciousness through creative social action . . . people construct their sense of self in ongoing processes of social engagement" (Elkjaer and Simpson 2006, 4). First, like Dewey, Mead considered that the "'meaning which our world has . . . lie[s] in what we are going to do with it' . . . It does not lie merely in what we know, in our typifications and knowledge schemas . . . Our attention is selective and tends to favor stimuli that relate to what we are doing" (Gronow 2011, 126; see Mead 1936, 90).

Second, Mead's theory of action is dialogical. Community and self are dynamically and symbolically intertwined. Mead considered the emergence of the self with the help of two identities he called the "me" and the "I." The "me" arises in relationship with a community's habits and norms, or what Mead called "the generalized other," and the "I" is the subjective response of self to social conventions represented by the "me"; the "I" is a source of spontaneity and creativity (Aboulafia 2016). From Mead's perspective, community and self are symbiotically related. It follows, third, that his understanding of community does not diminish the self. The perspectives people have of generalized others are "objective" in the sense that "they provide frames of reference and shared patterns of behavior for members of communities" (ibid.). Fourth, Mead's notion of action's creativity (see also Joas 1990b, 1996), which is related to the "I," led him to think of creative actions as mutations, neither of which can be predicted.

Mead left an indelible mark on evolutionary epistemology by exploring the emergence of consciousness via the concept of sociality – the overlap between the "me" and the "I" out of which creative action may come. According to Mead, sociality is the stage between the old order that has not yet disappeared and the new one that has yet to be fully formed. During this stage, mutual adjustments take place and creativity may result. More generally, in "a manner reminiscent of James's account of the stream of thought, Mead argues that the present entails duration (James 1890, 237–83). It retains the receding past and anticipates the imminent future" (Aboulafia 2016, n.p.). The phase of adjustment between past and new orders is a source of creativity (Mead 1932, 47).

Having become interested in the psychological implications of evolutionary theory, James disputed Spencer's ideas that the environment was omnipotent in determining the evolution of mind and behavior, arguing instead that subjective factors also played a critical role (James 1890). James's epistemology consisted of the notion, first, that there are forces within the mind that lead to change or variation in beliefs or ideas. These forces operate somewhat analogously to the spontaneous mutations that occur during genetic reproduction, meaning that an endogenous source of variation is the proximate cause of a change, and environmental selection mechanisms then determine which changes are preserved. According to James, the process by which new ideas come into existence is analogous to evolution (James 1890, 2–8);[20] creative ideas result from a selection process by which they are adapted to the intellectual environment and thereby maintained.[21]

Second, James linked the selective retention of ideas in human minds to their wider selective retention in society. Thus, "the evolutionary perspective explains how fundamental new ideas might be introduced both to an individual consciousness, which preserves those that accord

[20] "'It is far too little recognized,' he observed in an early essay, 'how entirely the intellect is built up of practical interests … Cognition, in short, is incomplete until discharged in act'" (Richards 1987, 447).

[21] According to James, "alternative 'possibilities' compete for 'attention' through 'the phenomenon of consciousness' … If the chosen response has a favorable outcome, the neural pathways that triggered the behavior are strengthened, which 'loads the dice … in favor of those of its performances, which make for the most permanent interests of their brain's owner'" (Macy 1998, 220).

with its already established interests, and to a larger society, which will select or reject them" (Richards 1987, 436). Finally, James argued that in "deciding what to do in a situation, the mind . . . becomes the playground for competing plans of action. When one idea finally dominates our attention to the exclusion of the rivals, action follows automatically" (James 1882, 65–66).

However, James's account of intellectual heredity was rudimentary. Baldwin tried to fill in the gap by suggesting a theory of the selective retention of ideas and their inheritance (1897a, 1897b, 1906, 1909).[22] Baldwin's theory of social heredity considered knowledge as being inherently social, in the sense that "when a thinker asserts to herself or to others that something is truly the case, she concomitantly conceives other people as agreeing" (Richards 1987, 475).[23] In other words, truth is socially confirmable. It is also social because "traditions of knowledge become established in a society and form the hereditary deposit for each generation. A tradition consists of ideas that are fit" (ibid., 476) According to Baldwin, fitness did not mean struggle, "but fitness for imitative reproduction and application" (Baldwin 1897a, 183). Thus, once ideas are selected and infiltrate a society, they become part of the environment against which the new ideas of those living in that society are selected. This argument anticipated the notion that knowledge is a social construction.

Baldwin also contributed to notions of social heredity by considering that the conceptual space of idea variation is constrained by levels of knowledge's hierarchical organization, namely that some knowledge is at a lower level, so people learn it first, and is more primitive. Habit plays a role in how knowledge hierarchical organization functions. As Richards put it, Baldwin argued that ideas

> will not be readily assimilated to our habitual knowledge ... but they must be familiar enough to allow some connections with that foundation, lest they not enter consciousness at all ... As new ideas pass this muster, they gradually enlarge the deposit of habitual knowledge. This legacy, then, becomes our guarantee of the real. Echoing James's conception of reality, Baldwin argued that to regard something as real was to make its idea "part of that copy system which hangs together in our memory, as representing a

[22] "In Baldwin's judgement, James' evolutionary epistemology . . . failed on two accounts: it ignored the social aspect of knowledge, and it seemed to deny any constraints on the production of mental variations" (Richards 1987, 475).

[23] "Our thought is ejective: it imposes a subjective state on others and then assimilates the construction of others against our own perception of the situation" (Richards 1987, 475).

consistent course of conduct and the best adjustment we have been able to effect to our physical and moral environment.'" (Richards 1987, 477; Baldwin's quote is from 1897a, 324)[24]

Baldwin controversially argued that the mind governs both natural selection and social selection,[25] thus stressing that evolution is not just a matter of blind selection, a physical matter.[26] This argument, known as the "Baldwin effect," represents an alternative to Lamarckian evolution for it means that consciousness, by being able to look with foresight, plays a role in the direction evolution takes. Organisms that lack congenital adaptation to a changing environment will survive only if they can accommodate themselves to the environment through conscious learning. Eventually, physical evolution replaces "learned traits with instinctive ones" (Richards 1987, 482–83). This argument led Baldwin to maintain that "societies within which individuals adopted altruistic practices would be selected for in competition with other groups of more egoistically disposed members" (ibid., 485). Following Baldwin's (and Dewey's) ideas on the interaction between habits and environment, more recently Richard Lewontin argued that "animals adapt and construct their environment as much as they become adapted to it" (ibid., 477 paraphrasing Lewontin).

The application of evolutionary thought to the social world later took a naturalistic turn. The main argument was that mind can be reduced to genetics and that even altruism is selfish and depended on genes (Hamilton 1964; Trivers 1971; Williams 1966). E. O. Wilson suggested *sociobiology*, which reduced mind, cognition, and the evolution of consciousness to genes and neurons. Our genes might explain aggressive or altruistic behavior, incest, morality, and ethics. Some in the scientific community, like Jay Gould and Richard Lewontin (1979), disputed arguments that moral evaluations and cognitive abilities may be exclusively explicable by "wires" and argued that we should consider other factors, such as cultural learning (ibid.; Richards 1987, 545).

Pragmatist psychologists and philosophers, by pointing to habits and routines that, while dispositional, can reflexively change through creative ideas and the relationship between mind and social practices, left an indelible mark on the "evolution" of evolutionary epistemology.

[24] Both Baldwin and Peirce emphasized that the selection system of science renders individualist epistemology inadequate (Campbell 1987, 436)

[25] A dominant current in philosophy and cognitive science adduces that mind is purely physical. See, for example, Smart 1978.

[26] This could be seen as a subtle reference to how Baldwin's position contradicts the naturalist position that Richard Dawkins takes in *The Blind Watchmaker* (1996).

Philosophers of science like Karl Popper (1963, 1974, 1982b, 1987), Stephen Toulmin (1972), and Thomas Kuhn (1970), as well as psychologist Donald Campbell (1960, 1974, 1987), went further by adopting an evolutionary general principle of knowledge to explain the evolution of science. Among their many contributions lies the notion of epistemic context that gives meaning to science and scientific practices.

Popper conceived of evolutionary epistemology as taking a succession of theories in science to be similar to the process of selective elimination in nature. He claimed that the highest creative thought, like animal adaptation, is the product of "blind variation" and "selective retention," or a product of trial and error, of conjectures and refutations (Popper 1963). Scientists make conjectures to solve scientific problems; they then test their conjectures against the evidence and rational criticism. Some theories are falsified and replaced by others, and theories that survive do so not because they are necessarily true, but because the rival theories are less fit (Richards 1987, 575). Science, in Popper's view, is thus a "shot in the dark," a bold guess that goes far beyond evidence, and for which justification is less important than the viability of theories or "mutations." Viability, in turn, depends on the ability of theories to solve more problems than their competitor theories.[27]

Popper's evolutionary epistemology had a seldom-recognized "constructivist" side. Echoing Peirce's (Haack and Kolenda 1977) pragmatist "fallibility" view, according to which whatever a community of inquirers takes to be true today may be refuted tomorrow, Popper argued that the survival of theories is no guarantee of eternal life; a species that has survived for thousands of years can still become extinct. A theory that has survived for generations can be refuted eventually. To show that his evolutionary epistemology is neither naturalist nor that it turns science into a subjective enterprise, Popper introduced the notion of cultural world, or "World 3" (see Chapter 2). As Geoff Stokes argued, Popper's

[27] While Imre Lakatos's (1978, vols. 1 and 2) theory of "scientific research programmes" aimed to show that the growth of science is rationally progressive, from the perspective of evolutionary epistemology, he essentially made two contributions. The first consisted of adopting scientific research programs that represent a larger unit of evolution than Popper's scientific ideas or theories, and that are more in consonance with Thomas Kuhn's concept of paradigm. Second, Lakatos amended Popper's concept of scientific selection. He suggested that theories do not become directly and immediately falsified, but rather that, as part of scientific research programs, theories accumulate anomalies. These anomalies are first deflected by means of auxiliary hypotheses, which protect a program's "hard core" and sometime use amended hypotheses to the hard core's benefit. But when auxiliary hypotheses are unhelpful in making predictions and alternative theories of a different research program can make better predictions, then the original program becomes "degenerating" and eventually falsified.

evolutionary epistemology took a hermeneutic turn when he claimed that "in any field of knowledge one must first search out any problems with the 'background' that is normally taken for granted" (1989, 500).[28] This means that science is never free from assumptions and that at every instant it presupposes a horizon of expectations or frame of reference that precedes and confers meanings or significance on our experience, actions, and observations.

Kuhn did not intend to contribute to evolutionary epistemology. He believed that successive stages in the developmental process of ideas are marked by an increase in articulation and specialization. Like Popper and the pragmatists, Kuhn did not take scientific knowledge as relative or absolute (Hutcheon 1995, 28–37), yet he regarded science as being made up of niches within which practitioners go about their scientific habitual practices (Pilström 2008, 26). He called these niches "paradigms." Paradigms are accepted scientific practices from which scientific traditions arise. Science as an activity, rather than as the product of an activity (Pihlström 2008), fits well with how pragmatists understand beliefs or habits of action (Dewey 1922).

Kuhn's (1970) concepts of "paradigms" and "scientific revolutions" helped show that, in any type of scientific discipline, collectively agreed-on sets of concepts and epistemological understandings create the framework for research by structuring the activity of science and scientists.[29] A paradigm leads scientists to reject evidence that is fundamentally out of line with the expectations it generates (Jervis 1972). We can therefore consider paradigms as cognitive structures that constitute what scientists consider as natural or taken for granted. It follows, then, that scientific communities give meaning to data and evidence in accordance with the paradigms that govern periods of "normal" science. During scientific revolutions – those critical moments when belief about scientific phenomena changes, not unlike changes in belief about religion, politics, and aesthetic interpretive communities – one paradigm replaces another, and a new period of normal science commences (Depew and Weber 1985, 240). The resolution of revolutions therefore takes place by the scientific community selecting the fittest way to practice science (Hutcheon 1995, 28–37).[30]

[28] "Popper's proposal that rationality consists of critical problem solving presupposes a prior consensus on values, ends, and interests . . . Epistemology must therefore suggest the social and political preconditions for the successful application of its epistemic norms" (Stokes 1989, 505).

[29] Ludwik Fleck (1979) had a large influence on Kuhn's idea of paradigmatic revolutions.

[30] Before Kuhn, Max Plank argued that "new waves of thought, new theories, usually do not 'overcome' the existing ones due to people changing their way of thinking, but

Taking evolution as a shift in the composition of a gene pool shared by a population, rather than specified in an individual, Toulmin (1972) created an explicit analogy between population genetics and the evolution of scientific disciplines. Substituting competing intellectual variants for genes, and identifying the collectivity of scientists as the carriers of selective variants, Toulmin argued that through processes of selective diffusion and retention some intellectual variants eventually become predominant (1972; see also Campbell 1987, 436). Others, in turn, are completely eliminated and still others do not remain viable but neither do they disappear and they may come back as circumstances change.

We can disaggregate Toulmin's evolutionary epistemology into two arguments. First, Toulmin thought that the objects of evolution or "species" are *scientific disciplines* rather than disembodied ideas.[31] The content of scientific disciplines adapts to the environment in two senses: the intellectual problems a discipline confronts and the social situations of its practitioners (Richards 1987, 576). What is passed on as heredity are, first, sets of specific substantive theories used in a given discipline and, second, sets of explanatory procedures, techniques, and practices that help tell science apart from ideology. Novice scientists, through active participation in their disciplinary communities, inherit the "specific and substantive ideas and theories, the special explanations and techniques that solve recognized problems at any one period" (ibid., 577) as well as the "explanatory ideals" of their discipline. Second, Toulmin described innovation and selection as coupled, which means that variations are not "blind" as in Darwin's evolution theory. Mutations, in Toulmin's words, "are pre-selected for characteristics bearing directly on the requirements for selective perpetuation" (1977, 337). According to Richards, this argument places Toulmin in the Lamarckian camp (1987, 578).[32]

Building on Popper's work, Campbell (1974) developed further evolutionary epistemology, which he also coined (Schilpp 1974). He used

mainly because the advocates of the old theories simply disappear from the scene" (Suteanu 2005, 114).

[31] "Each discipline has certain methods, general aims, and exploratory ideas that provide its coherence over time, its specific identity, while its more rapidly changing content is constituted of loosely related conceptions and theories 'each with its own separate history, structure and implications.' To comprehend the evolution of science so structured requires that one attend to the cultural environment promoting the introduction of new ideas, as well as to the selection processes by which some few of these ideas are perpetuated" (Richards 1987, 576).

[32] This argument is important only to those who through analogy strictly adhere to Darwinist theory.

the evolutionary concept to show that ideas, beliefs, and behavior change as a result of processes of "blind variation" and "selective retention." "A blind-variation-and-selective-retention process," he said, "is fundamental to all inductive achievements, to all genuine increases in knowledge, to all increases in the fit of system to environment" (Campbell 1974a, 421). Campbell assumed that scientists act creatively and intentionally to solve scientific problems, but that their initial introduction to the pool of scientific ideas may not be originally justified by induction or previous trials. He went further than Popper, Kuhn, and Toulmin did to explain "*creative learning*," which he conceptualized as "*cognitive evolution*," a concept I borrowed and then substantially changed the meaning of. The three requirements for cognitive evolution, as Campbell coined it, are (1) mechanisms for replication or reproduction, (2) variety in whatever is reproduced, and (3) mechanisms for selection that consistently favor one type of variation over others. Cognitive evolution, Campbell thought, provides the mechanisms for replication. We learn our ideas, beliefs, and behavior from other people. When variation is introduced into this kind of learning process creativity may result. Because in the social and cultural world there is "cross-lineage" borrowing – people can borrow ideas across disciplines (as I did with Campbell's concept of cognitive evolution), cognitive evolution becomes possible. This may help explain why, as in Gould and Eldredge's (1977) "punctuated equilibrium" theory (see also Somit and Peterson 1992), sudden jumps in creativity can occur, probably more often in the social and cultural world than in the natural world.

Building partly on Campbell's cognitive evolution theory, Robert Richards developed an evolutionary epistemology about how conceptual systems evolve as scientists continually strive to cope with constraints and solve problems in their changing environment. This approach means, first, that the unit of evolution – the lineage or species – is a conceptual system. Second, the evolution of conceptual systems exhibits sensitivity to historical situations and changes. Third, Richards argued that rather than producing a stream of infinite ideas without stop, scientists are constrained in their creative thoughts by education, intellectual connections, the social environment, psychological predispositions, and recently selected ideas (Richards 1987, 581). Finally, selection occurs with public scrutiny of scientific ideas once these ideas are shared. "To the extent . . . that the problem environments of the individual and the community coincide, individually selected ideas or theories will be fit for life in the community" (ibid., 582). The crucial factors affecting selection are logical consistency, semantic coherence, standards of verifiability, and observational relevance (ibid.).

In contrast to Richards, David Hull argued that selection in science results from social considerations associated with scientists' interests and that the evolution of conceptual systems results from the interplay between scientists and the contents and practices of science. Although individual scientists come up with new ideas, they must cooperate with other scientists because their success relates to how much other scientists use their ideas, cite their papers, etc. This leads to cooperation in science and the formation of "local" research groups or "demes" around which concepts collectively evolve. By promoting the scientists' professional interests and careers, demes allow innovative individual scientists to get their ideas selected by other scientists and future scientists, thus also promoting the interest of science itself. In other words, "demes ... enhance a scientist's conceptual inclusive fitness" (Hull 1988, 514). It follows that cooperative competition between scientists becomes a social force that, being internal rather than external to science, such as class, religion, and nationality, leads to the selection of conceptual systems. The structural success of particular scientific substantive ideas depends on the extent to which other scientists consider them useful.

Evolutionary epistemology, of the sociocultural kind I described, has not been widely applied to the social sciences. By contrast, the number of studies that have applied evolutionary analogies and metaphors, or that follow some version of "generalized Darwinism" (Aldrich et al. 2008; Hodgson and Knudsen 2006b) in the social sciences, is very large; their impact cannot be emphasized more. While most of these studies try best to apply Darwinian, neo-Lamarckian, or other types of evolutionary ideas to their own fields, not all of them explicitly adopt an evolutionary theory of knowledge. But even if they do not, we need to consider them part of the "evolution" of evolutionary epistemology.

Evolutionary frameworks, concepts, and mechanisms were applied to explain institutions (Pierson 2004; Steinmo 2010; Streeck and Thelen 2005; Thelen 2004, 2), rules (Burns and Dietz 1992), and technology (Dosi 1988; Rosenberg 1982; Ziman 2000). They also were applied in economics (Nelson and Winter 1982), business organization (Fligstein 1990), psychology (Cosmides et al. 1992), political science (Alford and Hibbing 2004; Axelrod 1984; Blyth 2006; Lieberman 2002), and IR (e.g., Adler 1991; Barnett 2009; Florini 1996; Gilady and Hoffman 2013; Modelski 1990; Pouliot and Thérien 2015; Spruyt 1994, 2001; Tang 2010, 2013; Thompson 2001).

Most striking are attempts to explain institutions from an evolutionary perspective. Thorstein Veblen argued that institutions are not only the result of a selective and adaptive process but are also efficient factors of selection (Hodgson and Knudsen 2010, 12). Hodgson (2007) followed

Veblen (Gronow 2011, 97) by taking institutions as the objects of selection and describing their evolution as resulting from variation, a heritability mechanism, and differential selection. Long before Hodgson, Conway Lloyd Morgan argued that institutions are emergent so they cannot be accounted for "by individuals' biological properties" (Gronow 2011, 97). Ernst Mayr, in turn, invoked institutions as sets of rule-like dispositions, which he called programs.[33] "Evolution involves both the adaptation of programs to changing circumstances and the elimination of other programs through selection" (Aldrich et al. 2008, 590). Aldrich and colleagues (ibid., 585) argued that the evolution of social institutions involves innovation, imitation, planning, and other mechanisms that are different from biological mechanisms. Pouliot and Thérien (2015; see also Axelrod 1984; Tomasello et al. 1993) refer to a "ratchet effect" in the evolution of institutions, according to which political struggles promote the accumulation of norms and practices over time.

Economists have used variation-and-selection ideas borrowed from evolutionary theories, resulting in a growing subfield known as "evolutionary economics" (Boulding 1978; Fagerberg 2003; Mailath 1998; Nelson and Winter 1982; Witt 1993; Ziman 2000), a term coined by Veblen (1919). One of the first economists to apply evolutionary thought to economics was Joseph Schumpeter (1934). He was then followed by so-called new Schumpeterians, most prominently Nelson and Winter (1982) and Nelson (1993). Schumpeter did not believe in a one-to-one analogy between biology and economics but he aimed at a theory of economic evolution that would take the place of economic theories based on static equilibrium. For Schumpeter, evolutionary change meant mainly "qualitative, economic change brought about through innovation" (Mailath 1998, 7). The main idea was looking at how innovation shapes economic evolution.

Nelson and Winter (1982; Mesoudi 2011, 180) suggested a theory based on culturally transmitted routines as an alternative to prevailing economic theories based on rational calculation. The central evolutionary notion is that, like genes, routines diffuse among members of firms; variation comes in the form of technological innovation and competition takes place at the level of both routines and firms. Those firms that acquire the most efficient routines make higher profits and survive preferentially; the less competitive firms disappear.[34]

[33] Boyd and Richerson (1985); Hayek (1979, 1989); and Hodgson (1993) also promoted the notion of cultural-group selection.

[34] According to Nelson (2006), Nelson and Winter's references to organizational routines as genes largely meant that they provide constancy to organizational behavior, not that

The use of habits, routines, and customs as gene-like structural replicators that are selected and inherited is widespread in economics (and sociology).[35] Thus, for instance, Aldrich and colleagues (2008, 587) suggest that "if we consider economic competition between firms, then the elimination of some and the prosperity of others leads to the differential copying (by collaboration or imitation) of routines, techniques, management procedures, and so on." In a similar fashion, Hodgson and Knudsen (2010) regard ideas as emergent expressions of habits that, like customs and routines, qualify as generative replicators (habits replicate at the individual level and routines replicate between organizations). Like Nelson and Winter (1982), Hodgson and Knudsen (2004) suggest that business firms are best considered as interactors, thus reinforcing the notion of group selection in economics. Whether firms or other entities "interact with their environments in ways that cause the differential replication of relevant stored information" (Aldrich et al. 2008, 586) remains an empirical question.

Building on the science of complex adaptive systems, Brian Arthur (1994) developed path-breaking evolutionary-economics theories based on the concept of increasing returns. This kind of work suggests an alternative to static equilibrium- and rational choice–based economic theory. Echoing path-dependence theories, such as the QWERTY effect (David 1985), increasing returns theories show that there is no guarantee of the selection of optimum alternatives. Complexity-based economic theories also describe change as emergent – very small changes in expectations may lead to significant changes in economic practices.

Evolutionary economics was also applied to corporate technological development and practice. Chandler (1960, 1990), for example, studied competing corporate firms and concluded that those that adopted efficient corporate styles outdid their competitors. Neil Fligstein, in turn, suggested an idea of corporate fitness, "which emphasizes responsiveness to changed legal regimes, public policies, and the climate of political opinions" (Nelson 2007, 83). Other studies focused on the evolutionary differences between technological innovation and business practices. Nelson says that "a rather extensive literature has developed on the difficulties of replicating business practices ... Among other things, it is clear that the broad understanding that underlies business practice is far weaker than

they were easily transferable. Nelson also argued that imitation plays a major role as a mechanism of replication. In market settings "firms and individuals who do well tend to be targets of imitation by those doing less well" (Nelson 2006, 88).

35 On the diffusion and replication of routines, see Aldrich and Martinez 2003; DiMaggio and Powell 1983; Levitt and March 1988; Rogers 1995; Stinchcombe 1990; Zucker 1987.

the understanding that underlies many modern technologies, and this makes both reliable imitation and successful innovation much more difficult for business practices than for technologies" (ibid., 83).[36]

Psychology also developed a thriving evolutionary-epistemology branch. Evolutionary psychology (Buss 2016; Cosmides and Tooby 1987; Cosmides et al. 1992), much more directly than economics, builds on naturalistic evolutionary epistemology. While this version of evolutionary epistemology is tangential to my interpretation of cognitive evolution theory, it illustrates how evolutionary epistemology (of the naturalistic kind) blended natural and cultural factors to generate an established subfield in a major social science discipline. It thus strengthens the social sciences branch that strives to establish the subfield on evolutionary epistemologies as an alternative to utilitarian, or reductionist, and structural normative, or holist, epistemologies. As I mentioned in Chapter 1, some evolutionary psychologists (Mallon and Stich 2000; Wilson 2005) have suggested that evolutionary psychology and social constructivism are compatible. This psychology version of evolutionary constructivism can be a ground for cross-fertilization with the different kind of evolutionary constructivism I suggest in this book.

According to Lopez, McDermott, and Petersen, evolutionary psychology "is an approach to understanding behavior that argues that the functional structure of the human brain has been designed by natural selection to respond reliably and efficiently to adaptive problems in our ancestral social and ecological environments. An 'adaptive problem' is any challenge, threat, or opportunity faced by an organism in its environment that is evolutionarily recurrent . . . and affects reproductive success" (2011, 50).[37] Evolutionary psychology identifies the adaptive problems human face and explains the psychological means designed to solve these problems. It asks, for example, how evolved psychological traits explain human warfare (Gat 2008) and aggression (Archer 1988), and how adaptations become efficient solutions especially to reproductive challenges (Lopez et al. 2011, 52).

[36] Nelson (2007, 86) cautions that evolutionary perspectives in economics, science and technology, and business administration must acknowledge the role of human purpose and intelligence, the notion that selection criteria seldom include issues of human survival and reproduction, that culture is more than practices and beliefs by individuals, and that how individuals and groups are involved with culture differs from how genes and living entities are related to the evolution of species (see also Levit et al. 2011).

[37] Evolutionary psychology assumes that "there has not been significant evolution in the human brain within the last 100,000 years or so, but that cultural evolution since the agricultural evolution 10,000 years ago has radically changed the environment within which humans make their behavioral choices" (Dunbar 2007, 35).

According to evolutionary psychology, emotions (like fear) may help humans improve vision and hearing, thus enhancing their reactions to danger. Evolutionary psychology also studies irrationality (McDermott 2004) and the evolution of cognition, which allows scholars to posit important questions about the sources of agent variation, such as genetic variation, preference complexity, and iterated interactions between agents' preferences and environmental factors (Lewis and Steinmo 2012, 331). The role of cognition in social evolution has figured prominently in the work of Peter Richerson and Robert Boyd (2005), for whom human advanced cognitive capacities and decision-making are key institutional selection mechanisms, and of Lewis and Steinmo (2012), who focus on human creative faculties and problem solving in variation processes.

In political science, a new field of inquiry called "genopolitics" has emerged (Alford et al. 2005; Deppe et al. 2013; Fowler and Dawes 2008, 2013; for a critique of the approach, see Charney and English 2013). It inquires whether, how, and why genes matter in politics; for example, whether genes determine people's votes for liberal or conservative parties. Does voting behavior, for example, vary whether a particular allele is higher among voters than among nonvoters (Fowler and Dawes 2013, 363)? Like evolutionary psychology, genopolitics is of the naturalistic, rather than of the epistemic, evolutionary epistemology kind so the relationship of genopolitics to my work is minimal.

As I mentioned in Chapter 1, Ernst Haas (1982, 1990; see also Haas and Haas 2002) pioneered the *explicit* use of evolutionary epistemology in IR. His distinctive approach was that "although knowledge is only accepted belief, not correct belief, correct beliefs may evolve over time, as progressively more accurate characterizations of the world are consensually formulated. By reference to internally formulated truth tests, contending groups may collectively validate their conclusions and their beliefs may converge intersubjectively in the medium run" (Haas 1989, 23).

A survey of evolutionary epistemology would be incomplete without mentioning Richard Dawkins's concept of "memes" (1989). Although inherently problematic and unhelpful for cognitive evolution theory, the concept represents an attempt to ground epistemology in evolution's micro-foundations. The *Oxford English Dictionary* defines memes as an "element of a culture that may be considered to be passed on by non-genetic means, especially imitation" (Blackmore 1999, viii, see also 17; Dennett 1995, 344; Heylighen 1992). "Examples of memes are tunes, ideas, catch-phrases, clothes, fashions, ways of making pots and building arches. Just as genes propagate themselves in the gene pool by leaping from body to body via sperm or eggs, so do memes propagate themselves in the meme pool by leaping from brain to brain via a process which, in the broad sense, can be called imitation" (Dawkins 1989, 192). Like replicating structures that store and transmit information, memes survive preferentially depending on whether "copies and copies of copies of them persist and multiply, and this depends on the selective forces that act directly on the various physical vehicles that embody them" (Dennett 1995, 348). Like genes, memes are "selfish" in that they "use" people's brains and other objects (for example, computers) to become selectively retained. Memes are not necessarily for the good of something, but they flourish because they are good at replicating (Dennett 1991, 203). According to Dawkins, this means that, like genes, memes have fidelity, fecundity, and longevity (1989).

Blackmore (1999, 17) points out several problems with the concept of memes, though I mention only two. First, the objective of specifying what exact cultural unit is really a meme is elusive at best. For example, is Beethoven's Fifth Symphony a meme, or are just its first four notes a meme? Second, we really know little about the mechanism or mechanisms for the transmission and storage of memes; Blackmore (ibid., 58) assumes that they are transmitted by imitation. Sperber (1996), in turn, argues persuasively that memes cannot be copied with the same level of accuracy as genes. "Such accuracy is not possible because the relevant aspects are the ones that are favored in learning" (Gronow 2011, 51). "Memetics" makes it easier to fall prey to extremely rigid analogies between genes and memes, which, in turn, can lead social science research down the path of naturalistic reductionism. This is particularly true because the meme literature tends to emphasize the notion that ideas can be reduced to brains and that ideas are replicated by "jumping from brain to brain." Cognitive evolution, on the other hand, does not refer to people "carrying" practices and institutions as they would carry a tune, but to collective understandings and practices that constitute who we are – that therefore carry us along. Besides, diffusion by imitation, which the theory of memes assumes, is only a tiny part of how cognitive evolution takes place. By emphasizing "cultural genes," "memetics" loses sight of individuals as knowledgeable and interpreting agents. To become useful for a theory of cognitive evolution, "memetics" would need to get out of the brain and into the social world, which is where the puzzle of human action mainly lies.

In sum, for more than a century, scholars of various disciplines have used evolutionary epistemology to describe and explain change and stability of the social world. One theme that runs across the entire history of evolutionary epistemology that is crucial for a cognitive-evolutionary theory of social orders based on practices and communities of practice is the notion that something like habits, customs, routines, and practices are the structural material that preferentially replicates and survives. Evolutionary epistemology, at the same time, points to the importance of creative variation and selective retention. One of evolutionary epistemology's most important points is the need to study change and stability as part of a single theory of knowing the world. As we will see, complexity theory's concepts of change and stability support and strengthen evolutionary epistemology.

Complexity Theory as Evolutionary Epistemology

Complexity theory has gradually been making inroads across disciplines to explain both natural and social phenomena.[38] Widely identified with the scientific activities of the "Santa Fe Institute" (Helmreich 1998; Waldrop 1992) and associated with the mathematics of nonlinear dynamics and the concept of emergence and chaos (Gleick 1988), complexity theory deals with systems that exhibit complex, self-organizing behavior (Rinaldi 1997).[39] Complexity theory is not really a single and consistent body of knowledge but a cluster of different theories, approaches, and methodologies. As such, it is "the interdisciplinary understanding of reality as composed of complex open systems with emergent properties and transformational potential" (Byrne 2005, 97). Complex (adaptive) systems, says Brian Arthur, "are systems in process that constantly evolve and unfold over time" (1999, 107). Complexity theory posits that agents constantly learn, adapt, and change even if their communities persist; they sustain continuity and change simultaneously (Rosenau 1997, 40). From a complexity perspective, evolution and stability are two sides of the same coin.[40]

In subsequent chapters, I selectively use complexity-theory concepts as part of cognitive-evolution theory in nonmetaphorical ways "'through a

[38] See, for instance, Arthur 1994; Gleick 1988; Holland 1998, 1999; Kauffman 1993, 1995; Nicolis and Prigogine 1989; Prigogine 1980; Prigogine and Stengers 1984; Thrift 1999; Urry 2003, 2005; Waldrop 1992. In the social sciences, see Axelrod and Cohen 2000; Byrne 1998; Elliott and Kiel 1997; La Porte 1975; Mingers 1995. In economics, see Beinhocker 2007; Padgett and Powell 2012. In IR, see Alberts and Czerwinski 1997; Cederman 1997; Cudworth and Hobden 2011, 2012; Geyer 2003; Gunitsky 2013; Harrison 2006; Hoffmann 2006; Jervis 1997; Kavalski 2007; Popolo 2011; Rosenau 1997, 2003; Walby 2009.

[39] For an accessible source on complexity, see Urry 2005. For an application of complexity theory to IR, see Jervis 1997.

[40] "Complexity science repudiates the dichotomies of determinism and chance, as well as of stasis and change ... Complexity elaborates how there is always order and disorder within physical and social phenomena" (Urry 2005, 238).

process of 'piecemeal replacement'" (MacKenzie 2005, 52).[41] But for now I will introduce these concepts and highlight their importance for, and complementarity with, evolutionary epistemology.[42] Rather than reducing understanding of social orders' change and metastability to natural processes, I am saying that because complex processes like emergence and nonlinear change *are features of the social world* (see, for example, Arthur 1999), we should enrich our theories by using them, carefully, selectively, and with epistemic awareness that their usefulness should be supported by logic and empirical research.

The complementarity between evolutionary mechanisms and process and complexity theory did not escape complexity theorists. According to Stuart Kauffman, we can explain evolution only by the complementarity between natural selection and self-organization. In other words, self-organization may generate structures that can benefit from natural selection. For selection we "must choose among ... various complex systems (rising from self-organization processes) the ones with characteristics better suited to survival and reproduction, and eliminate others" (1995, 188). As Kauffman puts it, "evolution is not just 'chance caught on the wing.' It is not just a tinkering of the ad hoc ... It is emergent order honored and honed by selection" (1993, 644).

As cognitive evolution theory shows, complementarity between evolution and complexity transcends natural-biological evolutionary mechanisms, such as natural selection. Cognitive evolution mechanisms, which are associated with practices and communities of practice and are therefore unrelated to natural selection, and complexity mechanisms and processes such as emergence, complement each other at the epistemological level. I find complementarity and consistency between evolutionary epistemology as a general principle of knowledge and complexity concepts such as emergence (and complexity theory's general understanding of the social world as characterized by nonequilibrium). Take, for example, the transformation of a social order with the concomitant replacement of one set of practices with another. The structural changes that agents observe and experience may then lead to new interpretations of the world (Lane and Maxfield 1997, 89) and to new rounds of cognitive evolution. I cannot improve on Kauffman, who suggested that we "invent concepts and categories that we use to carve up the world ... Having invented the categories, we carve the world into them and find ourselves categorized as well" (Kauffman 1995, 300). A small fluctuation in human interpretation, in a system where positive feedback may

[41] For a view that complexity theory is not conducive to theory creation, see Gunitsky 2013.
[42] For a different approach on complexity as epistemology, see ibid.

prevail, can thus lead to the construction of rules, roles, and expectations, which, after being constructed, then construct us. Thus, for example, due "to the creation of a legal system, I am able to enter into contracts. Because we can both do so, you and I can create a person that may live forever, the corporation, which takes on aims that survive and even harm the interests of many of those who found it. Thus the modern corporation is a collectively self-sustaining structure of roles and obligations that 'lives' in the economic world, exchanges signals and stuffs, and survives or dies" (ibid.).

The evolution of the corporate order illustrates one of the key cognitive evolutionary mechanisms I discuss in later chapters: the invention of new polities and institutions that give rise to new fields of practices. Economic, social, and legal innovation led to the evolution of the corporation and of corporate practices. These, in turn, constructed the social and economic corporate order, which now constructs us. It constitutes our practices, habits, and the environments that surround us where we live and work and move around.

One of the most important concepts associated with complexity theory that has major implications for evolutionary epistemology is emergence: that "there are system effects that are different from their parts" (Urry 2005, 5). "Weather is an emergent property; take your water vapor out over the Gulf of Mexico and let it interact with sunlight and wind, and it can organize itself into an emergent structure known as a hurricane. Life is an emergent property, the product of molecules, all obeying the laws of chemistry" (Waldrop 1992, 82; see also Kauffman 1995, 24). Once they cross a complexity threshold, complex natural and physical systems can spontaneously organize into more complex, self-sustaining, and self-reproducing structures.

Emergent structures and processes are also ubiquitous in the social world.[43] "From the interaction of the individual components of a system ... emerges some kind of property ... something you couldn't have predicted from what you know of the component parts ... And the global property, thus emergent behavior, feeds back to influence the behavior of the individuals that produced it" (Thrift 1999, 33–34). Take, for example, a business. It is "a complex system that interacts with a larger complex environment (the market) ... General patterns emerge and the business is able to adapt to changes in its environment, but exact predictions and explanations of how a change in the environment will

[43] Before complexity theory helped popularize the concept of self-organizing orders, Frederick Hayak (1948) referred to the market as a spontaneous social order.

affect the business, or the best strategies to survive in the altered environment, are impossible to know in advance" (Geyer 2003, 26).

Self-organization[44] is an evolutionary process "where the effect of the environment is minimal, i.e., where the development of new, complex structures takes place primarily in and through the system itself" (Heylighen 2009, n.p.). This means, first, that the environment instructs but does not determine the course of evolution. From an evolutionary-epistemology perspective, self-organization means that creative-variation and selective-retention processes in and between communities and institutions are to a considerable extent *endogenous*. Second, self-organization refers to the emergence of novel "entities or stable aggregate patterns of organization and behavior arising from the interactions of agents" (Maxfield 1997, 80). Third, self-organization helps explain the establishment of order in the presence of constant change. "Self-organization defines the response of complex systems to the unpredictability of emergence – that is, it reflects the search for stability in the instability that characterizes periods of emergence" (Kavalski 2007, 439). Self-organization thus also means that the essential structures of a system "remain intact even as their emergent properties continue to accumulate and mature" (Rosenau 1997, 36).

Another important complexity-theory concept, with broad epistemological implications for evolutionary knowledge of the social world, is nonlinear change. Nonlinearity reveals "dynamical behavior such that the relationships between variables . . . are subject to positive feedback in which changes are amplified, breaking up existing structures and behavior and creating unexpected outcomes in the generation of new structures and behavior. Non-linear changes, for example, extreme weather events, show how small changes in driving variables, through positive feedback, can produce very large effects" (Urry 2005, 7). In contrast to linearity, according to which "we can get a value for the whole by adding up the values of its parts," nonlinear interactions most often make the behavior of the aggregate more complicated than would be predicted by summing or averaging (Holland 1995, 23). Nonlinearity can thus create "instabilities, discontinuities, synergisms and unpredictability. But it also places a premium on flexibility, adaptability, dynamic change, innovation, and responsiveness" (Beyerchen 1997, 73). Nonlinearity implies,

44 A closely related concept is autopoiesis. Autopoietic systems are self-producing of their components and their boundary (Maturana in Mingers 1995, 84). Autopoietic systems, through their interactions, (a) "recursively regenerate the network of productions that produced them" and (b) constitute and specify its boundaries (Maturana qtd. in Mingers 1995, 15).

for example, that anticipating the result of a planned action may lead to the plan's modification (Saperstein 1997, 59). Self-fulfilling prophecies (Merton 1948), for instance, when the collective fear that a bank will run into insolvency tomorrow actually causes the bank to become insolvent tomorrow, illustrate nonlinear change. Nonlinear systems are difficult to predict, not because of the lack of sufficient information but because of the "system's sensitivity to initial conditions and the nonlinear rules that govern its dynamics" (Schmitt 1997, 107).

The notion of complex systems' evolution owes much to Ilya Prigogine's theory of evolving systems' self-organization in the face of permanent instabilities and fluctuations. Prigogine, a Nobel-laureate scientist, first explained why in the face of the inexorable Second Law of Thermodynamics (which predicts a state of increasing entropy or disorder as energy is consumed), in conditions of nonequilibrium, order and organization, such as life, nevertheless become possible – in other words, why order can spontaneously emerge from disorder.

The key to this puzzle, according to Prigogine, lies in two concepts, "order through fluctuations" and "dissipative structures." Prigogine showed that partially open systems in a state of sufficient nonequilibrium try to maintain their capability for energy exchange with the environment by switching to a new dynamic order whenever entropy[45] production becomes stifled in the old order. This is the principle of "order through fluctuations," which reverses some of the dynamic characteristics holding for closed systems and systems near equilibrium. "In general," says Prigogine, "fluctuations play a minor role in macroscopic physics, appearing only as small corrections that may be neglected if the system is sufficiently large. However, near bifurcations[46] they play a critical role because there the fluctuation drives the average" (1980, 132). In Alvin Toffler's words, "a single fluctuation or a combination of them can become so powerful by positive *feedback*, that it shatters the preexisting *organization*" and thus may lead to the creation of new orders (qtd. in Prigogine and Stengers 1984).[47]

At bifurcation points "it is impossible to determine . . . whether the system will disintegrate into 'chaos' or leap to a new, more differentiated, higher level of 'order'" (Krippendorff 1986). Prigogine called structures that exchange order instead of disorder "dissipative structures"; they

[45] Entropy refers to the process indicated by the Second Law of Thermodynamics by which the universe and everything in it tend toward exhaustion, decay, disorder, and chaos.

[46] We know bifurcations also as phase transitions.

[47] "Large fluctuations . . . are not necessarily triggered from outside the system, in exceptional ways, but are often created by the same category of mechanisms involved in small-scale changes" (Suteanu 2005, 126).

maintain continuous entropy production that is more than compensated by the flows of matter or energy from the environment. That is, these systems dissipate the accruing entropy. For example, take the system in question to be a city. Without compensating for its needs (arising from its increase in size and necessities) by drawing energy and materials from the environment, the city would decay and die. The system's fluctuations therefore dissipate to the environment, which compensates for them. The evolution of dissipative structures is "chaotic" or sensitive to initial conditions (Harvey and Reed in Elliott and Kiel 1997, 306) and self-organizing. Complexity may emerge from spontaneous small fluctuations or changes. But when instabilities approach a "threshold" they can drive the system to change. As Chapter 6 shows in more detail, the overnight fall of the Berlin Wall is a good example of a social order reaching a threshold, tipping, and leading to the collapse of the Soviet Empire, thus, to the evolution of the international security social order (Urry 2005, 251; see also Gladwell 2002).

Early pragmatists like Peirce, Dewey, James, and Baldwin could not know about complexity theory, chaos theory, or Prigogine's theory of nonequilibrium and order through fluctuations. So it is remarkable that their philosophical, sociological, and psychological pragmatist theories – which I mentioned as precursors of evolutionary epistemology – prefigured to some extent complexity theory's epistemology. This is the case with the notion that habits and environments constitute each other. Early American pragmatist theories are also consistent with notions of endogenous change in scientific communities and of nonlinear change involving the relationship of mind, ideas, and exogenous factors. While this argument may be an oversimplification, it drives the point that there is a lineage linking early American pragmatist theories and complexity theory – there is an evolving program of evolutionary epistemology. Cognitive evolution theory builds on this lineage or program.

Being sensitive to complexity-theory concepts, evolutionary epistemology suggests that "the link between determinism and predictability had been broken" (Nowotny 2005, 16). Since even a small change in initial conditions can substantially change social order evolution, it limits prediction in major ways. This means looking at the difficulty of prediction as a consequence less of inadequate methods or knowledge than of the nature of the natural and social worlds (Suteanu 2005). Evolutionary epistemology, enhanced by complexity theory, therefore replaces a variance-type predictive explanation with a historical reconstructive explanation of change and stability processes, based on abduction and analytical narratives. One kind of prediction that evolutionary theory cannot make "is the course of the development of particular species through time … if species are lineages, and lineages are historical entities, no one should expect to make predictions about particular species qua that particular species" (Hull 1988, 430). It follows, then, that we need to start "near 'the end' of a process … asking how it could have been produced" (Dennett 1995, 62), although it could have been produced otherwise. This is, of course, what I ask about international social orders: how and why they became what they are, although they could have evolved differently; how and why they are kept metastable; and through what mechanisms and under what conditions they might evolve once again.

4 Practices, Background Knowledge, Communities of Practice, Social Orders

Between American Pragmatism and Pierre Bourdieu

I would like to reimagine a practice-based theory of social action and social order informed by both Bourdieu's practice theory and American pragmatism's theory of action (see, for example, Dewey 1922), with an emphasis on pragmatism. To do this I make seven moves.

First, I substitute Bourdieu's concept of habitus, and pragmatism's concept of habit, with the concept of practice that is bound up with background knowledge. Remember, practices are socially meaningful patterned actions that, in being performed more or less competently, simultaneously embody, act out, and possibly reify background knowledge and discourse in and on the material world (Adler and Pouliot 2011a, 6). Practice-based theories, such as cognitive evolution, "do more than just describe what people do. Practices are, in fact, meaning making, identity-forming, and order-producing activities" (Nicolini 2013, 7).

Practices are characterized by recursive action. Ann Swidler says they are also the *infrastructure* of repeated interactional patterns. Practices "remain stable not only because habit ingrains standard ways of doing things, but because the need to engage one another" (Swidler 2001, 85) in communities of practice compels practitioners to rely on shared social structures. With the expansion of communities of practice across geographical and institutional boundaries, intersubjective background knowledge embedded in practices grows in size and becomes more difficult to dislodge, evolutionarily speaking. The more people practice the same practice and therefore share background knowledge, the more they reinforce the practice, thus keeping it preferentially selected compared with other practices.

The concept of practice suggests an ontology that challenges standard social dichotomies, such as materiality and meanings, agency and structure, and stability and change. Practices are both material and meaningful; they are suspended between agents and structures; they rely for their existence and efficacy on "background knowledge"; they help make sense of the combined role of individuals and collectives as part of "communities of practice"; and they inform change as much as continuity (see Adler and Pouliot 2011a). So following Latour's (2005) action-network theory, we can take material objects, agents, and meanings as interacting seamlessly, being mutually dependent and mutually constituted. Practices are agential not only because individuals perform them, but also because they are the source, simultaneously, of stability of inventiveness and the steadiness of change. Practices translate structural background intersubjective knowledge into intentional acts and endow those acts with social meaning. The performance of practices in socially recognizable ways is the source of ontological metastability in social life. And social change originates from practices (Adler and Pouliot 2011a).

There are many reasons to prefer practice over habit when theorizing social action (for the opposite view, see Turner 1994; in IR, see Hopf 2010, 2013). Social scientists criticize the habit/habitus concept, particularly for its shortcomings in explaining agency and change and for its low-level reflectivity (Emirbayer and Mische 1998; Miettinen et al. 2012, 348; Shusterman 2008; see also Knorr Cetina 2001, 175). Starting with the obvious, (1) habits must be practiced and (2) practices grasp better the performative aspects of social action. (3) Practices give practical knowledge a huge selective advantage over "theoretical" knowledge by allowing the practical to be tested and refined in practice.[1] (4) From a practice perspective, creativity means not only reflexive adaptation to a changing environment, as with habits, but also endogenous changes of social mechanisms and processes mainly within and between communities of practice. At every repetition of practice, there may be a difference because every repetition "occurs under already altered circumstances" (Shäfer 2014, 2). (5) Practices embody intersubjective, rather than only subjective, background knowledge, as is the case with habit. (6) Because they are patterned actions in socially organized contests, practices are not merely dispositions and are better able to catch the institutional side of social action. (7) The articulation process that mediates between agency and structure makes practice a more meaningful social concept than habit. (8) In contrast to habits that mainly highlight experience, practices also involve expectations of the future; the past pushes them but the future pulls them. (9) Unlike habits, practices are learned from others, and can be done well or badly, and correctly or incorrectly (Barnes 2001, 19).

Second, following Searle's (1995) concept of the "background," and to a lesser degree Bourdieu's (1977) concept of "habitus," I take background knowledge as being bound up with the execution of practices. In

[1] I thank Iain Wilson for this insight.

addition to being intersubjective knowledge embedded in practices, background knowledge is distributed in practitioners' subjective representations of intersubjectivity – mainly expectations, dispositions, or preintentional capacities – that make intentional states possible. Individuals and groups act within a dominant interpretive backdrop that sets the terms of interaction, defines a horizon of possibility, and provides the background knowledge of expectations, dispositions, skills, techniques, and rituals that are the basis for the constitution of practices and their boundaries. Background knowledge is far from tacit. It depends on individuals' reflexive, normative, and instrumental judgments to remain effectively institutionalized. Background knowledge remains institutionalized in practices rather than merely in collective memory. A greater emphasis on the reflexive rather than on the tacit quality of background knowledge characterizes cognitive evolution theory and differentiates it from other practice-based IR theories (see, for example, Pouliot 2016).

Unlike Searle (1995, 2010), who while referring to collective intentionality, ontologically locates background knowledge only in individual minds,[2] I take background knowledge also to be an "exosomatic product, independent of its installation of any particular human mind." This is the case with linguistically formulated knowledge stored in books, articles, and programs, "which are independent of any question about who believes them or originated them" (Bartley 1987, 434; see also Popper 1982).

Third, I avoid determinism and stress contingency by referring to practices/background knowledge as performative, where agents, such as theater actors, act out and interpret social texts and knowledge thus displaying "performative power" (Alexander 2011; in IR, see Ringmar 2012).[3] According to Alexander,

> cultural performance is the social process by which actors, individually, or in concert, display for others the meaning of their social situation ... it is the

[2] Also Bourdieu (1977) located the concept of habitus in individual minds.

[3] The concept of performativity is indebted to Clifford Geertz's (1973) studies of culture and to Erving Goffman's (1956) dramaturgical theory. But Geertz left little room for contingency and Goffman highlighted the instrumental dimensions of performativity (Alexander 2011, 19–20). Performativity theory comes in different, though related interpretations. There is, for example, L. Austin's notion that performative assertions produce their referents by means of the utterance, an argument that produced a very rich philosophical tradition linking language and social reality (Searle 1995). Philosopher of science Ian Hacking (1983) argued that we understand representations only with interventions in the world. He thus conceived of "interactive kinds," the looping effects concepts have once they have been performed in practice (Hacking 1999). Judith Butler (1990, 1997) took performative theory from philosophy to the field of gender, and Michael Callon (2007) applied performative theory to the field of science studies. According to Callon, economics is less a discipline that represents social reality than a field of practices and instruments that constitute the reality, including the actors, which it comes to represent (see also Mackenzie, Muniesa, and Siu 2007).

> meaning that they, as social actors, consciously or unconsciously wish to have others believe. In order for their display to be effective, actors must offer a plausible performance, one that leads those to whom their actions and gestures are directed to accept their motives and explanations as a reasonable account. (2011, 28)

Contingency, according to Alexander, stands on two main pillars. First, it relies on the extent of freedom from background representations, sometimes related to originality, that accompanies performances. Second, skepticism about one's own knowledge, or that of others, can lead to uncertainty and thus contingency. Performative power means using the contingency of interpretations and performances to impose their meaning onto others. It means that no matter what resources and capacities practitioners or performers have, "they must find a way to make their audience believe them" (Alexander 2011, 89).

Fourth, departing from Bourdieu's oeuvre, and following Barab and Duffy (2000), I substitute the concept of field, which refers primarily to arenas of power stratification and hierarchy, with the concept of community of practice (Brown and Duguid 1991; Coe and Brunell 2003; Lave and Wenger 1991, 1998a; in IR, see Adler 2005, 2008; Adler and Pouliot 2011a). A community of practice, as defined by Wenger (1998a; Wenger et al. 2002, 27, 29), is a configuration of a domain of knowledge that constitutes like-mindedness, a community of people that "creates the social fabric of learning," and a shared practice that embodies "the knowledge the community develops, shares, and maintains." The interaction of practitioners in communities of practice gives rise to emergent properties, which means that we cannot reduce communities of practice's properties to those of their individual and corporate practitioners (Hodgson and Knusden 2010, 171).

The concept of communities of practice catches a broad section of social life; communities of practice are intersubjective social structures that constitute the normative and epistemic ground for action, but they are also agents, made up of real people who make things happen in the world. So as I discussed in Chapter 2, they are real, ontologically speaking. Communities of practice subsume the traditional divide between ideas and matter. On the one hand, they are material insofar as they are doings enacted in and on the world and thus exist embodied in materials. At the same time, practices are also shot through with meaning. Language, communication, and discourse make relationships in communities of practice possible. As spaces of intelligibility (Schatzki 2002) where horizons of possibilities become, communities of practice are the site where social order change first takes place, and where metastability is also maintained. Communities of practice are learning communities where learning means participation in and engagement with the meanings, identities, and language of communities of practice and their members (Wenger 1998a, 13–14, 55, 86–102; see also Lave and Wenger 1991). Learning in communities of practice involves adopting a shared identity that is constituted through the forms of competence it entails. Thus, communities of practice are not about "habits mechanically reproducing themselves, though habits too must be taken into account because they have their place in the practice" (Wenger 1998a, 97). Rather, communities of practice are "a matter of investment of one's identity and thus of negotiating enough continuity to sustain an identity. From this perspective, practice is different from a physical system, because people do not merely act individually or mechanically, but by negotiating their engagement with one another with respect to their shared practice and their interlocked identities" (ibid.).

Although communities of practice are everywhere, they transcend our obvious classifications of social phenomena. We can think of them as social spaces organized around practices where meaningful social relations take place based on "weak ties"; where practitioners "are known only in one very limited respect and . . . may *never* be encountered face to face" (Granovetter 1973; Urry 2004, 116). Communities of practice are grounded in places and represented in the material world (Sassen 2000). Like "social figurations" (Elias 2000), "discursive spaces" (Foucault 1970), "fields" (Bourdieu 1977; see also Beckert 2010), "strategic action fields" (Fligstein and Mc Adam 2011), and "networks" (McLean 2007; Nexon 2009; Powell et al. 2005), communities of practice fuse or conflate "macro" and "micro" "levels" into a "meso level" (Brachthäuser 2011) that ontologically incorporates both social structure and agency. Like Heidegger's "clearings" (1971, 53), they possess intelligibility and spatial qualities. Unlike the concept of network, which emphasizes connectivity, community emphasizes identity (Wenger 2010, 10). While for Bourdieu (1977) and Fligstein and McAdam (2011, 17) relational factors are subservient to distributions of positions or hierarchies (see also Pouliot 2016), in the case of communities of practice, the meaning of power covers a spectrum between horizontal accountability and vertical accountability. Horizontal accountability is "associated with engagement in joint activities, negotiation of mutual relevance, standards of practice, peer recognition, identity and replication, and commitment to collective learning" and who gets to qualify as competent (Wenger 2010, 195).

Conceptualizing power horizontally does not mean that power is less effective than vertical hierarchies associated with capital differentials (Bourdieu 1977). Power also operates outside communities of practice. "Beyond a given community, successful claims of competence inherit the position of the community in the economy of meaning in which its practice exists as a claim of knowledge" (Wenger 2010, 189). Power is projected outside by reification processes, for example, via institutions, laws, and designs (ibid.). From this perspective, "power and learning are always intertwined and indeed inseparable" (ibid., 9).

It is important to reemphasize that communities of practice organize differences rather than generate uniformity. And their practitioners' differences play a role in the endogenous changes taking place within their communities. Practitioners differ regarding the institutional resources they possess and their interpretation capacities. Some practitioners are also better performers and thus have a larger effect on practices' epistemic practical authority (Pouliot 2016). One should take contestation as one of the most important attributes of communities of practice.[4] Contestation is necessary for learning in communities of practice. It is a process by which practitioners dynamically define their practice, adapt to environmental challenges, and adopt a common identity. Learning and contestation determine both the shared meanings with which practices are bound and the selective retention processes that depend partly on "who gets what, whom, and how" (Lasswell 1936) in and between communities of practice.

As boundaries form in and around practice, communities of practice link with their social environments and with other communities of practice to form community-of-practice constellations (Wenger 1998a, 129), for example, diplomats and security analysts, or brokers and financial consultants. Several communities can share objects and meanings – Wenger (1998a, 106–8) calls them "boundary objects" – through which coherence is developed in constellations of communities of practice (Büger 2014). However, communities of practice can be at odds with each other, particularly when new practices emerge, and when communities of practice form in and around practices, thus challenging competing practices and communities. We can also find some hybrid patterns of practice arrangements where competing communities of practice share practices, for instance, diplomatic practices. Finally, communities of practice are part of larger contexts or "landscapes of practices" (Wenger-Trayner et al. 2015) where practices are related to other

[4] On norm contestation, see Ba and Hoffmann 2005; Wiener 2014, 2018.

practices. Thus, social order can be associated not only with one community of practice but also with what communities of practice do to nonmembers, and vice versa.

Fifth, I take cognition as social: it is not reducible to the human mind but "instead emerges from within the dynamics of the interaction itself" (Krueger 2011, 643). My approach to cognition therefore does not focus exclusively on individuals and is not based on brain research, as important theories in cognitive psychology, widely known as "social cognition" (Fiske and Taylor 2013), are, and as to some extent Bandura's (1986, 2001) "social cognitive theory" also does.[5] Instead, I focus on the embodied, mediated,[6] and participatory aspects of social understanding – on social cognition as constituted by social interaction (Dewey and Bentley 1949; Fleck 1979; Goffman 1963; Vygotsky 1978), particularly within communities (Lave and Wenger 1991; Mead 2015). This approach has solid ground in recent research. De Jaegher, Di Paolo, and Gallagher say that "a shift is taking place in social cognition research, away from a focus on the individual mind and toward embodied and participatory aspects of social understanding. Empirical results already imply that social cognition is not reducible to the workings of individual cognitive mechanisms" (2010, 441; see also Tomasello 2009 and Tomasello et al. 1993, 2005). According to Engel, Maye, Kurthen, and König, in "cognitive science, we are currently witnessing a 'pragmatic turn,' away from the traditional representation-centered framework towards a paradigm that focuses on understanding cognition as 'enactive,' as skillful activity that involves ongoing interaction with the external world" (2013, 202; see also Bandura 2001; Krueger 2011; Lave and Wenger 1991; Lemke 1997; Resnick 1991; Wenger 1998a).

Lev Vygotsky (1962, 1978), Ludwik Fleck (1979), and more generally pragmatism were important precursors of a social cognition approach. In the context of a theory of child learning, Vygotsky (1962, 1978) argued that cognition occurs through interaction and as a result of socialization, namely, that culture plays an important role in cognitive development. What makes Vygotsky a notable forerunner of the social cognition

[5] Bandura's theory, focusing on the psychology of individuals (which is influenced by learning from social interactions), may also be interpreted as a nonreductionist and emergentist interpretation of human agency (Rottschaefer 1991). According to Bandura, "social cognitive theory distinguishes among three models of agency: direct personal agency, proxy agency that relies on others to act on one's behest to secure desired outcomes, and collective agency, exercised though socially coordinative and interdependent effort" (2001, 1).

[6] "Mediated means . . . that all practices are carried out through, and are made possible by, a range of ideational and material apparatuses, devices, and utensils that we draw from our cultural heritage or social milieu" (Nicolini 2012, 106).

approach is his relational ontology regarding intra- and intercommunity knowledge development.[7] According to Fleck "thought styles" arrive from "thought collectives"; thinking is a collective activity (1979, 39).[8] A thought collective is "a community of persons mutually exchanging ideas or maintaining intellectual interaction [that] … provides the special carrier for the historical development of any field of thought, as well as for the given stock of knowledge and level of culture. This we have designated thought-style" (ibid.). A thought style, in turn, "consists of the *active elements*, which shape ways in which members of the collective see and think about the world, and of the *passive elements*, the sum of which is perceived as an 'objective reality.' What we call 'facts,' are social constructs: only what is true to culture is true to nature" (ibid.; Sady 2016).[9]

Pragmatism, as I discussed earlier, was a pioneering approach as far as locating the source of cognitions in social transactions (e.g., Dewey 1922) and action. I cannot agree more with Hans Joas, a notable contemporary pragmatist sociologist, who argued that we should look at "cognition not as preceding action but as a phase of action by which action is directed and redirected in its situational context" (1996, 134). From a pragmatist perspective, as I show later in this chapter, social cognition's interactions are related to practices' reciprocity (Bratman 2014; Tomasello et al. 2005), which, in turn, is related to social orders' normative character.

Finally, on social cognition, it is crucial to emphasize that cognitive evolution theory does not embrace an unqualified "externalist" philosophical perspective (Putnam 1990) where meanings are not in the head but rather only in the external world (Wendt 2015, 254). While cognition does depend "intrinsically on social relations … this is not to say people do not have private thoughts in their heads" (ibid.). Unlike externalism, I suggest that while individuals' thoughts are mostly constituted by social interaction, as Searle argued (1983, 1995), individuals may also have different intentional contents.[10] This is because "there are always

[7] See also Jean Piaget's constructivist theory of stages of cognitive development that are related to social interaction (1952, 1954).

[8] Later, Thomas Kuhn (1970) built on Fleck's theory to develop his own theory of paradigms.

[9] Fleck's theory was instrumental for the development of the concept and theory of epistemic communities in IR (Adler 1987; Adler and Haas 1992; Haas 1992a).

[10] According to John Searle (1983), "intentional states are those having conditions of satisfaction … In the case of belief, these are the conditions under which the belief is true; in the case of perception, they are the conditions under which sense-experience is veridical; in the case of intention, the conditions under which an intention is fulfilled or carried out" (qtd. in Siewert 2017).

conditions of satisfaction that we go by and that we can be said to have and to have set in our minds, even if we have to reflect about them" (Wenzel and Hsien 2004, 409). Thus, individual reflexivity and judgment may matter for social cognition. This does not mean that intentionality's background knowledge, as Searle argued (1983, 151), is reducible to the body. Rather, background knowledge is simultaneously a social structure, thus collective and intersubjective, and distributed in practitioners' dispositions and expectations, both of which are propensities realizable only through practice and social interaction. Social interaction and individuals' intentionality are therefore mutually constitutive and co-evolve together as part of social orders' practices.[11]

Sixth, I suggest a social-order approach that highlights a plurality of and often contesting social orders. Thus, for example, we can refer to the post–World War II European social order(s), the current Southeast Asian social order(s), the corporate social order(s), the emerging cyberspace social order(s), as well as Canadian health order and French art's social order. Cognitive evolution theory thus simultaneously examines the stability and transformation of mutually coexisting and sometimes overlapping constitutive fields of practice that cut across geographical and functional boundaries. As I discuss in Chapter 5, we can and should apply cognitive evolution theory to better understand the concept of world order (in IR, see Bull 1977; Ikenberry 2001, 2011; Phillips 2011; Reus-Smit 1999, 2013a). I conceive world orders as *social orders* (see also Reus-Smit 2013a; Skidmore 1997) whose boundaries globally span functionally differentiated agents and functionally and territorially delineated fields of practices and knowledge, whose authority refers mainly, but not exlusively, to horizontal epistemic practical authority.

Finally, I use the concepts of practice, background knowledge, performative power, and communities of practice not merely to show that "practice matters" or to introduce yet another communitarian advocacy group of people that "does things," but because these concepts are the building blocks of cognitive evolution theory. In taking theories of action as being consistent with theories of social order, and considering that action theories involve theoretical assumptions about social order theories, I follow pragmatism (Gronow 2011, 11). Because cognitive evolution's mechanisms better grasp social action's relational aspects than pragmatist mechanisms do, I also partly depart from how pragmatists theorize change and stability.

[11] I discussed the ontological implications of intersubjective social structures and individuals' dispositions and expectations in Chapter 2, in the section on "Karl Popper's 'Propensity Theory' and 'World 3'".

Why American Pragmatism?

As we can see from my discussion of the various philosophical and sociological approaches that had an impact on practice social theory, probably none has been more influential than American pragmatism and Bourdieu's theory of practice.[12] Pragmatism is an established philosophical school with ontological, epistemological, and methodological claims, some of which transcend this chapter's focus.[13] Here, I am mainly interested in pragmatism's theory of action.[14]

(1) Pragmatism's main argument is the primacy of practice (Hellmann 2009; Putnam 1995, 52). John Dewey maintained that we know and understand through action and practice (Amin and Cohendet 2004, 64). Knowledge is not only a by-product of activity (Menand 2001, 322) but also an instrument of successful action (Dewey 1916; see also Menand 2001, 361). It is productive – a tool for interacting in the world (Cook and Brown 1999, 393). According to pragmatism, "habitual action is the major explanation for the emergence of social structures ... their production takes place when action is habitualized, that is, when we develop the disposition to act in a certain

[12] Practice theory's philosophical roots can be traced to Hegel (2007 1830]) and later to Marx's theses on Feuerbach (1888), followed by Heidegger (1962) and the late Wittgenstein (1953). In the later part of the twentieth century, practice theory had a renaissance when social scientists and philosophers abandoned functionalist (e.g., Durkheim 1915) and structural functionalist theories of action (Parsons 1951), as well as methodologically individualist rational choice theories (Elster 1983), to begin conceptualizing social action as "a creative enactment over time of *social practices*" (Gross 2009, 359). Practices "are at the heart of Bourdieu's (1990) theory of social fields [and habitus], Foucault's discursive practices (1970), Butler's (1990) analysis of the performativity of gender, Giddens's (1984) theory of structuration, Charles Taylor's (1975) conception of social reality, Knorr Cetina's (1999) investigations of 'epistemic cultures' of science and modern society, Ortner's (1984) efforts to reground anthropological understandings of culture, and Sewell's (2005) contributions to historiography" (Gross 2009, 365–66). Some of the most recent contributions to practice theory were made by Hans Joas (1996), Andreas Reckwitz (2002), Joseph Rouse (2007), Theodore Schatzki (1996, 2001a, 2002, Schatzki et al. 2001), and Ann Swidler (2001). Practice-based approaches were adopted across the social sciences, for example, in sociology (Alexander 2006; Archer 2000; Fligstein and McAdam 2011), organizational studies (Brown and Duguid 2001; Nicolini et al. 2003), science and technology studies, most notably in Bruno Latour's "actor-network theory" (2005; see also Pickering 1992), and IR (Adler 2005; Adler and Pouliot 2011a; Büger and Gadinger 2015; Neumann 2002; Pouliot 2010, 2016).

[13] The literature is extensive. Important overviews of pragmatism include Bernstein 1985; Haack 2006; Menand 1997, 2001; Misak 1999, 2007; and Putnam 1994.

[14] I abstain from referring to pragmatism as a philosophy of science and thus as an alternative, for example, to positivism, scientific realism, and relativism (see Jackson 2010), or a methodology, such as abduction (in IR, see Ruggie 1998a) and semiotics (in IR, see Drieschova 2016).

manner in familiar environments" (Gronow 2011, 10).[15] Dewey considered institutions as embedded habits (Dewey 1922, 77), customs as "wide-spread uniformities of habit" (ibid., 58), and practices as helping to turn thinking into knowledge (Dewey 1916, 334). William James concurred: "'It is far too little recognized … how entirely the intellect is built up of practical interests … Cognition … is incomplete until discharged in act'" (qtd. in Richards 1987, 447).

(2) The creativity of action and human reflexivity are at the core of pragmatism and are the other side of the coin of habit, custom, and practice (Joas 1996).[16] Action, "as a response to problem situations, involves an alternation between habit and creativity" (Gross 2009, 366). While social action relies on habitual dispositional knowledge and expectations that are embedded in social practices, both endogenous and exogenous factors awaken and stir human reflexive creativity (Archer 2007), which leads to the transformation of practices and the knowledge that is bound with them.

(3) We owe to pragmatism the view that both dispositional and reflexive knowledge do not precede but are bound up in the execution of practices. Scientific and social reasoning are therefore not "causal" forces antecedent to practice but instead its "laborious achievement" (Dewey 1922, 198). Contrary to the classic view that individual mind and intersubjective understandings form social groups' habits, customs, and practices, the arrow also goes in the opposite direction; both knowledge and practices are reciprocally constituted.

(4) Pragmatism's theory of social action is communitarian. Communities of practice are practices' "containers" (Büger 2014, 6) and the locus for knowledge creation. We can understand thinking, deliberation, judgment, and interpretation only as taking place within and by communities of practice whose members socialize one another and learn from each other by and through practice. According to Peirce, inquiry is a communal activity; the fixation of belief results from a limited local convergence by a particular

[15] The "essence of habit is an acquired predisposition to *ways* or modes of response" (Dewey 1922, 42).

[16] "According to Peirce, it is human capacity for spontaneity that allows novelty to emerge … James argued that knowledge arises in human actions through the projection of experience into the future … Dewey argued that thinking is a method of generating working hypotheses, the consequences of which may then be tested through their imagination or concrete action … [and Mead was] concerned with the emergence of human consciousness through creative social action … in ongoing processes of social engagement" (Elkjaer and Simpson 2006, 4).

community at a particular time (Hausman 1993, 216). Dewey's – as well as Mead's – communitarianism sees that "sociality does not crush individuality and is not restricted to particular 'topics.' Dewey argued that 'individuals grow to a sense of self-consciousness *through* the communities in which they live, not simply *in* them'" (Gronow 2011, 68).

(5) We partly owe to pragmatism the notion that social learning is a communal and practical endeavor. Within communities, practitioners learn competent skills, acquire new meanings, and adopt new identities. Communities, "characterized by conventions of meaning and communication and the cultures of action and interpretation ... act as learning environments in their own right" (Amin and Cohendet 2004, 66).

(6) Pragmatism takes individuals' habits, customs, traditions, and practices as the structural makeup that is passed on in replication, thus becoming the building blocks of the social world. Habits, customs, traditions, and practices are transmitted within and between communities, most often with an increment of meaning that becomes the baseline for the next step in the process of constructing social worlds (Dewey 1922). Communities, as vehicles of practice and of the background knowledge they nurture, account for both the social world's stability and transformation.

Bourdieu (1977) charted new roads to understanding the relationship between social structure and social action, human dispositions, power, the state, and, perhaps most important, social practices. Bourdieu's theory of action features several key concepts, the most important of which are "field" and "habitus." Field incorporates the objective component – a relatively autonomous social microcosm, for example, economics or law, in which social positions are hierarchically structured. These positions are occasions for struggles for several types of "capital" – another Bourdieu key concept – accumulated in the fields; "the amount of capital one has determines one's position in a field, and power tends to accumulate in certain positions" (Gronow 2011, 57). The habitus consists of the embodied historical experiences of individuals that constitute their dispositions and strategies for positioning in the field. The *habitus* is the origin of the practices that reproduce the existing structures of the *field* – it is through these practices that individuals come to experience the *field*, which makes up their *habitus*.

Some social scientists distinguish between Bourdieu's theory of practice, which scholars often identify with "the practice turn in social theory," and pragmatism's action-based theory (in IR, see Büger and

Gadinger 2015; Schmidt 2014). I prefer not to. Bourdieu's inspired-practice theory and pragmatist-action theory are both pillars of the "practice turn" (Pratt 2016; Schatzki et al. 2001). While I have profited from both sets of theory, I find pragmatism more useful.

There are obvious points of convergence between Bourdieu's theories and pragmatism's theories, particularly an emphasis on the practical and habitual nature of social action. These commonalities have been amply stressed (Aboulafia 1999; Dalton 2004; Emirbayer and Goldberg 2005; Shusterman 1999). As Gross argues, "Bourdieu himself noted that 'the affinities and convergences are quite striking' and that his approach like Dewey's 'grant[s] a central role to the notion of habit... and reject[s] all the conceptual dualism upon which nearly all post-Cartesian philosophies are based" (2009, 367).

However, there are important differences between these theories. First, Bourdieu exclusively ties his "analysis of practices to questions of social-structural production and reproduction" (Gross 2009, 367; see also Boltanski 2011, 18–22). Second, Bourdieu's logic of fields is about "relentless competition and struggle over hierarchical social positions" (Gronow 2011, 114). Bourdieu "is first and foremost a theorist of the way in which we differentiate ourselves from others ... pragmatism ... is interested in such sociability which does not preclude identifying with others" (ibid., 54). Third, Bourdieu mainly refers to habitus in relation to socioeconomic differences, whereas to pragmatists habits "relate to all regularities in action" (ibid., 55). Fourth, pragmatists have much more to say about creativity (Joas 1996) than Bourdieu does.[17] Fifth, unlike Bourdieu pragmatists ignore issues of distribution, but Bourdieu places too much emphasis on the strategic dimensions of action (Gross 2009, 368). Sixth, in Bourdieu's framework, "practices tend to be seen as subscribed to the notion of relatively autonomous identity commitments ... Yet evidence suggests that factors of identity, morality, or tradition can certainly underlie the adoption of a social practice by a group, as well as shape individuals' enactments of it" (Gross 2009, 384). Seventh, because Bourdieu pitches his key concepts of habitus, fields, and capital at the individual level, he neither confronts the problem of collective action, such as institutions and communities, nor theorizes how fields are formed (Fligstein and McAdam 2011, 19–20). Eighth, while Bourdieu theorized that change takes place when conventional wisdom or "doxa" comes into question, his theory is really

[17] "Bourdieu subsumes creativity within the habitual and embodied action but leaves creativity as a residual capacity" (Dalton 2004, 620).

about explaining stability rather than change. Ninth, while Bourdieu's concept of "field" introduces to practice theory a welcome spatial dimension (see also Fligstein and McAdam 2011) that pragmatism lacks, we need a spatial concept, such as communities of practice, that can grasp both struggle and collective learning. Finally, according to Bourdieu, the knowledge bounded with practices is mostly tacit rather than reflexive (Knafo 2016).

Social Orders

A Practice-Based Conception of Social Order

Let us remind ourselves that social orders are fields, configurations, or "landscapes" (Wenger-Trayner et al. 2015) of practices and communities of practice, whose *epistemic practical authority* assigns functions and status (Searle 1995) thus organizing, stabilizing, and managing social life (Schatzki 1996, 2001a, 2002). My definition builds mostly on Schatzki's although I revise it and add other concepts. For Schatzki (2001a, 43) social order refers to "arrangements of practices." Order is a feature of a field whose components are responsible for the establishment of order. More specifically, he defines social order as "arrangements of entities through and amid which human existence transpires, in which the entities involved relate, occupy positions and enjoy meanings" (2002, 24). But what makes the social world hang together are practices – the organized nexuses of doings and sayings that are linked by practical understandings, rules that people adhere to when practicing a practice, and ends, projects, tasks, and emotions (ibid., 70–88). In other words, practices are the context within which people govern their identities as well as meanings and their arrangements.

Political orders, in turn, are social orders that involve both political and nonpolitical practices "in which people join together to oversee and direct their and others' affairs" (ibid., 252). Because communities of practice are the vehicles of the practices that constitute social orders, and because learning and contestation characterize emerging power relationships and processes within and between communities of practice, we can say that all social orders are also political orders; they are rooted in political relationships and processes.[18]

[18] While Schatzki (2002) conceives the site where sociality takes place as a mesh of practices and orders, in my view, sociality takes place in communities of practice.

From a sociostructural perspective, social orders rest on practices, the intersubjective background knowledge that sustains them, and communities of practice and the material resources that nurture them (Adler and Pouliot 2011a). From an agential perspective, social order rests on practitioners' dispositions and expectations, which keep practices organized and metastable, and on intentional commitments to, and mutual affirmation and defense of, core practices. Social orders are neither exclusively material nor mental phenomena, but ontologically exist as human action and transactions. As sources and carriers of meaning, language, and normativity, practices constitute agents' identities and interests, and agency. Recursively, practitioners lock in structural meaning in time and space and insert it within a social context. Social orders therefore exist only when as organized as communities of practice, and adhering to shared constitutive dispositions and expectations, practitioners competently act in ways that their performances are recognized as social objects of a particular sort (Rawls 2009, 508; see also Adler and Pouliot 2011a). Social orders are therefore what communities of practice have learned to become. In communities of practice learning and contestation occurs, sociostructural and agential propensities congeal and become established practices, and mutual recognition (Kessler and Herborth 2013) of competence takes place.

Within communities of practice the meanings of practices may change, for example, from collectively understanding the abortion practice as constituted by pro-life/pro-choice meanings, to becoming a public health concern (Greenhouse 2016). Or take climate change as another example. Global warming's main problem may have been framed as rising sea levels. In this case, most of the practices (and the politics about) managing climate change would have been related to the rise of sea levels. Instead, from the start, the meanings created and spread in and through communities of practice were about the rise of carbon dioxide levels in the atmosphere. Most practices developed to manage global warming, and the politics associated with them became therefore related to reducing carbon dioxide in the atmosphere. Technology facilitates the rapid spread of practices, for example, corporate practices (Drieschova 2017), but only as mediated by communities of practice.

Social orders and communities of practice, while intrinsically related, are not the same thing. While social orders are the steady organization and arrangement of the social world by practices, communities of practice are, simultaneously, (a) social and spatial structural sites where the emergence and selective retention of practice takes place and (b) collective agents whose actions may matter for social order's metastability or, alternatively, its evolution. Social orders are thus practices plus communities of practice, but only communities of practice (their practitioners and materials) have agency – they act. Social orders are likely to incorporate several communities of practice or, as in the current European social order and the cyberspace social order, conflicting ones.

On this point, it follows that social orders are in a constant state of becoming, but this does not mean that they are constantly evolving. First, social orders may be metastable. While subordinate and regulatory practices, as carried by communities of practice, may be incessantly changing, "anchoring" (Swidler 2001), or core, practices may remain in a metastable state. Second, social orders can also be in a state of betwixt and between, when "old" practices and communities of practice are being discarded, but "new" practices and communities of practice have still to fully take their place. We may therefore grasp change in social orders as an overlap between practices that might be declining and fading in terms of their epistemic practical authority and emerging practices that may be taking their place (Adler and Greve 2009). Some analysts and practitioners mistake this state as "disorder," rather than a transition between or the "balance" of competing practices.

A social order might feature a balance of practices for extended periods. The state of betwixt and between seems to describe the international order in present times. The liberal international order, created after World War II under US leadership, is threatened and being transformed, but has yet to be replaced by an alternative illiberal populist and partly authoritarian international order that perhaps is taking its place. This state of social order can be highly unstable. After a critical mass of changes has taken place, even a small fluctuation through amplification can reach an intersubjective cognitive threshold, tip, and bring about the evolution of a social order.

When a set of practices, particularly anchoring practices (Swidler 2001), and communities of practice replace an existing set of practices and communities of practice, social orders evolve. Once a new social order has evolved, changes in practices and background knowledge, and within communities of practice, do not stop. Whether they will reach a metastable condition or evolve again will depend on the mutual influence between practices' resilience and their capacity to change within a metastable trajectory. (I have more to say about practices' resilience and changes within a trajectory in Chapter 9.)

We should distinguish between a practice-oriented concept of social order and abstract structural understandings of sociality, such as "assemblages" (Deleuze and Gauttari 1987; see also DeLanda 2006). Assemblages describe emergent unities of "things" and "sayings" that come together in a single context and respect the heterogeneity of their components. The component can be detached from an assemblage and "plugged into a different assemblage in which its interactions are different" (DeLanda 2006, 10). For example, while the wasp and orchid create a "becoming or symbiotic emergent unit" (Smith and Protevi 2015, n.p.), the wasp can be detached from the orchid and, together with a nest, "become" a different assemblage. Assemblages actualize or concretize abstract structures, or "schemas," that define the unique and indeterminate assemblages, including their contents and expressions.

Cognitive evolution theory takes us farther than assemblage theory. First, assemblage theory lacks constitutive and causal mechanisms to explain how abstract structures actualize themselves into assemblages (Schatzki 2002, 94). Thus, assemblage theory misses the "sixty-four-thousand-dollar question": why do assemblages acquire one form rather than another? Second, in contrast to cognitive evolution theory, which conceives socially and epistemically organized practices to be based on real propensities to "become" (Popper 1990; see Chapter 2), and actions and sayings as presupposing practices (Schatzki 2002, 96), assemblages are abstract, "virtual" (ibid., 95) structures that concretize themselves. Third, according to assemblage theory, "becoming" accounts for only the organization and disorganization of assemblages' elements. It therefore misses the historical and evolutionary dimensions of coming about. Fourth, assemblage theory's explanation of change is obscure and lacks a clear concept of stability. Fifth, assemblage theory misses the normative, ontic, and value-related dimension of social reality, where a grain of sand may become "dirt" in my house (Thompson 1979). Finally, assemblage theory is hard to generalize, which makes it unsuitable for the social sciences, including post-positivist social science, and particularly for IR theory (but see Acuto and Curtis 2014; DeLanda 2006).

There are merits associated with the concept of social order, as I have conceptualized it here. First, social orders are organized and maintained not merely by the distribution of material and social power (Bourdieu 1977; Pouliot 2010, 2016) among social actors within a field, but also by how they interconnect – by what they *do* together, the quality of human interactions, and their social and normative achievements. Second, while social life's arrangement and organization depend on authority, shared values, and norms, authority rests neither exclusively on material power, and the "legitimacy" material power endows to powerful social actors' values and norms, nor on the notion that social actors have similar or even the same values and norms in their heads. Rather, the authority to arrange and organize social life rests primarily on practices, and on the communities of practice that serve as practices' vehicles. It is primarily practices and communities' *epistemic practical authority* and fixation of meanings that helps arrange and organize social life.

Third, my definition of social order is amenable to a constructivist evolutionary perspective. Social orders' change and stability are not mutually exclusive, are socially reinforcing, and involve practices' creative variation and selective retention processes. Fourth, as Barry Barnes argues, practices "are based on something observable" (2001, 20). Fifth, practices are observable not only because of their materiality but, as Charles Taylor (1971) argued, also because they are spatial. This means that social orders are something more meaningful, palpable, and researchable than if we conceive them as the aggregation of utilitarian individual choices, or the aggregation of social norms in people's heads.

Finally, defining social order as fields of practices that arrange and organize social life manages to encompass, subsume, and incorporate much of what alternative definitions of social order consider relevant. This is the case with definitions of social orders as normative structures (Parsons 1951), regularities (Giddens 1984), stability (Durkheim 1938), integration and interdependence (Giddens 1984; Habermas 1987), activities that discourses arise from (Laclau and Mouffe 1985), and the result of individuals' habits (Turner 2001). Schatzki is therefore correct that other notions of social order "mark dimensions of order, that is, characteristics of arrangements. A given arrangement can be regular or irregular, stable or unstable, and these in different regards and to different degrees. Arranged entities can also be symmetrically and asymmetrically dependent" (2002, 24).

My definition of social order also encompasses Erving Goffman's (1956) conception of "interaction orders," or "micro" social orders that result from individuals' interactions and invisible unspoken norms and rituals in face-to-face encounters that affect the self. Goffman (1956; see also Pouliot 2016) thought that the norms, rules, rituals, and practices that make up the interaction order, rather than intentions and motives, drive agents. Moreover, social order's constitution and change are mostly autonomous from sociostructural influences in the sense of stratification of material-power resources. Like Goffman (1956) and Pouliot (2016), I conceive social order as being "interactive." But interactions or, better, transactions in Dewey's sense (1922) do not constitute social order merely by shaping social ranks and roles, and the resulting interactional structures do not only "feed on a never-ending struggle for practical mastery" (Pouliot 2016, 21). Instead, interactions/transactions also create interconnectedness, constitute epistemic practical authority, and play a key role in how practices and the background knowledge associated with them are preferentially selected, spread across spatial and functional boundaries, and inherited by future practitioners. From a cognitive evolution theory perspective, interactions/transactions bind agency and structure, thus constituting practical and epistemic systems that govern both metastability and change. We should understand interactions and transactions as taking place between individual practitioners within formal structures, such as institutions and organizations (ibid.), and primarily within and between communities of practice.

Social Orders; "Anchoring," Subordinate, and Regulative Practices; and Constitutive Values and Norms

Because, as Ann Swidler argues, structures "are multiple and intersecting," because background knowledge "can be generalized to new situations," and because the background knowledge bound with practices "can be 'read' in multiple and sometimes competing ways, transformation as well as continuity of structures is possible" (2001, 79). For Swidler practices are "simultaneously material and enacted, but also patterned and meaningful," both because they enact background knowledge and because we can read for the transposable background knowledge bound with them (ibid.). This is why practices cannot be applied only to various fields and expand geographically – they also can be inherited by future generations of practitioners.

However, as Swidler (2001, 81) rightly argues, some structures are more fundamental. While all practices constitute social order, some constitute other practices, or in Swidler's terminology, some practices "*anchor*" others (ibid.; see also Sending and Neumann 2011). "Anchoring practices" – patterns of social activities that constitute social contexts and orders by rendering possible and defining the criteria used in more specific practices – play an important role in social order's evolution. Anchoring practices define social entities; other practices come to rely on them; and they "cannot be changed without disrupting collectively established realities" (Swidler 2001, 86, 90).

We may therefore consider social order as resulting from, and changing with, a combination of three kinds of practices. First, anchoring practices configure, organize, arrange, and stabilize social life around core constitutive rules. These practices are also the main source of communities of practice's epistemic practical authority. In the context of the European order, anchoring practices of a security community, transnational polity, and free movement of goods and people across open borders have become increasingly institutionalized in the institutions and treaties of the European Union to the extent that Europe itself has become a set of novel, constitutive practices that are both geographically and historically sui generis. The anchoring practices of the European order are, in effect, constitutive of epistemic practical authority, which is fundamentally different from the sovereign state model. In the case of the currently emerging and continually fluctuating cyberspace order, anchoring practices revolve around the extent to which territoriality practices are bounded or unbounded. In the corporate social order, important anchoring practices, such as the legal personality extended to corporations, the limited liability of their shareholders, and the separation between ownership and management define not only what a corporation is but also its organization and parameters. It also defines the relationship between those who control and own it, the relationship between the corporation and the state (which enables its creation but as a rule cannot entirely control it), and what remedies are available to those who are affected by its economic and social impacts.

Second, anchoring practices constitute more specific or subordinate epistemic and normative practices that establish practitioners' explicit epistemic and normative dispositions and expectations and thus their reasons to act. To continue with some of the same examples, encryption practices (in the case of unbounded territoriality anchoring practices) and filtering and censorship practices (in the case of bounded territoriality anchoring practices) illustrate subordinate practices of the cyberspace order. In the corporate order, investment and finance practices (undergirding the availability of capital to corporations, households, and others), the practices in the sector of business education (ranging from master of business administration [MBA] programs and schools to the adoption of business ideas and practices by universities), and corporate social responsibility (CSR) practices illustrate a set of subordinate corporate practices.

Third, epistemic and normative-related practices sustain regulative practices, for example, about learning and contestation in communities of practice, teaching skills to new practitioners, the diffusion of practices across geographical and functional boundaries, practitioners' attempts to change material and social environments to enhance practices' survival, and more. This is the case with cybercriminal practices and corporate practices, respectively. The EU's processes of enlargement after the Cold War reified the practical authority of the EU's institutions and member states' domestic experiences of "Europeanization," which turned outward to accession states in Central and Eastern Europe. These, in turn, simultaneously changed the social environments in new European states and attempted to assimilate the social, economic, political, and territorial practices of those states into the European order (see Schimmelfennig and Sedelmaier 2005).

Accession was fundamentally dependent on the geographic spread of anchoring practices by teaching and conditioning actors in those states how to behave as members of the European communities of practice across the range of Europe's sociocultural and material rules and practices.

According to Swidler, anchoring practices "operate as enactments of 'constitutive rules,' acquiring their power to structure related discourses and patterns of activity because they implicitly define the basic entities or agents in the relevant domain of social action" (2001, 86). Constitutive rules make practices and social orders possible (Frost and Lechner 2016a; Schatzki 1996, 2002). Constitutive rules, however, are not formulated explicitly in background knowledge as rules (Swidler 2001, 83). This is the case, less as Bourdieu (1977) argued, because they are "taken for granted" in individuals' minds,[19] but because practitioners enact rather than "follow" rules. This reading is consistent with David Bloor's (2001, 104) interpretation of Wittgenstein's (1953) concept of rule following, where rules are institutions, and rule following is participation in the relevant institutional practices.[20] Practices and rules are thus part of the same ontology. Understood as self-referential institutions, constitutive rules exist because of collective agreement, and practitioners are aware of them through their actions (Bloor 2001; see Searle 1995). Norms, as we will see in more detail in the next section and Chapter 10, also constitute practices, intersubjective understandings of competence, and "better" practices' conceptions.

While rules, norms, and values affect the world through the three types of practices discussed here, social order does not take the form of practices plus rules and norms. Rather, rules and norms are internally accessible and acquire their intelligibility (Nicolini 2013, 163; Schatzki 2002, 75) to others as part of practices' background knowledge. From a practice perspective, therefore, the efficacy of rules and norms and their constitutive roles come to play a part of the background knowledge that sustains practices. While it is "understanding [that] makes practice possible, it is also true that it is the practice that largely carries the

[19] "Bourdieu's underlying imagery leads us to think of an individual person carrying around with her the habitus of her childhood, the skills and dispositions she learned there, mobilizing them strategically as she encounters new social situations" (Swidler 2001, 86).

[20] For Wittgenstein "meaning (and mind) cannot be properly conceived of as properties of individual consciousness, and instead should be understood relationally as the result of the practical activity of sensuous and engaged agents" (Nicolini 2013, 40).

understanding" (Taylor 2004, 25).[21] The selective retention of what practitioners consider relevant to solve a problem and engage with fellow practitioners in communities of practice is partly what makes practices a creative force in the social world (Knorr Cetina 2001; Joas 1996). What practitioners consider relevant, in turn, relates to the objects of knowledge and to practices' trajectory within and between communities of practice, namely, how practices unfold over time (Knorr Cetina 2001, 182–83).

Conceiving constitutive and associated rules, norms, and values as part of practices' background knowledge helps underscore the notion that the evolutionary construction of collective agreements that constitute social orders, which are social facts par excellence (Searle 1995), is governed by background knowledge's rules and norms, as enacted in and by practice. In other words, practices constitute social facts, and therefore agency, agents' meanings and identities, and collective intentionality (ibid.). It also follows that because what makes sense to practitioners develops in communities of practice at the point of action (Rouse 2007; see also Nicolini 2013), deontic powers (Searle 1995), namely the rights, duties, obligations, requirements, permissions, authorization, and entitlements that establish social facts, rest in communities of practice and their practices' epistemic and normative background. Anne Rawls is correct to refer to social orders as "constitutive orders of practice"; people make choices "in the context of the constitutive domain of practice they are currently acting within" (Rawls 2009, 517). This way they simultaneously make choices in the context of practices' constitutive rules and associated rules, and of their normative content.

Social Order's Normative Content

While all practices that constitute social order are normative (as I will argue more in detail in Chapter 10), only some normative practices are *ethical*, and therefore can endow social order with a pragmatic normative conception of the "better" (Rawls 2010; Thévenot 2001). Better practices, at the minimum, carry values of a "common humanity" and life's worth. They are usually related to informal horizontal systems of rule and interconnectedness-related politics (Arendt 1965, 174; 1970, 44), practitioners' mutual commitment and accountability to practices whose background knowledge carries conceptions of "the better," and how

[21] It is not the case that knowledge "causes" practices, but rather knowledge, for example, Wittgenstein's (1953) rules of the game, can be understood only "through their use" (Collins 2001, 107; Frost and Lechner 2016b; Schatzki 1996).

actions are considered to be answerable to norms of correct performance (Rouse 2001). The argument I want to defend is that practitioners, when engaging the world with their practices, may carry normative background dispositions and expectations about what is good and what is better.[22] As MacIntyre argued,

> the sense of good that one introjects while being absorbed in a practice includes a range of acceptable and correct ends, tasks, and beliefs, a sense of which tasks are appropriate to achieve which ends, a set of discursive resources to account for what is appropriate, and even what are acceptable or correct emotions that should accompany the practice. (qtd. in Nicolini 2012, 85)

An important argument for why practices are normative is Schatzki's (2001a, 52). He maintained that practitioners act in the world with orientations toward ends, and act affectively (Bially Mattern 2011; Schatzki 1996, 2002), as if what they do matters to them, to their community of practice, and to others. In most cases, practitioners value their performances, which they would like to improve, and also value solving problems and doing things better than in the past, better than others, and better than alternative communities of practice, not only for efficacy reasons, but also because what they do is deemed to be appropriate. "Practice," Nicolini contends, "is the bedrock of normativity, as rules are literally grounded in practices" (2012, 176). This also explains practices' authority. "Basing rules and norms in publicly accessible activity can help explain their authority and force" (ibid.). Nuclear arms control, for instance, is the recurrent performance not only of controlling nuclear arms but also of preventing war because nuclear war can be devastating. Environmental practices possess normative content about protecting the environment for future generations. Environmental practitioners are therefore willing to pay a price today for a better tomorrow. Internet practices are not merely routines about acting in cyberspace, but also about producing goods, such as interconnectedness and/or national security. Similarly, CSR practices attempt to reconcile the profitability motive and the economic advancement of the corporation with a more modern sensibility toward the solution of social and ecological problems.

When practitioners learn how to perform a practice, and contest practices' nature, scope, and reach within communities of practice, they use normative knowledge to engage reflexively in practical reason and judgment (Aristotle's "phronesis"). They also justify their own performance compared with others' (Boltanski 2011, 2012; Boltanski and Thévenot 2000,

[22] According to MacIntyre (1981), practices carry both cognitive and moral and affective aspects of learning.

2006). This enables normative alignment.[23] It is only a short distance to argue after Charles Taylor that the image of order may carry "a definition not only of what is right, but of the context in which it makes sense to strive for and hope to realize the right (at least partially)" (2004, 9).

A notion of social orders as arrangements or fields of practices – understood as regularities of competent performances and as embedded in normative understandings – underscores the argument that "actors share a practice if their actions are appropriately regarded as answerable to norms of correct and incorrect practices" (Rouse 2001, 190–91). These norms rest on collective intentionality (Searle 1995). As Rouse argues, "what a practice is, including what counts as an instance of a practice, is bound up with its *significance*, i.e., with what is at issue and at stake in the practice, to whom it *matters*, and hence with how the practice is *appropriately* or *perspicuously* described" (2001, 193). Normative practices have a temporal dimension too. "What those practices are *now* depends in part upon how their normative force is interpreted or taken up in subsequent practice" (ibid.).

For example, current cyberspace practices depend on their propensity to constitute either a global cyberspace community or, alternatively, impenetrable national shields against cyberattacks. CSR practices, on the other hand, were a product of the postwar period, building on concerns about the potential impact of businesses and economic activity on individuals, society, and the environment that go back at least to the nineteenth century (Carroll 2015, 87; Carroll and Shabana 2010, 85; Ratner 2001, 446). Carroll argues that although they were previously dependent on the personal charity of industrial magnates, CSR activities gradually changed to involve more formal programs that reflected the interests of the corporations themselves (2015, 88). In the United States, this process responded mostly to changes in background knowledge brought about by the social movements of the 1960s and 1970s, especially the civil rights and environmental movements (Carroll and Shabana 2010, 87; Eweje 2006, 28; Jaffe et al. 1995, 132). CSR practices were designed to address the complicated balancing act and reconciliation of "pressures, demands, and expectations of home and host country stakeholders" (Carroll 2015, 88). As corporate practitioners institutionalized CSR practices, they also became more common, formalized, and more deeply integrated into business practices (ibid.).

[23] "Justification can become conventionalized, taken-for-granted beliefs about why certain acts and practices are normal and right. Justifications allow people to move forward without actively calculating and defending each action, feeling psychologically affirmed" (Biggart and Beamish 2003, 456).

Reciprocity is crucial to understanding practices' normativity, let alone better practices. With Anne Rawls (2010, 96; 2009; see also Boltanski 2011, 2012; Boltanski and Chiapello 2006; Boltanski and Thévenot 2000; Thévenot 2001) I argue that constitutive orders of practice can sustain a normative conception because objects "exist only when, and as, participants in situated practices, adhering to constitutive expectations that are shared, perform such acts, in such a way that other participants in the same situated practice recognize their performances as social objects of a particular sort" (Rawls 2009, 508) This promotes horizontal systems of rule, interconnectedness, and practical reciprocity. If constitutive social orders of practice entail a normatively based reciprocity dimension – that both mutual intelligibility and conceptions of oneself depend on (Rawls 2010, 96) – a minimalistic and pragmatist perspective of "better practices" can be defended. As I will show in Chapter 10, these considerations enter into practitioners' and communities of practice's conception of a common humanity.

In other words, as long as practices' background knowledge includes a conception of the better, it generates propensities, though not certainties, of practitioners' mutual commitment within communities of practice to better practices. The European order is a distinct case in point. While scholars disagree over decision-making logics and incentives behind pooling sovereignty in the EU's institutions (i.e., constructivist, intergovernmental, neofunctionalist, etc.), the European order relies on a notion that European practices are *progress from* the horrors of the first half of the twentieth century. Thus, they amount to a novel experiment in integration and nonviolent conflict resolution. The contemporary European order is framed as an "Area of Freedom, Security, and Justice" where states devolve and upload competences to new communities of practice. And in the process they "gain in problem-solving capacity, particularly since many societal problems, such as environmental pollution, drug trafficking, or migration, are no longer confined to the boundaries of the nation state" (Börzel 2013, 516). These communities of practice's spread is *normatively centripetal* insofar as they rely on the promise of *progress* through the adoption of novel practices.

It is only in and through practice that normative phenomena constitute social orders, their metastability, and their evolution.[24] The notion that can collectively justify that some practices are better than others – for example, that mastering one's destiny is better than slavery, well-being

[24] As Wittgenstein argued, "contents of any sort (e.g., linguistic or mental) [such as norms] are unable by themselves, i.e., in absence of established ways of using/applying them, to govern activity determinately" (qtd. in Schatzki 2001b, 8). See also Frost and Lechner 2016b; Hofferberth and Weber 2015.

better than poverty, happiness better than suffering (Barnett and Stein 2017), and health better than sickness – represents an added value of referring to social orders as arrangements of practices (see Chapter 10). This notion improves markedly on referring to the arrangements of ideas in people's heads, or of constraining institutions.

Although alternative practices will replace discarded practices, not every breakdown of practices that sustain social order means necessary "disorder." When the social order legitimizing slavery broke down, a new social order that proscribed such practice replaced it. But not every evolution of social order will be for "the better." If Hitler had won World War II, there most likely would have been a "new European order," for the worse; Hitler's "new world order" would not have been constituted by values of common humanity and life's worth, let alone of freedom, democracy, and human rights. This is true, of course, for people who value liberty over oppression, and practice pluralism and human rights rather than racism, and democracy rather than totalitarianism. *This is the nature of bounded progress: it transpires within and for communities of practice, although these may have the propensity to evolve into national, regional, and global communities.* But unlike Steven Pinker (2011), who portrays the control of violent practices throughout history as a secular progress, I take progress as limited in space and time, reversible, and contingent on technology, other material resources, and performativity.

Part II

Cognitive Evolution Theory and International Social Orders

5 International Social Orders

A Plurality of International Social Orders

Earlier, I defined *international* social orders as configurations or "landscapes" (Wenger-Trayner et al. 2015) of practices and communities of practice that straddle a spectrum between interconnectedness and dis-association. Their *epistemic practical authority* assigns functions and status (Searle 1995) thus organizing, stabilizing, and managing social life (Schatzki 1996, 2001a, 2002). I also mentioned that unlike most studies in IR, which focus on *a* or *the* historical, contemporary international, or global order (e.g., Bull 1977; Ikenberry 2001; Phillips 2011; Reus-Smit 1999, 2014), cognitive evolution theory focuses mostly on a plurality of spatially, temporally, and functionally overlapping international social orders that cut across domestic, international, transnational, and supra-national boundaries. For example, we may refer to the post–World War II European social order(s), the Southeast Asian social order(s), the corporate social order(s), and the emerging cyberspace social order(s).

IR scholars have conceived order in the international and global context as core rules of the game and related institutions that become authoritative and therefore constitute consent. This is, among other reasons, because they are imposed by the international system's most powerful states (Ikenberry 2001, 2011), because of the systemic influence of material economic and technological structures (Cox 1986), because of normative collective understandings and identities (Hall 1999), and because of international society's primary goals (Bull 1977). A few IR scholars have taken broad historical views that focus on "big structures and large processes" (Tilly 1984), such as those associated with modernity, capitalism, and broad ideologies, for instance, liberalism, socialism, and nationalism (Buzan and Lawson 2015), or with systemic configurations of authority, constitutional norms, and fundamental rules and practices (Reus-Smit 1999, 2013a, 2013b).

IR scholars have also looked at regional orders (Hurrell 2007b) and at functional "islands" of orders, which were defined as "international regimes" (Krasner 1982). The concept of regional order not only is eliciting academic interest but is also having a comeback in practice (Hurrell 2007b). Recent apparent changes in the current international order have led some scholars (e.g., Kupchan and Trubowitz 2013) to argue that we may be heading toward international orders breaking into regional orders. The best days of the international regimes concept, at least as it was originally conceived, seem to be over. The concept of regional orders has the advantage of describing multiple orders at the international level, but it does not spell out the relationship between multiple orders and world order adequately; plain aggregation does not an international order make.

Vincent Pouliot (2016) has recently developed a theory of "international pecking orders." These are multiple and serve as the source by which practices and practitioners' interactional performances constitute hierarchical orders within global and regional institutions. While Pouliot's theory of international order is consistent with my understanding of international order as social and constituted by practices and interactions, it is also mainly about power hierarchies that social interaction constitutes by means of diplomats' performances within multilateral international organizations. Cognitive evolution theory, instead, looks at the notion of order, less from a hierarchical perspective, than resulting also and primarily from horizontal arrangement of practices. Straddling interconnectedness and disassociation, it generates either contestation among communities of practice or their moving, dynamic, and temporary alignment as "balances" of practices.

The study of international order turned in recent years to explain its management or governance; the emphasis, though, has been on "global order" (Rosenau 1992, 2003). This order includes both nation-states and nonstate actors and individuals at the world level (Bull 1977). Soon after, "global governance," as this field of study came to be called, moved to explore multiple and layered sets of rules and institutions. The concept of "multilevel global governance" (Hurrell 2007b; Zürn 2010) thus aggregates a multitude of international, transnational, and supranational rules, norms, and institutions into one global system of governance that manages and provides stability and continuity to global order. While the multilevel global governance concept in my view improves on the concept of international regimes, and accords with my understanding of international social order(s) as being diffused and decentered, it differs in almost every other way (see this chapter's third section) from my theory, starting with the fact that its notions of order and governance are socially limited and relatively static.

These approaches have enhanced our understanding of international, global, and regional orders. The concept of a single international or global order, however, flies in the face of the existence of a multiplicity of international orders, and aggregating regional orders into one world or global order does not go far enough. These approaches explain stability *or* transformation but not both. That said, a notion of multiple international social orders, constituted by practices, knowledge, and communities of practice, has several benefits. First, by describing manifold organizing anchoring practices (Swidler 2001) that dynamically constitute different sources of political authority, a cognitive evolutionary approach enhances our understanding of the international order's pluralist nature. The EU, for example, relies mainly on practical and epistemic sources of authority that differ from those of the corporate international social order, the human-rights international social order, and the global financial order.

Second, my approach introduces the concept of practical and epistemic differentiation among international social orders. The social structures and agents and the transactions or processes that constitute practices, knowledge, and communities of practice across social orders differ from social order to social order. Like states whose interactions are characterized by "dynamic density" (Durkheim 2014 [1893]; Ruggie 1983), or the quantity, velocity, and diversity of interactions, international social orders are also differentiated by the quantity, velocity, and diversity of transactions within and among communities of practice, and by the nature of the epistemic and practical authority of their practices and background knowledge. However, social order differentiation also rests on the variety of normative backgrounds of the practices that constitute specific international social orders and on communities of practice's social power, material resources, identities, and learning processes, which help select certain practices over others and spread selected practices across spatial and functional boundaries. Thus, for example, the normative and epistemic thickness, depth, and reach of nuclear weapons' anchoring practices differ markedly from those of the cyberspace's warfare practices. Nuclear weapons' international social order has come to rest on relatively strong normative taboos (Tannenwald 2007) – although this may be now changing – which are far from being applied in the case of the cyberspace international social order. The two international social orders increasingly overlap. There have been notable efforts to disrupt nuclear programs through cyberattacks such as those directed against Iranian centrifuges at Natanz (Sanger 2013) or North Korean missiles (Sanger and Broad 2017). The normative background encouraging the use of so-called left-of-launch cyberattacks may undercut nuclear controls and deterrence itself (Gartzke and Lindsay 2017). It is also telling that despite the increased overlap between the cyberspace and the corporate social orders, because of the dominant role that corporations such as Google and Facebook play in both, there is a palpable tension between the normative understandings held by activists and the views of corporate practitioners who want to capitalize on the information they have about users and habits to increase profits.

Third, cognitive evolution theory takes practices as being indivisible from the constitutional norms and fundamental rules (Reus-Smit 1999, 2013a, 2013b) that organize international social orders. Thus, it is not rules *and* practices (Reus-Smit 2013b), but instead practices that carry both constitutional norms and fundamental rules, embedded in background knowledge. The material and normative resources of what Caporaso (2007) calls "mediating institutions" in the process of European regional integration have significant effects on the European order's communities of practice, which act as the vehicles of anchoring practices both within Europe and in its influence on competing or concurrent orders. The selective retention of practices embodies, and *lives in*, the corpus of European laws and institutions. These anchoring practices become tangible and achieve deontic and performative power in their practice. The process of accession, while not always tidy and most definitely not uniform among states, means that offering membership incentives is through conditionality wherein candidate states accept the penetration of Europe's institutions and communities of practice in all manner of domestic institutions. In effect, accession means that candidate states accept the criteria for becoming part of the European order (Schimmelfennig and Sedelmaier 2005). Despite what Olsen (2002) calls the "varieties" of Europeanization, selective retention in member and accession states alike means adapting to the constitutive practices embodied in Europe's institutions and joining Europe's communities of practice, which imbue those institutions with constitutive and regulative power. Understanding the expansion and deepening of the European order thus means recognizing a plurality of temporally and geographically concurrent social orders. The selective retention of European practices reifies the deontic power of European institutions, in particular, the European Court of Justice, European Central Bank, Court of Auditors, European Commission, Council of Europe, European Council (Council of Ministers), and the European Parliament.

The variety of ways by which practices' normative background knowledge are preferentially selected and retained across international social orders helps explain why inequality practices have varied across social orders. For example, while institutionalized slavery has almost disappeared as a human practice in the last century, inequality practices are very much alive when it comes to economic and social relationships within and among nation-states. Such variation may also explain the distinct views that practitioners and the public hold about the role experts play in the corporate social order. In the corporate order, experts have a positive image. In domestic politics more generally, however, there are widespread fears of "regulatory capture" and the "revolving door" by means of which policy-makers and bankers can easily transfer from one sector to the other, particularly in the United States (Binder 2015; Binder and Spindel 2013).

Fourth, a multiplicity of international social orders, with their different sets of practices, background knowledge, and communities of practice, reflects the difference in the quantity and quality of fluctuations in specific international social orders, how resilient they are, and how fast fluctuations within an order might approach intersubjective epistemic thresholds that can bring about the orders' evolution. For example, while changes away from democratic practices toward authoritarian and populist practices may indicate that the liberal democratic international social order is evolving, the capitalist international (actually now global) social order, in spite of its multiple manifestations, may prove to be more resilient. The corporation has spread to and survived in different social settings with different social, economic, and political configurations. International order or world order covers the entire globe, neither because all states more or less dance to the tune of a superpower's authority nor only because most states around the world share rules and norms. Instead, practices and their background knowledge, including rules and norms, become selectively retained and authoritative across communities of practice in many if not most international social orders.

Finally, it would be more accurate to describe world order or global order as consisting of a configuration of international social orders that differentiated communities of practice constitute. This perspective is consistent with the recent view that the international order has become pluralistic, decentered, and diffused, and that polarity does not apply to the contemporary international system and international order (Buzan and Lawson 2015; Kupchan 2012). Since the nineteenth century, power and wealth have become concentrated in a few Western powers and international rules and institutions were diffused around the world (Buzan and Lawson 2015), but in recent years military power has diffused even to a few individuals armed with lethal weapons, and economic power is diffusing to China and other so-called emerging markets. In my view, for most of modern history, international order consisted of different international social orders, whether geographically or functionally differentiated. Some overlapped while others did not. Even at the height of American power after World War II, and after the fall of the Soviet empire in 1989, international order consisted of a plurality of international social orders. Notice that the post–World War II liberal order was neither a global liberal order nor a world liberal order but was confined geographically only to the West and functional mainly to economics and security. I will return to this point in more detail later.

International Regimes

The concept of international multiple social orders as fields of practice that emerge in and through what people do, and constitute the expectations and dispositions that sustain ordered social life, differs markedly from the concept of international regimes (Krasner 1982, 1983).[1] The concept of international regimes suggested an institutional approach to world politics that transcended the classic focus on international organizations like the United Nations (Kratochwil and Ruggie 1986) that was in vogue until the 1970s. The key notion behind the international-regime concept was rule-based cooperation across a variety of issue areas, such as trade, energy, security, the environment, etc. IR scholars differed about the reasons that promoted and constrained normative or rule-based cooperation. Realists emphasized the imposition of institutions and practices by the materially powerful on the rest to advance their interests (e.g., Krasner 1982, 1983). Neoliberals (e.g., Keohane 1984) argued that powerful states explicitly create and use institutions to increase their welfare and avoid suboptimal/Pareto inefficient outcomes, for instance, by lowering transaction costs. Another school of thought (e.g., Powell 1991) focused on the nature of the strategic environment within which international regimes lay their roots. Other scholars emphasized processes and institutional bargaining (e.g., Young 1982), intersubjective normative and epistemic meanings (Kratochwil and Ruggie 1986; Ruggie 1982, 1983), and consensual causal and normative knowledge (E. Haas 1982, 1983; P. Haas 1989).

In the last couples of decades, the international regime-research program gave ground somewhat. This was partly a result of Susan Strange's

[1] Stephen Krasner's consensus definition of international regimes involves "implicit or explicit principles, norms, rules, and decision-making procedures around which actors' expectations converge in a given area of international relations. Principles are beliefs of fact, causation, and rectitude. Norms are standards of behavior defined in terms of rights and obligations. Rules are specific prescriptions or proscriptions for action. Decision-making procedures are prevailing practices for making and implementing collective choice" (1982, 2).

(1982) admonition that the concept was too abstract and "woolly." Friedrich Kratochwil and John Ruggie's (1986) seminal insight that there was a major inconsistency between the concept's intersubjective ontology, such as norms, and the positivist epistemology that most scholars used to study regimes also played a major role. Theoretical differences about explaining international regimes and a refocusing of scholarly attention toward nonstate actors, networks, and global governance placed the international regime concept on the back burner. It recently had a comeback around so-called regime complexes (Alter and Meunier 2006, 2009; Raustiala and Victor 2004), which Raustiala and Victor defined as "an array of partially overlapping and non-hierarchical institutions governing a particular issue-area" (2004, 279). Because boundaries and linkages between regime complexes can be renegotiated and reconceptualized, regime complexes suggest a more dynamic approach than the classic concept (Kuyper 2014). Neither "international regimes" nor "regime complexes" suggest viable dynamic approaches to the concept of social order as I defined it here.

A few international-regime studies evoked the concept of international social order, as I understand it. Thus, for example, Kratochwil and Ruggie stressed the notion that actors "not only reproduce normative structures, they change them by their very practice" (1986, 770) and that we can identify international regimes only through performative acts that carry normative intersubjective knowledge. Oran Young (1982) linked international regimes to higher classes or categories of social order – spontaneous, negotiated, and imposed – and uncovered mechanisms of regime transformation, such as inner contradictions, underlying power structures, and exogenous factors. Michael Lipson (2001) instead used "sociological institutionalism's" organizational field theory (e.g., DiMaggio and Powell 1991; Scott 1995) to explain institutional isomorphism across organizations and practices.[2] More specifically, interactions between organizational elements of different international regimes within an organizational field cause isomorphism across these regimes (Lipson 2001, 14). While these studies were suggestive, they did not have much influence on persuading mainstream international-regime scholars to study international regimes from a more dynamic, practice-oriented, and social–order–based perspective. Lately, Reus-Smit (2017, 876;

[2] Institutional isomorphism's key notion is that it occurs within spatial organizational fields (evocative of communities of practice), through which – by coercion, imitation, and expert knowledge – mechanisms, organizations, and practices acquire legitimacy (Powell and DiMaggio 1991).

2018) has argued that to meet cultural diversity challenges, "international orders develop 'diversity regimes': systems of norms and practices that simultaneously configure authority and construct diversity." While the regime concept is useful for explaining the influence of cultural diversity on international order, and while Reus-Smit insists that his concept of regime is not according to common usage, it is not entirely clear why he finds the regime concept useful. A concept of social order, as a configuration of constitutive practices coupled with constitutive rules as part of the same ontology (Swidler 2001), might work better than the concept of regime for explaining cultural diversity in the international order.

Studying social orders as fields of practices that create interconnectedness and configure, organize, arrange, and stabilize social life suggests an alternative to studying "islands" of social order understood as international regimes and international-regime complexes.

(1) According to my conception of international social order, *practice rules*. Thus, practices are prior to and intertwined with norms and rules. We know rules, as Kratochwil and Ruggie (1986) argued, only through performative acts. Practices are therefore not, as in the international regime literature, merely the intended or unintended outcomes, or outputs, of international regimes. They constitute social order. In fact, they *are* social order.

(2) *Social orders, including international social orders, are processes rather than entities.* While they may remain in a metastable state, their practices and knowledge nevertheless continually fluctuate; practitioners learn and negotiate practices and their competence to engage in them. The community of practice organized around business education in the corporate social order, and the process of bringing new states and their bureaucracies and domestic institutions in line with the European order through institutional conditionality and social learning, exemplify this point.

(3) Communities of practice, rooted in and across institutions and organizations, help diffuse practices and normative knowledge. While institutions and organizations result from practitioners' creativity and the need to solve problems, and from learning how to deal with them, once institutions and organizations become established, they are sites of practices and can generate novel practices and knowledge on which basis new social orders can evolve. The diffusion of practices across institutions and organizations, therefore, is an open-ended process, according to which intended and unintended consequences may affect the evolution of, or alternatively the maintenance of metastability in, international social orders.

Institutions neither emerge solely for the sake of pursuing egotistic interests and achieving more efficient outcomes (Keohane 1984), nor are they the main objects of evolution (Steinmo 2010; Thelen 2004). As enduring arrangements of multiple practices across space and time, institutions help configure the nature and boundaries of social order – for example, the nature of postwar European order, the corporate social order, and the cyberspace order – and help constitute practitioners' dispositions and expectations. For example, the Tallinn Manual Process was an effort among an International Group of Experts (IGE) to articulate how international law would apply to cyberconflict and thereby define the legal scope of armed conflict in cyberspace (Schmitt 2013). Accession through "twinning"[3] relies on the exchange of member state bureaucrats with accession states, but their practices acquire both normative and procedural power as vehicles of background knowledge and practices embodied in the deontic power of EU institutions (see Grabbe 2002; Papadimitriou and Phinnemore 2004).

(4) In contrast to international regimes, which were commonly understood to be about international "cooperation" in an anarchic international system, international social orders are about all sorts of ways that humans organize and configure themselves around practices and background knowledge that move along a spectrum between interconnectedness and disassociation. When practitioners engage in corporate practices, they are not necessarily "cooperating," but rather enacting corporate knowledge, thus sustaining the corporate-social order. When Europeans organize themselves as a union, their integrative practices do not represent "international cooperation," but interconnectivity that configures their identities and affirms and defends their mutual solidarity. Similarly, connectedness rather than cooperation reflects the practice and background knowledge associated with hacking and the dual-use nature of malware where practitioners can use the same practices in developing or exploiting malware for different defensive or offensive ends (Stevens 2017). Hacking is typically defined by shared intrusion and exploitation practices and background knowledge but the distinction between black-, white-, and gray-hat hacking captures connectedness rather than cooperation.[4]

[3] "Twinning is a European Union instrument for institutional cooperation between Public Administrations of EU Member States and of beneficiary or partner countries." European Neighbourhood Policy and Enlargement Negotiations, available at https://ec.europa.eu/neighbourhood-enlargement/tenders/twinning_en.

[4] I differentiate between interconnectedness, which I use as a normative concept, and connectedness, which I use as a descriptive concept.

(5) Contrary to the old and new international-regime literature, expectations are not "waiting" in people's minds to "converge" around changing norms and rules. Expectations are emergent, even when social order remains in a metastable state. The emergence of CSR practices in the wake of and response to the social and environmental movements of the 1950s and 1960s exemplifies this. Expectations rest on practice and performance, which means that they drive social order as much if not more than the norms and rules that are bound with practices.

(6) The same can be said of international regimes' concept of issue areas, such as security and trade – they emerge through practices that constitute them. Unlike the international regimes' literature, I do not take issue areas to exist unambiguously or to depend exclusively on the perceptions of participating individual actors (Efinger and Zürn 1990, 68). While the international-regime literature was well aware that issue areas are objects of contestation (Hasenclever et al. 1996, 191) and that knowledge and problem definition compelled actors to link issues in particular ways (E. Haas 1980), it stopped short of arguing that issue areas do not exist until they are constituted in and by practice. Issue areas do not depend for their continuous configuration on only the subjective minds of participating individual actors, but also on their institutionalization in communities of practice, material objects, and discourse.

(7) Unlike the concept of international regimes (according to which political actors choose institutional instruments to advance their particular interests and/or for functional reasons) social orders, and more particularly international social orders, are neither "chosen" nor merely the result of practitioners' intended preferences. They result from sometimes long processes of creative variation, the selective retention of practices, practices' background knowledge, and transactions within and between communities of practice. For instance, we can trace corporate social order's anchoring practices – the limited liability of shareholders and the separation between management and ownership – to medieval, Renaissance, and early modern types of commercial association, such as the *commenda* partnership in the Italian city-states and fifteenth-century Florence (Hillman 1997, 621; Kessler 2003, 513). There is also a lineage from the earlier joint-stock companies used during the seventeenth century in the Low Countries for the exploration of long-distance trade routes to Asia and the Americas (Gelderblom and Jonker 2004, 649) and the French *société en commandite simple*, a form of limited liability partnership established in the 1670s (Kessler 2003, 518). The modern form of the corporation is a result of a long process of negotiation, culminating in the institutionalization of such core practices in legal statutes in the United States and the United Kingdom.

The adoption of the limited liability core practice in particular was far from certain, and was resisted and negotiated for most of the nineteenth century. In the United Kingdom, the debate about limited liability raged through the whole first half of the nineteenth century (Blumberg 1986, 583; Hillman 1997, 627) and was eventually settled with a number of acts culminating with the Joint Stock Companies Act of 1862 (Blumberg 1986, 584; Gillman and Eade 1995, 30; Turner 2009, 122). In the United States, personal shareholder liability in some form or another survived in many states until the twentieth century, especially for financial institutions (Blumberg 1986, 594, 600). Contrary to some interpretations of international regimes (Keohane 1982) that assume they *do things*, social orders do not possess agency. Instead, practitioners, organized in communities of practice, are the agents of both change and stability across time and space.

(8) International social orders are neither purely spontaneous (Hayek 1973; Young 1982) and detached from practitioners' dispositions and expectations nor the exclusive result of human design. They result from emergent processes *within* communities of practice. While packet switching was a product of network design, the cyberspace social order was emergent as users began developing and designing applications like email not anticipated by network designers. Fundamentally, "through grassroots innovations and thousands of individual choices," the computer science community would come to view ARPANET "not as a computing system but rather as a communications system" (Abbate 1999, 111).

Similarly, continental Europe's practice of limited liability before the nineteenth century emerged mainly because it allowed a partner in a business venture to remain hidden from the general public. For instance, the old *commenda* system in Italy helped moneylenders to disguise insurance or lending transactions at a time when charging interest on capital had social and (many times) legal repercussions – there was widespread condemnation of *usury*. Kessler (2003, 516–18) argues that the limited-liability partnership may have been used also in *ancien régime* France because it allowed the French aristocracy to invest in partnerships without the stigma attached to commercial activity and labor, including the moral and legal prohibitions of usury and the risk of losing noble status. However, in the American and British contexts during the nineteenth century, the practice of limited liability was reinterpreted and started to be applied in ways that could never have been anticipated in seventeenth-century France, let alone in fifteenth-century Italian city-states. Kessler argues that in the United States the practice began to be defended based on the principle that it democratized the acquisition of wealth by allowing less-privileged individuals to invest in business ventures and highlighted the "American" character of hard work, entrepreneurship, and equality under the law (Kessler 2003, 540). In the United Kingdom, the defense of the adoption of limited liability rested on the benefits it would confer to the working classes. This is not only because it potentially allowed anyone to invest in productive activities without the fear of putting their assets at risk (Halpern et al. 1980, 118; Saville 1956, 423; Turner 2009, 117) but also because it would make capital for productive investment more abundant (Blumberg 1986, 584; Saville 1956, 424). Whether some of the advantages attributed to the practice of limited liability ever came to fruition is debatable, but it is undeniable that as one of the hallmarks of the modern economy it increased the importance of financial markets as the engines of capitalist production.

(9) Because practices have to be learned and can be contested because of standards of competence, social orders cannot result solely from coercion based on material power. Material power is a useful resource of communities of practice as they compete with each other for practices' selective retention. However, without social purpose (Ruggie 1982, 1983) and social power, particularly deontic power (Searle 2010), and performative power (Alexander 2011), material power is neutral and aimless.

(10) International social orders' normative content, which is part of background knowledge, determines its legitimacy. This idea did not escape some international-regime scholars (Hasenclever et al. 1996, 187) who conjectured that international regimes facilitate legitimate bargains and raise transaction costs of illegitimate bargains (Keohane 1984, 90). However, the intersubjective legitimacy of social orders is associated neither with utilitarian-functional considerations nor with the mere fact of their embeddedness in institutions. Foremost, it rests with practices' capacity to create interconnectedness and practitioners' mutual commitment to their practices. This is particularly so when this capacity is sustained by intersubjectively normative understandings that enhance practitioners' security, welfare, and well-being. For example, our discussion of cyberspace has focused on two competing communities in cyberspace sustained by respective normative commitments to security and privacy. Likewise with regard to corporate practitioner attempts to reconcile CSR with profitability (Carroll 2015, 89; Carroll and Shabana 2010, 88; Esty and Porter 1998, 36), in the sense that it can yield tangible returns that justify the expenditures made by the corporation (Carroll and Shabana 2010, 92). Recent developments in Central and Eastern Europe's post-Soviet states have shown that the European order's

deontic power faces challenges precisely around the normative content of practices. In both Poland and Hungary, for example, responses to the 2015 migration crisis were both demonstrably anti-liberal and framed as against the core practices and the practical power of the EU's institutions. The practices and practitioners in these states illustrate differing background knowledge as related to outsiders and minorities. As Grabbe argues, Europe's transformative power is "strong in guiding and supporting reformers, but weak when nation-based populism dominates domestic politics" (2014, 45). Commitments to the European order and its anchoring practices would not offer politicians and public servants the same electoral gains as border fences, nativist rallies, and transhistorical appeals to civilizational struggle.

(11) While the international-regime literature had plenty of insights on the creation of international regimes, and on why they remain stable and transform, it failed to recognize the potential of studying the stability and evolution of social orders as part of the same analytical framework. It took the existence of international regimes as stability and their creation and demise as change. As in Young's (1982) study of international regimes, the mechanisms that enter into the creation and transformation of international regimes are different.[5]

(12) International regime scholars, most prominently Keohane (1993, 27), complained about the difficulty of penetrating the human mind to know whether principled and normative shared understandings are there. The concept of international social orders, defined from a practice perspective, helps break the "other minds" (Hollis and Smith 1991) barrier – what other people have "in mind." A social-order approach, understood as fields of practices, might help find a solution to this problem. Accordingly, principled and normative shared understandings are part of the background knowledge that is bound with practices that have a material presence, are outside the mind for us to "see" and research, and can be said to possess a higher chance of survival than theoretical or mental knowledge because we can put them collectively to the test. Thus, international legal experts have wrestled with the problem

[5] Young's argument that international regimes transform or decay because of inner contradictions, underlying structures of power, and exogenous factors is important but insufficient. Contradictions may be necessary, but without individual and collective agency, contradictions cannot effect change. We can make a similar argument about material power: without social purpose, material power is only a propensity for, rather than a condition of, change. Finally, exogenous factors, such as technology, may force communities of practice to learn to creatively adapt to changing environments. In and by themselves, exogenous factors create only propensities rather than determinants of change.

that "cyberweapons are not themselves physical in any natively comprehensible fashion" so one must look to their effects on "physical processes, entities and events" (Stevens 2017, 2).

Multilevel Global Governance

The concept of multiple international social orders can also supplement and improve on the concept of global governance,[6] especially when conceived as multilevel governance (Zürn 2010, 2018) and as political order (Enderlein et al. 2010, 9). As Enderlein et al. understand it, multilevel governance is a "set of general-purpose or functional jurisdictions that enjoy some degree of autonomy with a common governance arrangement and whose actors claim to engage in an enduring interaction in pursuit of a common goal" (2010, 4). Global multilevel governance, in turn, refers to the "sum of all institutional arrangements – be they international, transgovernmental or transnational – beyond the nation state … the global level must be autonomous [and] must be part of a system that is characterized by the interplay of different levels" (Zürn 2010, 81).

This conception of global governance did not solve all the problems of previous attempts to define it (Rosenau 1992). First, the concept of global multilevel governance authority is static because it stands on fixed institutionalized entities, with the capacity to regulate and control interactions across nation-states. What is novel is the multiple and changing institutional sites of authority at different "levels" and their autonomy degrees. Much of what I said about international regimes' lack of attention to processes and transactions and to the emergent character of international order also applies to the concept of multilevel global governance. The alternative is to take knowledge and practices, as carried by communities of practice, as becoming authoritative across institutions and organizations, depending on background knowledge's and practices' change over time. Second, we should understand multilevel global governance as the organized management of knowledge and practice required for keeping international social order resilient and metastable. Finally, while the literature on global multilevel governance acknowledges that it has normative implications (Zürn 2010, 2018), they are limited mainly to the nature of, and relations between, institutions, for

[6] The concept of global governance "looks at the sum of international regulations and goes beyond the issue-area-specific orientation of regime analysis. In doing so, the problem-solving orientation of international regimes was supplemented by a look at the political order" (Enderlein et al. 2010, 8).

example, to the question of whether institutions and processes are democratic or not. A wider approach should look at the normative content of practices, such as the constitutive norms that are bound with anchoring practices and provide insights into the question of what "better" practices mean and are.

The key notion I suggest is that practices constitute the regulations, institutions, organizations, and norms associated with global governance. Processes and transactions among practitioners constitute the actors or agents and institutional social structures of global governance and not the other way around. When it comes to the management of international social orders, practices "are combined and become crystalized into something definable and consistent" (Powell and Sandholtz 2012, 379). Thus understood, governance affects the "ways in which practices relate to each other . . . the careers and trajectories of practices and those who carry them and . . . the circuity of reproduction" (Shove et al. 2012, 146).

Practices, background knowledge, and communities of practice cut across national, regional, and global social structures and agents. Communities of practice, for instance, generate and help frame the politics of institutional and organizational learning and contestation, and institutions and organizations' performative capacity. By combining practices across institutions, organizations, and "levels," and by helping spread practices from one community of practice to another across "levels," communities of practice are also the engine of practices' invention and innovation (see Chapter 8). I refer to so-called levels because from a cognitive evolution theoretical perspective, and in contrast to the multilevel global governance literature (Enderlein et al. 2010), state, regional, and global "levels" are not really levels in any meaningful ontological sense. The meanings of spatial and institutional boundaries emerge from constitutive rules and anchoring practices, such as sovereignty, nationalism, integration, and global pluralistic legality (Cohen 2012). Similarly, while I agree with multilevel-global governance theorists (Zürn 2010) that global-governance authority is not hierarchically ordered but distributed across functional boundaries, as I show in more detail in Chapters 6 through 9, authority is distributed, frequently horizontally, among the practices and communities of practice that constitute international social orders.

Multiple International Social Orders, Global Order, and Global Governance

My discussion raises the question of whether and how multiple international social orders relate to each other and might amount to one world social order. As we saw earlier, Andrew Hurrell (2007a, 2007b), for example, argued that one-world forces play out across different regions and vice versa. Regionalism and regions, in his view, occupy a middle ground between the English School "solidarist," cosmopolitan conception of governance and the "pluralist," sovereign state-based and power-related, conception of governance (Hurrell 2007a, 9). At the regional level, different sources of authority overlap while values and power are in contestation. Regions are "containers for diversity and difference ... poles or powers ... levels in a system of multilevel global governance ... [and] harbingers of change in the character of international society (Hurrell 2007b, 136). Hurrell's regional approach is very useful, but it is in my view not dynamic enough. Thus, for example, the European social order gains coherence through metastable yet ever-changing communities of practice whose anchoring practices are contained within and reified through its supranational institutions.

A slightly different but complementary perspective on global order and global governance is Jean Cohen's notion of a dualist world order. In this view, international society overlaps with "the legal and political regimes and global governance institutions of the functionally differentiated global subsystems of world society" (2012, 5). Its "institutional structures, decision-making bodies, and binding rules have acquired an impressive autonomy with respect to their member states and one another" (ibid.). Against the view that the world is evolving to a global, perhaps also cosmopolitan law, Cohen suggests "constitutional pluralism":

> a plurality of constitutional sources of authority and competing claims to jurisdictional supremacy by autonomous, interacting, and overlapping public (state and supranational) legal orders, whose relationships must be also characterized as heterarchical and which creates the potential for constitutional conflicts that have been solved in a non-hierarchical manner. What is involved here is a complex of political communities within an overarching political association of communities, each of which has its own legal order of constitutional quality. The core claim is that the interrelations between the constitutional legal orders of states with that of the overarching political community, of which they are members, can be characterized as legal, even constitutional, without preemptive closure, imposition of hierarchy leveling unity, or final resolution of ultimate supremacy claims. The EU, on this analysis is the prime example of constitutional pluralism. (Cohen 2012, 70)

There is much to like in this approach, particularly the notion of "political communities within an overarching political association of communities" (ibid.). However, the contribution of my notion of overlapping, complementary, and functionally and spatially differentiated international social orders for understanding global order and multilevel global governance does not rest only on the aggregation of, and organization between, international social orders. Nor does it identify authority as residing at different "levels," such as nation-states and global institutions and legal systems, or take regions as the loci where global order and governance norms and institutions are dispersed. Rather, we should consider world order as a constellation and landscape of practice configurations and communities of practice, some of which overlap, others that complement and depend on each other, and still others that are in contestation for material and cultural resources, and for the selection of practices and the background knowledge bound with them.

Cutting across multiple international social orders are *global anchoring practices and their constitutive background-knowledge rules.* Global anchoring practices straddle a spectrum between interconnectedness and disassociation. However, as I mentioned in the prologue, there are no ideal types or "pure" interconnectedness and disassociation anchoring practices. Thus, for example, multilateral diplomacy and contractual international law are closer to the interconnectedness pole in the spectrum. National security and mercantilism anchoring practices, on the other hand, are closer to the disassociation pole in the spectrum. Characteristic of most international social orders is the contestation between different and sometimes opposite anchoring practices, the constitutive rules bound with them, and communities of practice. Cyberspace, for instance, is bursting with contestations between "multistakeholdering" or global-commons anchoring practices versus national-domain anchoring practices. In other words, we may better understand the constitution of global orders by way of anchoring practices that spread across communities of practice and international social orders, thus having systemic or global effects, than by aggregations of levels, regions, legal systems, and global institutions.

Global anchoring practices permeate and penetrate and help constitute not only multiple international social orders' anchoring practices and background knowledge but also supplementary and regulative practices and background knowledge. In cyberspace, to use the same example, we might find supplementary practices of encryption, on one hand, and surveillance, on the other. In the corporate social order, we can find supplementary practices such as those of investment and corporate finance, business education, and corporate social responsibility. These practices, and the communities of practice that build around them, also help establish the institutions and mechanisms for managing global social order.

Think metaphorically about global social order and governance as a computer whose operating system, such as Windows, organizes, controls, and manages how the computer "hangs together," what it does, and what we see. Every other software program, such as Office, anchors in the computer's operating system. "Software," according to this metaphor, refers to practices that carry rules (and identities) in their midst. While we can bring up a variety of "windows" and leave others behind, and while software programs change and are replaced all the time, as long as the computer operating system, with some upgrading, remains the same, the computer resembles a metastable global social order. But if we replace the operating system, how the computer "hangs together," what we see changes, and we also need to replace and update the rest of the software programs. In this case, the computer resembles an evolved global social order. The global order "operating system" is usually a hybrid between interconnectedness and disassociation, between the ideal types of a cosmopolitan world society and tribalism, which happen to be in a dialectical relationship to each other, what John Ruggie called "*the complementarity of contradictory tendencies*" (1978, 399, my emphasis).

Understanding global social order and global governance requires us to identify the anchoring practices and background knowledge that are dominant across international social orders. It requires identifying whether contestation between two or more anchoring practices and background knowledge, and carried by contesting communities of practice, characterize global social orders, or whether a global social order is undergoing a phase transition from one global social order to another. These procedures are both descriptive strategies and empirical research instructions.

In Europe and the United States, and also in other parts of the world, and across functional areas, the main contestation appears now to be between nationalist and populist anchoring practices, background knowledge, and communities of practice, on one hand, and liberal internationalist anchoring practices, background knowledge, and communities of practice, on the other. Is this contestation only a temporary phenomenon, or are we in the midst of the evolution of international order, in a "betwixt and between" phase of transition between a liberal international social world order and a nationalist and perhaps authoritarian social international order, to some extent, *back to the future*? At the time of writing, the contemporary international social order has not evolved, and there are some positive signs of its resilience.

It is also not evident whether the contestation between nationalist and liberal communities of practice is occurring with equal intensity across all international social orders. It is unlikely that all international social orders will become *either* fully liberal or nationalist. One of the reasons is cultural diversity between states and regions (Reus-Smit 2017, 2018), which is rooted in "multiple modernities" (Eisenstadt 2000; Katzenstein 2010); the liberal international order has really been a Western liberal order all along. Another reason is the differentiated impact of neoliberal policies, waves of immigration, and jihadist terrorism, all of which are salient causes of the current anti-liberal backlash. This makes the concept of multiple and pluralistic world order more appealing. Take, for example, the crises of democracy, liberalism, and rule of law in Central and Eastern European states, particularly Hungary and Poland, against the background of EU membership and its supposed "transformative power" over domestic politics (Börzel and Risse 2009; Grabbe 2014). These countercurrents occur against a facile Euroskeptic, xenophobic, nativist populism for domestic political ends, but are also illustrative of divergent lessons about, and practices derived from, the same historical events of the mid-twentieth century and the Cold War context. The background knowledge derived from these historical events includes the normative drive of competing communities of practice and perhaps conflictual, even mutually exclusive, social orders.

I am not claiming that cognitive evolution is a deterministic and final purpose-oriented evolutionary process from one set of global anchoring practices to another, for example, from nationalism to liberal internationalism, or vice versa. As I discuss in more detail in Chapter 10, because some practices may be *better*, while reversible, indeterminate, and confined to communities of practice in space and time, bounded progress may be possible. I will ground the criteria for judging bounded progress, however, less on the existence of universal principles, on reason, or on communitarian ethics. Instead, horizontal systems of rule and the contingent, reversible, and practical *path-constructing* (as opposed to path-dependent) selective retention of practices, whose background knowledge has evolved, for example, carry normative conceptions of a common humanity and, more specifically, of peaceful change and well-being. Take, for example, the European Union's practices of peace as embedded in its anchoring practice of the security community, particularly compared with balance-of-power and spheres-of-influence anchoring practices. It would not be an exaggeration to claim that it amounts to bounded progress. While not applicable anywhere and at all times, and while reversible and context contingent, some communities of practice may thus evolve to practice *better* practices. It is far from global progress, perhaps, but preferable to no progress at all, or ethical relativism.

Theories of International Order Change: Distributional, Transformative, Frictional, and Evolutionary

Four categories of theories of international orders' change – distributional, transformative, frictional, and evolutionary – help situate cognitive evolution theory in IR literatures. Most theories of international, global, and regional order deal with change *or* stability, but not with both at the same time. With some outstanding exceptions (e.g., Cox and Sinclair 1996; Nexon 2009; Phillips 2011; Pouliot 2016; Reus-Smit 2013a), theories of international order are mainly about stability, the maintenance of order, and institutionalized patterns of behavior rather than change. It is difficult to classify international order theories according to specific categories of change because they may capture more than one category, and because some theories may cut across ontological boundaries, such as material and ideational, and agency and structure features, and some epistemological boundaries, such as exogenous and endogenous explanations. While it may be possible to conceive other categories or modes of change, I believe I can capture most categories of change with my four broad categories. We may interpret change as differentiation, for instance, as being part of the broader category of distributional change, and dialectical change and interactive change as being part of the broader category of transformative change.[7]

A relatively small but important literature on change in international relations has inspired IR scholars on this subject.[8] Overall, this literature has mainly focused on international systems (e.g., Gilpin 1981; Holsti et al. 1980), foreign policy (e.g., Buzan and Jones 1981), global governance (e.g., Rosenau 1992, 2003), and sovereignty and territoriality (e.g., Ruggie 1986, 1993). The application of theories of change to international order, however, is more sporadic.

Distributional Change

Distributional theories of change of international orders take them to be a matter of how material (Gilpin 1981) and economic (Wallerstein 1974) power is stratified (Gilpin 1981), and as power transitions (Kugler and Organski 1989) that trigger long-cycle changes of global politics (Modelski 1978) and economic cycles of the world economy (Kondratiev and

[7] For another classification of categories of IR change, see Holsti 2016.

[8] Buzan and Jones 1981; Czempiel and Rosenau 1989; Gilpin 1981; K. Holsti 1998, 2016; O. Holsti et al. 1980; Jones 1981; Katzenstein 1989, 1990; Rosenau 1990, 2003; Rosenau and Czempiel 1992; Ruggie 1986, 1989, 1993; Walker 1987.

Stolper 1935; see also Modelski and Thompson 1996). This is also the case with the development of international hierarchies produced by changes in material and institutional power (Lake 2009). According to this mode of change, the idea of equilibrium – sometimes used merely as metaphor, sometimes taken in a literal sense – has been prevalent in representations of balances of power. This approach also resembles change as conceived by Newtonian physics, as a matter of objects moving in space and time affected by their mass. Most conspicuously missing are the capacities for novelty, for self-transformation, and for conceiving systemic changes as resulting from causes other than major wars (but see Gunitsky 2017; Modelski 1990). While it may sound oxymoronic, from this perspective, change in the order of things is therefore "static."

It is hard to understand *social* order without incorporating social factors, particularly cultural factors, such as practices, knowledge, norms, identity, and human agency. While material power distribution among great powers at the international or regional level (Waltz 1979) can give us a clue about what is permissible, possible, and impossible, it cannot say much about what power is good for, the content of social order, which practices are adopted and rejected, and how practices generate strategic interaction.

Robert Cox's (1986) theory on the transformation of global orders, while more dynamic than the theories I mentioned, conceives of world orders as a combination of material capabilities, ideas, and institutions that develop historically as a result of hegemonic and counterhegemonic structures' competition for means of production and forms of state. This mostly socioeconomic and materialist understanding of social order change is about the distribution of means of production and the differentiation of social classes and forms of state.

Intuitively, Ikenberry's (2001b, 2011) important theory of international order, which involves norms and institutions that the most powerful states expect the rest of the world to follow, should not be classified as a distributional theory of change. According to Ikenberry's liberal theory, the sustained liberal rules and institutions of the United States, which most states adopted as their own, guided international relations since the end of World War II. In Ikenberry's view, however, a weakening of material power can crush widely accepted rules and institutions. This theory suggests changes in international orders that usually apply to hegemons or at least great powers. Ikenberry's theory of change of international order is about the loss of material power by the "top dog" or, worse, its replacement by another "top dog." It is, after all, a theory of the international distribution of power. Recently, however, Ikenberry adopted the view that liberal internationalism, which characterized US-led international order, "is not simply a creature of American hegemony" but a way of responding to modernity (Ikenberry 2018).

Today's international order appears to be changing, but not as a result of the loss of US material power.[9] While less hegemonic than in the past twenty years, the United States is still the most powerful state in comparative terms and has not been replaced by another world power with different norms and institutions. The appearance of change in international order seems to be occurring not because of an alteration in the world's distribution of power but because of a move from liberal interconnectedness to nationalist disassociation, as illustrated by Brexit and US President Trump's departure from liberal norms of democracy, the rule of law, and human rights. As a liberal scholar, Ikenberry could argue that international order change is taking place due to domestic political changes. Actually, Ikenberry used a domestic argument when explaining change toward a US-led international order (Deudney and Ikenberry 1999).[10] But anti-liberal Donald Trump's arrival to power did not result only from domestic political, economic, and ideological forces. It is intrinsically related to global factors like globalization, the largest wave of immigration since World War II, and Islamic terrorism. What binds domestic and global "levels" is not just material power but more importantly the practices and communities of practice that are empowered and disempowered by a combination of national, regional, and global factors.

Transformative Change

Transformative theories of international order change point to shifts in the "order of things" (Foucault 1970) – not change in the position of existing "things," but in the creation of new "things," their renewal, or their modification. Transformed "things" are seldom entirely new but exhibit elements of past "things" that take new forms (Holsti 2016; see also Pouliot 2016). By "things," I mean not only material objects and environments, but also collective ideational structures, intersubjective

[9] Ikenberry recently admitted this point, saying that "the great threats [according to my theory] were supposed to come from hostile revisionist powers seeking to overturn the postwar order ... Instead, the world's most powerful state has begun to sabotage the order it created" (2017, 2).

[10] Hendrik Spruyt (1994), for instance, suggested that domestic coalitions played a role in the selection of the state from other alternatives because of the domestic coalitions' comparative economic capacity and efficiency. Etel Solingen (1998) considered that internationalizing, rather than inward-oriented, domestic coalitions may produce cooperative international and social orders.

understandings of space, agency, social reality, as well as normative ways of organizing social relations. Transformative theories of international order may also involve macro-historical accounts of how global orders come to be. For example, Buzan and Lawson (2015) examined the origins of the current global order, which they traced back to modernization, more concretely to industrialization, state-bulding, and ideological processes that took place during the long nineteenth century.

Transformative theories of international order change may refer to changes in the principles necessary for organizing systems of rule and for allocating political authority (Reus-Smit 1999, 2013a; Ruggie 1993). It can also involve changes of deep norms that constitute the nature of actors and their interactions (Reus-Smit 1999, 2013a), changes in scientific cosmology (Allen 2018), and changes in the purposes for which material capabilities are used (ibid.; Phillips 2011). This type of "remaking," according to Ruggie, "involves a shift not in the play of power politics but of the stage on which the play is performed" (Ruggie 1993, 139–40). It might also involve changes in imaginaries for organizing the world (Phillips 2011), actors' identities, and fundamental or primary institutions (Bull 1977; Buzan 2005). Thus, for example, focusing particularly on how Europe transformed itself from a feudal order to an order of sovereign states, Ruggie (1993) argued that the raw materials Europeans used to effect such grand transformation were material environments, strategic behavior, and social epistemology, the latter referring to changes in collective and institutionalized ways of understanding social reality.

According to Reus-Smit's (1999) sophisticated explanation of international orders, transformation results from a combination of changes in (a) systemic configurations of political authority, (b) fundamental institutions and practices that enable coexistence and cooperation between loci of political authority, and (c) deep constitutional intersubjective norms and principles that define legitimate political agency. Reus-Smit (2013a) also argues, correctly, that changes in international social order result from contestation about configurative principles and deep norms. He thus persuasively shows that, during the last five centuries, through concrete struggles that generate crises of legitimacy, revolutionary ideas about individual rights were at the root of the demand for sovereignty and delegitimation of empires and also the expansion of international systems and the evolution of international order.

Andrew Phillips (2011) made a closely related argument that "order is produced through the combined influence of communicative and coercive forms of social power, and is manifest in shared and authoritative and coercive institutions, including ritual and law, on the one hand, and feud and war on the other" (ibid., 43). According to Phillips, international order changes with the rise of insurgent belief systems and forms of collective identity, processes of institutional decay and breakdown, and material increases in agents' destructive capabilities (ibid., 9). These changes destabilize social imaginaries that in turn shatter the normative consensus social order relies on and thus its legitimacy.

Daniel Nexon (2009) takes transformation to mean deep changes of international relations' structure, what he calls a "network of networks" of sorts that results from the dynamics of prevailing actors' performances and new actors' pressure and resistance. Focusing on the transformation of the European international order in early modern Europe, he traces the undermining of imperial rule, and the epochal transformation of the preexisting order, to the Reformation and a transnational cross-class network surrounding religious beliefs and identities that diminished the ability of empires to resist challenges against their rule (ibid., 4, 22, 24).

I drew inspiration from these theories when conceiving cognitive evolution theory. While I agree with Nexon that new forms of rule result from relational processes, missing in his case is the key role social epistemology plays. Ruggie, Reus-Smit, and Philipps, on the other hand, do not take social epistemological changes to their logical conclusion. Changes in collective "epistemes" do not precede but occur in tandem with changes in political practices, which in turn emerge via new forms of interconnectedness (and disassociation). Thus, for example, the post–World War II European order became constituted and organized not only around new epistemic ways of conceiving space and authority in Europe, but concomitantly with new ways to interconnect within the European space. Integration-relational processes drove differentiation of units, to a great extent, rather than the reverse.

Frictional Change

I name this category of change after Robert Lieberman's argument that "friction" between orders promotes change. He says that "viewing politics as situated in multiple and not necessarily equilibrated orders suggest[s] a way of synthesizing institutional and ideational approaches and developing more convincing accounts of political change. In this view, change arises out of 'friction' among mismatched institutional and ideational patterns" (Lieberman 2002, 697). I extend the insight to other types of "friction." Frictional theories of international social change interpret change as a rupture between two different "states" or circumstances – as a break, mismatch, disjuncture, and dissonance between subjective and objective reality, competing understandings of reality, social structures and processes, individual and collective identities, pressure and resistance, communicative and coercive forms of social power, and the past and the present.

Philpott's (2001) theory of the disjuncture or dissonance between heretical identities and the existing social order, and Hall's (1999) theory of a social dissonance between agents' understandings of order coconstituted by individual and collective identities and the existing order structure exemplify "frictional" theories of international order change. We can also consider Bukovansky's (2002) theory of international political cultures' contradiction in establishing the normative and strategic terrain where legitimacy contests between hegemonic and counterhegemonic regimes take place, and Phillips's (2011) theory on social imaginaries and the existing social order as belonging to this category. Other friction-type theories of change focus on the pull and push of pressures and resistance (Nexon 2009), "activators" and "inhibitors" – the forces that push for and against policy innovation in the global order – (Brachthäuser 2011), and "incumbents" and "challengers" within "strategic action fields" (Fligstein and McAdam 2011). There are also theories of "hysteresis," inspired by Bourdieu (1977), about the mismatch between practices and the fields in which they are performed (Drieschova 2016; Pouliot 2010). Because of their emphasis on practices and process-oriented change, they are particularly relevant for cognitive evolution theory.

Closely related to friction-type theories are theories that primarily or partially use crises to explain international order change. Philpott (2001) and Reus-Smit (2013a; Phillips 2011), among other IR scholars, have argued that while a combination of ideational and material factors explain why a change in international order might take place, change requires legitimacy crises that drive the change from one order to another. Because of crises' collective cognitive effects on people's practices, which is why I once referred to crises as "cognitive punches" (Adler 1991), crises can play a role in bringing about the evolution of social orders. The end of the Cold War clearly exemplifies how a legitimacy crisis in the Soviet Union and among its allies prevented the communist regimes from taking actions to defend their regimes, thus leading the Cold War order to its end and to a new social order.

It was not only the Cold War crisis but also the buildup of a critical mass of fluctuations across multiple international social orders that created the conditions for a crisis that tipped the international social order. Sometimes relatively minor, uncoordinated, and unintended actions can build up to a critical mass of small changes that, close to intersubjective thresholds, force the social order into tipping and evolving (Schelling 1971). Because crises are socially constructed, we need to understand better when a crisis or a cognitive punch will lead to change and when it might lead to further entrenchment in existing practices.

Evolutionary Change

The final category of change in international order is evolutionary. According to Daniel Dennett (1995), natural evolution is an algorithm[11] involving variation, selection, and inheritance (in IR, see Tang 2010, 2013; Thompson 2001). Even if we disagree, as I do, with the premise that variation, selection, and inheritance processes amount to an algorithm, these processes are still at the core of what evolutionary theories of change are about, and what differentiates them from positional, transformative, and frictional explanations of change, and, more generally, rational choice and structural-functionalist explanations of change. Evolutionary change, particularly when applied to the social sciences, has been misunderstood and misrepresented. For example, evolutionary change need not be deterministic, teleological, or directional, or necessarily represent a progression toward greater complexity or universal "progress."

Most evolutionary theoretical understandings of world politics purport to explain, for example, change in international systems (Gat 2009; Gilpin 1981; Thayer 2004), cooperation (Axelrod 1984), institutions (Blyth 2011; Lewis and Steinmo 2012; Steinmo 2010; Thelen 2004), norms (Barnett 2009; Florini 1996), the emergence of international actors (Cederman 1997), and political ideologies (Shelef 2010). In some cases, evolutionary theories of IR (Axelrod 1997; Cederman 1997) build on complexity concepts, such as "emergence."[12] However, the few evolutionary theories that explicitly focus on international order change (Modelski 1996; Spruyt 1994, 2001; Wendt 1999), perhaps with the sole and partial example of Wendt (1999), refer either to Darwin or Lamarck or both by means of metaphor, analogy, or direct correspondence. Sterling-Folker (2001) is right that realist and liberal IR theories build on *implicit* evolutionary understandings of international order. But for

[11] According to Dennett's algorithmic logic, evolution theory's causal power depends less on the material used than on the algorithm's mindless and foolproof logical structure and procedure (Dennett 1995; see also Dawkins 1983; Lewis and Steinmo 2012).

[12] Robert Axelrod (1997) applied emergence to the study of competition and cooperation, while Lars-Erik Cederman (1997) studied international actors' emergence. Both used computer simulation, known as "complex adaptive systems," to explain systems-emergent properties.

the most part realist and liberal evolutionary assumptions do not refer explicitly to international order change. Moreover, IR scholars frequently use the concept of evolution as a synonym of development or mere historical change. We should be careful to distinguish between this loose use of the concept and an explicit use of the mode of evolutionary change.

Alexander Wendt's (1999) seminal theory of change in international politics addresses change of international order as changes in systemic "cultures." However, his evolutionary theory's mechanisms and processes, which emphasize learning, do not fully explain how learning and identity change at the individual level become changes in systemic cultures. Ernst Haas (1982, 1990, 1997, 2000; see also Haas and Haas 2002), and Peter Haas (1992a) contributed to explaining cultural and social evolution from a constructivist perspective. Like my theory of cognitive evolution, they do not borrow from natural evolution's mechanisms and processes, but focus mainly on the evolution of scientific consensual understandings and their effects on institutionalized ways of solving international problems.

Recently, Ikenberry has built on historical-institutionalism theory's insights (e.g., Thelen 2004), most particularly path dependency and interest-oriented mechanisms and processes, to develop some insights on the evolution of international order. In his own words,

> International orders, at least in the modern era, do exhibit a contingent evolutionary logic. Specific historical moments are created by hegemonic wars, but the "problem of order" that is thrown up at these instances is defined and shaped by the longer-term problems generated by the Westphalian state system and the liberal ascendancy. Order building states have found themselves building upon, extending, and modifying these deeply entrenched state-system and liberal internationalist frameworks of world politics. (Ikenberry 2016, 550)

These brief remarks require further development. I have more to say on historical institutionalism and their take on evolutionary change in Chapter 9. So here I will leave it that path dependency is too deterministic and that the historical-institutionalist literature remains committed to at least a "light" rationalist and materialist perspective on power and to arguments that actors are guided by past attachments and prospective opportunities (Fioretos 2011, 372). Institutions work mainly as constraints and opportunities, and selection takes place mostly through changes in domestic political coalitions. Existing theories of international order evolutionary change, except to a degree Wendt's evolutionary theory of change, and Ernst Haas's (1997, 2000) conception of procedural progress, are closer to "being" than "becoming."

Cognitive evolution theory, as I mentioned, is neither Darwinian nor Lamarckian but adheres to "Campbell's rule of a *general model of evolutionary change*, for which organic evolution is but one instance" (Blackmore 1999, 17; see also Campbell 1965; Durham 1991; Ridley 2015). This means that while biological evolution and knowledge evolution belong to the same "family" of explanations, they need not necessarily be isomorphic and, therefore, that the power of one theory need not depend on a strict analogy of the other.

6 Cognitive Evolution Theory

Social Mechanisms and Processes

> History emerges in an unintended shape as a result of practices directed to immediate practical ends. To watch these practices establish selective principles that highlight some kind of events and obscure others is to inspect the social order operating on individual minds. (Douglas 1986, 69–70)

Cognitive evolution is an interactional theory that explains the change and metastability of social orders, including international sociopolitical orders, by practitioners' practices, the background knowledge bound with them, and the communities of practice that serve as their vehicles. It refers to relational and interactive processes of becoming that, beginning with the awakening of consciousness to something new and to novel ways to practically solve social and political problems (Joas 1996), create propensities for social orders to either be kept metastable or evolve.

More precisely, cognitive evolution refers to a collective-learning process that takes place within and between communities of practice and through their action in their broader material and social environments. Learning, rather than natural selection and the survival of the fittest, is cognitive evolution's main social driver. As will become clearer in the following pages, learning refers not to adaptation-like arguments associated with Lamarck's evolution theory (Nowacki et al. 2008; in IR, see Sterling-Folker 2006) but to structural and agential mechanisms and processes that are strongly associated with social power.

Before turning to cognitive evolution theory's structural mechanisms and processes, and to the agential mechanisms and processes in the next chapter, let us remind ourselves of the theory's main concepts and their relationships. *Practices*, and the *background knowledge* that sustains them, are the *structural makeup that is passed on in replication.*[1] *Background knowledge* is simultaneously intersubjective knowledge embedded in

[1] For a different argument that practices are the objects for which social evolution selects, see Runciman 1989. For an argument that social evolution selects for the cognitive resources that give rise to practices, see Harré 1993.

practices and practitioners' subjective dispositions and expectations. *Communities of practice* are practices' "*vehicles*" that, interacting with the environment, make selection and (albeit variable) replication differential.[2] At the same time, they are the spatial field where practititoners' transactions take place. *Institutions* are emergent yet persistent social structures that manifest materially and meaningfully as a collection of practices (see Wendt 2015, 264). Institutions usually incorporate multiple communities of practice, help promote metastability, manage relationships among practitioners, and disseminate practices/constitutive rules in time and space.[3] *Organizations*, and more broadly *polities*, are *corporate practitioners* that incorporate background knowledge and populate particular social orders. The *environment* consists of cognitive evolution's *sociocultural and material contexts. Social orders evolve over time.*

Cognitive evolution explains how communities of practice establish themselves preferentially and how their practices and background knowledge spread and become institutionally selectively retained through practitioners' transactions with stakeholders outside their communities. It also explains how their members' expectations and dispositions survive in practitioners' minds and therefore how social orders remain in a metastable state or evolve. Social order evolution usually happens over time, when a critical mass of changes in practices and background knowledge builds up, when, for example, the prevailing social order is in decline, but when a new social order has yet to take its place. But social order evolution is concretized rapidly, with the "crossing" of an intersubjective cognitive threshold, when prevailing practices, background knowledge, and communities of practice are substituted by alternative practices, background knowledge, and communities of practice.

The differential selection in and among communities of practice is at the same time the differential transformation of practices and background knowledge that are deposited as sediments in practitioners' dispositions and expectations and incorporated as corporate practitioners' organizational and corporate routines. The selective retention of novel practices and background knowledge explains the structural survival of communities of practice and the survival of expectations and dispositions in practitioners' minds.[4] These subjectivities then become the reasons for

[2] I owe inspiration for these concepts to Hull 1988, 408–9. See also Shove et al. 2012.

[3] In a nutshell, institutions are reified and metastable collection of social practices.

[4] Practices at any given time are "reflected both in the ideas, beliefs, and convictions held by agents (individuals and groups), and in the ideologies, creeds, doctrines acquiring more objectified, super-individual existence. Changed consciousness feeds back on the capacities of agents (redefining what actions are possible) and on the potentialities of

the actions of practitioners who keep the practices and background knowledge selectively retained. Because communities of practice are not only the collective knowledge that sustains practice over time, but also the aggregation of agents who practice what they know, the active spread of practices by the organizations and polities within which communities of practice become embedded promotes the selective retention of new subjectivities. As mentioned earlier, social structures endure in human subjectivity and are simultaneously reflected back as practices (Wendt 2015, 269).

For example, European social order evolved after World War II. Because that order's evolution entailed mainly transformed fields of practices, and the background knowledge bound with them, practices and background knowledge, carried by communities of practice, engendered new dispositions and expectations in people's minds, particularly of European elites, but to some extent people more generally. These dispositions and expectations, in turn, engendered new types of institutions and organizations that transformed the polity and the social order.

Communities of practice's survival, namely, the selective retention of practices and background knowledge, is governed by a set of social mechanisms and processes at the collective level that are at work and occur only in consonance with agency. This means, first, that collective structural processes, such as selection in and between communities of practice, and agential processes, such as changes in practitioners' dispositions, expectations that result from learning and meaning negotiation, and in an experience of identity, are constitutively related as practice flows that take place in and through communities of practice in space and over time. As Wenger argued, the "duality of identification and negotiability" within communities of practice "provides a sophisticated way" to look at "the individuality-collectivity dichotomy by recasting it in terms of processes of identity formation. Neither identification nor negotiability is inherently collective or individual. Yet their interplay in specific settings is what defines the meaning of the collective and the individual as an experience of identity" (Wenger 1998a, 212).

Second, and following from this, communities of practice and background knowledge intersubjectively manifest themselves, or are instantiated in space and over time, by practitioners' individual practices and their dispositions and expectations. Practices and background knowledge

structures (specifying what structural arrangements are feasible). In effect, the agency is significantly reshaped. In its actualization, it results in changed praxis at a later time, and this in turn brings about changes in consciousness" (Sztompka 1993, 228).

stabilize social structures and fix subjectivities in people's minds (or determine the dominant ideas that corporate practitioners focus on at a given point in time), thus constructing practitioners' agency.

Practices and background knowledge integrate both structural and agential mechanisms and processes, and therefore support their mutual constitution and causation, both diachronically and synchronically.[5] Whereas, on one hand, the dispositions and expectations of communities' practitioners sustain background knowledge and practices, on the other hand, collective social mechanisms, such as the selective survival of communities of practice, constitute practitioners' dispositions and expectations and therefore their practical reasons. Collective social mechanisms and processes constitutively come to bear on communities of practice.

Learning and Power

Individual and collective learning processes drive cognitive evolution; they constitute each other. Learning is what produces, helps reproduce, and changes the social-structural processes that sustain social life. While both learning, on one hand, and negotiation and contestation, on the other, are vehicles for the evolution of practices and international social orders, we should understand negotiation and contestation as an intrinsic part of collective and individual learning. Cognitive evolution is a collective learning process according to which social orders evolve with the change of intersubjective and subjective background knowledge and practices. By collective social learning I do not mean the internalization of ideas by individuals through socialization and persuasion, but rather primarily the selective retention over time of collective meanings of reality in practices, thus, also, in a community of practice's background knowledge. At the individual level, learning is what changes practitioners' ability to engage in practice, the understanding of why they engage in it, and the resources they have at their disposal to do so (Wenger 1998a, 95–96).

[5] First, individuals' *reasons*, thus *intentional acts*, at time t_1 are explained as a product of practices and background knowledge, which were socially constituted at time t. Individuals' intentional acts constitute a social reality by endowing physical and cultural processes and their outcomes with epistemic and normative meanings, as well as with functions, status, and emotions (Searle 1995). Second, individuals develop the dispositions and expectations they do because they conform to communities' practices and background knowledge that both present and future generations of actors will draw on. Third, the practices and background knowledge that become selectively retained at time t_2 will be causally related to individuals' dispositions and expectations, therefore, to their intentional acts (as well as to their acts' unintended consequences) at time t_1 (ibid.).

Take, for example, the learning process of "twinning" between EU member-state bureaucrats and EU personnel with candidate countries for accession (Hronešová 2016). In this process, technocratic practitioners work hand in hand with relevant counterparts in accession countries to help prepare the administrative capacities for the implementation of the EU *acquis communitaire* – the corpus of common EU laws and regulations that bring states "in" to the European order (Bailey and de Propis 2004; Papadimitriou and Phinnemore 2004). Adhering to the *acquis* is a mandatory process for "Europeanization" (Börzel 2013; Schimmelfennig and Sedelmaier 2005) – the broad and deep impacts of EU regional integration on the domestic political, social, and economic structures of member states, old and new. Beyond the grand narratives of "becoming" or "returning to" Europe, the functional spread of the European order at the agency level is fundamentally predicated on collective learning by communities of practice, which are the vehicle of background knowledge and the change of sociocultural and material contexts. Reformed bureaucratic practitioners in "new" European states act as both the recipients and corporate practitioners of the European order, embodied in, and given power through, institutions and organizations. Their initiation, as it were, into the ranks of European technocracy involves new epistemic, ontological, and normative orientations to their political world. Accession into the European order means entirely new orientations toward security practices, territoriality and borders, and the relationship between states and the exercise over finance, markets, currency, and citizenship. These radical changes require new communities of practice and collective learning.

Another illustration comes from the intersection between the corporate and the finance communities of practice in the United States during the twentieth century. Despite the recurrent financial crises that followed in the wake of burst investment bubbles, only after the Great Depression did US federal officials and policy-makers attempt to regulate in more detail how market professionals (dealers, brokers, investment bankers, salespeople) interacted with the broader public. Because of scandals and disruptions, the practice and theory of stock market trading had very low prestige and remained unattractive to economics PhDs until the late 1970s (MacKenzie 2008, 46). Changes in practices and background knowledge, including in the prevailing ideology during the 1970s – from a more interventionist view on the state's role to a neoliberal perspective that defended deregulation and liberalization of markets – brought renewed interest to the academic study of stock markets (Chancellor 1999, 241).

Economists both in business schools and in economics departments started applying statistical and mathematical innovations to the study of markets and the economy.[6] Their research led to the development of the "Efficient Market Hypothesis,"[7] which established itself as background knowledge of business and financial practice and the basis for price forecasting models. More importantly, the hypothesis reinforced the already existing background knowledge (and ideological claims) about the efficiency of financial markets and the advantages of financial liberalization, which eventually became important even in official circles, particularly when bankers and officials are trained in the same schools and traditions and move back and forth between public office and private jobs. Corporate communities of practice, including practitioners both outside and inside academia, selectively retained the innovations that took place in the practice and background knowledge of stock markets through learning processes.

Individual learning means acquiring competence in, and knowledge about, a community of practice's meanings and in how to negotiate to make them dominant. In other words, transforming newcomers into oldtimers in communities of practice "becomes unremarkably integral to the practice" (Lave and Wenger 1991, 122). Learning also involves what Wenger calls reification, "the process of giving form to our experience by producing objects that congeal this experience into 'thingness.' In so doing we create points of focus around which the negotiation of meaning becomes organized" (1998a, 58). This is why I argue that institutions are reified practices.

Learning changes practitioners' ability to engage in the solution of problems.[8] Perhaps more importantly, learning within communities of practice may allow their members to be disposed to expect "better" international problems, such as how to manage relations diplomatically in a security community, rather than "worse," albeit more classic international problems like winning a war. From this perspective, practitioners in EU communities of practice expect better problems than their grandfathers did.

[6] Harry Markowitz was a pioneer with his work on efficient portfolios and portfolio selection (MacKenzie 2008, 48–50). Other important researchers were Eugene Fama, Robert Merton, and Robert Lucas (Shiller 2003, 84).

[7] In short, since investors are fully rational and intent on maximizing their wealth, and all the information they need to make informed decisions is contained in stock prices, market movements are random, and the work of investors exploring price mismatches (arbitrage) will help markets return to equilibrium (Chancellor 1999, 242; MacKenzie 2008, 42; Shiller 2003, 83).

[8] Lachmann makes the useful point that practitioners can perform a practice badly and may learn not to learn (n.d., 3–9).

Policy-makers make choices, bureaucrats and other political actors implement policies, and they all engage in strategic interaction. But policy-making, policy implementation, and strategic interaction take place in a context within which practical rationality emerges and reasoned actions take place, not only of those people whose judgment helps adopt and institutionalize a practice, but also all those people whom, later, by means of learning, a community of practice will grow on. What largely explains contemporary European practices' selective retention, and their relative resilience against major crises, is not merely practitioners' formal or institutional power or expertise, but the epistemic practical authority of their practices, which, institutionalized in communities of practice through learning, possess deontic power and performative power to constitute day-to-day dispositions toward and expectations of "better" problems.

While deontic power helps background knowledge to remain in a metastable state of flow, learning, by changing background knowledge or the rules of the game, sometimes in dramatic ways, can lead to the mobilization of new biases, the constitution of new functions and status, new notions of competence, and thus practitioners' effective moves (Guzzini 2016). Because learning involves the negotiation of meanings within communities of practice, it encourages practitioners to borrow resources from their environments while they also disseminate their practices and background knowledge to wider environments. In this sense, we can compare background knowledge to a "dissipative structure" (Prigogine 1980). Practitioners who are constituted into a community of practice because of what they do and what they collectively have learned[9] borrow social, cultural, and material resources from environments that make their practices and knowledge more selectable, while "over time, the joint pursuit of an enterprise creates resources for negotiating meaning" (Wenger 1998a, 82). At the same time, communities of practice disseminate their practices and knowledge to wider environments, thus increasing the propensities for practices' and background knowledge's survival.

[9] Another way to understand a community of practice, beyond its classic definition (see Chapter 4), is to take it as involving "the explicit and the tacit . . . what is said and what is left unsaid; what is represented and what is assumed. It includes the language, tools, documents, images, symbols, well-defined roles, specified criteria, codified procedures, regulations and contracts that various practices make explicit . . . but it also includes all the implicit relations, tacit conventions, subtle cues, untold rules of thumb, recognizable intuitions, specific perceptions, well-tuned sensitivities, embodied understandings, underlying assumptions, and shared world views. Most of these may never be articulated, yet they are unmistakable signs of membership in communities of practice and are crucial to the success of their enterprises" (Wenger 1998a, 47).

Communities of practice coexist and overlap with formal actors. They cut across organizational boundaries and constitute institutions and organizations, or corporate practitioners. The interaction between communities of practice and formal organizations increases social orders' complex processes and may be a reason for social order evolution. The dynamics of interorganizational relations depends largely on how boundaries emerge between communities of practice. Because of emergence processes, boundaries conform to complex nonlinear processes and thus change over time. As they change, they affect the relationships between organizational practitioners, which specific organizational practices and background knowledge also affect (Bicchi 2014; Lachmann n.d.). What appears sometimes to be duplication processes between organizations may be related to the sharing of the same practices and practitioners, and to how communities of practice engage each other and share intersubjective background knowledge and symbolic and material resources. Communities of practice often emerge and coexist in "constellations" that, characterized by convergent or complementary practices, are affected by, and in turn affect, learning and contestation processes.

According to Wenger, constellations emerge out of shared historical roots, geographical and functional proximity, overlapping discourses, and more (Wenger 1998a). European security practices, for example, helped sustain a constellation of communities of practice that cut across organizational divides, such as NATO, the EU, and the Organization for Security and Co-operation in Europe. In the corporate social order, a constellation cutting across functional and geographical boundaries (and thus prompting a recurring renegotiation of those boundaries) also emerged, connecting communities of practice in the legal profession, state bureaucracies, finance, accounting, organizational studies, education, and beyond. Cybersecurity practices have moved beyond technical computer science and engineering communities to national security organizations, public sector and private corporations, and even human rights NGOs as they become aware of similar risks in and through cyberspace (Deibert and Rohozinski 2010; Nissenbaum 2007).

Community-of-practice constellations can be symbiotic (Adler and Pouliot 2011a) and hierarchically related to each other. During the Cold War, for example, the nuclear-arms-control community was embedded in a community of nuclear-deterrence practice (Adler 1992). This community-of-practice constellation played a role in keeping the Cold War cold and in bringing about its demise. Both a disarmament community of practice and a "nuclear fighting" community of practice actually competed with the community of nuclear-deterrence practice constellation *and lost.* The history of the relationship between the finance and the corporate-administration communities of practice provides another example of such symbioses and hierarchical connections (along with shifts in the more influential pole of the relationship). At the same time that finance enabled the rise of the modern corporation, it also benefited from the expansion of market capitalism and the corporate demand for capital, including by adopting corporate practices and the corporation model to its own business ventures. Since the 1970s, this process has come full circle with the increased control of corporations by financial interests, whether in the form of private equity firms, the use of leveraged buyouts,[10] or the increased emphasis on creating "value" to shareholders (i.e., increasing dividend payouts).

To get back to the main point, power permeates individual and collective learning. As Wenger says, "the definition of the regime of accountability and who gets to qualify as competent are questions of power" (2010, 8). Wenger differentiates between vertical accountability, which, as in Bourdieu's (1977; see also Pouliot 2016) case is associated with hierarchy, and horizontal accountability, "which is associated with engagement in joint activities, negotiation of mutual relevance, standards of practice, peer recognition, identity and reputation, and commitment to collective learning" (Wenger 2010, 13).

Horizontal accountability and social power are important for learning, the negotiation and contestation of meanings, and identity change, both within and between communities of practice. Learning is associated with the development of shared identities in communities of practice, though it also involves negotiation and contestation so is inherently political (Schatzki 2002, 251) and thus it constitutes the building blocks of governance through practice. In contrast to the received view of governance, which is associated with the management of social relations by institutions and organizations (Enderlein et al. 2010), governance may be also comprehended as the organization and management of social reality by means of practices and the intersubjective background knowledge that are bound with them. Thus understood, governance can partly help "flatten" hierarchical relationships in and between communities of practice.

Interconnectedness and horizontal accountability are closely related. The closer a social order's practices are organized and characterized by horizontal accountability, the more propensities for learning take place,

[10] A leveraged buyout is a financing strategy in which a group of investors buy all of a company's publicly owned stock and take it private (Holmstrom and Kaplan 2001, 124; Kaplan and Strömberg 2009, 121; Shleifer and Vishny 1997, 766), usually against the wishes of its management and employees.

the more practices they tend to integrate and cut across borders, and the "flatter" relationships in and between communities of practice will be. In such orders, power is not absent but is distributed among practitioners. Arendt (1965, 174; see also Bernstein 2018, chapter 8) already made a similar argument years ago; power is mainly about a plurality of individuals acting together. This is particularly evident in democratic politics. While democracies involve conflict and hierarchies, they nonetheless distribute power to make decisions among many individuals and institutions. The closer a social order's practices are organized and arranged by vertical accountability, the fewer propensities for learning, the more practices will tend to emphasize disassociation, such as strong nationalist practices, and the more hierarchical relationships in and between communities of practice are going to be. As I mentioned in the prologue, international social orders tend to vary along the interconnectedness–disassociation continuum so international social orders, while closer to one pole or the other, are likely to exhibit, in different measures, both horizontal and vertical or hierarchical forms of power. We may even see the partial flattening of relations in certain communities where ordinary dissociating pressures around national lines exist. For example, just as in the "high politics" world of foreign intelligence, professional standards act as "peer constraints" among the Anglo-American Five Eyes intelligence community, pushing cooperation closer to legal compliance (Deeks 2016).

The enactment of law also contributes to horizontally conceived power or governance by practices (Brunnée and Toope 2010, 2011b), so it similarly tends to flatten social and political interactions to a certain degree (excluding the power of courts). The notion of horizontal power I refer to may be partly related to legal authority – which may also be a source of reciprocity among practitioners and of learning – and to the processes of negotiation, contestation, and learning that instill in practitioners a sense of sociocognitive and normative reciprocity. The partial flattening of hierarchical relations through normative reciprocity processes is essential in communities of practice, especially in the discourse of normative justification that aims at achieving shared ways of skillfully performing normative background knowledge (Boltanski 2011; Kornprobst 2014).

The EU's common acquis, reciprocity, common norms among member states, supranational commitments to the fundamental freedoms of EU citizens, and communities of practice within the EU's seven fundamental institutions constitute, as it were, the European polity and the embodiment of background knowledge among and between overlapping communities of practice in the European order. While hierarchical power over certain issue areas is never absent – for instance during the 2008 and 2015 Greek debt crises – intra-EU bargaining is characterized by a remarkable degree of horizontal reciprocity (Lewis 2014; Naurin and Wallace 2008). The European order's evolution is unique to the extent that some argue that the depth of its regional integration, that is, Europeanization, is sui generis (Börzel 2013; Olsen 2002). In other words, its evolution is the result of practice-selective retention through the sociocultural mechanisms of endogenous change among, and competition between, communities of practice.

Scientific background knowledge may also help partly flatten hierarchical relationships in communities of practice. For example, although power struggles among states about climate change are extensive, compelling consensual scientific evidence concerning climate change, though it cannot entirely overcome power struggles, can force states – President Trump's disregard for scientific knowledge notwithstanding – to take common action. Finally, deontic power, which collectively creates entitlements and affects collective intentionality, makes social reality even before the distribution of formal authority positions kick in. While corporations, states, and international organizations might struggle about how to make corporate practices more ethical, the power of the corporation qua corporation, to practice within and across states, is an entitlement that corporations owe to the attachment of status and function to legal and social reality (Searle 2010).

In fact, states' regulatory and legislative action confers status and functions to the corporate order, whether in important areas where they have no interest to act or by laying the institutional groundwork for corporate existence and activities (legal personality, protection of rights, law enforcement, and so on). The anchoring practice of legal personality, enshrined in domestic legislation by the state, is a case in point. It confers to corporations a separate legal personality from that of its shareholders or owners, with its own rights and obligations (Blumberg 1986, 577; Turner 2009, 117), allowing it to have a separate "life" and to continue in perpetuity, surviving the death or retirement of its shareholders (Kessler 2003, 528). As it gives personality to corporations, it also has a number of practical consequences. It enables corporations to sign contracts with suppliers and distributors and to access the courts (Chandler 1992, 483) and it confers to them a number of rights and obligations that are usually the prerogative of individuals, such as the right to own property.

Power is also associated with communities of practice's material and institutional resources, for instance, objects and technology that members of a community of practice share (Fox 2000). Material power increases propensities of communities of practice to spread in space and time, thus for practices and background knowledge to be selectively retained. When two or more competing communities of practice jointly affect institutional and political processes without one community overcoming another, a "balance of practices" (Adler 2010; Adler and Crawford 2006) may be temporarily created, which can help keep practices and background knowledge preferentially selectively retained over time, thus keeping a social order in a state of metastable flow. From an agential perspective, power enters practitioners' competence and performative capacity to transform their communities of practice endogenously, as well as to affect the boundaries of their communities of practice, and endow material and social processes with collective meaning, particularly functions and status, thus creating entitlements (deontic power).

Let us now take a closer look at how social power manifests itself. Together with learning, these manifestations are crucial for creative variation and selective-retention processes (which I describe in detail in Chapters 8 and 9) and thus for social orders' change and stability. First, power "involves a tension – a kind of inherent double bind ... between identification and negotiability" (Wenger 1998a, 207–8); there is therefore a tension between sharing and contesting the nature of practices and the competence by which they are performed:

> When a style or a discourse spreads through a vast community or constellation, claiming ownership of its meaning becomes a source of power by the very fact that such style or discourse is a source of widespread identification ... Rooted in our identities, power derives from belonging as well as from exercising control over what we belong to. It includes both conflictual and coalescing aspects – it requires or creates some form of consensus in order to become socially effective, but the meaning of the consensus is something whose ownership always remains open to negotiation. (Wenger 1998a, 207)

At a broad level, for example, the open architecture of cyberspace where power is distributed has created widespread expectations about the availability, integrity, and confidentiality of information. In the early days of the ARPANET, computer science researchers' practices of decentralized network design and open sharing defined an open and free consensus. But once the US Department of Defense in the form of the Defense Communications Agency again regained control of the ARPANET in 1975 and reoriented the network to more immediate military operational concerns, this open consensus was contested by curtailing the common practice of copying files without the owner's explicit consent, imposing network access control practices (Abbate 1999, 136–39). Ordinary users and other grassroots open-source communities across the globe identify with this open consensus and continue to participate in ways that make it resilient. However, this global associated consensus about cyberspace remains open to negotiation by others who approach it with distinctly local experience like national security or law-enforcement communities seeking to impose "architectural regulation" (Tien 2007). Specifically, intelligence agencies like the National Security Agency can request back doors from service providers into products and services using technologies like encryption that can thwart collection efforts.[11] The FBI, for instance, successfully pushed to expand the Communications Assistance for Law Enforcement Act (CALEA) to include Internet broadband and voice over Internet protocol providers to facilitate lawful interception of growing digital communications (Hancock 2007).

Second, while collective learning affects deontic power, that power simultaneously facilitates learning (cum negotiation and contestation) and how it affects creative-variation and selective-retention processes. To begin with, endowing social and material reality with new functions and status promotes creative variation: it generates propensities for communities of practice to innovate, such as developing new practices or finding new ways of performing existing practices, and performing well. It also affects the negotiation and contestation processes that help in the selective retention of innovations. For example, many common institutional objects, such as money, can be reproduced in cyberspace as digital artifacts (Brey 2014). The ability to conduct financial transactions online spurred innovation in the corporate sector by inventing "e-business as the new organizational model" (Castells 2002, 67). These e-commerce and e-banking practices were selectively retained only after the dot-com boom that created Internet giants like eBay, Amazon, and others that offered online services and products. This, in turn, generated more innovation where money-transfer services like PayPal were established (which eBay subsequently acquired in 2002 to facilitate online transactions). More recently, the invention of crypto-currencies like Bitcoin by Satoshi Nakamoto, which use a blockchain or public ledger to verify transactions, has the potential to reinvent money more radically by removing intermediaries like central banks or other financial institutions.

Third, "performative power" plays a major role at both the collective and individual levels via contestation processes, where performances of resistance and subversion may flourish (Alexander 2011). Performative power is galvanized when practitioners "orient themselves toward others as if they were actors on a stage seeking identification with the

[11] A back door is a method of surreptitiously obtaining access to a computer system by bypassing normal front-end authentication.

experiences and understanding of audiences" (ibid., 8). According to Jeffrey Alexander (ibid., 89), being really powerful means that no matter what resources and capacities social actors possess, they must find a way to make their audiences believe them. From the perspective of cognitive evolution theory, practitioners should be able to make their performances believable to other practitioners, thus enhancing their competence in other practitioners' eyes. They also use performative power to establish the dominant meaning of a practice, thus, the community of practice's identity.

Brexit illustrates how European integration-related communities of practice have recently lost some of their performative power: they have had difficulty putting on an act in front of British domestic audiences to persuade them that European integration is in their interest. Performative power relies on the better performance in front of publics rather than on the transmission of facts. Disassociation-related communities of practice, and particular practitioners among them like Boris Johnson and Nigel Farage, put on a better "act," often using "alternative facts" (lies) and steering emotions to persuade their audience of disassociation's benefits. By contrast, the resounding defeat of Le Pen's Front National in France was not so much a rejection of a nativist Euroskepticism than the result of the performative power of Emmanuel Macron, an anti-establishment candidate with no history of holding elected office. Macron enlisted his anti-establishment performance in support of the status quo of European integration, while offering an alternative to rightist, centrifugal social forces.

Similarly, national "security communities"[12] following the Snowden disclosures faced a challenge to their performative power, or to their ability to assuage credibly the American public's concerns about surveillance. In particular, Snowden describes that the "breaking point was seeing the director of national intelligence, James Clapper, directly lie under oath to Congress . . . Seeing that really meant for me there was no going back" (2014). National security communities may face unique challenges in actualizing their performative power given the demands of state secrecy.

Performativity (Adler 2010; Alexander 2011; Ringmar 2012) increases the contingency of processes and outcomes both within and between communities of practice. Performative power acquires its efficacy as processes of meaning communication and via the imposition of meanings by some practitioners on communities' practices. Practitioners thus

[12] Here I use this concept meaning communities of security practitioners.

continually negotiate meanings while striving to make their own meanings stick (Alexander 2011, 11).

Close to intersubjective cognitive thresholds, when the possibilities for a social order to be kept metastable or to evolve might depend on small nonlinear changes, performativity can play a large role in which way the social order will go. Because of the contingency of practices, at thresholds, a performative innovation, or small changes in the performance of key practitioners, might make the difference between a social order remaining metastable or evolving. Victor Turner, who contributed to performative theory, used the concept of "liminality" – representing "the midpoint of transition in a status-sequence between two positions" (1974, 237) – to express the view that contestation grows and practitioners have more performative agential freedom to effect change under liminal conditions.[13] It is in liminal situations and times, close to intersubjective cognitive thresholds – when disenchantment with practices grows, when practices are seen as failed symbolic performances, when they lose legitimacy, when the function status on which practices depend weakens or disappears, and when identities are undermined or transformed – that social order can evolve.[14] At such times, only as a result of resilience and "homeorhesis" (change to a flow or trajectory, rather than to an equilibrium point) (Waddington 1977),[15] both of which can be associated, for example, with individual and institutional practitioners' performances and/or institutional symbolic and material strength, a given social order may manage to remain metastable. The unstable, but still not transformed, European order is a case in point.

Close to intersubjective cognitive thresholds, social-order evolution can also take place because of the weakening of "anchoring practices" (Swidler 2001; see Chapter 4). The Hungarian government's push against the European Court of Justice and the commission's oversight, and new laws to tighten rules against NGOs, universities, and asylum seekers turned Hungary into the site of significant contestation between illiberal communities of practice and the anchoring practices of the European order.

[13] According to Alexander, "liminality, which represents ideal sites for contestation, and pragmatism . . . are natural theoretical bedfellows" (2011, 21). For an alternative concept of liminality mainly applied to territorial and identity boundaries, see van Gennep 1961.

[14] Similarly, from a complexity theory perspective, innovations may be amplified to such an extent that social orders may encounter bifurcations, at which time emergent orders, through positive feedback processes, can replace existing ones (Haken 1990; Prigogine 1980).

[15] I discuss these two factors in more detail in Chapter 9.

Less pivotal practices that depend on anchoring practices may then follow the way of the anchoring practices. At such a time, a "tipping point" (Gladwell 2002; Grodzins 1957; Schelling 1969) might be reached when functions and status can be withdrawn from people, institutions, and organizations, thus leading to social order evolution. For instance, as states became aware of the implications of open access as well as user demands for local content delivery, global end-to-end cyberspace practices weakened and became increasingly challenged in the late 1990s (Goldsmith and Wu 2006).

While the number of practitioners who continue to practice a practice may be important, at thresholds, like the case of the fall of the Berlin Wall, even a small number of individuals can lead a social order to tip and evolve. If each individual's expectations depend on what other individuals expect, and if each of these individual's expectations depend on their collective background knowledge, then a change affecting even a small number of key individuals can become self-reinforcing and lead to changes of background knowledge and practices and thereby to structural change (Adler 2008, 203; Arthur 1995). It is very difficult to determine what circumstances and what time process might reach a tipping point, for example, what circumstances if any will undo the European social order. But the countervailing forces are clearly competing, mutually exclusive communities of practice exercising control over the meaning and mobilization of Europe's ghosts.

Learning and power come together through the negotiation of meaning within and between communities of practice. Said otherwise, practice's power rests on practitioners' propensity to shape and change identities. Pairing identity and community is an important component of power's effectiveness. Even in cases of material power imbalance, social power like performative power can come to bear through participation in the community of practice and thus offset material–power imbalances. Power also manifests itself as practitioners' politically competent performance to align competing coalitions on behalf of their practice.

As Nietzsche said, "the evolution of a thing, a custom, and organ is thus by no means the *progressus* toward a goal, even less a logical *progressus* by the shortest route and with the smallest expenditure of force – but a succession of more or less profound, more or less independent processes of subduing, plus the resistances they encounter, the attempts at transformation for the purpose of defense and reaction, and the results of successful counter reactions" (qtd. in Dennett 1995, 465–66). Learning, including contestation, negotiability, and identification processes within communities of practice, and social and material power always go together and contingently establish which and whose performances become socially and politically authoritative.

Structural Social Mechanisms and Processes

Social orders cognitively evolve according to three distinctive structural social mechanisms (Sewell 2005) and related processes.[16] First, they evolve when endogenous learning processes involving negotiation, contestation, and identification within communities of practice result in transformed background knowledge and new fields of practices along with their constitutive effects.[17] "Descent," in such case, takes place with modification from a common community-of-practice ancestor. Selection through negotiability entails contestation, whereas selection through identification entails commitment, affinity, and allegiance (Wenger 1998a). There are many reasons, all of them context related, that practitioners negotiate and contest their practices. These might include disappointment, disenchantment, or the loss of confidence, differences of interpretation, especially regarding what works and allows practitioners to keep solving problems, and practitioners' unequal competence and performative power. Practitioners may also contest their practices because of changes in deontic power, differences regarding their creativity and innovation[18] capacities, and individual and corporate interests, such as state interests. By promoting individual and corporate

[16] I follow Gross's definition of social mechanism with a twist. The definition says that a "social mechanism is a more or less general sequence or set of social events or processes analyzed at a lower order of complexity or aggregation by which – in certain circumstances – some cause X tends to bring about some effect Y in the realm of human social relations. This sequence or set may not be analytically reducible to the actions of individuals who enact it, may underwrite formal or substantive causal processes, and may be observed, unobserved, or in principle unobservable" (2009, 364). The twist is that the generation of social phenomena refers to both causal and constitutive processes. Both constitution and causation are part of the same epistemology. Because, as I argued in Chapter 2, I rely on processual and relational ontological premises, we can understand cause and constitution as the way processes become, and as based on patterns of interaction (Brachthäuser 2011; Nexon 2010).

[17] My view of endogenous mechanisms of cognitive evolution differs from the view of endogenous change in the literature of institutional change, where it is associated with game-theory equilibria (Greif and Laitin 2004), path dependence (Thelen 2004), feedback, and punctuated equilibria (Streeck and Thelen 2005; Thelen 1999, 2004. See also Lewis and Steinmo 2012). It differs from Lamarck-based adaptation (Sterling-Folker 2006), which is at odds with my constructivist understanding of collective and individual learning. For a different, but still constructivist, view of endogenous change, see Widmaier et al. 2007.

[18] "By virtue of originality, the novel event cannot be explained or understood in terms of prior interpretations of the past. The past, which by definition can only exist in the present, changes to 'conform' to novel events" (Aboulafia 2016).

practitioners' interests and careers, state communities of practice enable innovative and powerful practitioners to get their interpretation of practices selected, thus leaving a mark on practices' interpretation and performance, and on stability or transformation. I will unpack some of these reasons in Chapters 8 and 9.

Endogenous processes are most relevant when newly evolved social orders involve novel anchoring practices and existing, albeit altered, practices. Altered practices, and the communities of practice that serve as their vehicle, amount to new types of social arrangement and organization. Cognitive evolution in this case occurs when people suddenly become aware of something new and of the political, social, and economic implications of knowing and acting, regardless of whether the knowledge is objectively "true" or whether the acting is "efficient" or not. It takes place when a community-of-practice's practitioners become aware of their awareness and adjust their conscious insights accordingly – when consciousness becomes learning and when self-awareness turns a nonissue into a political issue. In short, cognitive evolution manifests itself in "hierarchical restructuring of our conceptions; and the derivative system of thought, institutions, etc., through which we achieve coherent integration" (Markley and Harman 1982, 132).

Public awareness of a new virtual reality in cyberspace expanded when users could intuitively participate through user-friendly graphic interfaces and applications, most notably the World Wide Web (Abbate 1999). The open architecture of cyberspace, which empowers users, endows cyberspace with a "plastic" quality where users themselves can introduce innovations in combining applications (Clark 2010). Facebook, Twitter, and later mobile applications, for example, represented novel ways to combine databases with applications to produce "dynamic content generation" by users themselves (Clark 2010). The background knowledge new Web users relied on was the open and distributed communications early Internet pioneers built into ARPANET. As a result, users reacted with growing discomfort in light of these open dispositions and expectations when actors, such as states, Internet service providers, or others, tried to police or monitor content. This self-awareness of cyberspace's reality has turned purely technical nonissues like managing root and domain names into contested political issues, for example, when the US government threatened legal action against computer scientist Jon Postel to surrender his root authority privileges (Goldsmith and Wu 2006). There is an important note here about the historical and geographic context in the spread of background knowledge. The fastest growing Internet populations are in the Global South, and "unlike the early adopters of the Internet in the West, citizens in the developing world are plugging in and connecting after the Snowden disclosures, and with the model of the NSA in the public domain" (Deibert 2015, 12). This may mean that new users in the developing world may be as committed to the background knowledge of the early Internet and not aware of threats to it.

New fields of practices and background knowledge usually start with the discovery of new problems about natural, social, and political phenomena, for example, climate change or social and economic dislocations, which require new solutions. Practitioners then engage in practical innovations, including institutional innovations. In the environmental case, it was the 1992 "Agenda 21," and in the corporate social order, the rapidly expanding field of CSR, that responded to these problems. Once epistemic change is bound up with practices, communities of practice develop around these practices and the background knowledge bound with them. Practices and background knowledge then endure and become publicly recognized and reified as institutions and organizations, which helps keep practices and knowledge in a metastable state of flow.

Behind the bilateral and multilateral diplomacy that states engage in, for example, on climate change or sustainable development, are communities of practice whose practitioners, in and by practice, constantly negotiate and struggle over meanings and what counts as competent and normatively proper performances (Brunnee and Toope 2010). As this occurs over time, the environmental social order might continue to change in part because of exogenous factors like natural developments – though the Hurricane Katrina and Harvey disasters in the United States did not do the trick – or because of competing communities of practice, the development of new scientific knowledge (Adler and Haas 1992; Haas 1992b), the failure of existing practices, and "path dependence." But one of the main reasons is the endogenous processes within communities of practice associated with learning, negotiation, contestation, and identity change. The current very thin climate change social order has not yet cognitively evolved into a full-fledged environmental-protection social order – not only because of US President Trump's denial of climate change – according to which an extensively new configuration of practices and background knowledge have begun organizing social life and creating increased interconnectedness in environmental affairs.

Endogenous interactions can keep communities of practice in a metastable state, in spite of the fact, or actually because, social environments and communities of practice affect each other. As Schatzki (2002, 245) argued, the default and predominant state of practices in human life is incremental change. In the corporate social order, the emergence of CSR practices illustrates endogenous change. The struggles about corporations' social and environmental responsibilities gave rise to new ways of understanding and practicing inside the corporate community of practice, which helped keep the corporate order metastable during a period of social contestation and turmoil in the 1960s and 1970s.

The emergence of endogenous changes, such as new practice interpretations, practice contestation, and challenges and struggles about meanings of competence and of communities of practice's identities may get fluctuations within communities of practice closer to intersubjective cognitive thresholds where, through positive feedback, even some small changes can bring about social-order change. Because endogenous changes are characterized by nonlinearity, at thresholds, complex phenomena can lead either to the maintenance of metastability or to social-order change. Predicting whether and when a tipping point will occur and whether it will lead to social-order change is a difficult enterprise, and there may be times when the new order "has not fully developed, and therefore has not yet modified its environmental niche. In this situation the old order has not disappeared, but neither has the new one been established" (Aboulafia 2016, n.p.). Because of emergent changes, which I discuss in more detail in Chapters 8 and 9, the betwixt-and-between state is a feature of processual and relational reality (ibid.).

For example, endogenous learning and contestation in communities of practice were key drivers in how the cyberspace social order evolved into multiple, competing orders. As wider public awareness about the Internet was reaching a threshold in the formative 1990s, distinctly localized communities began learning and contesting this emerging consensus by pointing to the growing challenges for law enforcement, intelligence, and national security through critical infrastructure vulnerabilities. These government initiatives to contest the growing cyber order were both technical – for example, the NSA-proposed Clipper Chip that would serve as a back door to decrypt voice communications – and legal, for instance, FBI-led efforts to promote the CALEA to President Clinton's Executive Order 13010 on Critical Infrastructure Protection (Kaplan 2016). At the same time, privacy advocates were vocal in opposing these efforts by promoting commercial encryption and Europeans raised alarms about a global espionage network code-named ECHELON, leading to EU directives on data protection and more developed privacy and human rights laws.

Because of the difficulty practitioners face understanding long chains of complex cause–effect processes and interactions, practices tend to rely on cause–effect intersubjective background knowledge as learned in communities of practice. These cause–effect collective understandings change, as I mentioned, through new theoretical knowledge, as understood in the epistemic community literature (Adler 1991; Adler and Haas 1992; Haas 1992a), but primarily in and by practice (Adler 2014).

Over time, learning and competition within communities of practice affect dispositions and expectations and therefore what practitioners do the next time around. Empirically, we can see that the Snowden disclosures about mass surveillance had a "chilling effect" on Wikipedia traffic to privacy-sensitive topics (Penney 2016). This may suggest that awareness of surveillance can affect users' dispositions and expectations about online privacy. Because communities of practice have a temporal dimension – they fluctuate even when the social order is metastable – they sustain what Luhmann called the "temporalization of complexity" (1978; see also Knorr Cetina 2005, 217). In other words, communities of practice become part of a temporal stream that dynamically "exists" behind apparently stable structures, such as organizations, states, nonstate organizations, etc. By looking at the temporalization of complexity, we might better explain what communities of practice do and why and empirically trace their paths over time and analyze their effects.

The second mechanism by way of which social orders evolve is when communities of practice establish themselves preferentially vis-à-vis competing communities of practice, and their selected practices and background knowledge are passed on to future practitioners. More specifically, evolution of social order takes place when prevailing practices lose their authoritative attraction and pull, practitioners lose their status and functions (Searle 1995), and communities of practice lose their legitimacy, naturalness, normative appeal, and access to material, institutional, and symbolic resources, while the practices and background knowledge of competing communities are selectively retained preferentially.

For example, a major struggle between two communities of practice in cyberspace is currently raging. It pits one community of practice whose individual practitioners and corporate practitioners take cyberspace to be global and for the benefit of all humankind against another community of practice whose individual practitioners and corporate practitioners take cyberspace as extensions of states and as serving their (mostly) security interests. While one community of practice has not yet eliminated the other, the state- and security-oriented community definitely has the upper hand (Deibert 2013).

A similar debate has been raging between communities of practice in business education. At least in theory, a business school should aim "to train men [*sic*] for the practice of management (or some special branch of management) as a profession, and to develop new knowledge that may be relevant to improving the operation of business" (Simon 1967, 1). Much of the debate and contestation about the role of business education thus revolves around questions about performance, relevance, how it connects to particular values and ideas (background knowledge), and what it is or should be about. One axis of contestation is between those who do "academic" research and those who think that business education has lost touch with the "real" world and the real problems affecting businesses and managers (Khurana and Spender 2012, 621, 633). A second axis of contestation focuses on practices' adequacy in view of wider background knowledge. "There are … important questions about the models and values of management that emanate from the business school … Business school research that has most impacted practice has been around financial management … and the diffusion of this 'knowledge' into practice via the medium of the MBA has been a major factor in the market for mergers and acquisitions, leveraged buy-outs, the dot-com bubble, [and] the activities of management consulting firms" (Starkey, Hatchuel, and Tempest 2004, 1523). A third axis of contestation involves the "Americanization of business education," which highlights some resistance to the geographical spread of practices as an increasing number of non-American business schools have adopted the "American" business school model (Juusola et al. 2015, 347). Whether the embrace of the US model of business school is desirable or "conducive to better techniques," some question whether it can provide the intellectual framework to support the economic development of regional or national economies (Starkey et al. 2004, 1523).

Nowhere is the contestation between communities of practice about regional order more evident than in the current case of the EU. Take, for example, the meeting of twenty-seven heads of state and heads of the European institutions in Rome, on the sixtieth anniversary of the Treaty of Rome, to sign a new document called "The Rome Declaration."[19] The declaration, signed, of course, in the Hall of Rome, is essentially a commitment to the European order and a claim about the proper interpretation of Europe's history and the need to maintain both the *trajectory* of anchoring practices and the *meaning* of the background knowledge that informs them. Europe's political elite sought to mobilize the aspirational discourse of the European security community to renew faith in Europe's supranational institutions. In this sense, it sought to connect actively Europe's anchoring practices – economic integration, security

[19] Rome Declaration, www.consilium.europa.eu/en/press/press-releases/2017/03/25-rome-declaration/?utm_source=dsms-auto&utm_medium=email&utm_campaign=The+Rome+Declaration.

community and coordination, the transnational polity, and borderless territoriality – with the ideational and material embodiments of the European social order. The context for the event was pressure from countervailing, illiberal communities of practice and shocks ranging from Brexit to the migrant crisis, to Central and Eastern European ethnic nationalism, to the electoral threat from Euroskeptic political parties. Communities of practice are thus the agents of both stability and change.

Selection between communities of practice[20] (their practices and background knowledge) involves power – material but primarily deontic and performative power. It also may involve practitioners' socially recognized competence and their ability to control competing authority claims through politics, the participation of key decision-makers as practitioners, and practitioners' political ability to align competing coalitions on behalf of their practice. Other potentially important factors may be practices' novelty or familiarity; their being publicly accessible; their timing; their attraction as focal points, for example, because of their scientific nature; commonalities with other practices; spillover to other communities of practice; and practices' normative attraction and influence.

Environmental factors, for example, external shocks like international crises, war, and the sudden increase in resource prices, seldom determine selective retention of specific practices and background knowledge but may play an important role in communities of practice's emergence, legitimation, naturalness, access to resources, and social power. For example, anti-terror legislation and widened intelligence and law-enforcement mandates often follow in the wake of terror attacks while simultaneously weakening the arguments of civil liberty and privacy advocates (Deibert 2015). Law enforcement has been more vocal in articulating how full disk encryption has thwarted criminal investigations (Vance et al. 2015). This was evident in a recent case between the FBI and Apple when the FBI alleged that iPhone encryption had threatened their investigation of the San Bernardino, California, attackers. Those communities of practice who are better at affecting their environments so that selection forces promote their practices and background knowledge are more likely to have the upper hand. The selection of their practices and background knowledge will be a detriment to other communities' practices and background knowledge.

[20] Because selection operates at the level of practice/background knowledge, my argument is consistent with arguments that selection operates at the cultural-group level. For cultural-group selection, see Boyd and Richerson 1985; Hayek 1979, 1989; Hodgson 1993.

Communities of practice whose practices and background knowledge manage to disable the selective forces arranged against them will tend to force processual changes close to intersubjective cognitive thresholds, when even small changes might bring about social-order evolution. Environmental fluctuations can also give rise to the development of competing communities of practice that create alternative "evolutionary niches," and may end up bringing about the evolution of social order that corresponds to the challenging practices and background knowledge of a community of practice. However, communities of practice that challenge the existing social order can often overcome their competing alternatives because the practitioners who sustain the social order are politically and institutionally replaced and may even disappear as practitioners from political, social, and economic scenes.

Social orders' resilience may prevent social-order evolution from taking place. Resilience can depend on the intensity of competition between communities of practice. The greater the contestation between communities of practice, the more cohesive communities of practice, and the more interconnected their practitioners may become. This might increase communities of practice's resilience. Competition in cyberspace between both national and global communities encourages further innovation of techniques to ensure information security through evasion strategies (Acquisti et al. 2007) and techniques that find and exploit vulnerabilities for national security ends (Greenwald 2014), in the end increasing both communities' resilience. Larger communities of practice – those that succeed in spreading across space and time – can generate more adaptive practices' creative variations, which might also increase resilience (ibid., 213).

Moreover, the challenge posed to European integration practices and background knowledge by a constellation of domestic, all-European, and other international nationalist populist and disassociation-oriented communities of practice and practitioners (e.g., President Trump's blatant anti-European deeds and words) has apparently enlivened, motivated, and empowered European liberal internationalist elites and ordinary people to rally around the European integration flag. The striking victories by Emmanuel Macron in France, the eventual success of Angela Merkel in putting together a governing coalition after the September 2017 German elections, and the understanding between these two leaders about the need to strengthen European integration practices exemplify the resilience of postwar European social order's practices, which was triggered by their being seriously challenged. So is the major setback experienced by the conservative party (which supported Brexit) in the June 2017 British elections, and an emotional response, at least in some Western European countries, that points in the direction of European solidarity.

It follows that social order resilience may ultimately depend on the challenge by competing communities of practice that can dialectically trigger a stronger defense of the current order's practices. But a challenge to the current order, thus to prevailing communities of practice, can also lead to the opposite result, bringing about its demise. Whether social order's resilience or demise take place is indeterminate. The propensity for one or the other outcome will depend on context and on how particular situations processually unfold (Popper 1990). As I will show in Chapters 8 and 9, however, the outcome will also largely depend on the differential purchase of epistemic practical authority. The latter, in turn, will depend on resourcefulness and innovation in creative variation processes, as well as on learning, contestation, and negotiation processes within, and deontic and performative power of, communities of practice in selective-retention processes, particularly when approaching intersubjective thresholds.

The third mechanism is the invention of new social actors. International social orders may evolve because of the invention of new social actors and/or the effects that the replacement of one type of political entity and organization by another may have on background knowledge and practices; on learning, contestation, and negotiation processes within communities of practice; and on the selection processes between such different communities. There must be some relationship between political entities, such as states, empires, or religious communities – in contemporary Europe's case the political entity is a *transnational polity* – and communities of practice. On one hand, communities of practice confer to political entities – corporate practitioners – the dispositions to *act* on behalf of the community of practice's knowledge, identity, discourse, and normative makeup in distinctive ways. On the other hand, by means of practice, political entities legitimize, empower, and institutionalize the community of practice's knowledge and discourse. The transformation of polities, of course, results not merely because of a change of ideas and institutions but also, as in the EU's case, because of the development of novel practices, such as border practices, and the concomitant struggles by communities of practice to negotiate meaning and identification and affect environments for the benefit of their practices. Because I am suggesting a processual explanation where the change of practices and their background knowledge enables a social order to be metastable or to evolve, my argument is not circular. The invention of the corporation in the nineteenth century led to the development of myriad corporate practices and communities of practice that constitute the current corporate order. These practices, in turn, led to the development of new organizations, such as the multinational corporation, which had a significant impact on the corporate order. Because new polities and organizations often mean new bases of epistemic practical authority, they may substantially replace practices (Schatzki 2002, 245) and constitute new or recombined communities of practice, all of which eventually can lead to the evolution of social orders.

In the minds of most people, the European social order has become virtually coterminous with the institutions of the European Union. These institutions are reified instantiations of anchoring practices of security communities, transnational polities, and novel forms of territoriality. The order evolved when communities of practice mobilized these anchoring practices. Anchoring practices existed in nascent forms as liberal internationalist ideas and ideals. But novel communities of practice organized EU practices – brand new technocratic competences were reified as supranational institutions' treaty-making processes and key sovereign state practices were subordinated. These practices included border controls, assigning migration and residence rights, monetary policy, judicial oversight, and market economics. European communities of practice cut across European institutions, thus protecting the treaties and expanding and deepening the European order.

Cognitive Evolution and Complexity Theory

Cognitive evolution theory, as enriched by complexity theory, supports the notion that social orders' change and stability depend on emergent fields of practices and background knowledge. While practitioners' capacity to break with entrenched practices through nonlinear positive-feedback processes may be one of the sources of social order's evolutionary change, their complementary capacity to stabilize social order through collectively agreed-on knowledge and practices may be the source of social order's metastability. International social orders thus can be considered complex emerging entities whose constituting practices are continually being contested and negotiated – in other words, characterized by "fluctuations."[21] The key idea here is that fluctuations are continuous and therefore that orders are in a state of nonequilibrium.

[21] We should contrast this concept of fluctuation with the received notion that change is ubiquitous because of the never-ending stream of events. A complexity perspective takes communities of practice as emerging entities that change in nonlinear ways, even if their structure persists in time. Their effects, therefore, are different from the combined effects of their individual practitioners' practices.

We can understand cognitive evolution as a simultaneous process of change and stability, where continuous fluctuations below a certain intersubjective threshold help keep social orders in a stable state of flow. Paradoxically, it is fluctuations, such as practice negotiation and learning, that help keep social order in a metastable state. Over a threshold, however, fluctuations can result in emergent new types of social orders.

Like swirls in a stream (Shotter 1983, 81) (or like New York City) that, given enough time, will replace all its constituent parts while still maintaining its basic identity, social orders are usually in a metastable state despite constant change. We should consider social orders as self-organizing. In and through practice, actors reproduce the knowledge that constitutes their identities, thus maintaining a social order in a stable flow. Once a particular social order stabilizes, although not always entirely – so long as change remains in a stable flow below an intersubjective threshold – it defines, constructs, and reconstructs identities.

Social orders remain metastable when communities of practice expand to other geographical and institutional environments. The integration of individual and corporate practitioners to communities of practice widens the physical and functional fields of practices that hold society together and, consequently, augments the number of practitioners holding similar dispositions and expectations that sustain a given practice or sets of practices. In return, communities of practice borrow from the environment material and institutional resources to sustain them, thus helping to keep social order metastable.[22]

The process of enlargement encapsulates quite neatly the simultaneity of change and stability in the European social order and the social mechanisms at play in the retention of social practices and the background knowledge bound within them. More succinctly, enlargement illustrates that the European social order has achieved metastability through the European Union's expansion. After the Cold War, communities of practice were able to affect (for a time) both the material and sociocultural environments in Central and Eastern European states in desired ways. It is telling that the Schengen *acquis*, which set out the laws and functional prerequisites of free movement – one of the constitutive elements of European order – were formulated *during* the accession process (Phuong 2005) and became European law only through the Amsterdam Treaty of 2005, *after* formal accession. European practices spread to Central and Eastern European states in part because of the utter absence of immigration legislation, institutions, and norms in the

[22] Dissipative structures "represent the *spontaneous emergence of order out of disorder*" (Smith and Jenks 2005, 145).

postsocialist enlargement states. European metastability was ensured as a process of change wherein communities of practice served as the vehicle of change/stability. The process of these states "returning to Europe," of course, meant fundamental changes in the European order, thus illustrating the dynamic nonequilibrium, yet below a threshold, of the European social order.

Similarly, the "open source movement" in cyberspace has enabled the global user community to become metastable in spite of changes. Open-source movements can potentially expand to a global community of programmers and users engaged in a collaborative effort to develop software. Importantly, the software changes through its everyday use in a community of peers where developer-proposed changes to the source code undergo a peer-review process. More recently, Bitcoin as a "peer-to-peer version of electronic cash" is a successful open-source initiative where transaction verification takes place by the community of users, rather than an intermediary (Nakamoto 2008).

Fluctuations in the form of new knowledge and learning processes help channel change into new practices and forms of organization that help keep a social order metastable. I am not alluding to homeostatic self-maintenance but rather to resilience processes. Resilience is the measure of a social order's ability to absorb change and remain metastable (Adler 2005; Holling 1976; Schoon 2006).[23] More specifically, resilience means the capacity of communities and their practitioners not only to creatively learn (Joas 1996) and change their practices when circumstances require (changes below a threshold) but also to reconstitute their environments to match their practices, so that challenges to practices, and the knowledge that sustains them, are prevented from reaching a threshold and thus from evolving. Practitioners react to current challenges and to what they imagine or expect to occur in the future. By taking measures to fulfill their expectations or defeat them, they construct present and future reality. They also can exercise some influence on social orders' resilience. What Tomasello, Kruger, and Ratner (1993; see also Axelrod 1984; Pouliot and Thérien 2015) called the "ratchet effect," the propensity of institutions to be cumulative and build on earlier norms and practices over time, may also contribute to a measure of resilience.

Open-source software communities are very resilient because of decentralized authority in a peer network. These communities face challenges like proprietary ones but are more resilient against the challenges presented by software vulnerabilities since an entire community will be

[23] For a literature review on resilience, see Martin-Breen and Anderies 2011.

looking for and patching bugs compared with an in-house software intermediary (which can be more readily leveraged by governments). In 2003, there was a Linux back-door attempt to make an unauthorized alteration to the source code granting root privileges. To take another example, since people mine crypto-currencies to verify transactions and leave behind a public record (rather than central banks issuing them), they are less susceptible to manipulation, regulation, and control. Its resilience worries law-enforcement communities that attempt to investigate money laundering or cybercrimes.

But resilience is no guarantee that changes in practices will remain under a cognitive threshold or that a social order will remain metastable indefinitely. Communities of practice are continually caught between background knowledge (as practitioners' dispositions and expectations) and practitioners' faculty to reflexively innovate and change their minds, reinterpret their knowledge, negotiate with other practitioners over the meaning and nature of the practices that link them together, and change meanings of what amounts to competent performances. The more practitioners digress from mutually agreed-on patterns of action, the more fluctuations there are that may approach a threshold, where a social order might tip and evolve.

Thresholds (Gladwell 2002; Granovetter 1978) involved in the tipping of social orders are socially cognitive and intersubjective.[24] Nonlinearity may help us better understand intersubjectivity, a concept that is not easily grasped (Adler 1997). Intersubjectivity means that we cannot reduce collective background knowledge, as embedded in practices, to either material reality – or in Popper's terms, World 1 (individuals' brains, bodies, and physical materials used in practice) – or exclusively to individuals' inner subjective worlds – in Popper's language, World 2. Rather, like Popper's World 3–type phenomenon, intersubjective background knowledge is embedded in practices and is more than the aggregation of the individuals who hold certain knowledge and who practice certain practices. Physical reality, subjectivity, and intersubjectivity are in a constant emergent relationship with one another (see Chapter 2).

[24] Social complexity is a perceptual and intersubjective phenomenon. Situational complexity is the understanding of many interdependent facts by the actors themselves. By contrast, analytical complexity refers to the collective perception of a set of interrelated elements, as perceived by the observer of action (Wilson 1975; Wilson 1978, 69–90). In increasingly complex systems, people may not be able to perceive all the interconnections between agents. This is one reason that these systems often surprise us: the fact that we do not see the connections does not mean that they are not there. If we add the synergetic effects of the interactions characterized by increased differentiation, interdependence, and plurality of interactions, we realize why it is implausible to understand social life other than as evolving in nonlinear ways.

Near thresholds – think of the fall of the Berlin Wall – a single fluctuation (or a combination of them) can become so powerful by positive feedback that it tips and shatters the preexisting order, leading to its evolution – the substitution of the old order by a new one. Tony Barber, reviewing historian Mary Alise Sarotte's book on the fall of the Berlin Wall (2014; see also Lohmann 1994) recounts Sarotte's conclusion that

> beyond any doubt . . . the Wall did not fall by the design of western, Soviet or East German political leaders, or because East Germany's fast-growing opposition movement had some master plan to bring it down. Rather, the Wall fell because of "a remarkable constellation of actors and contingent events" on the evening of November 9 "that came together in a precise but entirely unplanned sequence." In particular, had it not been for the bumbling Günter Schabowski, a Politburo member who mistakenly told a news conference that East Germany had decided to permit immediate free travel abroad, it is inconceivable that thousands of expectant GDR citizens would have massed at the Wall that night, obliging border guards at the Bornholm Street crossing to open the frontier. (Barber 2014, n.p.)

These events were preceded by peaceful demonstrations in Leipzig on October 9, 1989, one month before the Berlin Wall fell. Sarotte concluded that "a bloodbath was avoided largely thanks to a mid-ranking communist party functionary in Leipzig named Helmut Hackenberg, who happened to be in charge that night and was brave enough not to follow the usual practice of putting down the demonstration with violence" (Barber 2014, n.p.).

No doubt the propensity for the events to occur in Leipzig and later in Berlin was preceded and enabled by a critical mass of reactions against the Soviet and East European regimes, which can be traced back to the 1975 Helsinki Final Act (Adler 2008; Thomas 2001). The act helped create expectations of, and desires for, freedom, democracy, and economic prosperity (see Chapter 9) and heightened the Soviet and Eastern European regimes' delegitimation. Thus, even if a social order can tip and evolve very fast after approaching an intersubjective threshold, it still requires a critical mass of delegitimizing and weakening of deontic power events to precede the tipping event. The critical mass of delegitimizing reactions against the Soviet and East German regimes actually constituted the intersubjective threshold in the late 1980s. Cognitive evolution occurs as a result of changes in function status (Searle 2010; see Chapter 2), and a loss of legitimacy and performative power by communities of practice, endogenously or against others.

Exogenous crises may also play a role in helping push a social order over the threshold. The current and ongoing Middle Eastern crisis, particularly due to the Syrian civil war, by causing millions of Middle

Eastern individuals to seek refuge in Europe, consists of an exogenous crisis for the EU's social order and may end up playing a role in its demise. The court is still out on whether these events will bring the European social order close or toward the threshold. As of the summer of 2018, the EU is under increasing exogenous pressure as a result of President Trump's anti-EU policies, and it is also experiencing an internal legitimacy crisis because several Eastern European governments, most strikingly Hungary and Poland, are quickly abandoning EU practices and rules. At the same time, Germany and France have so far been successful in weathering the crises. Because legitimacy and illegitimacy are socially constructed (Reus-Smit 2013a, 2013b), however, an evolutionary constructivist approach may help us to get a grasp, albeit not accurately to predict, whether and when crises may accumulate to a critical mass leading a prevailing social order to reach a threshold, tip, and evolve.

To recap, even small changes that might start with very low self-evidence and authoritative meaning may, because of positive feedback and emergent attributes, reach a "bifurcation point" (Prigogine 1980) (really a stage or process), when social order remains in a metastable state of nonequilibrium or, alternatively, crosses an intersubjective and political threshold, tips, and evolves. The Berlin Wall events are a vivid example of how a sociocognitive and intersubjective threshold, the Communist social order in East Germany, and later in the entire Soviet empire, tipped, collapsed, and was replaced by a new social order.[25] Other empires, such as the Habsburg, Ottoman, and Romanov empires, also "suffered comparable swift collapses" (Ferguson 2010).

The notion that nonlinear interactions might lead to the generation of emergent social systems "with the potential to evolve in time" (Coveney and Highfield, qtd. in Thrift 1999, 33) is particularly relevant for understanding social order's change and metastability. Practitioners' nonlinear interactions often produce an emergent variety of practices, as well as the selection-retention processes that can stimulate the evolution of social orders from new practices. Because of emergent conditions, the evolutionary path that a social order can take is "often surprising because it is difficult to anticipate the full consequences of even simple forms of interactions" (Kavalski 2007, 439). Even if we were able to know all the interconnections between practitioners, we can still fail to predict whether social orders close to intersubjective thresholds will evolve or

[25] As Urry argued, "if a system passes a particular threshold with minor changes in the controlling variables, switches occur such that ... a large number of apathetic people suddenly tip into a forceful movement for change" (2005, 5).

remain in a state of stable flow. The reasons for a practice's emergence are likely to differ from the reasons for its subsequent use and usefulness. The social world is emergent not only because of the unintended consequences of interactions but also because humans can reflexively and often surprisingly affect their own and others' actions with knowledge. We can therefore describe the social world as a set of complex social orders, among other reasons because human knowledge can produce instabilities that lead to emergent properties and to propensities for self-organization.

Complexity theory's notion that far-reaching transformations in structure and order can arise from just a few practitioners interacting locally and shaping their environment for their purposes can sensitize us to what Lane and Maxfield called "generative relationships" (1997, 92). They allude to instances or episodes of formative interactions from which, through social communication, new ways of defining social reality emerge, for example, the joint US-Soviet seminars on nuclear arms control of the 1960s, the Helsinki Final Act negotiations in the early 1970s, and the negotiations that preceded Stockholm's first global environmental conference in 1972. These "generative relationships" to a certain extent forged and shaped the evolution of practices of nuclear arms control, cooperative security, and sustainable development.

Cognitive evolution theory, which is sensitive to complexity theory concepts, can help us better understand the emergence of collective new phenomena, relationships, patterns, arrangements, interconnectedness, and organization, which would not exist without cognitive-evolutionary processes. Our history books usually record the leaders who won the big battles, built empires, or founded states. However, the Alexanders, Napoleons, George Washingtons, Lenins, and Maos create eddies in the stream (Boulding 1978, 266) but do not transform the nature of social orders, *as long as practices remain the same.* The real catalysts of transformations that affect the relations between practitioners constituting social orders, and those constituted by them, are knowledge and practices' innovators. They create a greater variety of practice forms, which are subject to selective retention. Practices' innovators, as agents of change, do not make eddies in the stream but, echoing Heraclitus (see Chapter 2), *are* the stream: they provide it with direction. It is common to think that charismatic political leaders – Adolf Hitler comes to mind (Donald Trump?) – sometimes can trigger a change in social order. Even in cases when leaders come to power with radically changed and/or radical agendas, practices constitute their agency, rather than the opposite.

Cognitive evolution theory therefore helps transcend the duality of structure and agency and the linear understanding of cause and effect.[26] For example, practices that exhibit emergent and nonlinear properties are both individual and structural. Practices and communities of practice have structural properties. But they are also agential because both practitioners and communities of practice perform them. Structure is not determinative and leaves room for practitioners to fine-tune their performances, and their interpretations and interactions with other practitioners, to constitute emergent structures in unexpected ways. At the same time, practices are iterative, which epistemologically means that causes simultaneously become effects (Hoffmann and Riley 2002).

A cognitive evolution theory of international social orders, characterized by emerging structures and positive feedbacks, befits a becoming ontology and is therefore truly dynamic. It also does not resemble sociologies that take change only as a rupture between stable structural patterns (Elster 1983; Giddens 1984), an issue that I take on in the next chapter.

[26] Agent–structure processes "are better understood through the concept of 'iteration' rather than 'recurrence.' Iteration means that the tiniest of 'local' changes can generate, over many repeated actions, unexpected, unpredictable and chaotic outcomes, sometimes the opposite of what agents thought they were intending. Events are not 'forgotten' within the analysis of such systems. Complex changes stem from how agents iteratively respond to local configurations. Agents may conduct what appear to be the same actions involving a constant imitation of, or response to, the local actions of others. But because of what can be tiny adaptations of other agents, iterations result in transformations in even large-scale structures" (Urry 2005, 243).

7 Agential Social Mechanisms

Four agential[1] processual social mechanisms[2] account for cognitive evolution. First, there are practice-driven changes and stability of dispositions,[3] expectations,[4] and therefore of practical reason.[5] Second, there are learning, negotiation, contestation, and identification-shaping processes that, taking place within communities of practice,[6] dynamically

[1] "In very general terms, an agent is a being with the capacity to act, and 'agency' denotes the exercise or manifestation of this capacity" (Schlosser 2015, n.p.).

[2] Alternative micro-mechanisms refer, for instance, to rational choice (Elster 1983), socialization (Checkel 2005), persuasion (Risse 2000), imitation (Börzel and Risse 2009), normative structures (Parsons 1977), knowledgeability of actors (Giddens 1986), habits (Dewey 1922), and individual learning (Levy 1994).

[3] Propensities of practitioners to act in certain ways because of beliefs based on experience and habits (see also Bourdieu 1977, 34).

[4] Expectations are images of the future bounded by what is physically, humanly, and socially possible. When they exercise forethought, people motivate themselves and guide their action anticipatorily. "By representing foreseeable outcomes symbolically, people can convert future consequences into future motivators … Cognized futures thus become temporarily antecedent to actions" (Bandura 1986, 19). The meaning of action is constituted within a knowledge background that anticipates the future. According to Luhmann, social structures are expectation structures and action is always oriented by expectations. In his view, expectations play a double function. They help select meanings out of a totality of possibilities, thus reproducing "the complexity built into meaning without destroying it," and they bridge "discontinuities … so that expectations can still be needed when the situation changes" (1995, 97, 292–93).

[5] The notion that action is based on reasons is philosophically contested. Recent experiments with CT scans have shown that unconscious brain processes are seen before any conscious decisions to act (Hodgson and Knudsen 2010: 143; see Kahneman 2011). The notion that intuition and emotion may play a significant role in *decisions* does not invalidate the fact that people *act* for reasons, even if intuition and emotion affect them. As Hodgson and Knudsen argued, "humans do act for reasons. But reasons and beliefs themselves are caused and must be explained … Thus we need to look at cognition not as preceding action but as a phase of action by which action is directed and redirected in its situational contexts … Human cognitive capacities are, thus, irreducible to individuals alone; they depend on social structures and material cues" (2010, 134, 198).

[6] Wenger suggests the following agential indicators of the workings of communities of practice: (1) sustained mutual relationships – harmonious and conflictual; (2) shared ways of engaging in doing things together; (3) the rapid flow of information and propagation of information; (4) absence of introductory preambles, as if conversations

constitute communities of practice' practices and boundaries. Third, I refer to agents' reflexivity and judgment, which are necessary to change practices and the background knowledge bound with them. Finally, there is practitioners' capacity to affect material, cultural, and social environments in desired ways. These social mechanisms are intrinsically related.

The *first* mechanism refers to dispositions and expectations' resilience and propensities for change. Because identities are conferred on practitioners by the workings of communities of practice, practitioners' participation in evolving forms of mutual engagement, their struggle "to define what the enterprise is about, reconciling conflicting interpretations of [it], … inventing new terms and redefining and abandoning old ones, creating and breaking routines" changes perceptual and linguistic interpretations (Wenger 1998a, 96). It produces a particular set of experiences with a narrative and a sense of familiarity and generates motivational dispositions and expectations that structure experience (Searle 1995, 33–36).

Thus, for example, the development of the ARPANET or the early Internet illustrates how background knowledge, as part of both communities of practice and practitioners' dispositions and expectations, increasingly stabilized over time. Graduate students, sent by their advisors to represent their respective research institutions to develop standards and protocols and evaluate the network, largely ran the Network Working Group (NWG). A number of these PhD students, such as Vinton Cerf and Jon Postel, not only designed important host software but also became important figures defending the open-design principles of the Net in the 1990s. While network traffic was increasing, ARPANET's demonstration at the First International Conference on Computer Communications in 1972 "was a watershed event that made people suddenly realize that packet switching was a real technology" (Abbate 1999, 179). Following ARPANET's public success, "detailed accounts of the ARPANET in the professional computer journals disseminated its techniques and legitimized packet switching as a reliable and economic alternative for data communications" (Abbate 1999, 81). A community

and interactions were merely the continuation of an ongoing process; (5) very quick setup of a problem to be discussed; (6) substantial overlap in participants' descriptions of who belongs; (7) knowing what others know, what they can do, and how they can contribute to an enterprise; (8) mutually defined identities; (9) the ability to assess the appropriateness of actions; (10) specific tools, representations, and other artifacts; (11) local lore, shared stories, inside jokes, knowing laughter; (12) jargon and shortcuts to communication as well as the ease of producing new ones; (13) certain styles recognized as displaying membership; and (14) a shared discourse reflecting a certain perspective of the world (extracted from Wenger 1998a, 125–26, and Cox 2005, 531).

began to form around ARPANET that through publishing findings, attending conferences, and shaping graduate education trained the next generation of computer scientists, all committed to end-to-end background knowledge.

Emotional attachment to particular objects and subjects and agents' foresight faculties may help sustain dispositions and expectations that induce metastability. Emotions affect primarily the desire's intensity and a person's willingness to stick with dispositions and expectations that dynamically maintain practices and intersubjective background knowledge selectively retained over time.[7] Edward Snowden in the documentary *CitizenFour*[8] expressed nostalgia and emotional attachment to explain why he had decided to leak classified materials and expose the surveillance state: "I remember what the Internet was like before it was being watched. There's never been anything like it in the world." Emotional attachments can help sustain expectations and normative commitments to ensure the metastability of a particular social order when threatened. An emotional reaction to their threatened identity as members of integrationist communities of practice, for example, by President Trump's anti-European discourse and actions, helped European elites and masses to rally around European practices and the background knowledge bound with them, thus strengthening their solidarity and practice communities' identities. Background knowledge, in turn, naturalizes itself as a self-fulfilling expectation. Individuals' ability to imagine the future allows them to take actions that can change the future in and by practice. The past is preserved in the present not only as "memory traces" (Giddens 1984), which is a subjective Popperian "World 2" experience that dies when we do, but mainly as practices that carry transformed background knowledge, a Popperian "World 3" phenomenon or institutionalized social fact. The future connects to the present through expectations – which, as I argued in Chapter 2, are propensities and thus contingent – rather than quantitative probabilities of self-fulfillment.

Values and norms do not determine social orders' change and stability but are and continually become a feature or fragment of practices' background knowledge. Values and norms depend on practices and affect social order in and through them. Communities of practice sustain, horizontally spread, and vertically learn values and norms, which are part of practices' background knowledge. Values and norms thereby

[7] On "emotional communities," see Koschut 2014. For an excellent discussion of the relationship between emotions and practices, see Bially Mattern 2011.

[8] *Citizen Four* was available on YouTube but has since been removed.

constitute social reality through communities of practice's joint enterprises, mutual engagement, and shared epistemic and material resources (Wenger 1998a; see also Gronow 2011, 102). As part of background knowledge, values and norms play a role in the social mechanisms that govern practices' selective retention, such as endogenous change in communities of practice or the innovation of new polities and institutions. Values and norms endow practices with normative content and conceptions of "the better," for example, lowering the propensities of war and epistemological insecurity and reducing poverty and inequality. Normative background knowledge thus permeates learning and contestation in communities of practice.

The pervasiveness of cyberspace in our everyday lives highlights how values and norms are bound up with background knowledge. As Goffman claimed, "a working assumption in everyday life is that one's surround will be 'dead' – that is, contain no recording and transmission devices" (qtd. in Brake 2014, 47). The majority of ordinary online users act with these expectations of privacy whether surfing the web, emailing friends, or posting photos to social media. Just as closing a door or whispering creates privacy but also invokes a privacy norm (Tien 2007, 46), norms and values must be realized in practice to be meaningful. The challenge in cyberspace is the ontological uncertainty of privacy because "privacy risks and privacy behavior (for example, taking precautions) are often invisible" (ibid., 52). In other words, the ontological certainty of closing a door is difficult to replicate in the digital realm. Similarly, clicking a malicious link that installs malware is often not as glaring a privacy violation as a passerby eavesdropping on a conversation. However, when there is widespread (and hence public) knowledge of privacy violations – as in the case with hacks or the Snowden disclosures – practices can change (Penney 2016).

There is no deterministic relationship between dispositions and expectations and social action. Because reasons associated with doing are sensitive to interpretation, the expression of an intention is a process of temporal unfolding, where contingency and indeterminacy are the rule. Intentional phenomena are thus sources of indeterminacy. Because people do "what is called for" on the basis of background knowledge – which emerges in historical and cultural circumstances (Harré and Gillett 1994, 33) – people's reasons and their intentional acts should be traced back to their actions and thus their background knowledge. While background knowledge does not determine action, it can nevertheless provide agents with meaning, purpose, direction, and function. Performativity, as I explained earlier, adds to the contingency and indeterminacy of human action.

The *second* processual social mechanism involves transactions within communities of practice – most important, learning to competently perform, negotiate, and contest meanings – that create cognition as social activity. Social cognition enables, promotes, or in Popper's words *creates* propensities for the selective retention of practices and the background knowledge bound with them. Because the cognitions of any one practitioner in a community of practice are intrinsically related to other practitioners' cognitions, transactions give rise to intersubjective background knowledge or a "thought collective" (Fleck 1979). The creation of social cognition within communities of practice takes place through the reciprocal transactions between practitioners. Knowing, as Lave and Wenger so eloquently put it, "is located in relations among practitioners, their practice, the artifacts of that practice, and the social organization and political economy of the community of practice" (1991, 22).

Communities of practice might consist of practitioners holding similar or, at least, complementary dispositions and expectations but who differ on the type of competence they possess and the interests that drive them, and therefore contest each other's performances. This variation in interests, performances, and knowledge attributes is nonetheless directly associated with communities of practice's joint enterprise, which provides shared meanings and commitments. For analytical purposes only, I can identify three groups within communities of practice, each with their own practice competences. The first group performs mainly theoretical or "knowing that" knowledge (Ryle 2009),[9] which is turned into practical or "knowing how" knowledge and actions. In the political-strategic field, for instance, these practitioners are the strategists, so to speak, the "Schellings" of this world (Aristotle's "theoria"). The next group is made of active practitioners (Aristotle's "praxis"), to use the same illustration, who are actively engaged in, for example, performing nuclear deterrence and arms control. Finally, there is the outer or productive group (Aristotle's "poiesis"), mainly policy-makers who produce political facts by means of decision-making practices. To continue with the same example, strategy theorists and strategy practitioners will be effective depending not only on policy-makers' deontic and performative power to constitute social facts but also on their practices, such as summit meetings, multilateral negotiations, track-two negotiations, etc. The three community-of-practice groups determine together what kind of competent performances are suitable as states or organizations' practices.

[9] Ryle (2009) referred to "knowing that" as knowledge that can be expressed "in propositions whose truth or falsity can be tested" (Cook and Wagenaar 2012, 14). "Knowing how" is practical knowledge "acquired over time" (ibid.).

In such a way, selection works on agency as the congruence and complementarity of different types of competence.

The mechanism, which I describe as transactions in a community of practice, differs from socialization. This is not only in Wenger's (1998a) sense of being a process of "apprenticeship" through learning, but especially because it involves meaning negotiation and contestation, and because its outcomes – metastability or evolution – are conditioned by emergent and reflexive innovations of background knowledge and performances (Gherardi 2008). Participating in communities' transactions not only enables judgments about what needs to be done to act successfully, but also about when and why to challenge engrained habits and rules (Karp 2009, 9).

The mechanism also differs from socialization and persuasion because it results in the changing and integration of identities rather than merely in the transmission of ideas "from mind to mind." According to Wenger, building an identity "consists of negotiating the meanings of our experience of membership in social communities" (1998a, 145). Building an identity is achieved mainly through processes of *engagement* (the active involvement in the process of negotiating meanings), *imagination* (creating images and perceptions that are revealed by personal experience), and *alignment* (the coordination of activities so that they fit into broader structures and contribute to broader enterprises) (Wenger 1998a, 173–74). Engagement is what allows individuals to conform to the norms of the community and to negotiate their participation in it. Imagination allows its members to link their experience with that of others. Alignment, in turn, allows them to combine their material and ideational resources for the sake of what they jointly practice.

Within the expansiveness of cyberspace, for instance, different communities of users, ranging from technical computer "security communities" to ordinary passive users, possess different competencies but they more or less engage each other ("hang together") because of complementary background knowledge. The growing realization of the importance of cyber alertness reflects how transactions within a global community align between competent members and ordinary users. Computer "security communities" stress that we should not look for technical panaceas but rather that users must be more alert to cyber risks and "best practices." In fact, the volume of cyberattacks that profit from computer vulnerability actually increases after a fix is released because most ordinary users do not regularly update their software or they use pirated copies (Bilge and Dumitras 2012). Cyber alertness requires engaging ordinary users about their membership and experience online as users of technology.

In the European context, the transactions within communities of practice are part of the metastability inherent in the "Europeanization" process, which takes place mainly in "Brussels' space" (Drieschova 2016). These transactions are not limited to penetration into national systems of governance. They also involve the development of authoritative institutions through what Olsen calls an "institutionally ordered system of governance" (2002, 922). Indeed, "Brussels," a space imagined by individual European integration practitioners and representing Europe's multiple communities of practice, has become a metonym for the centripetal force of European communities of practice. From this perspective, transactions and contestation within communities of practice are part of Europe's system of rule, thus maintaining the metastability of the European order. The treaties have granted the European Parliament increasing competence despite the long-term trend in declining voter turnout from 62 percent in 1979 to 42 percent in 2014. While successive treaties granted new competence to the European Parliament to curtail the activities of the Commission (and to a certain degree even the Council), in effect the engagement processes between EU parliamentarians and the technocrats in the executive are modes of identity building, even if the practitioners in both institutions often frame their relationship as adversarial.

The *third* processual social mechanism accounting for cognitive evolution combines reflexivity and judgment, both of which contribute to learning processes within and between communities of practice and thus to the evolution of practices and background knowledge. The large majority of the practice literature, especially that building on Bourdieu's work (1977, 1992; see, for example, Adler-Nissen 2013, 2014a; Pouliot 2010, 2016), refers to habitus and/or background knowledge as primarily tacit. I do not dispute that background knowledge is commonly tacit in the sense that people do not think all the time on the rules that constitute their practices or whether they are performing practices competently. However, practitioners reflect on their practice much more often than the Bourdieu-based literature concedes. My argument resonates with Wendt's (2015, 269) claim, which, in turn, is based on Teruaki Nakagami (2003), that individuals cannot participate simultaneously in all processes and relationships, although relationships exist as "potential" or, in my own lexicon, propensity. Thus, practitioners relate to social transactions according to two modes, "active" and "passive." The crucial switch from passive to active mode occurs as a result of attention (ibid.). This poses the question of what triggers attention. According to Dewey, who understood "practice and knowledge as a form of purposeful, flexible engagement" (Cook and Wagenaar 2012, 15; Dewey 1983), people reflect on their habits primarily when challenged by the environment. From this perspective, learning's triggers are exogenous and so akin to adaptation processes.

The EU's Copenhagen Criteria, for instance, set out prerequisites of fundamental European practices for "opening" chapter negotiations with accession states: rule of law, minority rights, democratic processes, and market economies. The Copenhagen Criteria were laid out in 1993, a year after Maastricht, when the end of the Cold War, German reunification, and the now post-Soviet sphere loomed large on the European policy agenda. The process of enlargement and the attendant geographical spread of the European social order spurred European communities of practice to reflect on, clearly define, and codify in prerequisite criteria the anchoring practices for the European social order. Similarly, because online privacy (and the risks to it) is not as apparent as privacy in real life, users may be unaware unless there is widespread (hence public) knowledge triggering attention like the Snowden disclosures or a large-scale hack.

Several other triggers of reflexivity are *endogenous* to interactions in and between communities of practice. This is particularly so in liminal situations, and close to cognitive thresholds, when disenchantment with practices grows within a community of practice, or when a community of practice loses its authoritative traction or pull – more precisely, loses its deontic power, performative power, legitimacy and authority, or credibility. Take, for example, the case of Europe's leaders meeting to bolster the historical moment of the Treaty of Rome on its sixtieth anniversary. The meeting of the heads of state and EU institutions resulted in a declaration that asks to reconsider the disenfranchisement with European practices in reference to the worst moments in European history. The March 2017 Rome Declaration was nothing less than a claim about the *right* and *good* interpretation of background knowledge from which Europe's anchoring practices derive their meaning and authority. The fact that such overtures have become necessary – that practices have become so plainly reflexive – is telling in terms of the potential for cognitive evolution and potentially proximate thresholds.

Among other endogenous reasons that the move from habit to reflexivity takes place,[10] I should first mention learning, which is not only an outcome of reflexivity, or what Janice Stein (2011) called bringing background knowledge to the forefront, but also a catalyst of reflexivity. I mean this in the sense that learning processes within communities of

[10] Referring back to Pierce, Geoffrey Hodgson argues that "habit is not the negation of deliberation but its necessary foundation" (2006, 7).

practice, which we should understand only socially and interactively, promote judgments about self and others' understandings and about what other practitioners do. These judgments turn background knowledge from tacit to explicit (Polanyi 1966, 1983; see also Sikkink 2011).

Second, contestation in and between communities of practice forces practitioners to reflect on their practices and background knowledge, make judgments about their performance and its outcomes and, if disenchanted, intentionally act differently from before. This is clear in the corporate social order as communities of practice formed around the practices of CSR and business education made reflexivity part of their raison d'être. The academic proliferation of studies on CSR was one of the main reasons behind the expansion of these practices (Carroll 2015, 95; Carroll and Shabana 2010, 85). This corporate community of practice is particularly self-aware about its role in shaping CSR and, more importantly, in using it to shape their broader communities of practice, but we can also see a similar process of learning in the business education community of practice. There has been a debate about the educational approach at business schools in the United States. The trend in favor of quantification and the predominance of rational choice in business education since at least the 1950s meant in practice the predominance of economists in business schools, in part thanks to economics' claim to scientific rigor, and in part thanks to its influence in the US government following World War II (Khurana and Spender 2012, 628). Herbert Simon, in particular, worried about what he considered the "colonization" of business education by the rational approach (Simon 1967, 12). Today, the predominance of rational choice approaches and quantification in business education is increasingly contested, and some fear that rationalism has become management education's paradigm to the detriment of other approaches (Khurana and Spender 2012, 620).

Third, as Boltanski argues, practices require both cognitive and normative justification, thus replacing "Bourdieusian power struggles of positioning in fields with the practical competences, critical capacities and an 'ordinary sense of justice' that actors mobilize in their daily struggles to reach agreements" (Büger and Gadinger 2014, 53). Fourth, creativity and innovation (Joas 1996; Pratt 2016), as socially collective phenomena, cannot occur without individual practitioners' conscious reflection and judgment. I have more to say about this in Chapter 8. Fifth, as Rawls (1955) and Karp (2013, 976) argued, practices condition and enable judgments about what participants need to do.

Sixth, practices such as arguing, proving, and achieving a compromise (Shäfer 2014; see also Schatzki 2002), which cut across several communities of practice, require practitioners' attention for how to specifically apply them in their own communities and contexts. Seventh, rigidities of institutions in which communities of practice are embedded can easily open a space for heightened attention, thus for the transition from a passive to an active mode. Ninth, emotions and identities can be reflexive; practitioners reflect on their emotions as triggered by practices and background knowledge, as well as on their understanding of self versus their practices and contexts (Knafo 2016). Tenth, uncertainty may generate reflexivity and self-awareness. If we take uncertainty as the normal condition in international affairs (Katzenstein and Seybert 2018), it follows that practices' reflexivity and self-awareness are the normal condition.

Finally, practitioners' imagination, foresight capacities, and expectations turn individuals into agents who think through and define what competence means in particular contexts. It is practitioners' performances that establish why, regardless of their apparent functionality or relative success, particular kinds of background knowledge and practices end up not being selected and inherited. Practitioners' talent to legitimate their practices – in the eyes of fellow community-of-practice practitioners and of practitioners in the broader social environment – and to construct their practices as focal points around which political coalitions can be formed, is directly related to learning, negotiation and contestation, and identification processes, which sustain cognitive evolution's agential foundations.

Cognitive evolution's *fourth* micro-social mechanism is social power, this time analyzed from individuals' social-cognitive perspective. Practitioners who are drawn to particular changes in their social and material environments that pose a challenge to their practices may utilize social power, for example, performative power, and institutional resources to intentionally affect their environments to solve problems (Gronow 2011, 24; Schatzki 2002, 97; see also Mead 2015). In this sense, individual and collective intentionality become propensities for enhancing practitioners' practices and background knowledge's survival across space and time. This notion loosely borrows from the so-called Baldwin effect, which refers to James Baldwin's pragmatist notion that "learning can change the environment . . . in such a way as to influence the selective environment for the learned behaviour or some closely related character" (Shettleworth 2004, 105).

Practitioners can actively change the environment to match their intentions because, as Searle (1995) has shown, intentions relate to the world in what he calls a "world-to-mind" direction of fit. When, for instance, beliefs do not match the world, people must change their beliefs. But when people approach the world with intentions, they must change the world to match their intentions. Intentional states function according to Searle (1995, 129) only given a set of background or dispositional capacities. Practitioners must bring these capacities reflexively to the "foreground" (Stein 2011; see also Nonaka 1994; Polanyi 1983). This enables learning and it changes the world. However, intentions are not predetermined and the directions they take are constituted in situations in and by practice (Joas 1996); they are propensities until they become actualized. In other words, "the actual reason for why an agent does X does not exist before doing X, but emerges with the latter" (Wendt 2015, 181)

It follows that when people perform with a desire or an intention to act, they attempt to change the world according to their reasons, thus exerting power onto, and control over, the world. Both expectations and dispositions are therefore important in the constitution of reasons but they play different roles. If we take reasons as tendencies or propensities, then a practitioner's expectation "corresponds to a tendency possessed," a disposition "corresponds to a tendency" that can be exercised, and "an action corresponds to a physical manifestation, "whether or not the want is realized" (Bhaskar 1998, 95). Because practitioners' dispositions and expectations are not only part of cognitive structures through which they interpret the world but also resources for changing the world, constitution – as in how practices constitute practitioners' intentions – and causality – as in causing intentional changes in the world – are part of the same nonrepresentational epistemology. In other words, action-constituted reasons are causes if they are likely to produce changes in the material world. Agency, as Schatzki argued, is the engine of becoming (Schatzki 2002, 189).

Cognitive evolution involves causal relationships and how and why practices, background knowledge, and communities of practice become the conditions of possibility for social orders' stability and change. In other words, a constitutive theory can, as part of its epistemology, harbor causal relationships when, for example, in the myth of the "samurai crab," a social structure causes changes in the material world, in this case, the differential proliferation of "samurai crabs."

In the interest of making a more comprehensive argument about agency, I will take a closer look at some of agency's other attributes. First, agency is processual and relational; our doings depend both on intersubjective background knowledge and on our relationships with others (Schlosser 2015). Second, agency is involved in individuals and groups of people's capacity to endow physical and cultural objects with meaning, thus constituting social facts (Searle 1995). Cognitive evolution thus requires "social actors to win the struggles that take place over the attribution of specific social meanings to particular actions" (Long 1992, 23–24). For instance, while ordinary objects like money "emigrate" to the virtual realm, it is often easy in hindsight to overlook users' reluctance to accept this until after e-business had legitimated its use. Similarly, there is an ongoing struggle to attribute crypto-currencies as a widespread medium of exchange.

Third, because cognitive evolution theory is about collective agency, which occurs within the bounds of communities of practice, it depends on practitioners' organizational capacities as part of other practitioners' doings. For example, the organizational capacities of law-enforcement communities compared with the more diffuse privacy community has enabled law enforcement to shape and expand key regulative acts on cybercrime such as the Communications Assistance for Law Enforcement Act (CALEA) and Convention on Cybercrime (2001).

Fourth, agency may have unintended consequences that also affect the world (Giddens 1984, 9–10). Fifth, agency can be constrained: certain physical activities may not be possible and practitioners may consider some practices or their mixture "unthinkable." The actions of other individuals and their ability to threaten, sanction, or punish can also be powerful constraints (Dietz and Burns 1992, 192–93). For instance, the design, deployment, and regulation of information and communications technologies (ICTs) can take some practices off the table and constrain others. Architectural regulation is not necessarily visible to the public. It is typically accepted as normal or given and "we cannot easily exit large-scale sociotechnical systems like telecommunications" (Tien 2007, 48). In effect, technological architecture structures conditions for action (ibid., 39). To take an obvious example, if the government requires service providers to be able to turn over user data or even decrypt communications, the potential lack of anonymity or privacy that enables agency is constrained through chilling effects.

Sixth, agency is dynamic and can be creative. It is dynamic because it depends on social transactions. Because agents' dispositions and expectations rely on interpreted rather than determined meanings, it ensures that transaction processes involve transformation. Agency can be creative because before there can be social structures, agents must construct them, and before social structures constitute individuals' reasons for action, agency must be awakened or become aware of their existence. Finally, agency can be creative because intentions, rather than being predetermined (Joas 1996), emerge in and through practice in specific situations. Agency thus constitutes propensities for, rather than determinants of, change. The Internet's open-source movements show agency's dynamism and creativity. "Open distribution of the source codes allows anyone to modify the code and to develop new programs and applications, in an upward spiral of technological innovation" (Castells 2002, 38).

Seventh, endowed with the capacity of collectively expressing intentions or collective intentionality (Searle 1995), entire communities may act for similar or the same reasons. When a community endows material and social processes and relationships with collective meanings, social communication, deliberation, and discourse become vehicles for fixing meanings – for selecting some meanings from others. Once collectivities, such as communities of practice, constitute themselves as a "we," their members do what they do, consciously, in the sense of doing something *together*. At the very least, they are aware of what other practitioners are doing and how their practices are similar or differ from their own. In some cases, the actions of other practitioners (Shotter 1995, 59) satisfy a practitioner's intention. Take, for example, a soccer game: when player X kicks the ball ahead of where playmate Y is, who must run ahead to catch the ball, X's intention to make a goal will be satisfied only by the actions of playmate Y.[11]

Eighth, people enact their background knowledge, which consists, among other things, of rules. For example, people are now willing to intervene on behalf of human rights, not because they consciously or unconsciously follow human-rights rules. Instead, they become disposed to behave the way they do because, first, background knowledge on human rights has changed and has become selectively retained. Learning occurred both in people's minds and in a community of human-rights practice. Second, people became disposed to intervene on behalf of human rights because this background knowledge conforms to human-rights rules (Searle 1995).[12]

So rather than rules mechanistically "telling" people what to practice, actions and background knowledge work by enabling linguistic and perceptual interpretations or by structuring consciousness (Searle 1995, 32–33). Most people standing on a polluted beach in 1925 would have been aware of and talked about their feet getting dirty and oily. Back then, however, there was hardly any background knowledge about, and actions to prevent, human damage to the natural environment, so conversations about global environmental protection would have been very rare. However, several generations later, people in the same situation would still talk about their dirty feet, but also and primarily about the damage that oil tankers do to the global environment. Had someone

[11] For an interpretation of agency as a network, see Schatzki 2002.
[12] For a different interpretation, see Beitz 2009.

asked Frederick the Great whether he protects the human rights of the peoples of the territories he conquered, he would have sent that someone to the nearest psychiatric hospital. Except there were no psychiatric hospitals in the eighteenth century, only "lunatic asylums."

Finally, if we take performativity as what practices are about, it follows that rationality is a practice (Cabantous and Gond 2011) that helps fulfill expectations (ibid., 578).[13] More specifically, rationality is the performance of what people collectively and intersubjectively consider to be rational as part of their background knowledge. In most cases, "theories" of what rational knowledge is about remain tacit and become part of background knowledge, although at other times these "theories" are reflexively brought to the forefront (Stein 2011). In other words, people perform rationality and consider their actions "rational" because the actions confirm their intersubjective background knowledge and their individual dispositions and expectations. Cognitive evolution, in both its metastable and transformative manifestations, is the context within which practical rationality emerges and reasoned actions take place, not only of practitioners whose judgment helped develop a practice but also of those who later join a community of practice. The capacity for rational thought and behavior is above all a background capacity (Searle 1995). The evolution of practical rationality takes place both in agents' heads and from learning in communities of practice.

Thus understood, "rational choice" is also a practice that some functional fields like economics engrain more deeply culturally than in other fields, such as law, and in some societies based on impersonal relations, such as the United States, rather than in traditional societies. The European order relies on sui generis anchoring practices and background knowledge, which – despite what some scholars paint as Europe's transformative aspirations to replicate the European project in other regions – have little effect outside that context (see Acharya 2012; Bicchi 2006; Börzel and Risse 2009). The European Neighborhood Policy all but failed in its aspirations to foster even the most basic of rights and governance reforms without the promise of eventual membership and even in those Balkan countries with membership incentives is experiencing a distinct lack of influence and domestic penetration in recent years (see Grabbe 2014; Haukkala 2011; Mungiu-Pippidi 2014; Noutcheva 2013). It is increasingly evident that the functional rationality of

[13] In economic sociology, a theory is said to be *performative* when it influences social reality in such a way that its premises, even its predictions, become true (Cabantous and Gond 2011, 578).

European practices may be confined geographically to spaces where the background knowledge lends them culturally distinct rationality.

Practitioners' actions, their intersubjective background knowledge in and across communities of practice, and their dispositions and expectations thus sustain rational choice practices. For example, there is a struggle for the meaning of the rational and responsible course of action between cyber communities of practice on the disclosure of zero-day vulnerabilities.[14] Technical security experts urge the public disclosure of such vulnerabilities since it makes ordinary users and systems more secure, while intelligence communities may choose to keep some vulnerabilities secret for their intelligence value.

To summarize the agential social foundations of cognitive evolution theory:

1. Background knowledge is Janus-faced: one side faces social structure, while the other side faces individuals' dispositions and expectations. Action is "pushed" by the past from background knowledge's dispositions but is also "pulled" toward the future with foresight, anticipation, and expectations.
2. As individuals practice something they enact background knowledge's dispositions and expectations, which become the spring of their reasons for action.
3. The transformation in and by practice of background knowledge becomes practitioners' new dispositions and expectations. Although practices and background knowledge constitute individuals' intentional acts, they do not determine it. They are sensitive to interpretation, reflexivity, and learning.
4. Individuals act intentionally with a world-to-mind direction, trying to change the world according to their intentions (Searle 1995). However, practitioners' experiences may be better portrayed, less as static representational pictures or schema in people's minds, than as streams of dispositions and expectations.
5. Cognitions are social (Fleck 1979; Tomasello 2009) – they emerge from a social and communal context.
6. As Searle (1995, 2010; see also Mitzen 2013) argues, intentionality is collective, in the sense of "we intend." In communities of practice, individuals act with collective intentionality, which they draw from the same practical experience and shared background knowledge. When practitioners act strategically they usually know what "game" they are

[14] Zero-day vulnerabilities are those software vulnerabilities unknown to a vendor that can be exploited by another party.

playing, which other practitioners are friend or foe, and why and how to proceed.

7. Practitioners exercise social power to shape the character and boundaries of their communities of practice and to affect material and cultural-social environments in desired ways.
8. Finally, performances are indeterminate; thus, practitioners' actions are contingent.

Cognitive Evolution Theory: Beyond Elster and Giddens

Cognitive evolution theory attempts to transcend exclusively social functionalist and intentional theories. On this count, I am in full agreement with both Jon Elster and Anthony Giddens. Functionalist theories would unreasonably take us close to natural evolution theory (Elster 1983), while intentional theories avoid social structure and structuration processes (Giddens 1984). Intentional theories would also take us away from practice-oriented evolutionary theories. Cognitive evolution theory can add to and improve on these largely influential theories by Elster and Giddens. A sociocognitive evolutionary theory that is neither rational choice theory nor psychological theory but still possesses a phenomenological component need not rely on sociofunctionalist (let alone natural evolution) mechanisms.

Jon Elster (1983) sought to escape the trappings of functionalism in the social sciences, but the result was an intentional theory of rational choice. Anthony Giddens's elegant "structuration" theory (1984) was also anti-functionalist in character, but he ended up with a theory that only marginally accounts for agency and that is better at explaining social stability than social change. The theory Elster settled for is ontologically restrictive, while Giddens's theory is epistemologically impaired. Cognitive evolution theory purports to account for both structure and agency and the material and ideational worlds. It explains both social change and the selective retention of creative variations and it is amenable to empirical research.

In Elster's view, functionalism is appropriate to explain biological evolution. But when it is applied to the social world of, say, an institution's evolution, existence, and persistence, an institution's function works as a causal explanation only if we assume a "feedback loop through the consciousness of individual agents," thus falling "prey to an individualist account" (Elster 1983, 57; Hollis and Smith 1991, 404). Troubled by the epistemological challenges that a feedback loop through human cognition would raise, Elster preferred the more comfortable foundation of an intentional, or rational-choice, grand theory instead. Elster suggested a general sociological theory that, superficially at least, resembles

Giddens's theory of structuration between agents (Elster's individuals) and structures (Elster's macro-states):

> Preferences and desires are explained endogenously as a product of the social states to the generation of which they also make a contribution ... This theory would include (i) the explanation of individual action in terms of individual desires and beliefs, (ii) the explanation of macro-states in terms of individual action, and (iii) the explanation of desires and beliefs in terms of macro-states. (Elster 1983, 86)

Predictably, Elster's emphasis was on the individual. He argued that agents must exhibit *judgment* and *autonomy* (ibid., 88). He also said that invoking social structures to explain practices requires a causal loop through human consciousness, that is, explaining how thinking individuals combine to create a collective good. However, echoing Giddens (1984) and Archer (1995), he argued that the explanation also requires tracing the agents' judgments and intentions to social structures (Elster 1983, 86). Thus, Elster supplemented the theory of collective action with a collective cognitive element.

Elster's second move was to drop this general theory and settle instead for a rational-choice explanation for the social sciences: "intentional explanation of individual actions together with causal explanation of the interaction between the individuals" (ibid., 84). In other words, Elster thought that to make his general theory operational would require supplementing intentional action with two additional causal explanations: a macro explanation of desires and beliefs in terms of macro-states and a "sub-intentional explanation" of individual action in terms of individual desires and beliefs (ibid., 84–85). In Elster's own words, this general theory "appears to be light-years away" (ibid., 87).

Because of this second move, Elster (1989c) explained normative behavior from a rationalist perspective. His results were ambiguous. He argued that rational choice can explain some cases, while norms, which he reduced to ideas that defy rationality, can explain other cases (ibid.). This argument amounted to putting the epistemological cart before the ontological horse. An intentional paradigm, according to which norms mean only irrational internalized preferences, cannot make sense of reasoned practical behavior that is rule and norm driven, let alone practice and background knowledge driven. By taking identities and preferences for granted, rational choice overlooked questions such as where preferences come from, why people develop the practices they do, and how practices dynamically affect people's preferences to begin with.[15]

[15] In Alex Wendt's eloquent words, rational choice models isolate "an important moment in the social process, the moment when actors choose actions on the basis of identities

Like Elster's rational-choice theory, Giddens's structuration theory's point of departure was a deep suspicion of functionalist-social theories. For Giddens, functionalism fails to conceive of societies as constituted by people's practices, or attributes needs to systems; it fails to acknowledge the negotiated character of norms and values and neglects the role of power (see Baert 1998, 96).[16] Trying to rectify these shortcomings, structuration theory, as sustained by the principle of the "duality of structure," maintains that "structures, as rules and resources, are both the precondition and the unintended outcome of people's agency ... people draw upon structures to proceed in their daily interaction" (ibid., 104; Giddens 1984). Thus, when people draw on structures to know how to go on and, in practice, also to act, they also reproduce these structures. "So structure allows for agency, which in turn makes for the unintended reproduction of the very same structures" (Baert 1998, 104).

Giddens conceived structuration theory as an agent-based theory where agency does not mean intention to act but the actual capacity or power to do something – to affect causally something in the world. Giddens's knowledgeable and reflexive agents get their bearings and act accordingly by drawing on social structures. But these agents are far from being structural "idiots." They are the social constructors of their own practices and structures and bear identities, rights, and obligations in their own consciousness. While agents act according to institutionalized rules, they also act according to their interests (Cohen 1987, 302). Because of Giddens's suggestion that "the properties of agents and of structures are both relevant to explanations of social behavior" (Hollis and Smith 1991, 396), his theory is more ontologically comprehensive than Elster's. Unlike Elster, Giddens (1984) does not drop the constitutive impact of social structures on agents and he turns this causal link into one of the essential features of his theory. He also claims that through reflexivity agents can change their own structures.

However, Giddens's structuration theory is epistemologically handicapped. First, by placing structure and agency, rather than practices, in

and interests which are at that instant given. But in making those choices actors are simultaneously reproducing themselves as 'givens,' which only a constructivist approach can grasp" (1987, 368).

[16] For example, Giddens argued that functionalist theories are teleological – they assume that systems evolve toward some state and do not specify the mechanism that explains differentiation and integration in evolutionary processes. Functionalist theories presume a set of fixed stages that societies have to pass in their evolution, and are adaptation-based theories, even though adaptation is a vacuous and diffuse concept that can mean everything. Societies themselves cannot adapt, only institutions can, but empirically, this does not seem to be the case. Finally, functionalist theories have not made the case that natural selection is applicable to the social sciences (Giddens 1984, 228–80).

the driver's seat, Giddens analyzed agency and structure as separate ontologies, though with equally ontological status, which presuppose each other. This, as Archer argued (1988, 97), created a problem in how Giddens's concept of "duality of structure" can encourage empirical research. It discourages a historical or evolutionary constructivist analysis of social orders whose histories and trajectories can be empirically traced and researched. Second, Giddens's concepts of agency and structure are problematic; agency neglects the role of intentions, expectations, and emotions, while structure refers to "invisible" memory traces of rules. Third, structuration lacks a theory of norm and practice selection and diffusion. Finally, structuration is a theory of how orders remain stable rather than how they change.

Roy Bhaskar's argument that agents "inherit" social structures that they did not play a role in producing (1998, xvi) improves on structuration theory. This argument ontologically distinguishes between agents and structures. By invoking the principle of "duality of praxis" – where social construction and reproduction are separated in time "and may well involve different agents altogether" (Archer 1998, 369) – Bhaskar claims that agents can help constitute a social structure that only future generations of agents can draw on for their practical action.

In similar fashion, Margaret Archer's "morphogenesis" theory (1988, 1995, 2007) takes structure and agency as being capable of independent variation and evolution. With the addition of a time variable, the morphogenesis concept means "that structure necessarily pre-dates the action(s) which transform it; and that structural elaboration necessarily post-dates those actions" (Archer 1995, 76, 247, 257; see also Carlsnaes 1992).[17] This move enables empirical research into social recursiveness over time – "real" and measurable time, rather than, as in Giddens, looping or circular time (Archer 1995; Carlsnaes 1992). Archer's morphogenesis theory also purports to correct one of the most important problems of Giddens's structuration theory: the lack of specificity about when actions will recursively replicate social structures and when they will bring about transformation. Archer suggests that explaining action requires focusing on the conditions that make change more or less likely (1995, 209).

[17] With particular reference to foreign policy, Carlsnaes added that to explain an action, a dynamic model based on morphogenesis must consider "not only its underlying structures, but also previous actions and both the structural effects *and* structural antecedents of the latter … Accounting for the causes underlying policy change will involve an examination of how this policy has evolved from the past to the present" (1992, 264).

Both Bhaskar and Archer bring intention back into the picture. The very framing of intentions, Bhaskar argues, could not take place without people drawing on social structures, but intention "demarcates agency from structure," since people's intentional behavior is caused *for reasons* (Archer 1998, 372). Although Archer is careful not to fall for arguments that denote voluntarism, she nevertheless claims that the social and material causes of actions can transform agents' efficient actions (ibid., 369–70). Thus, she argues that the "way forward consists not only in viewing structural conditioning as a supply of reasons for actions but additionally in showing why agents tend to regard them as better than other courses of actions which also may be considered good" (Archer 1995, 209).

Bhaskar's and Archer's theories represent a step forward. But Bhaskar's theory is naturalistic and, like Giddens's, refers mainly to the recursiveness of social life. Archer's time-bounded theory is linear, and while perhaps it is better able than Giddens's theory to deal with "upward causation" and "downward causation,"[18] neither Bhaskar's theory nor Archer's can explain how and why certain practices survive rather than others, and why social orders evolve.

Cognitive evolution theory overcomes functionalism by assuming that practitioners – who as members of communities of practice draw on symbolic, material, and organizational resources – collectively and individually enact their background dispositions and expectations concerning what they are doing through competent performances. Structural and agential social mechanisms and processes explain both the differential, albeit variable, replication of the practices of communities of practice and of their background knowledge, their selective retention in space and time, as well as social order evolution. Whether social orders evolve or remain metastable is contingent on both the structural and agential mechanisms I referred to earlier, and the creative variation and selective retention processes, which I discuss in the next two chapters. However, it is also contingent on processual and interaction flows occurring close to intersubjective cognitive thresholds, and at "bifurcation points" that, while indeterminate, depend to some extent on a combination of social orders' resilience and "homeorhesis" (Waddington 1977), in short, a stabilized flow.

Although cognitive evolution theory has an intentional component, it is not a psychological-based theory. Psychological explanations fall short when we move from the human mind to the social world and require

[18] "The procedure of reducing the one component of the actor-structure linkage to explanation in terms of the other" (Carlsnaes 1992, 249).

auxiliary mechanisms to explain how, for example, individual cognition and emotions may be able to spawn regional and global practices. Thus, experiments that social psychologists perform with rats, or with students in labs, and most recently with the help of brain CT scans, are no doubt useful for explaining human behavior, but insufficient to explain social orders' change and stability. The focus should therefore be on interpreting agents who perform (Alexander 2011) their background knowledge, rather than on the psychological processes inside people's heads. We also cannot reduce cognitive evolution to rational choice. A theory of cognitive evolution subsumes rational choice because strategic action, which takes place at time t_1, occurs as a result of practices and background knowledge that were socially constructed at time t_0. Rational actors live and act in a socially constructed world. Practitioners do not only recursively reproduce background knowledge, on which practices rest, as in structuration theory (Giddens 1984), but they continually change it through their practices.

8 Creative Variation

In the last two chapters, I suggested both structural and agential mechanisms that help explain international social orders' metastability and change. In the next two chapters, I unpack these mechanisms to argue that they depend on, and are sustained by, *creative variation and selective retention* processes. These processes establish how and why fluctuations or evolutionary variants occur, and how and why they become selectively reproduced, retained, naturalized, and institutionalized. These processes also show the role of communities of practice in both the reproduction of practices and knowledge and their evolution. For descriptive reasons I analyze creative variation and selective retention processes separately in two chapters. However, nonlinear and nonsequential relationships, interactivity, synergisms, and positive and negative feedback characterize these processes. Creative change, for example, plays a role in both innovation and selective retention processes.

One of the consequences of relying on evolutionary epistemology, and within it Donald Campbell's (1965) "general model of evolutionary change," for building my theory is, as I argued in Chapter 3, that organic evolution is only one instance of this principle. This is why cognitive evolution theory and its mechanisms do not follow a "generalized Darwinist" (Aldrich et al. 2008; see also Lewis and Steimo 2012; Lustick 2011) path, are not concerned with whether cognitive evolution theory is Darwinist or Lamarckian, and do not rely on natural evolution's mechanisms from identity, homology, analogy, and metaphor's perspectives (Cohen 1993, 1994; Ma 2016). Whether we are trying to explain the evolution of institutions or, as I do, of social orders, creative variation and selective retention are necessary processes for evolutionary explanations of change and stability. They distinguish evolutionary explanations, in my case cognitive evolution theory, from other social models of change or stability, such as rational choice and normative models.

In this chapter, I discuss creative variation processes. Following Hans Joas (1996), I show that variation from a cognitive evolutionary perspective is creative, that creative variation arises from the contingency of social life, rather than only from intentions and choices, and that because of the processual nature of variation, epistemic and practice innovation are propensities rather than determinants of change. This is because variations depend on selective retention processes to congeal into institutionalized practices and because they arise in contingent practical situations. I also argue that individual creation and innovation becomes social innovation.

An Analysis of Creative Variation

Nascent forms of awareness that lead to the development of new practices; endogenous social interaction processes in, and exogenous processes to, communities of practice; and a variety of additional creative variation sources, such as the emergence of new radical ideologies, new scientific knowledge, normative changes in background knowledge, and disruptive practitioners, generate processes of *creative variation.* Creative variation is also associated with incremental changes in the performance of practices within communities of practice. Although often unintended, this type of variation is creative because it has the propensity to generate changes in practices' meanings, in the materials that meanings attach to, and because it creates new standards of competence. Communities of practice, as emergent structures and agents that are neither inherently stable nor randomly changeable (Wenger 1998a, 49), are a particularly crucial source of creative variation, namely, of new and transformed practices and their background knowledge. Emergent creative processes are the springs of new social orders, but not all instances of creative variation emerge as new or transformed social orders – only those that are selectively retained and that replace existing social orders. Variations are "blind" only in the sense that human knowledge is always imperfect and untested, and that practices, as knowledge's practical material and meaningful side, are contingent, fragile (Knorr Cetina 2001), and context dependent. I distinguish my concept of creative variation from approaches that take a naturalistic turn and reduce variation to genetic factors (Alford et al. 2005; Dawes and Fowler 2009; Fowler et al. 2008) and to cognition, understood from a psychological, rather than from a social, perspective (McDermott et al. 2008; Richerson and Boyd 2005). I also distinguish my concept from approaches that focus primarily on ideas as a primary ontological and epistemological category (Berman 1998; Blyth 2002; Hall 2003; Lieberman 2002) and institutions (Steinmo 2010; Thelen 2004).

The Awakening of Consciousness

Creative variation sometimes starts as the irreversible unfolding of collective consciousness and knowledge (Mead 1967 [1934]). The importance of knowledge lies in its becoming social, collective, and interactive – it congeals into, and becomes bound with, social practices. Consciousness and new collective knowledge awaken to new situations and possibilities, affecting peoples' expectations and dispositions, and their capacity to do things, to engage in new practices, and to participate in social transactions, such as learning, meaning negotiation, and contestation in communities of practice. These nascent forms of awareness, some of which may be normative, scientific, or ideological, can be associated with, as I mentioned in Chapter 6, "generative relationships" (Lane and Maxfield 1997, 92). One prominent example is the active support provided in the 1950s and 1960s by the Ford Foundation to universities that were willing to push their business or management education in the direction of a statistical and rational choice approach, which led to the development of the modern business school model. Likewise, creativity, innovation, and discovery are central to the practice of hacking in open-source software communities (Castells 2002, 41–49), in other words, to instances and episodes of formative interactions that facilitate the emergence of new practices and communities of practice.

Although single individuals might invent new theories or conceive new knowledge, creative variation, or *social innovation*, is always a social, collaborative, and collective phenomenon "enacted in networks of social relations" (Coe and Brunell 2003, 438), such as communities of practice. Creative variation depends on individual practitioners' alignment between individual and collective meanings, imaginations, and identities (Wenger 1998a), as well as their reciprocal mutual engagement and interactions, where knowledge gains currency and can be tested in practice. What matters is less the act of invention in the mind of one individual or several individuals than the validation and epistemic practical authority that innovative practice meanings acquire within communities of practice.

The origins of cyberspace reveal how invention and innovation of packet switching was a collaborative endeavor. Following Sputnik, President Eisenhower created the Advanced Research Projects Agency (ARPA) within the Defense Department to fund defense-related research and development. With the founding of its Information Processing Techniques Office (IPTO) in 1962, ARPA became a major funder of the nascent field of computer science by establishing several university computing research centers. ARPANET was "born from an inspiration and a need" to link these research centers and more efficiently pool computing resources (Abbate 1999, 43). In 1966, the director of IPTO, Robert Taylor, tapped Lawrence Roberts to link the research community by managing ARPANET. Roberts knew that linking computers through long-distance telephone lines would be prohibitively expensive and prone to line failures. He was aware of packet switching but not yet sure how to implement it in large networks until he read Paul Baran's *On Distributed Communications* and "would describe this as a kind of revelation: 'Suddenly I learned how to route packets'" (Abbate 1999, 38). The "most distinctive" characteristic of ARPANET was its development and use of packet-switching principles to transmit data. It was through ARPANET's demonstration at the First International Conference on Computer Communications in 1972 that packet design could be tested and legitimated among the growing computer science community. By extension, a process of peer review and revision validates and authenticates technological innovation resulting from creative hacking in open-source communities (Castells 2002, 46).

Practical application in contingent situations is a source of creative action. New knowledge emergence depends on how it is expected to intervene in practical life (Fleck 1979; Hacking 1983), on the particular situations in which knowledge is performed, on its timing, and on the ability of practitioners, who hold particular interpretations of a practice, to anticipate the exigencies and needs of the political structures involved in selective-retention processes. The awakening of consciousness and its social consequences also occur through reinterpretation. Patterson gives the example of human rights practitioners who, seeking "to improve the status of women in patriarchal societies," discovered the value of "reinterpreting traditional gender ideologies that have been used to legitimate male domination and discrimination against women" (2010, 147).

Creative Action

According to Hans Joas (1996), human beings' most basic form of action – which all other forms of action like rational choice and intentionality are related to – is *creativity*.[1] This creativity is not just an occasional action. It involves all cases of social action and, therefore,

[1] Colapietro understands Joas's argument as entailing a "radical revision of our understanding of human action as "an ongoing, creative process in which the very terms of identification and description ... cannot be defined either in advance of the process ... or apart from the process of ongoing activity" (2009, 13).

agency. Creativity arises as the most basic form of action in situations calling for solutions to problems – when certainties are shattered and also "when new forms of acting take on the form of changed routine" (ibid., 139). Creativity increases instability but aims to reduce uncertainty (Katzenstein and Seybert 2018).[2] It reduces entropy (disorder) by creating propensities for the establishment of new orders (Poutanen 2013, 217). Contingent cognitive evolutionary variations thus rely on social creativity. Creative action accords with a becoming ontology, where change is the basic condition of social life (see Chapter 2). Out of continuous fluctuations arising from learning, negotiation, and contestation in and among communities of practice, creative actions emerge. Creative variation is also consistent with another of my key arguments, social cognition, namely with the "irreducible sociality behind all individual acts" (Joas 1996, 189; Mead 1967 [1934], 7).

Joas's view of creative social action (1996, 155, 158) rests on the argument that goals are not externally determined and that intentionality is not teleological. Instead, goals and intentionality *emerge* in shifting situational contexts that improvisational practitioners face, which result from reflection, aspirations, and dispositions that are constituted in and by background knowledge (ibid., 129). As Joas says, "our perception is directed . . . towards our being able to use in practice in the context of our action that which we perceive" (ibid., 158). The argument that *situations* constitute action accords with Popper's assumption (1990, 17; see also Katzenstein and Seybert 2018) that situations are indeterminate. Propensities, rather than being properties inherent in an object, are inherent in physical and social situations, *in what people do or practice*, and therefore in the particular ways in which situations change (see Chapter 2). Situations thus generate indeterminate propensities on which creative action is based.

Practitioners' goals and means, and the enactment of background knowledge, such as norms and values, depend on creativity. "Creativity is needed to give norms and values a concrete form in practice; the existence of values depends also on there having been a creative process by which values were formed" (Joas 1996, 233). In other words, normative background knowledge is instantiated in practice through creative processes. The interactive negotiation of practices in communities of practice, as practitioners attach more or less value, including political value, to practices, plays a role in normative creative-variation processes.

[2] Katzenstein and Seybert (2018) suggest the concept of "protean power," which refers to a structural form of power that is based primarily on creativity and experimentation to cope with uncertainty. Protean power stands in contrast to power as control.

Take, for example, the process of negotiating iterative European treaties and developing common themes through Council meetings. Over time, treaty negotiations (or "amending treaties" in the European parlance) and Council meetings developed into a practice of Intergovernmental Conferences (IGCs) and Council communications on the deep and pressing issues facing the European project writ large. IGCs and Council meetings are moments when member states' raison d'état comes to the fore and they are, at times, deeply conflictual. These conflicts are a normal part of doing business. Member state interests are often negotiated to the point of common ground in the interest of the European order. This common ground involves a statement and retrenchment of anchoring practices around common markets, freedom of movement, and security practices that are synonymous with the European order. Communities of practice, in fact, can influence normative interpretations of collective practices "more powerfully than individual actors" (Beckert 2010, 619).

Creative variation combines, on one hand, consciousness awakened, inspiration, and imagination and, on the other hand, "the rational production of something new in the world" (Joas 1996, 254–55; Maslow 1962). It also involves both new combinations of existing meanings – for example, protecting the natural environment and human rights, which did not exist one hundred years ago – and the continuous experimentation with meanings that are put to the test practically. Like competition in economic markets that spurs market innovations and wealth creation, dissent and contestation in communities of practice energize creativity. Nemeth and colleagues (2004) have shown that dissent, debate, and competing views boost creative group work (Poutanen 2013). For example, we can consider the European Union either as one big experiment in social order or as a creative social order consisting of a large number of novel and ongoing experiments that sometimes overlap, sometimes compete, but are at their core deeply experimental in the history of international relations (Nicolaïdis and Howse 2002).

Creative Variation in and between Communities of Practice

Having now established the key role that creativity plays in cognitive evolution's variation processes, let's look at communities of practice where creative variation usually takes place. Discontinuities and instabilities arise from endogenous processes in communities of practice mainly because of learning, and the negotiation and contestation processes that accompany it. Learning, in the agential sense discussed in Chapters 6 and 7, is about acquiring the knowledge and meanings necessary to practice competently, as well as an identity.[3] Building an identity consists "of negotiating the meanings of our experience of membership" in communities of practice (Wenger 1998a, 145). Meaning negotiation takes place through three main processes – "engagement," "alignment," and "imagination" – each of which separately, and combined, is a source of creative variation.

While engagement is what allows practitioners to conform to the community's practices and background knowledge, it also contributes to the negotiation of their participation in it; this encourages creative variation. Imagination allows practitioners to connect their experience with that of others, and to innovate and learn. Alignment, for example, in the case of the environmental movement, allows practitioners from different backgrounds (for instance, the natural and social sciences) to bring together their material and ideational resources for the sake of what they jointly practice. Resources help keep the community in a stable state of fluctuation, but also work on behalf of innovation. Through alignment, practitioners straddle boundaries between different communities of practice and translate meanings from one to the other (Wenger 1998a, 182, 185, 186, 192). Wenger describes community identity as a trajectory that accumulates competences and is contingent on external events and on the regime of competence that the community settles to through negotiation and contestation (2010, 5). Creative variations that affect the trajectories' direction punctuate these trajectories.

Communities of practice's boundaries are important for creative variation because they produce synergisms between practices, and because they are not necessarily "congruent with the reified structures of institutional affiliations, divisions and boundaries" (Brown and Dugiud 2000; Wenger 1998a, 118–19). Boundaries mediate between different organizations, and as meanings spread and are translated across communities' boundaries and organizational boundaries, they become the source of creative variation. The positioning of individual practitioners within and between several communities of practice and organizations is also an important source of creative variation (Müller and Ibert 2014). Boundary practices can bring two practices together, for example, nuclear deterrence and nuclear arms control, or corporate law and corporate finance. Their combination, however, is more than the sum of its parts. Because it is emergent, it might also create symbiosis with other practices, such as research and development and military budgeting. In business education, it can lead to changes in social organization. More important, "boundary encounters" (Wenger

[3] Learning "creates emergent structures: it requires enough structure and continuity to accumulate experience and enough perturbation and discontinuity to continually negotiate meaning" (Wenger 1998a, 227).

1998a, 112–13), such as diplomatic meetings and visits, can create opportunities for strategic interaction and international cooperation efforts. When practices overlap, the common space they share enables and promotes changes in the performativity of practices and definitions of competence. This is the case, for example, with macro-economic and finance communities of practice, which remain separated but their overlap has led to changes in local and global economic social orders.

Boundary encounters involve "boundary objects" and "brokering." The former refers to "artifacts, documents, terms, concepts, and other forms of reification around which communities of practice can organize their interconnections" (Wenger 1998a, 105). Because institutional and organizational effects often transcend the communities that created them, the reification of practices into institutions and organizations can be a source of creative variation. "Brokering," in turn, refers to "connections provided by people who can introduce elements of one practice into another" (ibid.), as in the case of multilateral task forces handling the military, economic, and political dimensions of international terrorism. Eventually, community of practice constellations or constellations of interconnected practices might form (ibid., 126–28). Constellations create continuities among practices but can also be the source of practice variation arising from cross-organization cleavages (Lachmann 2010).

The translation of meanings (Benjamin 1977) across community-of-practice boundaries is also an important source of creative variation. According to Michel Callon, translation "involves creating convergences and homologies by relating things that were previously different" (1981, 211; see also Latour 1993). While the "translator's" objective is to find the closest meaning, creative changes often take place in translation processes, which can affect learning and negotiation within and between communities of practice. I have more to say about translation in Chapter 9. Here it will suffice to say that what on the surface appear as "diffusion" of ideas and policies among formal organizations are really translation processes that take place within and between communities of practice. These processes become the source of both practice replication and creative variations, especially because of what is "lost" or gained "in translation."

Creative Variations and the Birth of New Social Orders

The following illustrations provide insight into why creative variations take place.

(1) Contestation and meaning change during practice-emergence processes can lead to creative variations. Take, for example, the postconflict

settlement of disputes. According to Michal Ben-Josef Hirsch (2014), a change in the content of an emerging norm made the practice of establishing truth-and-reconciliation committees more persuasive and appealing, thus easier to adopt. They started as a weak compromise to trials. But because of contested changes in normative background knowledge, the truth-and-reconciliation practice became a tool for social and political reconstruction, democratization, and a strong alternative to political trials.

Likewise, a change in practitioners' understanding about the content and purpose of CSR practice also led to wider acceptance by the community of practice. In the 1970s and 1980s, corporate practitioners pushed back against the idea that corporations had social responsibilities (Carroll 2015, 87, 91; Carroll and Shabana 2010, 87; Shleifer 1997, 751). This was because they thought that management's sole responsibility was to increase profitability (Carroll and Shabana 2010, 88; Friedman 1970, 33) or because managers were not equipped to make socially oriented decisions (Carroll and Shabana 2010, 88; Friedman 1970, 122). In the 1990s and 2000s, however, practitioners started to propose that CSR could be reconciled with profitability (Carroll 2015, 89; Carroll and Shabana 2010, 88; Esty and Porter 1998, 36). The "business case" for CSR – that a company will be financially rewarded by consumers for adopting socially or environmentally responsible practices (Carroll 2015, 89; Carroll and Shabana 2010, 86, 92; Eweje 2006, 28; Jeppesen and Hansen 2004, 265; Lindgreen and Swaen 2010, 3; Reinhardt 1999) – helped promote CSR's acceptance among business and management communities of practice.

Similarly, contestation and concern over the warrantless wiretapping program of the National Security Agency (NSA) has led to creative variations in intelligence collection that try to reconcile widespread privacy concerns. Specifically, the NSA in the United States and its Five Eyes partners (Australia, Canada, New Zealand, and the United Kingdom) have focused on their collection of metadata and minimizing the identities of citizens caught up in incidental collection as a way to reduce its impact on civil liberties. Indeed, traffic analysis of metadata is the "core of what surveillance is about in the digital age" (Geer 2007, 32). Despite the considerable contestation over the privacy impact of metadata itself (Forcese 2015; Schneier 2015), a National Research Council Report concluded there are no technical alternatives to bulk data collection (Sanger 2015). In an effort to assuage these continued privacy concerns, the Office of the Director of National Intelligence has begun to release annual transparency reports.

The failure of the European Neighborhood Policy (ENP) to meet its own goals of fostering a ring of stable democracies around its near abroad (evident, for example, in the Arab Spring and Russia's annexation of Crimea) signaled a change in European practices through contestation over the meaning and spatial extension of the European order. While not normatively progressive, the 2015 "Revised ENP" signals the outcome of contestation from member states, through the Council, to the commission's "external" priorities (see Bouris and Schumacher 2017). Program funding for democracy promotion always paled in comparison to other forms of engagement (see Balzacq 2009). But the shift to a "pragmatic" and "differentiated" approach to the post–Arab Spring neighborhood policy signaled the shift from the logic of "democratic peace" to a commitment to stability and the reemergence of statist practices as the driving force in European foreign policy (see Tömmel 2013).

(2) Creative variations sometimes take place in translation processes to local conditions (see also Acharya 2004). For instance, the translation of European security-community building practices, such as regional forums, to the Association of Southeast Asian Nations (ASEAN) "exposed a background of hostile relations, for example, between Singapore and Malaysia, inconsistent with security community practices" (Adler and Greve 2009, 77). This occurred not only because of cultural differences between the two regions, but also mainly because of a different mix between cooperative security practices and balance-of-power practices in both regions (ibid.).

(3) Disruptive practitioners, because of their creative action, can open new possibilities for knowledge and practices' transformation with the potential of changing social order. By making public the NSA's surveillance of citizens worldwide, including Americans, Edward Snowden intensified the contemporary contestation between communities of practice on the nature of cyberspace order. This contestation is taking place between practitioners who regard cyberspace as a national domain that should be at the service of state security and practitioners who take cyberspace as global and constituted by transparency and global governance practices (Deibert 2013).

We might also consider US President Donald Trump, for example, as a disrupter practitioner who has done and said enough for experts and observers alike to question the stability of the international order that has been in place since the end of World War II. But the Trump effect has less to do with American material power (or lack thereof), Trump's ideology (or lack thereof), or some of his psychological attributes. Instead, it has to do with what he has done and said: the practices and background knowledge he has empowered, which are at odds with long-standing political national and international practices and their constitutive rules. But while Trump has been actively undermining the liberal international order's norms and practices, he has hardly promoted or developed new ones; he has been a "destroyer of worlds" (from the Hindu *Bhagavad-Gita*) rather than a creator of new ones. While deontic power made it possible for Trump, the outsider, to disrupt widely accepted practices and background knowledge, his performative power has been an intrinsic part of his practices' disruptive effects.

Disruptive background knowledge also has creative variation potential. In the corporate social order, for example, the development of financial economics in the 1970s and economic models that characterized the separation between ownership and management as a "conflict of interests" was equally disruptive.[4] More to the point, these developments provided the justification and theoretical template for the leveraged buyout, merger and acquisitions, restructuring, and "junk bond" waves of the late 1970s and early 1980s. This occurred as "corporate raiders" and financial actors claimed that they were "unlocking shareholder value" by removing incompetent managers and making big, sleepy public corporations more efficient and profitable.[5] A feature of corporations that appeared positive in the past or, at a minimum, irrelevant from a commercial point of view gradually changed into a problem of "control," a conflict of interests between shareholders and management worthy of investigation by academics and action by shareholders.

(4) Inventions of new social, political, and economic practices depend in large measure on definition and classification strategies about how to frame new practices and related epistemic backgrounds. This is the case with the invention of "operational risk" for the regulation of banking activities in the 1990s (Dumouchel 2016; Power 2005). Operational risk "is a label for a collection of practices that sets minimal capital standards and embodies both qualitative and quantitative requirements for risk management ... the adequacy of the control environment and systems ... and the nature and extent of bank disclosures about the process used to manage and control risk" (Power 2005, 582–83). Beginning from a low epistemic status, the operational risk bundle of practices now organizes and manages the global financial social order (Dumouchel

[4] Ciccotello 2014, 8; Cooper et al. 2010, 692, 712; Fama and Jensen 1983, 304; Jensen and Murphy 1990, 226; Kaplan and Strömberg 2009, 130–31; Shleifer and Vishny 1997, 738, 740.

[5] Chancellor 1999, 258; Holmstrom and Kaplan 2001, 121, 127; Kaplan and Strömberg 2009, 131–32; Shleifer 1997, 756, 766; Wruck 2008, 9.

2016; Power 2005). However, major differences remain about defining and classifying how risk management delimits jurisdictions (Abbott 1988a) and about data collection and quantification (Power 2005, 586, 590). Definitional issues, data collection, and trust in the "numbers" are a source of creative variation in the development of operational risk-management practices. As I showed earlier, similar processes in the corporate social order were behind the creation of the corporation itself, but also practices of CSR and others.

(5) Radically new ideologies can be a source of creative variation. Key to understanding their role in creative variation is the performativity of such ideologies. Knorr Cetina (2005) has admirably explained how Al Qaeda, which she describes as embodying a complex dynamic "global microstructure," helped constitute global terrorist practices. As a novel community of practice, Al Qaeda displays a combination of global reach with a global micro-structure: complex, emergent, self-organizing, fluid, processual, and aterritorial fields of practice (Knorr Cetina 2005, 214). Practices are created and recreated in situations, or "in-going-along" (ibid., 215, 222), so they are a dynamic source of social innovation. For instance, practices of temporalization ground actions in transformation situations, which include terrorist cells that appear and later disappear. Al Qaeda's media (re)presentations motivate creative variations by linking its "few thousand" active members to millions of supporters united by diasporic history and imagination (ibid., 228).

(6) Individual leaders can be a source of creative variation by using political, economic, and social practices whose legitimacy has long passed its "expiration date," or so it seems. I do not mean that individual leaders come up with new ideas – this would be a banal statement – which in any case would require public and collective legitimization to become practices. I mean that to get the support of masses who desire political change, individual, usually populist and authoritarian leaders challenge the status quo with "innovative" practices that otherwise seem anachronistic and normatively unacceptable. Populist leaders from Hungary, Poland, and the United Kingdom have wedded their domestic populism to anti-Brussels, Euroskeptic attitudes, where the very nature of the European social order has become a foil against which they can help ensure domestic electoral gain. In turn, European communities of practice must toe the line on identity issues around borders, refugees, and the meaning and scope of national destiny – potentially legitimizing practices seen as fundamentally anachronistic and contrary to the anchoring practices of the European order.

Likewise, when former US Secretary of State John Kerry said after Russian President Vladimir Putin had decided to annex Crimea that "you just don't in the twenty-first century behave in the nineteenth-century fashion by invading another country on completely trumped up pretext,"[6] he was indirectly saying that the annexation was a variation from current and best international practices. Likewise, when President Trump reverts to mercantilist economic policies that Western liberal market democracies have long discarded, he is taking an "innovative" initiative, and challenging the current international order, by moving forward to the past. Creative variation, in short, might occur not only with the introduction of new knowledge and practices but also with the restoration of practices and knowledge that have collectively been normatively delegitimized. In these illustrations, the knowledge and practices have become normatively nonlegitimate *only* in communities of liberal democratic practice. As I show in Chapter 10 in more detail, progress or a move to better practices is bounded in space and time.

(7) New scientific theories and their empirical confirmation are an obvious source of creative variation and social innovation. Scientific knowledge about climate change, for instance, linking the rise of greenhouse gases to the rise of global temperatures, has become the source of creative variation through performativity of the scientific theories and data that support them. Partly because of the stalemate in negotiations by formal organizations, an important source of innovation in this area has been experimenting with novel practices aimed to counter climate change's harmful effects. "These innovations are pushing the envelope of climate action and demonstrating what is possible" (Hoffmann 2012, cover). Thus, changing the conceptual categories that are required to transform both human consciousness and state practices for the protection of the global environment may require persuading policy-makers of the normative and causal implications of the new science, as epistemic communities (Adler and Haas 1992; Haas 1992a) would. But it mainly requires performing and socially and legally experimenting with science and translating it across communities of practice's boundaries. Experimentation and translation become a source of learning in, and creative variation of, communities of practice (Adler 2005, 2008; Never 2012).

Another example of expertise spurring the development of new practices comes from business education. The post–World-War II period set the stage to contest the role of business education in the corporate order, especially how it could contribute to economic activity and the

[6] Reid J. Epstein, "Kerry: Russia Behaving Like It's the Nineteenth Century," *Politico* [blog], March 2, 2014, www.politico.com/blogs/politico-now/2014/03/kerry-russia-behaving-like-its-the-19th-century-184280.

improvement of corporations. Those who affirmed the superiority of "proper" natural science methods interpreted the type of business education taking place in older schools and programs as lacking in academic coherence and scientific rigor (Khurana and Spender 2012, 622). This movement sought to "legitimize" the social sciences by making them "objective" and "neutral" through quantification and the use of statistics (ibid., 622–23). It also followed the experiences of economists and other social scientists who worked in planning and management for the allies in World War II and who thought that "rational choice" and the concepts and techniques developed during the war were viable for the study of management and improving business firms' performance (ibid., 624). Khurana and Spender also relate the rise of this particular view of business education in the United States to the highly bureaucratized society of the postwar years and the rise of the conglomerate, which put a premium on forecasting, planning, and coordination skills (ibid., 624–25). In the 1950s and 1960s, the Carnegie Corporation and the Ford Foundation sought to apply these "revolutions" in the behavioral sciences to the management of education (Augier and Prietula 2007, 508; Khurana and Spender 2012, 624). Some business schools also received assistance from the US government and the defense complex.

(8) A major source of creative variation is the transition from one form of political institution to another. This is true when, as in the EU, states give up part of their sovereignty and integrate themselves into a transnational polity that novel transnational practices help constitute. Far from being "blind mutations," EU innovation of economic, security, citizenship, borders, human rights, and membership practices resulted from learning processes that instilled in Europeans novel ways of identification. In Nicolaïdis and Howse's words, Europe has been and still is a work in process, a "EUtopia," or "laboratory where options for politics [and governance] beyond the states are generated" (2002, 768, 771). However, the space of Brussels is also a byword for Euroskeptic agendas that turn on a narrative of imperial overreach and undermining authentic polities and modes of self-determination from the Pyrenees to the Carpathians.

(9) Finally, there is the settling of complex processes in unexpected dynamic ways, where emergent and small nonlinear processes have huge consequences. The 1975 Helsinki Final Act and the Conference on Security and Cooperation in Europe (CSCE) (the latter resulted from the former) unleashed creative variation processes, in both human rights and international security, that unintentionally resulted in the end of

the Cold War.[7] We learn two lessons from this case. First, "cultural innovations do not emerge full blown all at once but may be the result of years and decades, and for this reason have a sequential effect on their own development" (Wuthnow 1989, 7). Second, creative variations, such as human rights and confidence-building measures, may undergo amplification processes that can deeply affect the epistemic practical authority on which the existing social order's practices rest.

In cyberspace, Tim Berners-Lee's "marriage of hypertext and the Internet" that created the World Wide Web was just one means of navigating the Internet, but it had profound effects for how we imagine the Web (Campbell-Kelly and Garcia-Swartz 2013, 30). The World Wide Web was selectively retained against competing directory systems, like Gopher and WAIS, and opened up creative variation with the development of MOSAIC web browser, a "textbook example of user-friendly, point-and-click software" (ibid., 30). The above illustrations do not exhaust the reasons that creative variations take place. After all, creativity turns variation into a source of constant, vast, and often unforeseen cognitive evolution possibilities.

[7] The Helsinki Final Act was a quid pro quo agreement between the West and the Soviet Union, according to which the West would accept the Soviets' post–World War II borders, and the Soviet Union would formally accept human rights norms. The Soviets did not suspect, however, that their token agreement to abide by human rights norms would end up mobilizing people and movements (Helsinki committees) across the Soviet empire in favor of human rights norms. The norms created a crisis of legitimacy for the Soviet Union and the entire Warsaw Pact, which eventually lead to "perestroika" and the end of the Cold War. Confidence-building practices promoted trust and enabled the dismantling of the hardware that the Cold War relied on. On human rights and the Helsinki Final Act, see Thomas 2001; on the CSCE, see Adler 1997, 1998.

9 Selective Retention

Epistemic Practical Selective Retention

Creative variation can make an existing social order stronger and more durable, or it can lead to instabilities that result in the evolution of social order. The phase transitions to a new order involve bifurcations close to intersubjective cognitive thresholds that, through positive feedback processes such as the case with the Helsinki Final Act and the end of the Cold War, can bring about a new social order, or in Prigogine's (1980) words, "order through fluctuations."[1] Whether communities of practice's trajectories and fluctuations bring about the evolution of social orders depends on selective-retention processes.

Selective retention is not an act of choice, let alone rational choice. It refers to processes by which the differential extinction or proliferation of communities of practice means also the differential extinction or, alternatively, the perpetuation of practices and the background knowledge that sustain them. One reason for not treating diffusion, selection, and institutionalization processes separately but as a single concept of selective retention, or *epistemic practical reproduction*, is that there is an intrinsic and synergetic relationship between these processes. Communities' vertical spread of practices and background knowledge, for example, is one way of selecting practices, but it also helps reproduce dispositions and expectations that "newcomers" learn to adopt. Institutions' diffusion, selection, and reproduction are the most visible set of processes, behind which lie deeper and more fundamental processes of practices' and knowledge's selective retention.

As Bockman and Eyal's fascinating study on the transnational roots of neoliberalism shows (2002, 311–14), what first might look like a diffusion process between Western "authors" of neoliberal ideas and passive

[1] Orlando Patterson refers to non-path-dependent positive feedback mechanisms that produce reproduction rather than change. He attributes this to what he calls "frequency dependent selection," bandwagon effects, or reinforcing expectations, where people disproportionally settle for a practice because of its frequency (2010, 144).

Eastern European "recipients" was also a selection process involving the emergence and enlargement of a pre–World War II *transnational network* of Western and Eastern European economists. The translation and alignment of this network's interests took place through the mobilization of "crucial new resources needed to reproduce it or to protect it from attacks" (ibid., 337; see also Latour 1987). During the Cold War period, this transnational network of economists "continued to be organized around attempts to connect the results obtained in the socialist laboratory with debates and struggles in Western economics" (ibid., 310). Thus, "the rapid adoption of neoliberalism in Eastern Europe after the fall of communism was simply another instance of this translation and alignment of interests" (ibid.). When we substitute transnational network for transnational community of practice, the more general takeaway is that it is not merely ideas or norms, as the institutionalization literature argues, that diffuse and become selected and institutionalized. Rather, by spreading across space and time via learning, translation, and alignment processes, the favorable selection of communities of practice takes place – their embedded practices and knowledge preferentially survive and become institutionalized.

Epistemic-Practical-Authority Selection Dynamics: Emergent Persistence, Regularity, and Change

Selection mechanisms explain both change and stability. As Patterson argues, we "need to study continuity, not only in its own right, but because a proper understanding of change itself is not possible without knowledge of the process of persistence against which it is measured and can only be properly understood" (2010, 149). For example, the creative variation of knowledge and practices that the evolution of new social orders triggers requires selective retention to remain metastable. But selective retention processes are necessary for one social order to replace another.

To the extent that practitioners enact their shared background knowledge over time, the propensity for the selection of communities of practice and their practices to politically survive increases. Selection is therefore active, and to some extent agential, not in the sense of a "rational choice" by practitioners, or as they consciously "follow rules," but as a result of practitioners' practical acts that, in and by practice, reproduce practices' and their background knowledge's authority.

Let's remind ourselves that by authority I do not mean merely social power that arises from iteration, competence, knowledge, and practices' legitimacy (Weber 1958), or power plus legitimate purpose (Ruggie

1982), although these factors play a role. Instead, I mean mainly epistemic practical authority: the capacity for practical meaning fixation or the structural and agential authoritative ascription of practical meaning to material and social reality to "stick," or to be authoritatively selected and retained.

Epistemic practical authority, which suggests the structural and agential capacity to reorganize social life, break new social ground, and offer previously unavailable modes of consciousness and discourse (Adler 2008, 203; Wuthnow 1989, 3), is the combined result of two types of social power and itself a cause of practices' selection and social orders' evolution.

Epistemic practical authority results first and primarily from deontic power (Searle 1995, 2010; see also Hall 2008, 9), which the community of practice confers on practices and their background knowledge,[2] and from performative power (Alexander 2011), which brings in audiences who affect practices' eventual capacity to be selectively retained. Based on collective intentionality, deontic power is the glue that keeps societies and social orders metastable. Because practices and knowledge's authority are really a process of becoming, longevity, reach (which is related to the spread of practices and knowledge), and the consent of stakeholders outside communities of practice are also important. In short, selection of communities of practice, survival of practices and background knowledge, and evolution of international social orders take place as a result of epistemic practical authority.

Epistemic practical authority is not located only in people's bodies and minds – it cannot mean merely knowing a justified belief or, as Zürn, Binder, and Ecker-Ehrhardt argue, "having special knowledge or moral expertise" (2012, 86). Instead, epistemic practical authority is intersubjectively located in communities of practice. The reason that practices and the background knowledge bound with them possess deontic power is easy to see: practicing or knowing in practice means competently acting because of status functions that a community of practice collectively creates, recognizes, and legitimizes. Knowing in communities of practice or, in Searle's (1995) words, possessing collective intentionality, invests practices and practitioners with status functions that rest on their collectively recognized normative power.

[2] Searle claims that humans can "impose functions on objects and people where the objects and the people cannot perform the functions solely in virtue of their physical structure. [The] performance of the function requires that there be a collectively recognized status that the person or object has, and it is only in virtue of that status that the person or object can perform the function in question" (2010, 7).

For example, human rights practitioners, nuclear-deterrence practitioners, and corporate practitioners, as well as their practices, remain selected over time because of the functions, status, rights, and obligations to which, as members of communities of practice, they become entitled. Deontic power involves practitioners' reciprocity in what their counterparts do, a commitment to get involved in future action because others commit as well, and often a need to justify each other's actions (Boltanski and Thévenot 2006). When, for example, Eastern European countries joined the EU after the end of the Cold War, their willingness to submit themselves to EU practices' epistemic practical authority was not because it rested on instrumental calculations nor because Eastern European countries were "following" norms. They submitted because the new practices (from an Eastern European perspective) created new status functions and normative entitlements whose authority was that of Eastern European practices, their background knowledge, and practitioners. This argument is consistent with Kathleen McNamara's (2015, 2) recent arguments that European symbols and practices constructed European political authority. However, legitimate political authority, understood as social control and compliance (Hurd 1999; McNamara 2015, 5), rests both on shared values, which therefore assure compliance, and on new practices, as performed and "governed" by practitioners.

The continuous selective retention of practices and their background knowledge depends on whether a sufficiently large number of members of a community of practice continue to recognize and accept the shared meanings on which such practices rely (Searle 1995, 117). As long as this occurs, practices become both "objective" and "exterior" – acts are "*objective* when they are potentially repeatable by other actors without changing the common understanding of the act, while acts are *exterior* when subjective understanding of acts is reconstructed as intersubjective understanding so that acts are seen as part of the external world" (Zucker 1977, 728). From this perspective, social order is not a goal pursued but an effect that occurs and a field of practices that continually becomes. But if deontic power diminishes because of endogenous processes within communities of practice, or because of exogenous factors, as was the case of the Soviet empire's collapse at the beginning of the 1990s (Searle 1995, 91–92), practices lose their epistemic practical authority and social order evolves: the configuration of practices that constitute it are replaced.

Epistemic practical authority is contingent on performativity. In other words, it depends on the capacity to present a dramatic and credible performance in front of local and global audiences (Alexander 2011, 89). Because practitioners' performances, including their competence, affect learning, negotiation, and contestation, and may strengthen or weaken the deontic power that keeps social orders together, performative power is part of the selection of communities of practice's dynamics, and of practices and background knowledge's effective retention. For instance, in corporate communities of practice, the performance of business school academics, consultants, and the business media influences their capacity to legitimize particular business practices. Performativity can also lead to disenchantment with practices, thus empowering alternative practices. The 2015 "Grexit" crisis showed that the capacity of neoliberal and left-wing economic communities of practice to negotiate "truly European" economic practices depended not only on material power, ideology, and economic knowledge but also on the performances of the most salient practitioners, like Angela Merkel and Alexis Tsipras, in front of their local, European, and global audiences.

The tension between identification and negotiability, or "between what is shared and what is contested" (Wenger 1998a, 207–8, 296), also plays a role in selection-retention processes. While sharing meanings and identity between individual practitioners and the communities of practice to which they belong inspires trust, "identification with a community makes one accountable to its regime of competence and thus vulnerable to its power plays . . . Short of the threat of violence, the efficacy of power depends on your degree of identification with communities and their practice" (Wenger 2010, 9). In other words, practitioners integrate themselves to a regime of accountability, to "what the community is about, to its open issues and challenges, to the qualities of relationships in the community [and] to the accumulated products of its history" (ibid., 6).

Accountability, in turn, as I mentioned in previous chapters, relates mainly, but not exclusively, to the horizontal dimension of power and social order. Because knowledge and competence are not equally distributed in communities of practice, and practitioners are accountable to political authority, organizational hierarchies, and bureaucratic regulations, communities' accountability regimes are also to some extent hierarchical.

However, it would be a mistake to think that the arrow goes exclusively from political and organizational authority to practitioners who are commonly taken merely as part of implementation or, at best, informal institutional processes. Rather, the arrow usually goes in the opposite direction. Institutions are reified practices, and organizations do what they do only because of the practices they bring together (Wenger 1998a, 243). Political and organizational authority, political interests, and organizational interests are what they are because practices and the background knowledge bound with them constituted them in the first place. Striving for the common good depends on material and organizational resources and formal rules and institutions (Zürn et al. 2012, 87). It is also primarily a function of practices' and practitioners' capacity to endow material (also digital) and social objects and rules with practical meanings and deontic power, which, because they have normative power that rests on communities' recognition, are seen as self-evident, and thus are not easily discarded. Practitioners learn about their "real" interests only as they are revealed in political campaigns, negotiations, bargaining situations, and collective action, all of which communities of practice helped inform. Interests and, more generally, collective understandings of the common good emerge as practitioners learn and negotiate meanings, justify their aptness to particular practical situations, and create powerful stories as the basis for engaging and controlling their social environment. For example, Internet organizations such as ICANN or the World Wide Web Consortium were constituted based on the tradition of a "communitarian approach to technology, as a way to learn and share" among peers and needed to be in order to be considered legitimate (Castells 2002, 33).

One should not discount the importance of controlling material and organizational resources for selection processes. Material and organizational resources come from the environment or as communities of practice spread horizontally. The EU, for example, was able to develop and perform its integrative practices by pooling material resources, reifying practices into supranational institutions, and developing organizations that became European integration's corporate practitioners. EU enlargement to the East also helped beef up EU organizational resources. However, as we witnessed in the last few years, integration-bound economic, security, social, and legal communities of practice have been challenged by countervailing practices embedded in nationalist, statist, ethnic, and even xenophobic communities of practice. The EU may achieve a dynamic balance of practices where opposite practices remain complementary, overlap, or even become dialectically symbiotic. Although this situation may not last for long, it could help keep the current European social order metastable for a while. Alternatively, the current contestation between European communities of practice could lead to the evolution of the current European order. This could happen particularly as a result of anchoring practices being challenged, such as European monetary union. One should interpret the 2015 crisis over the euro not only in light of economics and faulty institutions, but primarily as a reflection of a threat to European anchoring practices. If and when a threshold is crossed, and the European social order ends up evolving, it would be not primarily because of this or that crisis, but because of years of instability-creating variations, some of which are related to the EU's premature enactment of monetary union.

Technology has an impact on all the mechanisms I described in Chapters 6 and 7, but especially on endogenous changes in communities of practice, contestation between them, and the emergence of new institutions, organizations, and polities.[3] Take, for example, the international cyberspace social order. New technological developments like "the Internet of Things (IoT),"[4] is already transforming how people live, how business operates, the development of artificial intelligence (AI), national security, and day-to-day life. The interconnection of millions of devices without human involvement could represent a major asset for terrorists and cyberterrorists. The growth of networked devices, networked military operations, and demonstrations of these capabilities and vulnerabilities in prominent cyberattacks as far ranging as Estonia (2007), Georgia (2008), Israel's Operation Orchard against Syrian air defenses (2007), and the Stuxnet attack against Iranian nuclear facilities have spurred the creation of national cyber commands (Healey 2013; Stiennon 2015). Following these developments, we are witnessing the growth of supercomputing, machine learning, and AI along national lines and particularly in China with substantial R&D investments that promise to change the nature of cyberwarfare with "offensive and defensive AI algorithms doing battle" (King 2017; Knight 2017; Lee 2017). But the IoT also has the propensity to tightly interconnect the globe as a community. It will also likely spur the development of new organizations and institutions to manage and control it. For instance, the IoT, by helping connect medical doctors around the world and use AI to speed medical treatment, could help increase global health care and therefore well-being.

Relatedly, we should also consider the role of social and physical environments in the selection of communities of practice and in the corresponding survival of practices and background knowledge. By this I mean not as with natural evolution that the environment determines selection, but that environmental crises and other developments create propensities for change. They challenge agents to experiment with, and create, new practices. However, as in the case of cyberwarfare, practitioners do not always respond to challenges with experimentation and

[3] I thank Alena Drieschova for insisting that I highlight technology's role.

[4] "*The Internet of Things* (IoT) is a system of interrelated computing devices, mechanical and digital machines, objects, animals or people that are provided with unique identifiers and the ability to transfer data over a network without requiring human-to-human or human-to-computer interaction." http://internetofthingsagenda.techtarget.com/feature/Explained-What-is-the-Internet-of-Things.

innovation of practices or with action. The practices, the background knowledge bound with them, and communities of practice play the key role in cognitive evolution. Practitioners can play a role in, first, interpreting and discerning among environmental challenges and, second, purposively trying to affect the environment in ways that make their practices and knowledge more selectable. Social construction and context are decisive in shaping the success of environmental interventions.

Let's consider the role of physical and social environments in somewhat more detail as well as a few additional factors that could encourage communities of practice's selective retention. First, as I already mentioned, communities of practice are "dissipative structures" (Prigogine 1980) that "dissipate" to the environment meanings and practices considered to be destabilizing to the social order they sustain and, instead, borrow institutional, material, and symbolic resources from the environment to nurture their practices. This is why societies that are interested in modernizing import institutional resources and modern practices from abroad while they demystify and shun traditional and religious meanings and practices.

Second, building on what Robert Wuthnow referred to as the problem of articulation, agents do not only draw resources, insights, and inspiration from the environment, and do not only reflect on it, speak to it, and make themselves relevant to it. They also "remain autonomous enough for their social environment to acquire a broader, even universal and timeless appeal" (1989, 3). It is therefore up to practitioners to find the right balance of practices that can provide resilience to the social order from physical and social environmental shocks.

Third, innovations, which practices are based on, must be *reproducible* (Burns and Dietz 1992). Some social innovations, like human rights, may have little chance to be selectively retained in particular social environments, such as the wider Middle East today. Similarly, the EU's democratization and Copenhagen Criteria conditionality programs have little chance of replication in the Western Balkan candidate countries. On the other hand, corporate practices, such as corporations' legal personality and separation between ownership and management, are highly reproducible. The most dramatic growth in Internet usage and mobile device ownership is in the developing world (Deibert 2015). This reflects how participation in cyberspace is intuitive and local owing to cyberspace's plasticity as a platform for learning, development, and innovation.

Fourth, practices that are compatible with, or separable from, other practices are more selectable (Burns and Dietz 1992, 270). In other words, the clearer and more specified practices are, the more likely it is that people will adopt and reproduce them (Hirsch 2014, 815; Legro 1997, 34). The selection of open-network outcomes, such as TCP universal host protocols, LINUX, and the World Wide Web, occurred because they could be compatible with other Internet practices.

Fifth, timing plays a role in making practices more selectively retained. For example, there was only a very narrow political and symbolic window for the spread of democratic practices to the Middle East during the Arab Spring. When the window closed, selective retention of democratic practices there became unlikely, and the EU all but withdrew its aspirations for the long-term project of fostering a ring of democracy in the Middle East in favor of the immediate promise of autocratic stability.

Finally, there are environmental changes that practitioners may have a hard time controlling, for example, demographic trends, business cycles or economic fluctuations, epidemics, natural disasters, and unexpected wars. Even in such cases, however, the environment does not command practitioners, let alone determine how and what to practice, but rather defies and provokes them, and promotes experimentation with and innovation on how to overcome challenges. Because environmental events can have a measurable influence only as interpreted by practitioners, and based on their dispositions and expectations, practitioners will respond to social and physical environmental challenges differently. Thus, for example, it is indeterminate at what level of ecological catastrophe states would drastically change existing economic and environmental practices to bring about a new global environmental order. Said otherwise, it is not clear where the intersubjective threshold lies, but it is clear that it keeps moving. Ulrich Beck (2006, 2007, 2013), thinking about evolution toward a cosmopolitan Europe, argued that anticipating catastrophe may play a more transformational role than catastrophe itself. Whether it does or not depends on practitioners' willingness and ability to learn.

The Horizontal and Vertical Spread of Communities of Practice: Reach and Longevity

Through reproduction processes and mechanisms, practices become enacted in wider and different places and functional spaces such as organizations, bureaucracies, polities, and economic institutions. New practitioners who join existing communities of practice also begin to enact their practices, thus enabling their selective retention over time. According to cognitive scientists Philip Fernbach and Steven Sloman (2017), knowledge is not in our heads but shared: "Being part of a community of knowledge can make people feel as if they understand things they don't" (n.p.). With the expansion of practices that move hand-in-hand with intersubjective background understanding across space and time, chances grow that these practices will become selected and retained. More formally, practices and background knowledge are selectively retained with *horizontal* replication. Communities of practice expand across geographical space and organizations, and with *vertical* replication, pass on practices and background knowledge to their new practitioners. Horizontal and vertical replication in and by communities of practice take place structurally and are performed by agents.

The horizontal spread of practices and background knowledge occurs as they embed in communities of practice and in routines and public policies – for example, income tax policies that affect governments' legal systems, such as human rights law and universal suffrage – and simultaneously in individuals' dispositions and expectations. European integration, for example, enabled the establishment of new communities of practice that spread across existing and new institutions and organizations and geographical borders through integration practices and background knowledge (Adler 2010), thus engendering collective identities (Risse 2010) and creating novel communities of practice. Consumer groups, cultural fads, public intellectuals, cultural celebrities, customs, habits, rituals, and legal systems and innovation of public policies played a contextual role in the spread of European communities of practice.

Similarly, there was the steady expansion of corporation-oriented relations of production and the corporate order to areas that had previously fallen outside it, including those that were assumed to be core responsibilities of political communities and the state (defense and law enforcement) or that used to be conceptually allocated to different social orders or communities of practice (childcare, education). Emblematic of this spread, the corporate order was made possible by the state but came to dominate economic production to the point of constraining state action, leading to learning and adaptation as the creation of state-owned corporations or the adoption of corporate administrative practices by state bureaucracies. But we should be careful not to take the illustration too far. The corporation has not replaced the state. State and state-related communities of practice (legal, regulatory) were, and to a large extent still are, crucial to the support of the corporate order, whether by acting where the corporation has no interest or no capabilities to act (say, market failures) or by laying the institutional groundwork for the corporation (legal personality, protection of rights, law enforcement). Selective retention processes within and between all these communities of practice may shift the direction of the corporate order's expansion or even lead to its retraction.

Practices and background knowledge spread because communities of practice enable practitioners to learn together by sharing the way of doing things, thus acquiring collective identities that affect their dispositions and expectations. In other words, learning to do things together and sharing meanings across geographic and institutional or functional boundaries reproduces social structure and induces practical meaning fixation.

Because of legal norms' general obligational nature and deontic power, legal communities of practice nicely exemplify practices' epistemic spread and replication. According to Brunnée and Toope (2010, 2011a), legal authority rests on the practice of legality and its background knowledge, or criteria of legality, which they traced back to Lon Fuller's (1969) criteria. Carried and reproduced by and in communities of practice, through which law practitioners interact, the practice and criteria of legality account for the distinctive epistemic authority of law, including international law. The expectations about good and bad arguments of lawyers, who act as conduits of normative background knowledge, constitute legal communities of practice (Cohen 2015, 185, 193). Because legal communities of practice make claims in the name of law, this also helps mobilize and demobilize allies (Schotel 2013) and increases trust in the background knowledge behind legal practices.

Making a claim in the name of a collectively valuable practice, be it law, strategic stability, economic development, human rights, environmental protection, etc., rather than imitation or emulation (Börzel and Risse 2009; Nelson 2006, 88), as the common argument goes, facilitates communities of practice to spread their practices and background knowledge. *The more a claim in the name of a valuable practice, which is grounded on collective intentionality, is endowed with deontic power and performative power, thus with epistemic practical authority, the more the propensity for the horizontal spread of practices and background knowledge to take place.*

Political context is crucial for meaning negotiation and fixation within and between communities of practice, thus for practices' horizontal spread. The argument that practices spread because they "help solve problems" therefore makes sense only because "what works" is context-related and socially constructed through politics, learning, negotiation, and contestation within and between communities of practice. After the Cold War, for instance, NATO adopted CSCE's practices, such as partnerships, which became highly selectable because security and other experts credited them with helping redefine European security after the Cold War (Adler 2008). Not only were these practices highly context related, but Euro-Atlantic communities of practice also politically negotiated their "successful" status. Particularly after Russia ceased collaborating with NATO's security community expansion (Pouliot 2010), and other security threats such as international terrorism became salient, CSCE practices lost much of their highly selectable status. Likewise, the expansion of the European Order through the successive "big bang" enlargements in Central and Eastern Europe in 2004 and 2007 were dependent on the radical political shift away from a bipolar world international system. The horizontal spread of practices was wholly contingent on new political contexts but was made possible only because the communities of practice had the normative and epistemic weight of thirty years of European integration and the deontic power of European practices.

The current round of enlargement in the Western Balkans is arguably failing to produce similar democratic dividends precisely because the historical and political context is not about a thriving and successful EU, but a European order in crisis and facing significant competition from disassociation-related nationalist populist practices. The horizontal spread of practices through EU enlargement – which was and is still expected to make European practices highly selectable with the passage of time, and after recurrent crises, such as the 2015 potential Grexit, Syrian refugee, and the current Brexit crises – created challenges to their reproduction. The entrenchment of what, in a remarkable 2014 speech, Hungary's Viktor Orbán called "illiberal democracies," is premised on the rejection of fundamental European practices of rule of law, rights, and a free civil society.[5] Instead, both incumbents and serious challengers champion a more robust, exclusivist state based on "national foundations" (Ágh 2016). In his speech, Orbán cited the successes of China, Russia, and Turkey against the crisis-ridden EU. Ruling and contending parties from Poland and the Czech Republic have followed suit. Moves to curtail constitutional courts, free press, and universities and to strip minorities, migrants, and women of rights are not merely normatively worrying. These changes represent the potential for European practices' replacement in states whose accession into the European order was predicated on the prerequisites of membership laid out in the Copenhagen Criteria. More to the point, the Copenhagen Criteria codified Europe's normative anchoring practices *specifically for many of the Central and Eastern European states*, which are actively contesting their valence, arguing that the European order is unable to weather crises specifically because of its practices.

[5] Hungarian government, www.kormany.hu/en/the-prime-minister/the-prime-minister-s-speeches/prime-minister-viktor-orban-s-speech-at-the-25th-balvanyos-summer-free-university-and-student-camp.

In cyberspace, "what works" depends on where practitioners stand on cyberspace practices. Both cyberspace national-security-oriented communities of practice and global communities of practice take each other as part of the problem. While the spread of information controls in cyberspace as an anchoring practice is metastable, there are important variations in subordinate practices. What works for Chinese nationals to defend cyberspace cannot work for US or Canadian national security officials. There is an important difference between the use of the Great Firewall of China that censors content from users and the practice of collecting Internet metadata to monitor cyberspace by American and Western authorities (Lindsay 2015). They interpret the mass collection of metadata as a compromise that reasonably violates privacy, while still allowing intelligence services to monitor cyberspace (Hayden 2016).

After their emergence in the nineteenth century, corporate practices spread across geographical and functional borders like fire, partly because they helped to "solve problems" (they also created major problems) and partly because they were identified with increasing power and wealth. However, corporate practices' spread to global proportions (Ruggie 2017) was also associated with the creation of new negotiated and contested sources of identity and self-interest. Whether at the business office and the university or when flying, resting in a hotel, communicating through social media, and finding satisfaction in shopping at the corporate mall, these sources of identity "reinvented people" around the world as corporate practitioners.

Translation (Bockman and Eyal 2002, 314; Latour 1987, 108), as a practice and competence for devising *reinterpretations* of meanings and interests (that align with new practitioners across community of practice boundaries) is an important source of epistemic and practice fixation and spread. According to Orlando Patterson,

> a good part of the fascination with reinterpretation is that it can operate as a mechanism of both change and persistence, accommodation and contestation, and domination and counter-domination, depending very much on the perspective of the agents involved, the context in which the interpretation takes place and whether the issue is temporal connections in a single culture or lateral connections between different cultures. (2010, 146–47)

Dan Sperber (1996; see Patterson 2010, 145) argued that micro-variations in interpretation achieve macro-metastability by movement toward attractors.[6] Translation and reinterpretation thus help practices and background knowledge to settle around epistemic practical

[6] In any complex system, "attractors" are where dynamic states of flow eventually settle.

authority, which possesses deontic power. Translation practices can promote engagement – the coordination by communities of practice of multiple localities, competences, and viewpoints. Imagination, in turn, plays a role in conceiving new ways to translate practices across boundaries. Through alignment processes, translation practices also help empower some meanings over others; they establish a measure of hierarchy in communities' otherwise partly flat power structures.

Communities of practice have boundaries, and the fact that they often cut across institutional and organizational boundaries is closely associated with practices' and knowledge's propensities to spread and be selectively retained. As boundaries form around a practice, communities of practice develop synergisms with other communities of practice, thus producing a larger space for learning in community constellations (Wenger 1998a, 128–28), which then can spread across geographical and functional boundaries through institutions and organizations.

Different arrangements among communities of practice and their constellations are also important for the spread of practices and knowledge (Adler and Pouliot 2011a). For example, during the Cold War, the US nuclear-arms-control community (Adler 1992; Evangelista 1999) was hierarchically subordinated to a US community of nuclear-deterrence practice whose shared knowledge and practices spread to the Soviet Union, thereby promoting collective learning about how to prevent nuclear war across geographical and institutional boundaries. Communities of practice can also be complementary, such as security and economic communities engaged in wrestling with international terrorism across borders. Their shared engagement, imagination, and alignment help fix meanings about the nature of international terrorism to promote the spread of anti-terrorism practices across geographical and institutional boundaries. Economists and finance traders as communities of practice, who symbiotically depend on each other's knowledge and practices for the day-to-day conduct of financial transactions, facilitate their spread across the world. Similarly, complementarity in the form of public-private partnerships around critical infrastructure protection from cyberattacks (Deibert and Rohozinski 2010), or in developing surveillance dual-use technologies, has given rise to the "surveillance-industrial complex" (Ball and Snider 2013). To help clarify meanings about cyberwar's nature, international legal experts and military planners have shared engagement in the Tallinn Manual Process. Institutions, laws, plans, and public policies, through which power is projected toward stakeholders and nonpractitioners, also help create propensities for knowledge and practices to spread across geographical and functional borders.

The more congruence between communities of practice and organizations' boundaries, and the more knowledge and practice become entrenched in organizational rationalities and routines, the smoother the spread of practices across geographic and functional divides. As organizational bureaucrats adopt practices, they mobilize on behalf of the community of practice the organization's resources and technologies, reputation, and international legitimacy and, eventually, the practice's background knowledge. The dynamics of interorganizational relations plays a role in the alignment and translation of practices and knowledge. It helps create boundaries between communities of practice and may play a role in the negotiation and fixation of meanings within and between communities of practice, and in how communities of practice become reciprocally organized.

Communities of practice might belong to one organization, or they may have members in common in several organizations. The EU's institutions are a case in point. While there is significant bureaucratic competition within and between institutions over the function and competences, the "Brussels" space as a whole operates with the weight of a constellation of communities of practice, despite internal contestation over its meaning (Drieschova 2016). Regional proximity can promote the spread of practices and knowledge, as was the case in Eastern enlargement. However, as Ash Amin suggested, "organizational or *relational* proximity – achieved through communities of practice – may in reality be more important than geographical proximity" (Amin 2002, 393–94; Coe and Brunell 2003, 445). For instance, in the corporate social order, new "management ideas flow" across relational boundaries between consulting firms, celebrity managers and gurus, business schools, and management academics (Fincham and Clark 2009, 513; Starkey et al. 2004, 1524), and such flows may be as important as the geographical spread of practices between trading partners or inside the same trade group.

A post–Cold War constellation of Euro-Atlantic "cooperative security" communities of practice cut across international and supranational organizations, such as NATO, the European Community, and the OSCE. Although these organizations competed for resources and for playing the leading role in integrating Eastern and Central European countries and the former Soviet republics to Western institutions, the fact that the constellation of cooperative-security practices crossed organizational borders helped enlist organizational struggles on behalf of the temporary spread of cooperative-security practices. That said, the closer Russia identified cooperative-security practices with Western security institutions and their spread toward the East, the more it refused to engage, align, and imagine itself as belonging to the Euro-Atlantic security community (Pouliot 2010). Additionally, interorganizational competition, and different normative commitments of cooperative-security communities of practice, also became an obstacle for cooperative-security practices' horizontal spread (Lachmann n.d.). Likewise, in the open architecture of cyberspace, organizational and proprietary ownership sometimes slows the horizontal spread and retention of practices; the dramatic spread of computer networking was associated with open TCP host protocols, open-source operating systems like LINUX, and the World Wide Web (Castells 2002).

The spread of practices across geographical and functional boundaries can also involve people's movement from organization to organization, for example, from the World Bank to the International Monetary Fund, and from domestic organizations like a ministry of defense to international organizations like NATO and back. Similarly, there is often a close relationship between intelligence and defense officials and private contracting or consulting cybersecurity firms. While many former government employees will go on to lucrative careers in the private sector, "what most people don't realize is just the sheer scale of the intelligence workforce that is outsourced" (Rosenberg 2016). Edward Snowden and Harold Martin III, representing two of the biggest thefts of classified documents in US intelligence history, were contract employees from Booz Allen Hamilton. Similarly, there is a "revolving door" through which management gurus and academics can transition from business schools and academia to consultancy firms and vice versa (Fincham and Clark 2009, 513). The EU Commission's functioning is much the same. While civil servants' mandates are limited, they take with them the networks and lessons from previous postings and thus exercise significant power over policy-making (see Eppink 2007).

Because people perceive certain practices as a ticket for membership in prominent organizations, they adopt and pass them on to future practitioners. This was the case with the adoption of EU practices by Eastern and Central European countries immediately after the Cold War (Gheciu 2005). Through transactions in communities of practice, innovative practices sometimes produce emergent "focal points" around which future practitioners can converge. For example, practitioners constructed deterrence and arms control as focal points for strategic interaction during the Cold War (Adler and Pouliot 2011b). According to rational choice, expectations *converge around* focal points. For neoliberal institutionalists, institutions *are* focal points. Constructivists look at the *construction* of focal points by norms, identity, etc. According to evolutionary constructivism, however, focal points do not exist until practitioners dynamically create them through interaction, learning, negotiation, and contestation in and through practice.

Practices that are agreeable across a wide political spectrum can promote their spread and background knowledge. Practitioners might frame practices to appeal to both liberals and conservatives across state boundaries, thus promoting a broad political coalition on behalf of the practice. After the Cold War, for different reasons, both liberals and conservatives promoted NATO expansion to the East through cooperative-security measures. Such bypartisan support for NATO made it resilient to the point of withstanding President Donald Trump's early attempts to delegitimize it as being obsolete, until international events forced him to declare NATO was not obsolete anymore.[7]

Practices and knowledge sometimes spread because they advance practitioners' personal interests and careers, or because of their novelty and practitioners' familiarity with them. To a large part, the personal and career ambitions of the expanding European Commission's Directors General drive the practices' competences. Communities of practice's competences, however, are possible only through the shared background knowledge and agreement on the power of Europe's institutions. Practices' emotional and normative appeals can also be very important: an emotional appeal intends to elicit trust, which, in turn, helps achieve solidarity and cohesion inside and between communities of practice. Again, the expansion of the European order to the Central and Eastern European states after the Cold War relied on a common appeal of the region "returning to Europe." A normative appeal, by contrast, can become a source of epistemic practical authority, and so can consensual *scientific* knowledge background (Haas 1989, 1992), for example, on climate change or global pandemics. What expands in this latter case, however, is not an epistemic community that carries ideas but a community of practice that carries practices constituted by scientific background knowledge (Adler 2014).

When it comes to vertical replication in communities of practice, learning a new practice, and the knowledge bound with it, does not mean acquiring and possessing something in individuals' brains or minds, but rather is a process of social participation (see Lave and Wenger 1991, 29). Individuals enact knowledge, but it is "owned" by communities of practice. Because what matters most is what new practitioners learn in and through practice, social cognition emerges from, and evolves together, with practice. As practitioners enact their dispositions and

[7] "Trump Says NATO 'No Longer Obsolete,'" BBC News, April 12, 2017. Available at www.bbc.com/news/world-us-canada-39585029.

expectations, they spread their practical understandings to their communities' new practitioners.

The "induction" of new practitioners to communities of practice becomes a vehicle for the development and transformation of practitioners' identities. This means that, as Wenger so aptly put it, "there is no need for a separate mechanism, such as transmission, imitation or even internalization. Because practice is from the start a social process of negotiation and renegotiation, what makes the transitions between generations possible is already in the very nature of the practice" (1998a, 290). In other words, people do not join communities of practice the way they join a club or school. Instead, as practitioners learn a practice, in and through practice they adopt shared identities and background knowledge's dispositions and expectations, which are conducive to taking this practice as natural. The larger the number of members in communities of practice, and the more new practitioners adopt practices, the more practitioners possess dispositions and expectations that correspond to communities' background knowledge and practices. Negotiation and contestation about practices' meanings, particularly about competence, are also social forces that promote vertical replication in communities of practice. Because struggles within a community of practice may not lead to their demise but dialectically elicit consensus, contestation may actually work to strengthen practitioners' attachment to practices and so to the maintenance of a given social order.

For example, the pervasiveness of cyberspace in our everyday lives and how a global user community has suddenly come online suggests that for the vast majority of new users, the information and communications technologies on which cyberspace is based are taken as natural. Cyberspace is a landscape where ordinary and infinitely complex real-life social facts like friendship, money, and privacy are ontologically reproduced online (Brey 2014). This means that ordinary dispositions and expectations that we have about these social facts in real life carry over to cyberspace. Most ordinary users online act with expectations of privacy and take them for granted without considering the vast private and public infrastructure and intermediaries that communications must be routed through. What accounts for the dramatic expansion of the Internet and its applications is that the "timespan between the processes of learning by using and producing by using is extraordinarily shortened, with the result that we engage in a process of learning by producing, in a virtuous feedback between the diffusion of technology and its enhancement" (Castells 2002, 28). Learning by using and in turn producing by using open-source technology carries dispositions and expectations around openness that are taken as a natural foundation in the Internet community (Castells 2002).

The vertical spread of practices differs from socialization by highlighting neither social-psychological mechanisms (Johnston 2001) and ideas' internalization (Wendt 1999) nor persuasion, where newcomers are persuaded by oldtimers. Instead, newcomers learn practices and acquire the background knowledge associated with them through participation and transactions within and among communities of practice (see Gherardi 2009). Communities of practice are not just a place where learning takes place, but a social interactive medium where "situated and repeated actions create a context in which social relations among people, and between people and the material and cultural world, stabilize and become normatively sustained" (ibid., 523). Participation in communities of practice is emergent. Both knowledge and practices are reproduced or discarded through contingent and nonlinear creative variations and selective retention processes.

Institutionalization as Retention Processes

Institutionalization processes enrich selective retention. *Social institutions* are reified and metastable social practices. In contrast to practices, social institutions are "not strictly learned; they are enacted or performed" (Patterson 2010, 142). More specifically, they are social practices that incorporate established and prevalent social rules that constitute practitioners' dispositions and expectations, thus producing regular, albeit emergent, relational processes. Social institutions are simultaneously intersubjective and subjective. They manage practitioners' transactions and play a role in practices' spatial and functional dissemination (Hodgson 2006, 2; Kratochwil 2011, 42; Young 1989, 32). Designing institutions is important "but in the end it is practice that produces results" (Wenger 1998a, 243). More specifically, "institutions provide a repertoire of procedures, contracts, rules, processes, and policies, but communities must incorporate these institutional artifacts into their own practices in order to decide in specific situations what they mean in practice, when to comply with them and when to ignore them" (ibid., 245).

There is not a necessary sequence between practices and institutions. As Wenger argues, many communities of practice arise "in the process of giving existence to an institutional design[;] they may even owe their existence to the institutional context in which they arise" (ibid., 244). Even in these cases, it is not an institutional mandate that produces a practice but a community of practice (ibid.). Thus, both institutional design and practices are structuring sources. Organizations, in turn, are "the meeting of two sources of structure: the designed structure of the institution and the emergent structure of practice" (ibid., 244). In other words, "organizations are social designs oriented at practice." They "do what they can do, know what they know, and learn what they learn" through practice (ibid., 241).

Institutionalization is the process of reflexive reification of selectively retained practices and their background knowledge (ibid., 243). Institutionalization includes formal institutions and organizations, as well as public policies, standards, roles, laws, and bureaucratic procedures (ibid., 243). According to Wenger, "practice is where policies, procedures, authority relations, and other institutional structures become effective. Institutionalization in itself cannot make anything happen. Communities of practice are the locus of 'real work'" (ibid.). Through institutionalization, practices and background knowledge become both "objective" and "exterior" (Zucker 1977, 728).

From a cognitive evolutionary perspective, institutionalization means reproduction plus *inheritance* so it is not just one stage of selective retention but an emergent process of selective retention over time and space, which involves practices, background knowledge, and communities of practice. First, and foremost, institutionalization is a matter of degree. Second, because institutional and organizational categories do not define community of practice membership, and the boundaries between communities of practice, institutions, and formal organizations keep changing (Wenger 1998a, 119),[8] institutionalization means more than the persistence of formal institutions and organizations.

Third, we should refrain from reducing institutionalization to mental phenomena only, such as James Baldwin's notion of "ideas" becoming "part of a copy system" and "of the environment [of ideas] against which the new ideas of those living in that society are selected" (Richards 1987, 475, 477). While Mary Douglas (1986) introduced the useful notion, which I agree with, that institutions remain stable by gaining legitimacy so that they are distinctively grounded in nature and reason,[9] she perhaps went too far in arguing that the process of institution "naturalization" is only deposited in the "mind."[10] It resides also in practices.

[8] Actually, "communities of practice that bridge institutional boundaries are often critical to getting things done in the context of – and sometimes in spite of – bureaucratic rigidities" (Wenger 1998a, 119).

[9] An institution, said Douglas, affords "to its members a set of analogies with which to explore the world and with which to justify the naturalness and reasonableness of the institutionalized rules" (Douglas 1986, 112).

[10] In Douglas's own words "any institution then starts to control the memory of its members; it causes them to forget experiences incompatible with its righteous image, and it brings to their minds events which sustain the view of nature that is complementary to itself. It provides the categories of their thought, sets the terms for self-knowledge, and fixes identities" (ibid.).

Bourdieu (1977) replaced the reduction of reproduction plus inheritance to mind processes with a phenomenological perspective where reproduction takes place in the body and things. His "habitus concept does double duty, directly explaining cultural reproduction, which, in turn, explains 'the reproduction of structures'" (Bourdieu 1973, 71; Patterson 2010, 140). As I discussed in Chapter 4, however, Bourdieu's selective-retention mechanism is mostly about reproduction rather than change, and he neglected collective action in communities. With Bourdieu, I avoid a Cartesian ontology, like that of Giddens, who thought mental representations of material reality establish themselves as memory traces (Douglas 1986; Giddens 1984). While changes of individual practitioners' expectations and dispositions sustain changes of practices and intersubjective knowledge, as I have said, I take cognition as social phenomena (Fleck 1979; Vigotsky 1978). From a cognitive evolutionary perspective, practice means knowing, and knowing takes place in situated practices (Gherardi 2008, 523). This, in turn, means that knowledge's practical effect depends on how it intervenes and how practitioners perform and enact it (Douglas 1986; Fleck 1979; Hacking 1983). Practices, while embodied in physical "bodies" (Bourdieu 1977), are therefore not individually but collectively owned by communities of practice.

While with Douglas (1986), I suggest that institutionalization requires gaining legitimacy through a continuous process of naturalization, practitioners aim at naturalization not as a goal but as a process. Legitimacy is associated with practitioners' competence (Boltanki and Thévenot 2000, 215) and resides mainly in communities of practice where practitioners reproduce it through practice until it becomes built into the social order. Legitimacy depends on epistemic practical authority and deontic power. Institutionalization, or the selection of communities of practice and the survival of practices and background knowledge, therefore has less to do with efficiency, efficacy, truthfulness, and transhistorical and cultural reason than with knowledge and practices becoming authoritative (Goodwin 1978, 138–39). Take, for instance, the legitimacy of open-source software communities. It depends on the duties and obligations of everyone, from co-managers and contributors to technical excellence in support of community projects (Castells 2002). This means that practitioners view practices that support open sharing, access, and modification and redistribution as authoritative and legitimate in open-source communities. By contrast, practitioners view entrepreneurship practices used to develop proprietary and closed software epitomized by software giants, such as Microsoft and Apple, as betraying open-source commitments (Castells 2002, 47).

To summarize, practices are more likely to become institutionalized when, enacting their collective understandings, practitioners frame reality around epistemic practical authoritative meanings, help spread practices both horizontally and vertically, and gain control of the social support networks of politics, thus making it too difficult and costly for opponents to deconstruct their practices and background knowledge (Fuchs 1992). The institutionalization of practices requires that communities of practice withstand meanings, functions, and status that challenge the practices' existence. Contestation between communities of practice, in turn, requires institutional and material resources, the creation of constituencies and bureaucracies on behalf of the practice, and the formulation of public policies and the setting of legal systems that can help keep normative expectations metastable. When these processes take place, practices, communities of practice, background knowledge, and institutions align, and social orders are metastable. At this time, competing practices, communities of practice, background knowledge, and institutions may fail to bring about social order evolution.

Alternative Interpretations of Institutional Evolution

Many studies of the extant literatures on "old" and "new" institutionalism, some more explicitly than others, have invoked evolutionary concepts and mechanisms as metaphor, analogy, or "the real thing." While I have benefited from these studies in developing my concepts of creative variation and selective retention, I differentiate cognitive evolution theory from institutionalism studies. This subsection, therefore, aims less at reviewing some literatures than showing how their interpretation of institutional evolution sometimes accords with, but mostly differs from, mine.

Traditionally, the study of institutions focused on their enduring nature (Zucker 1977), thus marginalizing "the processes of conflict and innovation that are central to politics" (Clemens and Cook 1999, 442). From this perspective, otherwise known as "old institutionalism," change occurs only by exogenous shocks. Stephen Krasner (1984) expressed this understanding in evolutionary language when he likened the stable state of institutions (states) that were interspersed with exogenous sudden and dramatic changes to "punctuated equilibrium" evolutionary processes (Eldredge and Gould 1972). From this perspective, institutions are stable until disrupted (Clemens and Cook 1999, 447). Rational choice institutionalization clearly reflected this perspective by taking history as efficient and institutions as reaching equilibria "in which 'no one has the incentive to change his or her choice.' Consequently the only source of change is exogenous" (Levi 1997, 27; Lewis and Steinmo 2012, 323). More recently, rational choice institutionalism has posited an understanding of discontinuous institutional evolution (Weingast 2002, 692) and distinguided between endogenous and exogenous institutional reproduction and change (Greif and Laitin 2003; Streeck and Thelen 2005, 7). In IR, several studies (Donnelly 2012; Holsti 2016; Raymond 2011) traced sources of international-system change to institutions, although with no clear evolutionary theory in mind.

"New institutionalists," some of them called "sociological institutionalists," refuted these arguments and focused on both change and stability resulting from cultural and normative structures (DiMaggio and Powell, 1983, 1991; Meyer and Rowan 1977; Meyer and Scott 1983). Reflecting Martha Finnemore's (1996) advice not to overlook agency, this approach searched for the cognitive micro-foundations of stability, mainly cognitive "schemas" (DiMaggio and Powell 1991; Meyer and Rowen 1977) and ideas (Blyth 2002; Hall 1989; Hall and Soskice 2001). According to Meyer and Rowen, organizational forms "can be attributed not only to the complexity of 'relational networks' and exchange processes, but also to the existence of elaborated 'rational myths' or shared beliefs systems" (qtd. in Scott 1987, 497). With an emphasis on the diffusion of rules and practices across organizational fields and national boundaries, new institutionalists also began asking why different institutions become homologous or take similar forms. DiMaggio and Powell (1983, 1991) traced homology to emulation, new knowledge, and coercion mechanisms.

Overall, new institutionalist arguments about stability tacitly followed evolutionary imagery and analogies. Following an earlier lead by Berger and Luckman (1966, 54; Scott 1987, 495), who argued that institutionalization results from action being repeated over time and assigned shared meanings, Tolbert and Zucker (1996) argued that the perpetuation or retention of institutional forms is linked to the formalization of institutional procedures through "habituation, "objectification," and "sedimentation." Objectification requires consensus and actors taking institutions as a process in which a reality confronts the individual outside her- or himself. Sedimentation refers to processes that rest on historical structural continuity (Tolbert and Zucker 1996, 181–84).

For the most part, this literature pointed out how institutional change is incremental and endogenous and explained mainly by selection processes involving persuasion, learning, and socialization mechanisms. DiMaggio and Powell (1991; Beckert 2010, 615) argued that because institutional processes are never entirely coherent and complete, change in institutions is possible. As Clemens and Cook (1999) argued, we can explain institutional change by several mechanisms and processes, such as "mutability, or the loss of order," "internal contradictions," "multiplicity of institutions," and "collective learning." In all, endogenous change happens because of institutions' search for legitimacy. When it comes to explaining large institutional transformations, however, the literature points not only to exogenous challenges (drift, in evolutionary jargon) but also to changes of ideas (Blyth 2002) and narratives (Hay 1996). Fligstein and McAdam (2011, 2012), combining change and stability, suggest a contest between "incumbents" and "challengers" that takes place in "strategic action fields." Exogenous shocks can then lead to crises and ruptures that jumpstart episodes of contestation between incumbents and challengers, in turn, and either transform institutional fields or keep them stable.

"Historical institutionalism" (Carruthers 1996; Hall and Soskice 2001; Steinmo 2010; Streeck and Thelen 2005; Thelen 2004), which focuses "on long periods of time, variation and stability in institutional practice, and the 'heritability' of institutional structures across generations … has a particularly strong elective affinity for evolutionary theory" (Lustick 2011, 3). What distinguishes this institutional tradition from others is its commitment to the temporality of politics (Fioretos et al. 2016) – the assumption that preferences derive from endogenous historical processes rather than from static rational conditions or solely from "schemas" and beliefs supported by selection mechanisms, such as mimicry and coercion (Thelen and Steinmo 1992).

One of this tradition's first arguments, which reasoned by analogy from "punctuated equilibrium," was that change occurs at "critical junctures" followed by positive feedback or "reproduction" processes that reinforce change along the same path (Collier and Collier 1991; Fioretos et al. 2016). This approach was supported by the concept of institutional path dependence (David 1985), which Mahoney defined as "historical sequences in which contingent events set into motion institutional patterns or event chains that have deterministic properties" (2000, 507–8). Path dependence requires tracing institutional evolution to a self-reinforcing sequence of events, which we can find in early historical events that have disproportionate effects on later events (Pierson 2000, 74–77).[11]

[11] Among the path-dependent mechanisms, we can mention locking in power balances over time, the creation of new stakeholders who support extant institutional arrangements, and the self-reinforcing qualities of institutions as they engage with other institutions (Page 2006; Pierson 2004). Also relevant are "a steady increase in returns relative to once-feasible alternatives" (Fioretos 2011, 377) and the notion that ideas embedded in institutions "protect" institutions from being "invaded" by other ideas (Berman 2006).

Dissatisfied, however, with this literature's path-dependence deterministic arguments and the overall emphasis on stability rather than change, historical institutionalists (Shreeck and Thelen 2005; Thelen 2004) developed endogenous theories of incremental evolution, paying particular attention to dynamics caused by institutional logics (Beckert 2010, 615). For example, Thelen refers to "layering" – "the grafting of new elements onto an otherwise stable institutional framework" (Thelen 2004, 35) and "conversion" – "the adoption of new goals or the incorporations of new groups into the coalitions on which institutions are founded" (ibid., 36). Streeck and Thelen (2005; see also Mahoney and Thelen 2010) also refer to "displacement" – new institutional models that call into question the taken-for-granted qualities of previous institutional models – "drift," the ongoing reset of institutions in response to environmental changes, and "exhaustion," or institutional breakdown. Key to understanding Thelen's evolutionary institutional perspective is that "changes in the political coalitions on which institutions rest are what drive changes in the form institutions take and the functions they perform in politics and society" (2004, 31).

Comparative politics and IR literatures on international diffusion (Bennett 1988; Börzel and Risse 2009; Gilardi 2005; Jordana and Levi-Faur 2005; Simmons and Elkins 2004; Way 2005) and on policy convergence (Bennett 1991; Busch and Jörgens 2005b; Dolowitz and Marsh 2000; Drezner 2001) enhance our understanding of institutional evolution. Diffusion is "any process where prior adoption of a trait or practice in a population alters the probability of adoption for remaining non-adopters" (Strang 1991, 325). Policy convergence, on the other hand, refers to "the tendency of policies to grow more alike, in the form of increasing similarity in structure, processes, and performances" (Drezner 2001, 53). These literatures identify the agents of diffusion mainly as governments, epistemic communities (Adler 1992; Haas 1992a), think tanks, NGOs (Stone 2000), networks (Keck and Sikkink 1998), international organizations (Finnemore 1996; Jacoby 2001), and supranational organizations (Börzel and Risse 2007). Diffusion theory has been applied to policies (Dolowitz and Marsh 2000; Weyland 2007), institutions (Ramirez et al. 1997), regulatory practices (Radaelli 2004), organizations (Jordana, Levi-Faur, and Marin 2011), democracy (Gleditsch and Ward 2006; Starr 1991; Weyland 2009, 2010), international elections practices (Kelley 2008), suicide terrorism (Horowitz 2010), and integration practices and institutions (Börzel and Risse 2007).

Most importantly from an evolutionary perspective, the diffusion literature identified a relatively large number of mechanisms involved in diffusion processes, for example, costs and benefit calculations

(Simmons and Elkins 2004), regulatory competition (Scharpf 1997; Vogel 1977), public policies (Dobbin et al. 2007), international harmonization (Holzinger and Knill 2005), and coercion (Börzel and Risse 2012a; Busch and Jörgens 2005b). The policy-convergence literature also suggests the influence of domestic structures (Cowles et al. 2001; Solingen 2012). Social psychological explanations stress mimicking or emulation (Acharya and Johnston 2007; Bennett 1988; Börzel and Van Hüllen 2015), transnational communication (Holzinger and Knill 2005), persuasion (Börzel and Risse 2012a) and social influences, such as shaming and back-patting (Johnston 2001). Cultural mechanisms include the internalization of legitimized collective knowledge (Wendt 1999), ideational competition (Finnemore and Sikkink 1998), norm localization (or the process by which local recipients of norms reconstruct them to fit their own norms and local understandings) (Acharya 2004), learning (Hall 1993; Meseguer 2009; Stone 2000; Weyland 2004), and epistemic communities' construction of social reality (Adler 1992; Haas 1992a). The English School refers to diffusion as the expansion of international society (Buzan 2005), for example, by means of normative understandings of rights (Reus-Smit 2013a).

Unlike these literatures, Lewis and Steinmo (2012) and Lustick (2011) explicitly used Darwin's natural evolution theory to explain institutional evolution. For Lewis and Steinmo (2012; see also Blyth et al., 2011), the key unit of comparison is genes and institutions. Variation relies on three sources: genetics, decision-making malleability resulting from preference complexity, and the iterated interactions of agents with institutions and environments. Multilevel selection refers to governments' choices about institutional rules and decision-makers' interaction with their environment. Replication, which environmental selection partly determines, operates through internalization of ideas and cognitive schemas (Lewis and Steinmo 2012, 336). "Generalized Darwinism," therefore, with the addition of a nonequilibrium approach, "provide[s] a broad theoretical framework that integrates the study of cognition, ideas and decision-making with other literatures that focus on institutional change and human evolution" (ibid., 314)

Approaching institutional evolution as moving between similarity and identity, Lustick (2011; see also Ma 2016, 10) takes species and institutions as the unity of comparison. In Lustick's view, institutions are species, so applying Darwinian evolution to political science comes "naturally" and can greatly enhance our understanding of politics. In response to historical institutionalism's overemphasis on path dependence, Lustick recommends incorporating "mutation" or "sudden changes in variation arising from factors flying below the analytic horizon," for example, the meteoric rise of great leaders – and "genetic drift" – "fluctuations in the retention of information about the past associated with exogenous impacts" (2011, 24), for example, a plague.

In contrast to the literatures reviewed here, cognitive evolution theory refers to the evolution of social orders, including international social orders, rather than of institutions or organizations. Moreover, the structural "stuff" that is passed preferentially are not institutional forms or individual cognitions, but practices and intersubjective knowledge bound with them. I do not invoke by analogy, homology, and metaphor (Ma 2016) Darwin's evolutionary theory or "generalized Darwinism," but suggest a novel way to understand sociocultural evolution, which relies on the concept of evolutionary epistemology. Rational-choice institutionalism's assumptions are opposite to cognitive evolution's ontology, epistemology, and theoretical mechanisms. While game-theory modeling, based on crude Darwinian analogies of natural selection (Axelrod 1984), might help explain cooperation, it cannot explain the evolution and metastability of international social orders.

New institutionalism focuses primarily on reproduction and institutional stability and suffers from a Cartesian division between social and mental or cognitive phenomena. While DiMaggio and Powell (1983, 1991) gave an important impetus to the concept of networks, the concept refers mostly to information transmission, rather than to knowledge and practices. DiMaggio and Powell (1983, 1991) also refrain from bringing up community and power. New institutionalists lack a theory of how institutional fields and communities (of practice) emerge and are transformed. While the literature alludes to "entrepreneurs," it lacks a theory of active agency and places practices on the back burner (Fligstein and McAdam 2011, 21).

While the historical-institutionalist literature contributes to understanding evolutionary processes, it remains strongly committed to a rationalist and materialist power perspective and to arguments that past attachments and prospective opportunities guide actors (Fioretos 2011, 372). Institutions' importance lies in creating constraints and opportunities, and selection takes place mainly through changes in domestic political coalitions. This literature's ontology, thus, is closer to "being" than to "becoming." Second, the literature is also methodologically individualist, thus also dualist in nature. Third, when invoking meaning, the literature deals mainly with the role of "ideas," "policy paradigms," and cognitive frames. It therefore avoids notions of collective meaning and collective learning. Fourth, the historical-institutionalist literature argues that increasing returns capture only institutional reproduction (Thelen 2004, 293). So it ignores the complexity-theory-based notion that increasing returns are about nonlinear change and positive feedback. Finally, as Lustick (2011) rightly pointed out, the literature lacks emphasis on historical contingencies.

Lewis and Steinmo (2012) and Lustick (2011) make a strong effort to remain faithful to Darwin's theory. Lewis and Steinmo's (2012) suggestions, for instance, about variation being either genetically or cognitively (read naturally) determined, are closely related to the naturalist version of evolutionary epistemology, which I avoid. They suggest a rationalist understanding of selection that takes place through decision-makers' and environmental "choices," ontological dualism, and retention as "internalization" of ideas. I doubt that Darwinian natural evolution mechanisms like natural selection increase our understanding of the social and political world. Darwin's genius consisted in uncovering a general epistemological principle of change and stability, which he applied to the natural world. But as I have insisted, this epistemological principle does not mean that the same mechanisms that apply to the natural world also apply to the social world.

Selective Retention through "Homeorhesis" and "Resilience"

I end this chapter with an exercise[12] that juxtaposes the propensity of social orders to remain in a stable flow ("homeorhesis") and communities of practice's resilience to withstanding exogenous and endogenous shocks. The exercise can tell us something important about selective retention. It does not aim to predict, but to heuristically enhance our understanding of the propensities for social orders' metastability and evolution.

Homeorhesis, a concept coined by C. H. Waddington (1977, 105, 115–16), means a return to a stable flow or trajectory. It suggests an alternative to "homeostasis," which means a return to equilibrium. More specifically, homeorhesis means that a time-expanded course of change is maintained constant. Disturbances, in our case, countervailing processes, that put at risk the continuous selection of communities of practice and endanger the survival of their practices and background knowledge, do not work by returning the situation to where it was when disturbed (homeostasis). They work by returning to a changing but metastable trajectory (Jantsch 1975, 92). From a cognitive-evolutionary perspective, homeorhesis means that communities of practice cope with

[12] I build partly on Adler 2005, chapter 2.

endogenous and exogenous changes by maintaining a stable set of flows. We can therefore take homeorhesis as an alternative to "adaptation," a widely used concept in evolutionary thinking, especially inspired by Lamarck's evolutionary theory, as I discussed in Chapter 3.

Resilience is the measure of an order's "ability" to absorb change-driving variables and parameters and survive (Holling 1976, 73–92). The concept of resilience, which has attracted attention in recent years (Brand and Jax 2007; Lentzos and Rose 2009; Walklate et al. 2014), is fuzzy and contested. I take a common-sense sociological reading of resilience, which Adger defined as the "ability of groups and communities to cope with external stress and disturbances as a result of social political and environmental change" (2000, 347; see also Walklate et al. 2012, 190). From a cognitive evolutionary perspective, resilience is what enables social orders, and the practices that constitute them, to withstand exogenous *and endogenous* shocks and dynamically persist in time. Resilience does not prevent changes – it actually may encourage them. However, it might also prevent fluctuations from reaching a threshold, tipping, and bringing about social order evolution. As we saw earlier, the main factors that provide practices their resilience is their epistemic practical authority, their horizontal and vertical spread, and the agential competence to change the environment to make practices more selectable.

When high homeorhesis and high resilience characterize the state of affairs, social order remains metastable (see Figure 1, box 1). In the EU case, this was the situation right after the 1992 Maastricht treaty. Practices' fluctuations remained on a stable trajectory, and while the EU experimented with new integration practices, their resilience was high. Consequently, a stable flow of change characterized the EU social order.

When circumstances depict low homeorhesis and low resilience, the propensity for fluctuations to reach an intersubjective threshold and for the social order to tip and evolve (box 4) is very high. The EU is not there yet, but it has been close to the tipping point in recent years.

Box 3 reflects a situation where despite low homeorhesis (high unstable fluctuations), there is still a possibility of preserving social order metastable through practices' resilience. This is where the EU is now confronting a critical mass of crises. Low homeorhesis resulted from the magnified threat of Greece's exit from the Eurozone, Great Britain's decision to exit from the EU, and expectations that other EU members, such as Italy, will also leave. It also resulted from the Syrian refugee crisis's challenge to European norms, solidarity, and migration and border practices; from Eastern and Central European countries, especially Hungary and Poland, taking an illiberal turn; and from President

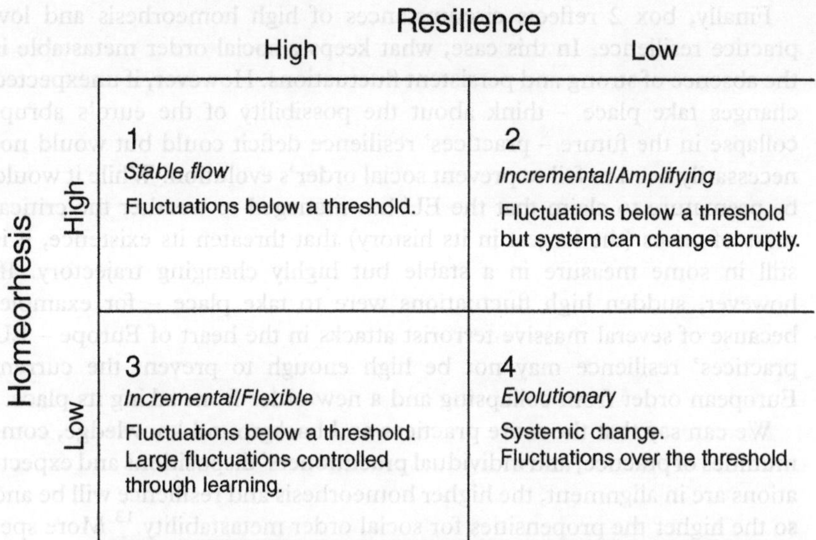

Figure 1. "Homeorhesis" and "Resilience": A Heuristic Exercise

Trump's challenge to EU practices and formal institutions. But EU practices and institutions have been resilient to withstanding the crises for now. While the countervailing pressures on the current European social order have been increasing steadily, the EU has not disintegrated, its practices are still in place (albeit with some large fluctuations), and the normative background knowledge that constitutes EU practices, while weakened, has not disappeared. The normative "glue" and solidarity that helped sustain European practices and institutions has weakened, but it has not entirely faded, and may be on the increase now because of intra-European and external challenges to European integration and European practices. It also received a "shot" of European optimism with the election of Emmanuel Macron in France, rather than Marine Le Pen, and of his understanding with Angela Merkel, Germany's chancellor, that European integration needs strengthening.

Perhaps with the exception of Hungary, racists (still) do not rule in Europe. Although they may rule in the near future, for now, illiberal democracy is considered objectionable, both on the left and to a substantial part of the liberal center right, for example, Angela Merkel. Europeans continue to practice peaceful change, and the rule of law and human rights still constitute EU practices and institutions. With the exception of Hungary, Poland, and Italy, the replacement of EU liberal internationalist practices with strong nationalist illiberal practices has still not occurred.

Finally, box 2 reflects circumstances of high homeorhesis and low practice resilience. In this case, what keeps a social order metastable is the absence of strong and persistent fluctuations. However, if unexpected changes take place – think about the possibility of the euro's abrupt collapse in the future – practices' resilience deficit could but would not necessarily need to fail to prevent social order's evolution. While it would be premature to claim that the EU has managed to weather the critical mass of crises (the largest in its history) that threaten its existence, it is still in some measure in a stable but highly changing trajectory. If, however, sudden high fluctuations were to take place – for example, because of several massive terrorist attacks in the heart of Europe – EU practices' resilience may not be high enough to prevent the current European order from collapsing and a new order from taking its place.

We can say that the more practices and background knowledge, communities of practice, and individual practitioners' dispositions and expectations are in alignment, the higher homeorhesis and resilience will be and so the higher the propensities for social order metastability.[13] More specifically, the propensity for metastability may increase given the following conditions. (1) Community-of-practice members possess high levels of engagement, imagination, and alignment, thus, strong shared identities and commitment to their practice and background knowledge. There are, therefore, no salient gaps between communities of practice and practitioners' dispositions and expectations.[14] (2) Practitioners' dispositions and expectations align with institutional and organizational practices and interests. (3) Practices and background knowledge result in strongly reified institutions, and institutional and organizational practices and interests correspond with communities' practices and background knowledge. (4) Clearly bounded practices, and the communities of practice that serve as their vehicle, constitute social orders. (5) Institutional and organizational practices and interests strengthen social orders. Obviously, the lower the alignment of these factors, the higher the propensities for social order evolution. See Figure 1.

[13] I was inspired for this argument by Beckert 2010.

[14] This argument differs from Bourdieu's concept of "hysteresis" (2000, 161; see also Pouliot 2010) where there is a gap between field and habitus.

10 Better Practices and Bounded Progress

> The birth of a new fact is always a wonderful thing to experience. It's dualistically called a "discovery" because of the presumption that it has an existence independent of anyone's awareness of it. When it comes along, it always has, at first, a low value. Then, depending on the value-looseness of the observer and the political quality of the act, its value increases, either slowly or rapidly, or the value wanes and the fact disappears. (Pirsig 1974, 280)

What follows is an intellectual experiment, a tentative venture into normative theorizing that international relations so sorely needs (Price 2008). In a more formal sense, it is a plausibility probe like the one Harry Eckstein suggested:

> At a minimum a plausibility probe into theory may simply attempt to establish that a theoretical construct is worth considering at all . . . Some ways of surmising the plausibility of a theory beyond that minimal point are nonempirical, and since they entail only the cost of thought, these should generally be used before, or instead of, empirical probes. (1991, 148)

I engage in this minimum plausibility probe with epistemic humility – normative theory has not been my research's main focus in the past. Because I am mindful that analytical evolutionary constructivism and cognitive evolution theory can and should open a door into practice-based and social-order-oriented world politics ethics,[1] I genuinely look forward to critical engagement with this probe and, with much anticipation, to future theorizing and empirical research. The analytical aspect of cognitive evolution theory explains how and why background knowledge, practices, and communities of practice purchase normative value. Both learning and deontic power – along with performative power, engagement, alignment, and imagination processes in communities of practice – play a major role.

[1] I thank Christian Reus-Smit, for encouraging me to go in this direction, and Charles Beitz, who, without him knowing, taught me much of what I know about international political theory.

As I suggested in Chapter 4, cognitive evolution theory claims that all practices are normative (see also, for example, Boltanski and Thévenot 2006; Büger and Gadinger 2015; Gadinger 2017; Kratochwil 1989; MacIntyre 1981; Nicolini 2012; Pouliot 2017; Rouse 2007). In this chapter, I build on that claim to develop a second, normative, middle-ground, theoretical perspective that transcends classic dichotomies such as practice approaches and normative approaches, "communitarianism" and "cosmopolitanism," transcendental and immanent values, the Enlightenment idea of progress and normative relativism, practice and discourse, and interconnectedness and disassociation.[2]

The normative middle ground involves identifying some practices as the repositories of ethical collective knowledge that are contained in, and spread by, communities of practice. *However, not all practices' normativity is necessarily ethical.* Rather, ethical normativity emerges and establishes itself when "common humanity" values (Stuurman 2017, 9), as part of background knowledge, constitute, and are constituted by, practices through transaction political processes – including negotiation, learning, contestation, and experimentation – in communities of practice.

Normative ethical values are immanent to practices, their background knowledge, and communities of practice. They have the *propensity* – however contingent, context-oriented, and reversible – to become universal when, dependent on and performed in practice (Raz 2003), communities of practice carry them to the global level. So while I do not buy into the notion of transcendental values (Kant 1998), ethical values still have the propensity to cognitively evolve and to become universal and, actually, they should. They therefore *appear* to be transcendental. My normative ethical theory thus overcomes the dichotomy between transcendental values and relativism (Raz 2003). It examines whether the common humanity value, which I identify as constituting *better practices* and *bounded progress*, may become transcendental.

Common humanity is "external" to practices only in the sense of being a worthy value that I associate with "better practices," "better social orders," and "bounded progress." Like Christine Korsgaard (1996, 2003), I believe that "all value depends on the value of humanity" (2003, 121). But in contrast to her I do not argue that values rest on human nature – they rest on the emergence and evolution of practices of common humanity. Thus, in my view, the fact that humans have naturally evolved to possess reflexive consciousness is secondary to the fact that humans have the propensity to value someone else's life as we value

[2] For my argument about constructivism as an analytical theoretical middle ground, see Adler 1997.

our own (Korsgaard 1996, 121). Common humanity values are immanent to practice, particularly to its background knowledge, and to communities of practice, where they are learned, and through which practice spreads. I mean this not only in the sense that a worthy value emerged through and in practice, with which a Kantian would agree[3] but still consider values as transcendental. Rather, also in the sense that "the existence of value depends on the *existence* of sustaining practices" (Raz 2003, 21) and their background knowledge.[4] In other words, the value of common humanity can persist and travel through history only because it is bounded ontologically with practice as part of its background knowledge. Later I explain the importance of the collective validity of what we consider knowledge, on which a "common-sense reality" (Ezrahi 2012, 106) is based, which I refer to as *epistemological security*. Without it, normative ethical principles cannot evolve and better practices and bounded progress become a chimera.

Considering better practices as acknowledging our common humanity highlights a distinctive liberal humanist, yet also realist approach to progress in international relations (Adler 1991). It's humanist because it takes values such as human life – and by extension, liberty, equality, and peaceful change – as reflecting our common humanity. And it is realist because it takes bounded progress as based on the evolution away from these values' antithesis: less domination, less poverty, and less violence, atrocities, and war. I use the word *realist* because better practices need not be those aimed at creating a global community, but only those that involve empathy (Crawford 1991, 456–58) with people beyond their own (national, religious, ethnic, etc.) identities and communities.[5]

Bounded progress is neither deterministic, unconditional, and teleological – a concept of progress usually associated with the Enlightenment idea of progress (Pinker 2018) – nor relativist, as in anything goes, or as in "good" is whatever I say it is. It does not follow from my approach that, as some notions of natural evolution argue, species necessarily evolve toward higher complexity and betterment or that, as the enlightenment idea of progress claimed, knowledge, justice, peace, and human

[3] I thank Reus-Smit for this observation.

[4] I disagree with Raz (2003, 21) that practices need not persist as long as the value does. While some of the original practices may disappear, people need practices to sustain values.

[5] Later I explain how a humanist-realist progress perspective differs from Linklater's notion of progress as a civilizing process defined as the avoidance of serious harm between political communities. Linklater's major works on civilizing progress and IR (2011, 2017), based on Elias's monumental sociology (2000), are two of only a few and the best works in IR on the subject of progress.

welfare advance together toward nirvana. The principle of practitioners' recognition of a common humanity is historically, culturally, and materially contingent and reversible. The recent shift from the liberal "end of history" (Fukuyama 1989) toward illiberal, historically identifiable, populist authoritarian regimes in former liberal democracies clearly shows this. The common humanity principle also rests on human epistemic and practical competence and practitioners' human willingness to experiment, create, and learn to control the negative effects of these environments (Frega 2012; Will 1997).

Exploring whether, how, and why some practices become better than others transcends the dichotomy between a classic cosmopolitan approach that places ethical standards exclusively in individual human reason (Beitz 1979; Rawls 1971) and a classic communitarian approach (MacIntyre 1981; Taylor 1985; Walzer 1990) that takes political community as the source of ethical standards (see also Morrice 2000). Resting ethical standards and the concepts I have mentioned on practices and communities of practice evokes the communitarian nature of my approach (see also Adler 2005).[6] My emphasis on "common humanity" as the basis of better practices, however, creates the propensity, even if unapparent now, that a few humanist practices, which develop in communities of practice, may become universally socially constructed.

Suggesting a normative theory that some better practices might expand to the global level via communities of practice means that cosmopolitans and communitarians alike can rely on cognitive evolution theory to examine practices and the trajectories of communities of practice. Cosmopolitan liberals might still argue that all cultures can, or eventually will, be steered to converge on a global community, so showing how communities of practice and their values, norms, and ethical standards evolve is of great significance. The empirical fact of a resurgent disassociation and reactionary right in so many bastions of liberal democracy adds impetus to the critical point that liberal democracies contain within them certain anti-liberal traps, meaning that their evolutionary possibilities matter in this debate.[7]

My normative ethical theoretical argument rests on what I call a practice principle. It differs from Jürgen Habermas's (1996) "discourse

[6] Communities of practice may be an ethical agent because through alignment, imagination, and engagement they can acquire collective moral responsibility. On the indirect moral responsibility of collectives, see Erskine 2003.

[7] I thank Simon Pratt for helping me see this point.

principle" (Bohman 2014), according to which the normative imperative of overcoming domination relies on a discourse where everyone is making a good-faith attempt to evaluate claims based on reason rather than self-interest. A normative directive is justified when it is consistent with the standards of discourse rightness or validity used by those involved. We should not, however, conceive of the two principles – practice and communication – in dichotomous ways. While Habermas treats communicative action as essentially distinct because of its embrace of truth seeking rather than of means–ends strategizing, I do not attribute it to, and classify practice into, essential characteristics. Communication and truth seeking are part of a wide range of practices that also have instrumental or strategic qualities. Truth seeking, in fact, is a better practice. Ultimately, Habermas is engaged in a Kantian project of transcendental and imperative values reasoning about special kinds of action, whereas I am engaged in a practical project of teasing out how all practice carries within it, as an empirically observable fact as well as a conceptual necessity, the potential for normative recognition (acknowledgment) and negotiation (democracy). Considering democracy as a better political practice than its alternatives, I regard the concept of "practical democracy" to be more comprehensive than Habermas's (1996) concept of "deliberative democracy." While the former, based on a common humanity, rests on experimental practices to match individual and collective interests, the latter rests on Habermas's discourse principle and transcendental normative theory.

Finally, while I have argued that bounded progress in international relations is associated with informal horizontal systems of rule (social power and accountability) and the politics associated with them – which, in turn, are more associated with interconnectedness, as the cyberspace case well exemplifies – interconnectedness can also be associated with harm (Linklater 2011). Nor do I take interconnectedness and disassociation as a dichotomy. Instead, I locate different, multiple, and sometimes overlapping international social orders on a spectrum, which is why some international social orders may be more progressive than others, and why it would be unproductive to refer to one globally progressive international social order.

In the rest of the chapter, I develop further the argument that ethics is located in practices' background knowledge. Then I explore the concepts of better practices, bounded progress, and humanist realism. Finally, I consider the concept of epistemological security as a condition for better international social orders and illustrate this with the concept of practical democracy.

Practice as the Source of Ethical Normativity

Normativity and Ethics

Normativity must not necessarily include better practices; performing a practice correctly makes it normative, but not necessarily ethical or moral. Better practices, from a humanist-realist perspective, are those that carry in their background knowledge constitutive ethical values about common humanity's worth and they are emergent in practice. In other words, practice (and practitioners) are makers of ethical values (see also Frega 2017; Frost 2003, 2009a, 2009b; Will 1997). For several centuries scholars debated whether organized slavery ended because of normative reasons (Crawford 2002, 167; Quirk 2011) or economic efficiency reasons (Williams 1944).[8] The practice of organized slavery slowly ended first in Western Europe and later in the rest of the world when, empowered by ethical values via transactions, including learning, contestation, and experimentation in communities of practice, slavery practices lost their deontic power and anti-slavery practices acquired epistemic practical authority. This empowered practitioners to overcome slavery's legitimacy and political resistance to abolition, which endured beyond the notion that, as Adam Smith argued (1981 [1776]; see especially Weingast 2016), slavery became highly economically inefficient.

The practice of organized anti-slavery slowly became universal neither because of the influence of civilizing, enlightenment, and humanitarian ideas through a rational choice mechanism (Pinker 2011) nor because individuals around the world turned into a community of discourse free of domination (Habermas 1984). Rather, practitioners in the communities of practice that *politically* sustained slavery learned in and through practice and political processes to endow all individuals with a common humanity status – to exempt individuals' statuses and functions from domination.

Background-knowledge-based values empower practices by endowing them with deontic power, that is, functions, statuses, and duties that they would not have otherwise. Performative power, subsequently, helps better practices to maintain epistemic practical authority as metastable. What matters for ethical normativity, which better practices build on, is primarily the creative variation and selective retention of practices. Carrying newly experienced background ethical values, practices spread in space and time and become selectively retained by political means of

[8] For a study that considers both normative and economic reasons, see Ray 1989.

negotiation, learning, and contestation in and between communities of practice. In other words, behind the daily wheeling and dealing about politics we are familiar with, politics and rule are primarily about epistemic practical authority – about getting the upper hand in creating, selecting, and retaining some practices instead of others. Practitioners, in turn, as members of communities of practice, play an active role in selecting ethical as well as competence standards.

Several points follow from this. First, discounting epistemological reasons, we should not distinguish between the sociocognitive and epistemic dimension, on one hand, and the ethical and moral dimension, on the other. As Nicolini rightly argued, "what is intelligible and what is right and wrong are apprehended together as something that makes it present to us in the performance of a practice" (2012, 176). Habermas (1990, 1996) did well to epistemologically deduce a normative theory from an analytical theory, although he stopped short by focusing only on communicative action.

Second, neither technological innovations nor practices' competence necessarily advance bounded progress; they easily can lead to regress. Thus, for example, being competent in bringing artificial intelligence technologies to the market does not necessarily imply bounded progress; it may lead to regress, such as greater inequality and organized violence (Harari 2016). Better (faster, more secure) transportation practices can lead to all kinds of material and sociocognitive improvements, for example, promoting trade and human welfare and expanding people's horizons about the world. But transportation practices, competently performed, also encouraged entrepreneurs to ship slaves from one continent to another, thus promoting slavery and detracting from our common humanity.[9] Only in and through practice do practitioners select ethical values with the propensity to promote bounded progress.

Third, common humanity values, which constitute better practices, create only propensities for the evolution of progressive social orders. To become bounded progress, better practices must be "responsive to the reality in which they are set, and this responsiveness provides the checks needed for us to introduce a reflective and critical distance from … current practices." This "mild realism," as Frega (2017, 497), describing Frederick Will's (1997) philosophy calls it, is pragmatically realist (see Chapter 2) because it depends on practitioners' learning and experimentation and on intersubjectively validating practices' background knowledge in and between communities of practice. As I have said throughout

[9] I thank Christian Büger for this illustration.

this book, this involves not only epistemic, cognitive, and sociological but also and primarily political processes. Learning, experimentation, and contestation, as well as the politics of adopting and/or replacing practices – as the uneven changes in the 2018 liberal international order show – are likely to be different across communities of practice. This partly explains international social orders' multiple character.

Pragmatist, Cosmopolitan, and Communitarian Ethics

The pragmatist argument that ethical standards rest on practices deceptively seems to contradict classical cosmopolitan arguments and communitarian arguments. In liberal discourse, the response to the question about where ethical standards rest is individuals who rationally choose among neutral and universal principles of justice (Rawls 1971). Morality makes sense only within the bounds of a cosmopolitan (thus universal) community of the human species (but see Brown 2010; Erskine 2008) in which individuals make a rational choice to pursue universally applicable principles of justice. States are free to pursue their interests as they care to define them as long as they abide by "universal" (Western liberal) principles of justice (Beitz 1979). In communitarian discourse, on the other hand, ethical standards rest on cultures, societies, and more generally community context-dependent perspectives (MacIntyre 1981; Taylor 1985; Walzer 1990). Communitarians, because they defend the view that the "common good or community interest ... is greater than individual goods and interests" (Morrice 2000, 237), argue that justice is possible only within the boundaries of a differentiated community. This means that human beings can fulfill themselves as moral beings only within states (Brown 1992).

Pragmatist ethics, while a less-distinct school of ethical thought than the other dominant approaches, views ethics not as a matter of seeking essential goods or conforming to essential principles but as processes of ends deliberation and the pursuit of contingent distributions of goods in response to concrete dilemmas. Dewey (1983, 194), for example, viewed moral experience and action as triggered by situations featuring an incompatibility of ends, to be resolved by something akin to scientific inquiry and experimentation (2008, 222; Anderson 2014). His theory of progress involves evolutionary growth:

> The process of growth, of improvement and progress, rather than the static outcome and result, becomes the significant thing ... The end is no longer a terminus or limit to be reached. It is the active process of transforming the existent situation. (Dewey 1988, 181)

It follows, according to Dewey, that "we test our value judgments by putting them into practice and seeing whether the results are satisfactory" (Anderson 2014, n.p.). While the first part of this sentence reflects the most important insight I take from Dewey's ethical political theory, I disagree with the second part because, when explaining evolution and better practices, Dewey places too much weight on the environment and, as with natural evolution, takes a functionalist approach – claiming better practices are the ones that work.

For Dewey the notion that, when challenged by the environment, individuals can change either their practices or their minds shows "that practical judgement is creative" (ibid.). This argument is consistent with cognitive evolutionary theory. While Dewey's ethical philosophy moves between psychological and sociological insights, as he showed in his political theory of democracy and education (1916), his main emphasis is on the social: "social ethics concerns the institutional arrangements that influence the capacity of people to conduct moral inquiry intelligently" (Anderson 2014). Axel Honneth, a pragmatist and communitarian, claims that a democratic community must have the reflexive ability to represent to itself its members' cooperative actions and common goals and subject its evolving trajectory to deliberation (1998, 774–77). Richard Rorty (2017), also taking both a pragmatist and communitarian perspective, argues that culturally and communally "thick" experiences of loyalty make it easier to engage in moral reasoning and that our relationships with and obligations to our fellow humans begin "thickly" and become "thin" as they expand to incorporate increasing numbers of people who are different from ourselves. Conceiving of justice as a larger type of loyalty would therefore provide us with a better vocabulary for engaging with distant others in the global context (ibid.).

How do I then reconcile my pragmatist argument that ethical standards rest on practices with my communitarian argument that ethical standards also rest in context-dependent communities and my cosmopolitan argument that these communities have propensities to become universal? In other words, how can my argument be simultaneously pragmatist, communitarian, and cosmopolitan?

The reconciliation between cosmopolitanism and communitarianism already occurred. Some of the key scholars who participated in the debate between cosmopolitanism and communitarianism have recognized weaknesses in their own theoretical positions and conceded some points to the alternative position (e.g., Beitz 2009; Habermas 1996; Rawls 1980; Walzer 1990). Thus, for example, Beitz (2009) concedes that human reason works in the context of communities of discursive practices. Walzer (1990), in turn, argued that the communitarian argument is only a correction to the liberal argument that liberalism tends toward instability and dissociation. If communitarianism is only a correction to cosmopolital theory, then cosmopolitanism and communitarianism are not necessarily at odds.

This standpoint has been widely acknowledged in IR over the last generation. Mervyn Frost (1996, 158), for example, suggested that people reason and engage in moral argumentation sharing language and normative understandings. Richard Shapcott, in turn, argued that expanding the boundaries of community to the universal level depends on a practice and ethics of communication that "takes from the … Kantian tradition the project of universal community … From the communitarian position it takes the premise that treating others in moral fashion requires paying attention to their particularity" (Shapcott 2001, 51). Mark Neufeld (1995) defended the Aristotelian view that the normative task in IR is to enlarge the *polis* – a political space within which the "good life" can take place through persuasion and through the pursuit of liberty and equality – to the global level. Andrew Linklater (1998, 2011, 2017) defended the view that a cosmopolitan order can develop thanks to the transformation of political community at the transnational and subnational levels. Erskine argued that it is possible to imagine a cosmopolitan aspiration that takes seriously communitarian views of culture and society (2008, 2).

A pragmatist, practice-oriented, ethical perspective is consistent with communitarianism (Adler 2005). Constructivism, and particularly evolutionary constructivism, is essentially communitarian. As I have shown, an evolutionary constructivist approach rests on the constitution of international social orders by practices, background knowledge, and communities of practice. This means that when we come to conceive of ethical standards embedded in social orders, our point of departure and focus of attention should be social action and transactions in communities of practice. At the same time, an ethical perspective that rests not only on communities of practice but also on constitutive background knowledge consisting of values of our common humanity transcends the differences between cosmopolitanism, communitarianism, and pragmatism.

Prominent political theorists of international relations have also recognized the overlap between cosmopolitanism, communitarianism, and pragmatism. Charles Beitz, for example, approaches human rights as a discursive and political global practice that "exists within a global discursive community whose members recognize the practice's [regulative] norms as reason giving and use them in deliberating and arguing about how to act" (ibid., 8). Practices provide converging reasons for purposeful behavior. People follow authoritative normative propositions because they possess authority rooted in the fact that they exist and are valuable (ibid., 11). Beitz's approach is cosmopolitan because it is based on a liberal assumption about how reasonable people behave and it considers the human rights order as a global political space based on public reasoning of international society's "liberal and decent peoples" (ibid., 100, 209). It is partly discursive because, in his view, the global human rights order exists within a discursive community in which, rather than blindly following norms, individuals use reasons for deliberating and arguing. It is also thinly communitarian because, while arguing that practice resides in communities and are emergent (ibid., 9), communities are not productive of a global normative order.

Mervyn Frost's, in turn, suggests a constitutive practice approach to international ethics. Frost argues that all international practices, actually all social practices, have a normative content (2003, 2009a, 2009b). In Frost's view, state and individual international actors are "constituted as actors of *a certain kind* within specific global social practices" (2009a, 19). It follows that the most important judgments actors make in international relations are on practices' ethical background (Frost 2003, 84). Equally important, practitioners support and sustain international practices because these practices have values embedded in them, which the practitioners are committed to and thus wish to uphold (ibid., 89). Frost argues that the best indicator of what is ethically universal is what actors have agreed on, or what is embedded in their practices. Participating in social practices thus "requires getting involved in the interpretation of normatively appropriate actions "from within the context of participants" (ibid., 91). But "in order to participate effectively in international relations, international actors . . . have to acquire a measure of . . . 'ethical competence' – that is, the skills necessary to protect freedom and diversity in the modern world" (2009b, 91). Freedom and diversity are, from Frost's perspective, the central values of the society of sovereign states (2009a, 95).

A pragmatist community of practice–based approach suggests that communities of practice, because they can expand both vertically and horizontally beyond their boundaries, make it contingently possible for ethical standards *that recognize our common humanity* to spread as part of practices' background knowledge – for practices to survive preferentially and for social orders to evolve to the global level.

A Normative Theoretical Exploration of Better Practices and Bounded Progress

My argument that all practices are normative, that ethics rests on practices and communities of practice, that ethical standards evolve in space and time, and that we may be able to identify better practices suggests the propensity for *bounded* progress.[10] Being contingent, partial, reversible, and constituted through practice and politics in transactions – including learning and contestation, in and among communities of practice – the notion of bounded progress stops short of the enlightenment idea of progress but goes beyond normative relativism. Contingency means lack of inevitability: practitioners need to take responsibility for what they practice. To take responsibility we need judgment and normative understanding of the situation. Normative understandings are constitutive of, and happen in, practice.

Bounded progress means that better practices and social orders may and *should*[11] cognitively evolve from the inside out in and from communities of practice. Better practices are those that *acknowledge*[12] (Markell 2003) a "*common humanity*" (Boltanski and Thévenot 2006, 74–78; Stuurman 2017, 9; Taylor 1992). By common humanity, I mean the socially constructed and emergent *acknowledgment* (Markell 2003) of most human beings as our fellow humans (Stuurman 2017, 10–12), which is derived from the value of life as "good" (Plato, *The Republic*, 1968) or "worthwhile" (Boltanski and Thévenot 2006) and from practices that constitute the value as a right. From a minimalist ethical perspective, "common humanity" means that all human beings, while not necessarily equal and culturally similar, and each having their primary allegiance to their community, belong to a meta-"imagined community" (Anderson 2003; Stuurman 2017) because life is qualitatively "good" or has "worth." From a more far-reaching ethical perspective, however, it means standards of empathy (Crawford 1991) with all humans qua humans, especially their suffering (Barnett 2011). As an aspiration or propensity only, the highest expression of this perspective, as articulated by the 1948 United Nations Universal Declaration of Human Rights, is "that all human beings are born free and equal in dignity and rights" (UN 1948).

Korsgaard claims that there are four sources of normativity: "voluntarism," namely moral claims deriving from some authority such as God; "realism," meaning that moral claims are normative if they are true; "reflective endorsement," according to which normativity is derived from

[10] For previous analyses of progress in IR, see Adler and Crawford 1991; E. Haas 1997, 2000; Linklater 2011, 2017; Price 2008.

[11] I thank Craig Smith for insisting that I emphasize the "*should*," especially because I am speaking to IR scholars as a particularly global community of practice who are, by dint of their pedagogical and public role, engaged in a normative pursuit of world ordering.

[12] I explain later why, following Markell (2003), I prefer the concept of acknowledgement to that of "recognition."

human nature; and "the appeal to autonomy," which rests normativity on the agent's own will (1996, 2003). Korsgaard derives normativity transcendentally and as an imperative from humanity itself, by which she means human nature (1996, 121). More concretely, she argues that because human beings have reflexive consciousness from which reasons arise, people should treat their humanity "as a practical, normative, form of identity," according to which humans value themselves as humans (ibid., 121). This, she argues, "puts you in moral territory. Or at least, it does so if valuing humanity in your own person rationally requires valuing it in the persons of others … valuing ourselves as human beings involves valuing others that way as well, and carries with it moral obligations" (ibid.).

I do not derive my notion of normativity from a religious perspective because "we are all creatures created in God's image" (but see Barnett 2011), nor from a realist perspective of truth or from Kantian (1998) appeals to agents' autonomy. Like Korsgaard, I derive my notion of normativity from our common humanity, not from human nature but from cognitive evolution, a historically evolved, still emergent (see also Beitz 2009), and socially constructed *acknowledgment* of *the "worth"* (Boltanski and Thévenot 2006), *"good"* (Plato, *Republic*, 1968), or "quality" (Pirsig 1974) of human life in and by practice. In other words, I refer to what Hannah Arendt (1958) called "the human condition," as derived from the "vita activa": action, practice, and practical experience. Social practices serve as the unit of transmission, and communities of practice are the conduit and repository of the value or quality of human life – of who we are and, thus, of our shared consciousness of common humanity – from which other values, such as liberty and equality, derive (Aristotle, *Nicomachean Ethics* 2000). If we consider, therefore, the UN Universal Declaration of Human Rights (UN 1948) as aspiration or propensity ("everyone has the right to life"), then better practices and the politics of practice in and between communities of practice may (yet not necessarily must, or will) turn propensity into a right and social reality.[13] I cannot improve on Michael Walzer, who, reviewing Stuurman's *The Invention of Common Humanity* (2017), wrote:

> Beginning with the American and French revolutions and developing in the early and mid-1800s, social and political movements committed to egalitarianism suddenly appear in Western Europe and the United States – "suddenly" given the scope of Stuurman's two-millennia history. Now movements that call themselves

[13] Dewey said that "we make moral progress by adopting habits of reflectively revising our value judgments in response to the widest consequences for every one of following them" (qtd. in Anderson 2014, n.p.).

> "internationalist" aim to draw all humanity into the struggle for equality. This is something radically new, and with it comes the idea that theories about humanity and equality must lead to a practice of humanity and equality … Abolitionism, the labor movement, feminism in its several waves, the civil-rights movement, and the gay-rights movement all have their origin in this moment when political action became, for people like us, obligatory. (Walzer 2017)

Several arguments follow from this discussion.

(1) An evolved consciousness of common humanity, leading to the understanding, for example, that death is worse than life, that insecurity is worse than security, that totalitarianism is worse than democracy, that despotism is worse than freedom, and that slavery and legally oppressive fanaticism should be opposed is a human *accomplishment* in practice. My argument is not that international social orders have already been constituted by better practices, certainly not globally and across all practices, but that *there is now a propensity for better ordering to occur, that it should occur, and, if and when it does, that it takes cognitive evolutionary processes to produce such an accomplishment.* With Walzer I believe that the emergence of common humanity in practices, and thus the propensity for bounded progress, follows the globalizing nature of practices over the last past two centuries. We can therefore characterize practices and communities of practice as sources of consciousness rather than as their outcome. As Stephen Toulmin argued, beyond

> sensibility, attentiveness, and articulateness of individuals, we should have recognized that the concerted plans of multiple agents manifest yet another, fourth aspect of consciousness. Agents who act as partners in a shared project, carried out jointly, with the intention of collaborating, and with each having full knowledge of the other's role in the project, are engaged in a conscious collaboration. They act as they do consciously – i.e., in the light of mutual understandings. (1982, 64)

(2) While better practices may not necessarily require, as moral cosmopolitans argue, the duty of care or aid to all members of the human species, this requirement can and should evolve in the future. Immanuel Kant may have been right that the project of universal community requires "treating all others in a moral fashion regardless of natural or communal boundaries" (Shapcott 2001, 51). He was perhaps too optimistic to believe that this moral value is transcendental, rather than a value with the propensity, not yet fulfilled, to become universal by means of the expansion of communities of practice. While constructivism shows against political realism that moral change is possible (see also Price 2008), evolutionary constructivism shows that while change does not necessarily mean progress, progressive social orders might still evolve

locally, or even globally. Progress may not happen but it still can happen. The roads toward progress have many obstacles; for example, progress in one practice may affect other practices negatively. This raises the question of whether identifying better practices helps practitioners to promote better practices.

(3) Practices become "better" not only because they are collectively accepted – at times, genocide was and still is accepted. Rather, better practices are endowed with what Robert Pirsig (1974) referred to as "quality." For Pirsig, quality as value is a perceptual category. This idea follows John Locke's notion of secondary quality (2009; see also Aristotle's *Categories* in Studtmann 2017); primary quality refers to an attribute that is intrinsic to an object.[14] To me, however, because I locate value in practices' background knowledge, quality is both subjective as part of practitioners' dispositions and expectations and also outside the mind – not necessarily only in an object or substance, but also as a socially constituted fact, in practice. Pirsig's (1991) differentiation between "dynamic quality" and "static quality" is useful for understanding this point.

According to Pirsig, "dynamic quality," which can be identified only in practice, rather than intellectually defined, is people's recognition of "good" when subjects become conscious of objects. From a cognitive evolutionary perspective, dynamic quality is largely what creative variation is about, a process that, consistent with process ontology, turns creative experience into social action and practice. "Static quality" refers to qualitative patterns that people can reason and define (ibid.). From a cognitive evolutionary perspective, it epitomizes metastabilizing processes of selective retention according to which better practices become institutionalized and communities of practice help maintain metastable. Without cognitive evolution, better practices, and better social orders, are impossible, but without social order, progress cannot last.

(4) Regarding the "*acknowledgment*" of a common humanity, I first thought of referring to the concept of "recognition" from a normative, rather than from a psychological, perspective. Charles Taylor (1992) famously discussed two kinds of recognition, universal and that of difference. Universal recognition goes back to the Kantian view that humans must give other humans the dignity and respect they deserve, the corollary of which is, of course, the equalization of rights. The politics of difference, which Taylor traced back to Jean-Jacques

[14] There is a controversy between intrinsic and extrinsic quality that, following my aversion to dichotomies, I avoid.

Rousseau, entails recognizing the cultural uniqueness of human groups. Neither concept fits my meaning of acknowledging a common humanity. In *The Phenomenology of Spirit*, Georg Hegel (1977) made one of the most important contributions to the concept of recognition when he suggested that human beings get their self-consciousness and self-identity when others recognize them as subjects. While this concept is more in line with my approach to practitioners as social beings, the Hegelian concept of recognition requires a level of sociality and normative progress that usually is not present when acknowledging a common humanity, particularly in relations of peoples across state, ethnic, and religious boundaries.

I also do not adopt Axel Honneth's (1992, 2007) well-known understanding of recognition, namely, as the development of a sense of oneself through rights, solidarity, and love. This concept is too maximalist to fit my very limited humanist-realist perspective. Equally socially and normatively ambitious, but ontologically limited, is Jürgen Habermas's discourse ethics, which relies on a form of speech that, at least in an ideal sense, recognizes all speakers as equally authoritative (Habermas 1992; Iser 2013).

The concept of acknowledgment, which I loosely borrow from Patchen Markell (2003), while still related to recognition, is less normatively "ambitious" than these other notions so it better suits my humanist-realist conception of better practices and bounded progress. To begin with, it assumes the unpredictable responses of other people (Markell 2003). While starting from a Hegelian perspective, in the sense that acknowledgment involves being self- rather than other-driven, it refers not to "one's own identity but one's own basic ontological condition or circumstances, particularly one's own finitude … a matter of one's practical limits in the face of an unpredictable and contingent future" (ibid., 38). Acknowledgment thus entails open-endedness, contingency, and aspiration. It cuts "across distinctions between individual and collective, contingency and particular … this would seem to deny the possibility of a *finally* satisfactory regime of recognition" (ibid., 15–16). Acknowledgment is therefore an ongoing process through shared practices of "recognizing" our common humanity, beginning with the value of human life (ibid., 33).

In this way we can interpret the "golden rule" differently and in a more minimalist sense: *value other human beings' lives as you value your own*. At a minimum, this is what accounts for our common humanity. Equality, liberty, fraternity, and mutual self-respect follow from this golden rule, albeit as a propensity rather than a determinist and teleological process. By engaging in shared practices that acknowledge our common humanity, practitioners generate processes that involve practitioners' reciprocity (ibid.), in the sense referred to in Chapter 4. To refresh the reader's memory, reciprocity is what practitioners' counterparts do. It is a commitment to get involved in future action because others commit as well, and it is often a need to justify each other's actions (Boltanski and Thévenot 2006; Kornprobst 2014). Most important, these processes encourage horizontal orders that promote negotiation, contestation, and learning. Some of the practices by which acknowledgment can be expressed are "taking a risk, withdrawing, speaking, listening, welcoming, polemicizing, claiming a right, refusing to claim a right, mourning, celebrating, forgiving, [and] punishing" (Markell 2003, 38). Yet acknowledgment "is not something that we owe to others ... At most ... others are its indirect objects and beneficiaries" (ibid., 180).

(5) There are multiple ways to realize values (Raz 2003), such as the value of common humanity, not only across communities of practice but also across cultures. For example, the value of common humanity can be practically realized as the avoidance of serious harm (Linklater 2011, 2017) among distinct communities, but also how the practice of protecting nature is performed across different cultures.

(6) Interconnectedness promotes the sharing of practices that enhance our common humanity, thus enhancing the propensity for the evolution of social orders based on horizontal systems of rule, rather than exclusively or mainly hierarchical systems of rule, in which domination and coercion are more likely. An important historical moment from a normative cognitive evolutionary perspective occurred at the end of the eighteenth century when the notion of social hierarchy and honor as a natural and/or God-given attribute (related to monarchy) was replaced by the modern and egalitarian notion of human dignity (Taylor 1992, 27). Looking into the future, we may see that interconnectedness and horizontal systems of rule become associated with better practices, thus bounded progress, *because without them it would be much more difficult to prevent nuclear war (life's worth), reduce poverty (equality), avert injustice and domination (freedom), and avert the irreversible damage of the environment (earth's worth).*

What Daniel Zimblatt calls "the soft guardrails of democracy," "mutual toleration," and "the responsible exercise of power" (Edsall 2017), as well as self-restraint, revulsion toward atrocities, and peaceful change – practices that resolve problems "without resorting immediately to violence" (Guzzini 2010, 317; Kratochwil 1989, 16) – illustrate practices imbued with collective knowledge of a common humanity. So do international human rights practices and global environmental practices, both of which place the quality of human life as a primary entitlement.

And so are poverty and hunger as conditions that, either inside national boundaries or worldwide, require overcoming.

Regarding the illustrations I use throughout this book, the European Union's security, human rights, citizenship, and environmental practices have been better than practices that were performed before the creation of the EU. Peaceful change has prevailed in Europe for the longest time in European history. Human right practices and institutions, such as the Human Rights Court, represent a major advance in the recognition of common humanity, and so do environmental practices and standards. Economic integration practices, on the other hand, have lagged behind. And while economic communities of practice have been at the vanguard of changes that occurred in the European order since World War II, when it comes to the contestation between social democratic and welfare practices and neoliberal economic practices, the neoliberal achieved the upper hand. European solidarity that once depended to a major extent on the welfare state has eroded – eating away at not only economic but also at political and social integration – and thus has become a major obstacle for overcoming the crises that the European Union has been confronting.

The spread of corporate practices, geographically and functionally, has resulted in the further strengthening of corporate communities of practice, which has helped weaken solidarity across porous European states' borders, and thus European integration. This clearly shows that bounded progress also consists in reducing the trade-offs between practices and communities of practice, which pull in different and often opposite directions. I do not mean only reducing trade-offs between values, but also that practices and values are subjected to creative variation and selective retention processes that can help reduce trade-offs between values. As part of economic globalization processes in the last decades, corporate practices and values account for much of the suffering (and anger) of those who have been on the losing side of globalization (Mishra 2017). We should consider the adoption of ethical standards by the corporate world in the last two decades as very limited and entirely reversible bounded progress. In large part, corporations adopted ethical practices for narrow financial interests. But this does not take away the value of corporations' partial and narrow move to adopt practices that enhance our common humanity. These changes in the corporate world would not have occurred without evolving human-rights practices that created the propensity for bounded progress to take place. This illustration shows how practices and communities of practice interact and intersect, sometimes complementing each other and at other times in contradistinction or even in opposition to each other. While it may be true that the road to hell is paved with good intentions, it may also be true that the road to heaven is paved with egotistic intentions.

Has bounded progress in cyberspace taken place? Have better practices been selectively retained? Is the cyberspace social order evolving away from practices that harm our common humanity? While we can trace the origin of cyberspace practices to US military technological innovations, cyber practices expanded to the entire world on the premise (and promise) of a world deeply interconnected by the Internet and that humans should communicate instantly around the world for the good of our common humanity. In the last generation, however, the contestation between communities-of-practice constellations that advance interconnectedness at the global level and those that advance national military, economic, and transnational corporate interests has clearly been leaning in favor of the latter. As cyberspace becomes increasingly associated with cyberwarfare practices and regulatory practices that harm horizontal rule in favor of hierarchical rule by governments and corporations, the Internet has been returning to its disassociation-inspired origins.

My revised version of the "golden rule" and the notion of common humanity do not go as far as promoting practices that enhance equality in a Kantian sense. It stops short of promoting common understanding the way Habermas's (1990, 1996) liberal discursive ethical principle does. Still, when better practices, which communities of practice carry, spread horizontally and vertically, perhaps even to the global level, they may constitute propensities for individuals, peoples, and states to move away from inequality, authoritarian rule, war, and human rights abuses.

Humanist Realism

An idea of bounded progress is distinctively communitarian because it takes normativity and ethical standards as being endogenous and immanent to communities of practice. Better practices and their constituting values (which make up background knowledge) acknowledge our common humanity and highlight a distinctive liberal humanist, yet also *realist*, approach to progress in international relations. In 1991 I called this approach "humanist realism." Back then, I argued that what I now call bounded progress in international relations "offers a pragmatic middle ground between the view that nothing changes" and "that everything is possible."[15]

[15] I am aware now that I came to the conception of a normative middle ground before the conception of constructivism as analytical middle ground. I also must concede that reading and teaching the English School probably affected my middle-ground normative and analytical views.

It depends on the emergence "of new values, redefinition of old values, and a change in the context of values that advances human interests. For progress in international relations to take place, the normative content of ... national interest as it is spread internationally must place a high value – relative to other values – on human beings, regardless of their nationality" (Adler 1991, 62). Second, I argued, progress in international relations can take place with a "change in expectations regarding the quality of the outcomes for the agent, including a redefinition of what exists, what can exist, what causes what, what the concomitants of desired actions are" (ibid.). The key question, I said, "is what causes expectations and values that enhance humanist interests across national borders to be politically selected, maintained, and spread at domestic and international levels" (ibid.).

After almost three decades, I have kept some of these main themes and arguments. However, while I may not have entirely answered all the questions about change in international relations, I believe that cognitive evolution theory can help provide a fuller answer. Some of the main innovations lie in highlighting the role of communities of practice, as both vehicle of practice/knowledge, and as a space where transactions, including learning and contestation as part of learning, occur. Cognitive evolution theory suggests novel forms of social power, the critical role that epistemic practical authority plays in creative variation and selective processes, horizontal systems of rule as part of social order, and how better practices occur and progressive social orders evolve together with the move from disassociation to interconnectedness. No less important, I have identified the mechanisms, both structural and agential, according to which processes congeal into practices and the complex nonlinear processes involved in turning metastability into social order evolution. I now take social orders, including international social orders, as multiple and overlapping.

From a normative perspective, I identify all practices as normative – as ethics located in practices. I also understand better practices and bounded progress as the evolutionary construction of cosmopolitan practices that are specifically identified by communities of practice and spread vertically and horizontally (see also Erskine 2008). I now identify ethical change with a principle of practice, rather than only of discourse (Habermas 1984), which entails a value of common humanity that derives first and foremost, but not exclusively, from human life in general as good, worthwhile, and as the value that carries most "value," from which other ethical values derive.

I also hold the view of bounded progress as a humanist view because it takes values such as human life and, by extension, practices of liberty, equality, and peaceful change as reflecting our common humanity. As

I said back in 1991, "progress in international relations … can be likened to climbing a precipice: slow, painfully difficult, fraught with setbacks, yet still humanly possible. In international relations we seldom climb toward the top, but mainly away from the abyss" (Adler 1991, 77).

International better practices require, for example, the evolution away from international policies that cause war, poverty, and human rights violations. From a human-realist perspective, these policy outcomes are "worse" than the ones that replace them after a progressive change has taken place. "Progress away from" means reducing the likelihood and scope of war, poverty, and human rights violations, rather than achieving peace, welfare, and justice. It also means that some conflicts can be controlled, that somewhere exploitation can be eradicated, at least temporarily, and that human suffering can be at least partially reduced.

My humanist-realist understanding of progress, while complementary to Linklater's (2011, 2017), differs from his view of progress as a global civilizing problem that occurs when political communities learn to avoid serious harm. Linklater believes that so far the solution to the problem of harm at the international level has been mainly "harm conventions" (Linklater 2011, 38). The view on whether civilization has progressed to stamp out mental and physical harm through international obligations is mixed. However, Linklater may be confining himself only to harm. By taking the avoidance of harm as the solution conflates problem and solution. In Linklater's own words, by "agreeing that the most fundamental duty of all is to avoid serious harm, the species may be moving closer to answering the question of how separate political communities can co-exist more harmoniously. If so, the harm principle can be regarded as the key element of a long-term global civilizing process" (2011, 76).

As a humanist-realist, I hold that what constitutes the propensity to avoid harm – partially, in some parts of the world rather than others, at different times, and with the propensity for reversibility – are values and practices of common humanity. While I agree with Linklater that interconnectedness can deepen the sense of moral community and reduce harm across communities (2011, 82), the missing link is the worth of life inherent in common humanity values and practices. For Linklater, progress means a directional and far-reaching global process by which our species becomes more civilized. For me, progress begins with, and sometimes does not go further than, the evolution of common humanity values and practices partially, locally, and reversibly, that help political communities to avoid the abyss.

Humanist Realism and Ernst Haas's Idea of Progress in International Relations

I now move to Ernst Haas's idea of progress, first, because I want to bring it back to the attention of our scholarly community; second, because it is where my notions of humanist-realism began; and finally because I want to contrast his idea of progress to mine. Haas's idea of progress is "directional change for the better" (Haas 1997, 9). "Things get better for us as our routines for choosing become capable of searching for solutions that get more sophisticated in recognizing complexity" (Haas 1997, 5). More explicitly, progress is "the improvement of every person's lot with respect to health, wealth, and peace. A country that has benefited from progress is one in which the citizenry lives free from the danger of war and civil war and enjoys a higher living standard and a better health ... than in the past" (Haas 2000, 2). Haas coupled this enlightenment feature with a rejection of Hobbesian realism and of an international anarchical system, although, like Elias (2000) and Linklater (2011, 2017), he argued that the pursuit of human welfare went hand in hand with the continuous desire for military security.

Haas believed that progress occurs because "social collectivities, including nations, are able to use knowledge as a result of systemic inquiry or scientific knowledge (1997, 4). Progress thus entails a learning process that Haas associated with the adoption of new meanings based on reason and consensual scientific knowledge. Applying formal reason based on scientific knowledge would help in finding solutions to collective problems – in other words, progress (2000, 3). Consensual scientific knowledge thus can, but not necessarily must, bind diverse cultures and nations, making them share meanings, "see" problems alike, and therefore lead to the solution of international problems. However, progress does not occur in a linear way, as Enlightenment philosophers thought, but dialectically: "suffering and disappointment are the stimuli that cause collectivities to examine past experience and reinterpret them" (1997, 5).

In modern times, Haas argued, cognitive structures based on science, which he associated with the concept of "cognitive progress," command respect and produce trans-ideological bridges (ibid., 14). By "substantive progress," by contrast, Haas meant the physical manifestations of cognitive progress, namely more health, wealth, and peace.[16] Showing the plausibility of his cognitive and substantive hypotheses about progress

[16] The subjects of both cognitive progress and substantive progress are individuals. For an earlier and different understanding of cognitive progress and substantive progress, see Adler 1986.

required Haas to ask how to achieve scientific consensus in view of the uncertainty concerning the status of scientific truth. Haas's answer was a pragmatist perspective, according to which knowledge is valid only for a community of actors, regardless of their ideological beliefs; temporary, based on socially constructed notions of cause–effect relationships; and an approximation, "always subject to amendment and even refutation" (ibid., 12). Only after truth claims associated with a given research tradition have passed an appropriate reality test can we consider them to be established, despite whatever ideological baggage or institutional bias they have been associated with in the initial research. Like most American pragmatists (see Chapter 3), Haas adopted an evolutionary epistemology where "science meant a process of selection among the viable and less viable variants of thought" (1997, 13). Haas's epistemology was also evolutionary because "older institutions and beliefs are thought to change (not only to adapt in the Darwinian sense) in such a way that people learn how to solve their collective problems to their increasing satisfaction" (ibid., 6). "Older institutions and beliefs 'evolve' into successors preferred by members of a society" (ibid.).

Haas's answer to the question of whether progress is cosmopolitan or communitarian was yes. He argued that progress might become global because scientific rationality "is being globalized by way of cosmopolitanism" (ibid., 4). At the same time, however, cognitive progress need not occur at the global level – "for it is more easily achieved among collectivities and individuals who already share a common culture" (ibid., 17). Substantive progress can occur only within local, national, or regional communities. On regional integration, Haas believed that different types of nationalist doctrines (or stages in nationalist development) explain the variance between Europe and developing countries' responses to interdependence (Haas 1986). He hypothesized, however, that only the kind of nationalism he called "liberal" is "consistent with the progressive transnational sharing of meanings" (Haas 1997, 19). He clarified that he associated liberalism less with a moral position than with a "certain procedure for making collective decisions ... liberal institutions favor learning because they admit the rational analytic mode of acting more than any other set of institutions. Liberal nationalism, more than any other, favors reason and progress" (ibid., 19, 21).[17]

Haas's idea of progress required agreement on both positive ends values and instrumental values. However, he did not choose arbitrarily

[17] Haas's conception of rationality was also minimalist in the sense of consisting "of the understanding that human beings are sub-optimizers, and that their collaborative arrangements are second-best" (1984).

among "good values" and adopted values whose universality and desirability very few people around the world would deny. Who, after all, would be against health, wealth, and peace as human values? Haas, however, did not specify the meaning of peace and was relatively mute about distributional issues. By eschewing notions of moral progress and focusing instead on the improvement of institutional and governance procedures, Haas took progress in international relations to be limited, reversible, and contingent. Progress occurs when, as a result of the increase of interdependence, disappointment and selfishness set in (Haas 1980, 1983). The increase of interconnectedness may after all be conducive to the improvement of people's lives and to peace, but only dialectically and when egoistic leaders, as in Europe after World War II, perceive the need to solve problems cooperatively at the international level and adopt new meanings of national interests. Like Max Weber (Schluchter 1981, 25), Haas believed that interests, rather than ideas, explained governments' actions (1990, 210). "We have no reason to expect," said Haas, "that increases in any kind of interdependence means a reduction of violence" (Haas 1997, 78).

Along the corridor of UC Berkeley's Barrows Hall's seventh floor, where both Haas and Kenneth Waltz had their offices, Haas was considered the "idealist" scholar and Waltz the "realist" scholar. But in light of Haas's pragmatist view of progress in international relations (which relies on a dialectical understanding of interconnectedness), compared with Waltz's persistent belief that disassociation, coupled with technological fixes and human reason in the form of nuclear deterrence, will assure "peace" (i.e., stability) better than international interdependence, I wonder who was the more realist.

In sum, Haas's view of progress built on the contradiction of opposites. He chose a sophisticated middle ground between a positive and, yes, optimistic view (for the discipline's standards), and a realist and, more than anything else, pragmatic and pragmatist approach to international relations that rejected the idea of universal progress. His cosmopolitan though not moral assumptions were full of stops and breaks and qualified by a measure of relativism arising from his understanding of how material and cognitive factors interact.

While I follow Haas's pragmatist notion of knowledge, an evolutionary epistemology, and a humanist-realist idea of progress, there are some differences between his and my conception of progress. Here, I mention only a few that might further help explain my interpretation of humanist realism and progress in international relations. Haas's approach to both cognitive and substantive progress was methodologically individualist, emphasizing individuals' physical conditions such as health and wealth.

By contrast, my approach refers to collective entities, better practices, and bounded progressive social orders. While we both emphasize peace, I depart from Haas's functionalist approach that argues that progress occurs merely because of the advancement of scientific knowledge and scientific rationality. Consensual scientific knowledge does not necessarily advance human values and our "common humanity" – some people may use such knowledge to gas millions of other people. Google can now predict flu epidemics and improve health around the world, but it can also help terrorists put together a nuclear device. Scientific consensus over the benefits of high-yielding varieties of grain gave us the "green revolution" and increased wealth, but it also caused desertification and other environmental catastrophes. I do not deny Haas's core idea that scientific reason offers the opportunity to create common meanings and thus promote international collaboration. What we need, however, is practical reason. Ethical and normative knowledge provides "better" practical meanings to social practices, including scientific practices. Without an idea of "the better," as it is related to a common humanity, scientific rationality is neutral.

While it takes science and technology to reduce hunger, increase health and wealth, and keep the peace (e.g., satellites), it also takes ethical practices. What is the point of achieving new scientific developments in education, for example, bringing computers to the classroom, if there is a bias in education, for example, in mathematics, toward men? What is the point of increasing wealth if it benefits only 1 percent of the population? What is the point of increasing human welfare, but only for people not considered "primitive" or unworthy? Can humanity achieve progress, defined as health, wealth, and peace, when ethnic nationalism and post-truth practices are rampant?

Other than his emphasis on the improvement of individuals' physical well-being, Haas's idea of progress was mostly instrumental. He looked at the advancement of international organization and global governance and focused on the possibility that scientific knowledge would have an impact on decision-making procedures that would lead to the solution of collective problems. By focusing mostly on procedure rather than ethics and the normative dimension, Haas left out better practices such as democracy, rule of law, and human rights. Perhaps it was hard for him to imagine that liberal nationalism, which was prevalent in developed democracies, could one day cave in to illiberal ethnic and religious nationalism, disassociation tendencies, and populism, all of which were characteristic of developing societies he studied, such as Iran, China, and India. Perhaps it was hard for him to imagine the current challenge to scientific knowledge and reason and, more generally the challenges to "truth," in the sense of "post-truth." Haas's conception of progress depended on the spread of scientific reasoning around the world. His emphasis on individuals and international institutional cooperation, such as international regimes (Haas 1982, 1983), left out the possibility that progress would be undermined, if not halted altogether, by the populist, coercive practice of Orwellian "newspeak" in its current version as "post-truth" practices. I believe that he overlooked the possibility that epistemological insecurity would undermine the very possibility of social orders.

Epistemological (In)Security, Practical Democracy, and Progressive International Social Orders

I have a bridge to sell you.

One of the worst threats to practices that contemplate our common humanity – the worst threats to better social orders and bounded progress – are "post-truth" practices. Those who use them as a power tool deliberately aim at undermining collective *epistemological security* for the sake of political domination.[18] Epistemological insecurity is a reason that we cannot and should not define progress as resulting from *only* scientific knowledge and reason, and why we need also a concept of better practices based on ethical humanistic values. Without epistemological security, better practices and bounded progress cannot take place, and social order is disrupted or can break down.

By epistemological security, I mean individuals' and communities' experience of orderliness, safety, and lack of threat to their physical integrity and identity, resulting from justified beliefs and trust in the knowledge on which their "common-sense reality" (Ezrahi 2012, 106) is based. In other words, epistemological security is based on the "socio-epistemological ground for determination of a public and commonsensical world of facts" (ibid.) or, in my own words, of reality as a condition of intelligibility. Hannah Arendt argued that "the result of a consistent and total substitution of lies for factual truth is not that the lies will now be accepted as truth, and the truth be defamed as lies, but that the sense by which we take our bearings in the real world ... is being destroyed" (1967, 78). The increasing selective retention of epistemological

[18] We should differentiate the concept of epistemological security, which I suggest here, from the concept of "epistemic security," which refers to the strength of the epistemic claims on behalf of self-knowledge, such as infallibility and omniscience. See Gertler 2017.

insecurity–causing practices poses a large threat to a social order based on common humanity values.

The main reason post-truth practices create epistemological insecurity and are therefore a challenge to social order is that their practitioners use deontic power to impose lies on material and social facts, which over time are held metastable as common-sense reality or scientific facts, to undermine, or supress completely, their status as facts. Equally, they use performative power (take, for example, President Trump) to persuade local and global audiences that their lies are true and factual. This disruption has two consequences. First, feelings or opinions disconnected from empirical facts, demagoguery, and, in a word, "bullshit"[19] prevent social and political consensus about functions, statuses, and constitutive normative rules. Practices like democracy that depend on socially constructed common-sense knowledge; promote learning, experimentation, and epistemic negotiation; and therefore encourage the selective retention of epistemic metastable conditions may succumb to epistemological insecurity. Social orders, most saliently liberal social orders, which rely on intersubjectivity and common-sense reality based on facts, learning, and experimentation, cannot therefore hold ground. When demagogues use post-facts[20] on behalf of control and domination, the result is populist authoritarian, or even totalitarian, regimes (Arendt 1973) that rely exclusively on hierarchical or vertical systems of rule.

The undermining of epistemological security prevents the survival and diffusion of better practices and therefore the diffusion of bounded progressive social orders. Epistemological insecurity prevents people from reaching political, social, and economic consensus; promotes deep clefts in society; and by intensifying disagreement about the conditions on whose basis people should validate knowledge, it notoriously undermines the reliance of public-policy decisions on science. As a consequence of epistemological insecurity, uncertainty increases, and so does the societal ambiguity about who governs and who should govern. People's ability to expect with some degree of confidence, let alone forecast, decreases. The influence of epistemological insecurity on

[19] "Not a Very Slippery Slope: A Reply to Fuller," European Association for the Study of Science and Technology, https://easst.net/tag/post-truth/.

[20] The issue is not whether practices rely on truths – religion and coercive power have their own version of the truth – but "false facts" that cannot be verified, are based only on emotions, and are aimed at control and domination. Even if they are socially constructed, facts, particularly scientific facts, rely on consensus and conditions of intelligibility. President Trump's claim that a million and a half people attended his inauguration was *his* truth, but it was not a fact. See Latour 1999; Latour and Woolgar 1986; Sørensen 2017.

practices pulls the rug from under practices' epistemic constitution. The rule of law, democracy, education, markets, trade, and peace, to mention some salient practices – all of which rely on tacit and/or explicit social epistemic agreement – break under the weight of epistemological insecurity, resulting in enhanced possibilities for violence, economic failure, surprises, people's physical harm and human insecurity, human rights violations, and individuals' poverty of imagination.

As important, epistemological insecurity literally does away with interconnectedness and with horizontal systems of rule; how else would people stay "connected" without a common social epistemic background? Under these conditions, a sense of common humanity becomes very difficult to achieve when populist authoritarian governments associate humanist-realist practices with "the enemy" or the "other." Because epistemological insecurity also creates radical uncertainty about who has rights and who should have rights, it undermines the possibility of better practices and social orders to evolve. Alvin Goldman and Thomas Blanchard say that "moral progress benefits from being organized in an egalitarian fashion, which occurs when all sides to a moral dispute are able to participate in the moral inquiry and to make their interests recognized" (2016, n.p.). In other words, horizontal systems of rule, which epistemological insecurity undermines, are more conducive to the development of practices based on moral background knowledge.

Epistemological insecurity radically undermines Habermas's (1984, 1996) condition for overcoming domination by means of his idealized conception of common understandings and practical discourse based on truth claims – understandings that all could accept without coercion. From Habermas's discursive perspective, epistemological insecurity may be the kiss of death for the liberal social order and "deliberative democracy." However, if we follow a practice-based principle where liberal practices sustain a liberal social order and democracy, post-truth, while a major threat to liberal order and democracy, *may not necessarily mean their end.* This is because the practice principle is inherently political, related to politics and rule, in other words, because the communities of practice that abhor and oppose post-truth are likely to contest the communities of practice that uphold it in the political arena. The judicial system and media institutions of the United States pushing back against President Trump's and his staff's lies attest to contestation. Epistemological insecurity, from a practice perspective, can also trigger creative variation in practices and new practices to counter post-truth. There is now an attempt around the world to develop new practices and technologies for double-checking the news and preventing the "fake news" phenomenon. Thus, a practice principle, as opposed to a discourse principle, encourages contestation. We see this in the areas of climate change, free trade, regional integration, and democracy. Social order is threatened, but it need not collapse. The end result may depend on the relationship between social order's homeorhesis and resilience (see Chapter 9).

To illustrate how and why epistemological insecurity–causing post-truth practices present a threat to better practices and social orders, I look at the liberal democratic social order and suggest "practical democracy," a normative concept I derive from cognitive evolution theory. Improving on Habermas's (1996) concept of "discursive democracy," practical democracy highlights the crucial notion that before and above anything else, democracy is epistemic and practical.

As of 2018, liberal democratic practices are eroding and being replaced by populist, semi-authoritarian, and outright authoritarian practices, often stylishly bunched together under the rubric of "illiberal democracies" (Zakaria 1997; see also Levitsky and Ziblatt 2018). Post-truth practices play an important role in constituting an illiberal democratic social order that aims to replace liberal democracies in non-Western states, which adopted these practices, but particularly in the West where liberal democracies first emerged.

I take my cues on practical democracy mainly from John Dewey (1916) and more recently from Honneth (1998), Christopher Ansell (2011), Roberto Frega (2017), Rorty (2017), and a growing literature on "epistemic democracy" that grounds the benefits of democratic practices on practices of truth rather than on norms and discourse (Anderson 2006; Estlund 2008). John Dewey strikingly referred to the benefits of the "public,"[21] understood as a "community of action rather than as a community of discourse" (Frega 2017, 727) in conceiving democracy as a creative activity and turning democracy into an identity, a habit, and a way of life, which is inculcated through education (Dewey 1916). He "stressed that for democracy to work, it was not enough simply to institute legal arrangements such as representation and periodic elections. Culture had to change too, so that citizens at large, interacting with one another in civil society, welcome diversity and discussion, and take an experimental attitude toward social arrangements" (Anderson 2006, 14). "The future of democracy," Dewey said, "is allied with the spread of the scientific attitude toward practical affairs" (ibid.). The public, according to Dewey, must be heard because it carries the practical knowledge and experience of a democracy based on cooperation. This means that the quality of democratic knowledge partly relies on public

[21] We should differentiate Dewey's concept of "the public" from the concept of public opinion.

experience and practice. At the same time, democracy depends on representative practices, such as the rule of law, and representative institutions, such as political parties, the parliament, and the courts. Democratic knowledge thus reconstitutes itself and democracy is renewed through experimental reflexivity. Practical democracy therefore encourages shared action, negotiation, and deliberation in a public political space, which is bred through experiential learning. Honneth argues that the "political sphere is not – as Hannah Arendt and, to a lesser degree Habermas, believe – the place for a communicative exercise of freedom but the cognitive medium with whose help society attempts, experimentally, to explore, process, and solve its own problems with the coordination of social action" (1998, 775).

Without epistemological security, the public is undermined and the practices, habits, and identities of democracy are challenged. However, because the public in democracies, as Dewey understood them, is a community of practice whose practitioners share meanings of competence and understandings of common humanity, a challenged democratic social order can be restored through contestation, learning, and experimentation. Epistemological insecurity, thus, may dialectically create propensities for bounded progress when communities of practice, which are constituted by the kind of democratic practices and identities that Dewey advocated, contest post-truth practices.

Epilogue
World Ordering

In this book, I suggested a systemic theory of world ordering: the study of world politics as ongoing dynamic processes of social orders' constitution, maintenance, contestation, evolution, and demise. Following a succinct definition of social order as configurations of practices that organize social life, we may refer to world ordering as the processes and mechanisms that drive the construction, evolution, and substitution of some orders by others. Cognitive evolution is an analytical theory of world ordering that aims to ascertain and explain the creative variation and selective retention of some social practices as opposed to others. At the same time, the theory's normative framework suggests how to conceptualize better practices and better social orders and, thus, bounded progress. Particularly when dark times for world ordering loom large, as they appear to do now, it is imperative to value and practice our common humanity. The theory's analytical component may then explain how and whether better practices and orders can creatively emerge and become selectively retained.

The analytical side of cognitive evolution theory breaks with most social explanations of evolutionary change in IR, political science, evolutionary psychology, and evolutionary economics that ground their theories in natural evolution and/or analogies and metaphors based on natural evolution. It also breaks with studies that have linked evolutionary processes to human progress or, alternatively, have dismissed the possibility of even limited and reversible human and social progress. Cognitive evolution thus takes a two-step (nonsequential) approach to evolution and progress. It first explores the social processes and mechanisms that explain creative variation and the selective retention of variants in nonteleological and nondeterministic ways, and as reversible processes. It then explores what collectively might count as better practices and social orders whose emergence and survival we can explain by social rather than natural mechanisms and processes.

Cognitive evolution theory, in particular, and world-ordering theories, more generally, are systemic theories of world politics. Rather than concentrating on international systems' stability and change – on international systems' constituents, their distribution, boundaries, and environments, and the interdependent and strategic interactions and decisions of entities such as states, as most IR theories do, cognitive evolution highlights the structural and agential mechanisms that dynamically enter the ordering of social and political life. It therefore attempts to promote the study of world politics as social-ordering dynamic processes. A world-ordering systemic theory helps clarify some past and current ambiguities in IR theory about the differences and relationships between the concepts of international system and international and/or global order. Both Kenneth Waltz's (1979) and Alex Wendt's (1999) celebrated IR theory books are about international systems, but they deal, albeit differently, with the concept of anarchy, which is an ordering principle. By contrast, John Ikenberry's (2011) theory of international order is really a theory about which major power institutes the rules of the game in a hierarchical international system.

Cognitive evolution theory is at least one level of abstraction higher than states and their interaction. It does not dismiss the centrality of states and material power for world ordering or the politics associated with it. But it places communities of practice at center stage, first, because they are the site where agency and social structures come together and where collective learning and political contestation take place. They are also the "backstage," or what lies behind the wheeling and dealing of political practitioners, between states, and in and between international and transnational organizations. They are the epistemic and practical background of how and why actors practice or perform world politics. Communities of practice combine the ontological and epistemological advantages of simultaneously studying material reality and knowledge, social structure and agency, and change and stability.

A theory of world ordering is systemic even when we direct our attention to regional social orders such as the European Union, functional social orders such as the cyberspace social order, and issue-specific international social orders such as the corporate order. In contrast to past international system theories, however, which made room for the study of "subsystems" like boxes within boxes, world-ordering theories, such as cognitive evolution, are about ordering complexity. They involve a multiplicity of social orders resulting from complex fluctuations that are characterized by emergence and nonlinear change. Theories of world ordering may be at least as structurally causal as international systems of times past were. Their comparative advantage, however, is to concentrate on both causal relationships and primarily on their constitution, in the sense of their conditions of possibility.

IR scholars may prefer studying world ordering from different theoretical perspectives than I do, for example, by focusing on norms or discourses, the "careers" or trajectories of institutions and organizations in global governance, policy-making, and the strategic interdependence between practitioners when rationally choosing practices and institutions. I would consider this a welcome move. However, this book shows the benefits of using a cognitive evolutionary approach for the study of world ordering. One of the benefits of studying world politics primarily as cognitive evolution is that scholars can approach the issues at hand at several levels and with the help of different methodologies. Another important benefit is moving the understanding of world ordering away from the concepts of anarchy and hierarchy, which mostly follow a vertical notion of order, toward more horizontal understandings of ordering, such as "interconnectedness" and "disassociation." While obviously not the only way of conceiving world ordering from a horizontal perspective,[1] concentrating on interconnectedness and disassociation (for example, on liberal internationalist and multilateral practices), on one hand, and illiberal ethnic and populist nationalist practices, on the other hand, is particularly salient and relevant for world ordering in our age. But this horizontal dimension of world ordering – mainly the overlap and a combination of interconnectedness and disassociation practices – has been crucial for understanding world politics since the dawn of nationalism and nation-states, if not before.

Transcending the dichotomy between evolutionary approaches and constructivist approaches for the sake of studying world ordering – and the politics involved with it, such as cognitive evolution theory – has other advantages. For example, it breaks with rigid and static – I would refer to them as Newtonian – ways of understanding change in world politics (for example, explaining the change from war to stability, and vice versa) as resulting from changes in the distribution of the systems' actors' "mass." Alternatively, consistent with its process-oriented ontology, cognitive evolution theory enlists Searle's concept of deontic power (1995), which, bringing together analytical and normative theory, explains fluctuations in the metastability of practices and social institutions and shows the importance of understanding political authority from a practical epistemic perspective. A dynamic approach to world order should explain, for example, how institutions make their appearance in the first place and remain metastable as long as people practice the same, or similar, practices, and understand via shared background knowledge how the world

[1] A related way is the flattening of international relations by international law.

hangs together. My systemic approach focuses on practices not because it is currently trendy in social theory and IR, but because practices are processes, relations, social structures, and agents congealed into substance and materials, and they thus capture a broader ontology and become more amenable to empirical research.

Studying world ordering could also provide IR theorists with alternative ways to understand power struggles, domination, and coercion, which are so entrenched in world politics. Thus, for example, the concept of a balance of practices can serve as a complement to the concept of balance of power when studying the role of power in world ordering because material power needs first to be turned into action and practice before having any significant effects. For example, a balance of practice, or lack thereof, between the disassociation practices of the United States under President Trump and the interconnectedness-associated practices of the EU can provide new ways of understanding the politics between these entities. Approaching world ordering from the perspective of deontic power, performative power, and epistemic practical notions of authority will help to better explain the dynamic social potential of practices and their background knowledge to keep the post–World War II liberal order metastable or, alternatively, promote its evolution, as appears to be occurring at the time of this writing.

Concentrating the study of international politics on world ordering would also open new ways of understanding and studying the impact of scientific and technical knowledge on world affairs. The epistemic community research program, for instance, which in the last generation helped frame international relations' understanding of the relationship between knowledge and power, has been so far singly conceptually driven and theoretically restrained. Its main emphasis has been on whether, how, and why epistemic communities help affect, cause, or constitute international public policy-making in fields where scientific and technical expertise is required. To some extent, my early work followed this path. A mostly overlooked alternative is conceptually pluralistic, driven to explain more broadly international politics from a systemic perspective, and therefore theoretically expanding. This alternative could conceive of epistemic communities, most likely together with other concepts, as part of a mechanism or mechanisms aimed at explaining world ordering more generally. Identifying epistemic communities as communities of practice, as I do now (Adler 2014; Adler and Faubert 2018), together with other mechanisms and processes, enables me to understand the effect of background scientific knowledge on conditions of possibility for the emergence of world-ordering practices, their selective retention, and the conditions for their long-term survival. Because practices are at the core of what epistemic communities are about, and what they would like to change, the concept of community of practice can play a major role in expanding the so far theoretically restrained research program on epistemic communities. Following an expanding theoretical agenda on epistemic communities, the concept of communities of practice can combine scientific knowledge, practices, material resources, and novel ways of understanding social power, authority, rule, and politics, as well as recruiting both systemic and agential factors to explain what makes world ordering and its evolution possible.

Some years ago, I wrote that constructivism lacks a theory of politics (2002). It was an inappropriate choice of words. As much as we cannot consider rational choice as social theory, or ontology and epistemology as a theory of politics, we cannot consider constructivism as social theory, or ontology and epistemology of the social world as a theory of politics. But evolutionary constructivist social theory can inform, guide, and ground theories of world politics, particularly of world ordering, because of its dynamic nature, especially because it takes change and stability as part of the same social reality. It also takes practices as the material and ideational manifestation of both agency and structure. While cognitive evolution may not be a "grand" theory of world politics, it nevertheless suggests a systemic analytical and normative theory of world ordering.

Cognitive evolution is about the politics within and between communities of practice, which is where and how new practices develop, through which practices and knowledge diffuse, and more generally where and how they are selectively retained. The politics of interconnectedness and disassociation – of internationalization and nationalism – goes to the core of world ordering. Just a quick look at world order changes in the last few years makes it amply evident that the politics of globalization, immigration, identity, liberal international institutions, free international trade versus mercantilism, democracy and authoritarian populism, and much more have everything to do with the contestation in and between communities of practice about interconnectedness and disassociation. This is not new to world ordering. Some remarkably similar processes occurred in the first half of the twentieth century, when the first wave of globalization and large waves of immigration created a reaction against them, which ended up bringing Hitler and Mussolini to power and forcing liberal states to escape from the grips of authoritarians. As I have shown in the book, better practices, namely those that highlight values and practices of common humanity, lack authority unless they are empowered by practitioners' performances. The politics of interconnectedness, which is contingently conducive to the institutionalization of common humanity practices and values, differs markedly from the politics of progress in one country we knew in Europe in the 1930s, and we know again now, with President Trump's policies of making "America great again."

Politics also enters world ordering and cognitive evolution by shaping the meanings of competent performances, in practice, and constituting social orders' conditions of possibility. Constitution, as processes through which social orders become possible, takes place only because of practitioners' performance, negotiation, learning, and contestation. Otherwise, constitution processes "constitute" propensities only. Politics and power, both social and material, are at the core of practices and background knowledge.

It is not enough to argue that politics permeates cognitive evolution processes, such as creative variation and selective retention, and mechanisms, such as contestation within and between communities of practice. Instead, following Martin Wight's (1960) understanding that a theory of international politics ought to have a normative component, politics, rule, and power are also about ethical epistemic authority and practices' normativity – about the conditions for the development of better practices founded on common humanity values, such as peaceful change. In other words, cognitive evolution's theory of politics is about the conditions of possibility of better social orders that flow not only from interconnectedness, communities of practice's spread, and practices' reciprocity but also from humans' will to perform "better," in terms of both their performance and the ethical quality or value of their practices. Cutting across comparative politics and international relations theory, cognitive evolution's theory of politics ought to demonstrate why practices (the "software"), rather than only institutions (the "hardware"), are crucial for constituting better practices. This is the case regarding the practices of democracy, understood from a Deweyan perspective, as an identity and way of being, which are promoted by negotiation and education practices, rather than by populist and coercive practices associated with authoritarian governments.

Beyond providing a general framework for studying world politics, theories of world ordering, in general, and cognitive evolution theory, in particular, also suggest specific tools for explaining how practices, institutions, and policies are selectively retained, where new practices come from, and why certain practices become prominent and institutionalized rather than others. Whether we look at cognitive evolution theory as a whole or through some of its components, for example, communities of practice, it can generate a research program on world ordering. A future research agenda on cognitive evolution might examine the theory's main claims as well as the various concepts, processes, and mechanisms on which it stands. More generally, the development of a research program on world ordering, whether based on cognitive evolution theory or on other dynamic theories (evolutionary or not), will be a positive and progressive development.

The agenda for future research can be quite vast; for the sake of brevity, I mention only a few items. First, while in this book I used illustrations, the development of case studies on various social orders will help test the arguments and the concepts I raised here, for example, deontic power, epistemic practical authority, common humanity, epistemological security, practical democracy, and many more. Second, the argument about the existence of multiple overlapping international social orders is debatable, and so is my way of portraying world order as a whole in light of the existence of diverse and overlapping international social orders. I can also think of fruitful avenues of research that consider world ordering and multilevel global governance. While I suggest multiple international social orders as a more social and dynamic concept than international regimes, the latter may still find its purpose in a theory of cognitive evolution in conjunction with a world-ordering agenda, for example, regarding competence regimes and regimes aimed at selecting, spreading, and institutionalizing practices that enhance our common humanity.

Third, the concept of community of practice, while it may be used in contexts and purposes other than cognitive evolution theory, raises a set of research questions. For example, future researchers could fruitfully examine the agency of communities of practice, their mutual relationships and reciprocal influence, constellations of communities of practice, the boundaries between them and with their environment, contestation and learning within and between them, power and authority as expressed in the politics of communities of practice, their relationship with formal institutions and organizations, and much more.

Fourth, the concept of background knowledge and its relationship to practices is contested and misunderstood. According to cognitive evolution theory, while background knowledge may often be tacit, it often is also reflexive. It is practical and about competence, but it also involves all epistemic and normative knowledge that constitute and maintain practices intersubjectively metastable. Rules, norms, and values are part of background knowledge as much as scientific knowledge and ideologies are. Can people and states, for example, practice practices of which they have no corresponding intersubjective understanding? What about individuals' dispositions and expectations about them? I doubt it, but scholars should more fully explore these questions theoretically and empirically test them.

Fifth, the mechanisms and processes of cognitive evolution theory might widen and deepen research on collective learning and contestation, the relationship between practices and background knowledge, practices' materiality, alternative notions of variation and innovation, processes and mechanisms of practices' spread across space and time, and the role of discourse and narratives in the evolution of social orders.

Sixth, my arguments on deontic power and performative power are worth a careful and critical look, as is the way I conceive of authority from a pragmatist and epistemic perspective. These concepts, of course, are also related to my notion of horizontal forms of rule in world ordering as part of international anarchy or, alternatively, of international material power hierarchies, as well as interconnectedness and disassociation practices. I think that studying world ordering along this spectrum can lead to the development of historical studies that look at how both interconnectedness and disassociation affected different international social orders. I am thinking, for example, of comparative historical studies based on cognitive evolution theory of world order change, such as between the first part of the twentieth century and the current age.

Seventh, we also may benefit from a research agenda on the pluses and minuses of using complexity concepts to explain world ordering. The notion of intersubjective thresholds and tipping points as explanations of sudden world-ordering evolution (the "fall of the Berlin Wall" phenomenon), of propensities rather than probabilities, and of the contingency that an indeterminate world evokes require additional theoretical development and empirical research. Prigogine's arguments about order through fluctuations may also require a more careful look regarding their application to the social sciences. I also consider it valuable to put to an empirical test the heuristic combination of the concepts of social orders' resilience and homeorhesis to assess social orders' propensities for metastability and/or change.

Eighth, cognitive evolution theory raises questions about the notion of constitution and causality and their relationship to power and systems of rule. There is still much more work to do on the methods necessary for tracing practices' trajectories retroactively and the political learning and contestation processes within and between communities of practice. Ninth, the entire "edifice" of cognitive evolution theory stands on process ontology and evolutionary epistemology foundations, which are contested in philosophy, sociology, and social change studies. Process ontology has only recently begun to gain ground in IR theory and so far has raised more questions than providing definitive answers. Some might argue that disregarding natural evolution, such as Darwinist and Lamarckian analogies to natural evolution, and referring only marginally to the coevolution between natural evolution and social and cultural evolution, as studied, for example, in evolutionary psychology, is misguided and that cognitive evolution theory has to be grounded in nature. I disagree, but the issue should be open to debate.

Tenth, there have already been animated debates between scholars who follow a Bourdieu-based approach to social practices and those who follow pragmatist philosophical and sociological approaches to practices. My book joins this debate by highlighting mainly pragmatism, although not entirely dismissing Bourdieu. I hope the book will constructively contribute to the debate, especially my argument that it would be regressive for a practice-based research program in IR to portray the two approaches as alternatives, let alone as mutually exclusive. Recent work by Adler-Nissen (2014a), Christian Büger and Frank Gadinger (2015), Alena Drieschova (2016), and Pouliot (2016) has shown that there is room for finding a common ground in this debate.

Finally, there is the normative agenda that I suggested in Chapter 10. As I said in the introduction to that chapter, I take my normative arguments as a plausibility probe. Still, I would like to defend and, if necessary, revise the normative "middle ground" arguments I raise there. The agenda on normativity, better practices, and common humanity; the concept of quality performance as an ethical companion to the concept of competent performance or practice; the notion of bounded progress; and my humanist-realist approach all raise more questions than answers. Because many of my thoughts in Chapter 10 are preliminary, I hope to return to them in future work, for example, exploring how epistemological insecurity impinges on what I call practical democracy. I also believe that the concept of epistemological security may have traction alone or in conjunction with the concept of ontological security. The current phenomenon of "post-truth," while not new, can enliven and energize an agenda on epistemological security. In sum, I welcome feedback and debate on cognitive evolution theory's normative framework and its relationship to the analytical side of the theory, and more generally to theorizing world ordering.

Years ago, Daniel Nexon and I were chatting leisurely over dinner. To his question about what I was working on, I said cognitive evolution. As I understood it then, this meant answering the question of why some international practices end up being adopted rather than others. He replied that this is the $64,000 question in IR theory, and wished me luck. Perhaps there are as many as 64,000 important questions in IR theory, but I agree with Nexon that this question is one of the most important. I know that this book is unlikely to provide a clear answer to the question, but I hope that I have nonetheless shed some light on where and how to find the answers.

References

Abbate, Janet. 1999. *Inventing the Internet*. Cambridge, MA: MIT Press.

Abbott, Andrew. 1988a. *The System of Professions*. Chicago, IL: University of Chicago Press.

1988b. "Transcending General Linear Reality." *Sociological Theory* 6 (2): 169–86.

1995a. "Sequence Analysis: New Methods for Old Ideas." *Annual Review of Sociology* 21: 93–113.

1995b. "Things of Boundaries." *Social Research* 62 (4): 857–82.

2001. *Time Matters: On Theory and Method*. Chicago, IL: University of Chicago Press.

2005. "The Historicality of Individuals." *Social Science History* 29 (1): 1–13.

Aboulafia, Mitchell. 1999. "A (Neo) American in Paris: Bourdieu, Mead, and Pragmatism." In *Bourdieu: A Critical Reader*, edited by R. Shusterman, 153–74. Oxford: Blackwell Oxford.

2016. "George Herbert Mead." *The Stanford Encyclopedia of Philosophy* (Fall 2016 edition), edited by Edward N. Zalta. Available at https://plato.stanford.edu/archives/fall2016/entries/mead/.

Acharya, Amitav. 2004. "How Ideas Spread: Whose Norms Matter? Norm Localization and Institutional Change in Asian Regionalism." *International Organization* 58 (2): 239–75.

2007. "The Emerging Regional Architecture of World Politics." *World Politics* 59 (4): 629–52.

2012. "Comparative Regionalism: A Field Whose Time Has Come?" *The International Spectator* 47 (1): 3–15.

Acharya, Amitav, and Alastair Iain Johnston. 2007. *Crafting Cooperation: Regional International Institutions in Comparative Perspective*. Cambridge: Cambridge University Press.

Acquisti, Alessandro, Stefanos Gritzalis, Costos Lambrinoudakis, and Sabrina di Vimercati, eds. 2007. *Digital Privacy: Theory, Technologies, and Practices*. New York: Auerbach.

Acuto, Michele, and Simon Curtis. 2014. "Assemblage Thinking and International Relations." In *Reassembling International Theory*, edited by Michele Acuto and Simon Curtis, 1–15. Basingstoke: Palgrave Macmillan.

Adger, W. Neil. 2000. "Social and Ecological Resilience: Are They Related?" *Progress in Human Geography* 24 (3): 347–64.

Adler, Emanuel. 1986. "Ideas of Progress in International Relations: A Conceptual and Theoretical Analysis." Unpublished manuscript, Hebrew University of Jerusalem.

1987. *The Power of Ideology: The Quest for Technological Autonomy in Argentina and Brazil*. Berkeley: University of California Press.

1991. "Cognitive Evolution: A Dynamic Approach for the Study of International Relations and Their Progress." In *Progress in Postwar International Relations*, edited by Emanuel Adler and Beverly Crawford, 43–88. New York: Columbia University Press.

1992. "The Emergence of Cooperation: National Epistemic Communities and the International Evolution of the Idea of Nuclear Arms Control." *International Organization* 46 (1): 101–45.

1997. "Seizing the Middle Ground: Constructivism in World Politics." *European Journal of International Relations* 3 (3): 319–63.

1998. "Seeds of Peaceful Change: The OSCE's Security Community-Building Model." In *Security Communities*, edited by Emanuel Adler and Michael Barnett, 119–60. Cambridge: Cambridge University Press.

2002. "Constructivism and International Relations." In *Handbook of International Relations*, edited by Walter Carlsnaes, Thomas Risse, and Beth A. Simons, 95–118. London: Sage.

2005. *Communitarian International Relations*. New York: Routledge.

2008. "The Spread of Security Communities: Communities of Practice, Self-Restraint, and NATO's Post-Cold War Transformation." *European Journal of International Relations* 14 (2): 195–230.

2010. "Europe as a Civilizational Community of Practice." In *Civilizations in World Politics: Plural and Pluralist Perspectives*, edited by Peter J. Katzenstein, 67–90. New York: Routledge.

Adler, Emanuel. ed. 2012. *Israel in the World: Legitimacy and Exceptionalism*. New York: Routledge.

2013. "Constructivism and International Relations." In *Handbook of International Relations*, 2nd edition, edited by Walter Carlsnaes, Thomas Risse, and Beth A. Simons, 112–144. London: Sage.

2014. "Epistemic Communities of Practice." Paper presented at the annual meeting of the American Political Science Association, August 30, Washington, DC.

Adler, Emanuel, and Beverly Crawford, eds. 1991. *Progress in Postwar International Relations*. New York: Columbia University Press.

Adler, Emanuel, and Beverly Crawford. 2006. "Normative Power: The European Practice of Region Building and the Case of the Euro-Mediterranean Partnership." In *The Convergence of Civilizations: Constructing a Mediterranean Region*, edited by Emanuel Adler, Federica Bicchi, Beverly Crawford, and Raffaella Del Sarto, 3–50. Toronto: Toronto University Press.

Adler, Emanuel, and Michael Barnett. 1998. *Security Communities*. Cambridge: Cambridge University Press.

Adler, Emanuel, and Michael Faubert. 2018. "Epistemic Communities of Practice." Draft, University of Toronto.

Adler, Emanuel, and Patricia Greve. 2009. "When Security Community Meets Balance of Power: Overlapping Regional Mechanisms of Security Governance." *Review of International Studies* 35 (S1): 59–84.

Adler, Emanuel, and Peter M. Haas. 1992. "Conclusion: Epistemic Communities, World Order, and the Creation of a Reflective Research Program." *International Organization* 46 (1): 367–90.

Adler, Emanuel, and Vincent Pouliot. 2011a. "International Practices: Introduction and Framework." In *International Practices*, edited by Emanuel Adler and Vincent Pouliot, 3–35. Cambridge: Cambridge University Press.

2011b. "International Practices." *International Theory* 3 (1): 1–36.

Adler-Nissen, Rebecca, ed. 2013. *Bourdieu in International Relations: Rethinking Key Concepts in IR*. London: Routledge.

Adler-Nissen, Rebecca, 2014a. *Opting out of the European Union: Diplomacy, Sovereignty and European Integration*. Cambridge: Cambridge University Press.

2014b. "Stigma Management in International Relations: Transgressive Identities, Norms, and Order in International Relations." *International Organization* 68 (1): 239–75.

Adler-Nissen, Rebecca, and Vincent Pouliot. 2014. "Power in Practice: Negotiating the International Intervention in Libya." *European Journal of International Relations* 20 (4): 889–911.

Ágh, Attila. 2016. "The Decline of Democracy in East-Central Europe: Hungary as the Worst-Case Scenario." *Problems of Post-Communism* 63 (5–6): 277–87.

Albert, Mathias. 2010. "Modern System Theories in World Politics." In *New Systems Theories of World Politics*, edited by Mathias Albert, Lars-Erik Cederman, and Alexander Wendt, 41–68. London: Palgrave.

Albert, Mathias, and Friedrich Kratochwil. 2001. "Conclusion." In *Identities, Borders, International Relations: Rethinking International Relations Theory*, edited by Albert Mathias, David Jacobson, and Yosef Lapid, 275–292. Minneapolis: University of Minnesota Press.

Alberts, David S., and Thomas J. Czerwinski. 1997. *Complexity, Global Politics, and National Security*. Washington, DC: National Defense University Press.

Aldrich, Howard E., Geoffrey M. Hodgson, David L. Hull, Thorbjørn Knudsen, Joel Mokyr, and Viktor J. Vanberg 2008. "In Defence of Generalized Darwinism." *Journal of Evolutionary Economics* 18 (5): 577–96.

Aldrich, Howard E., and Martha Martinez. 2003. "Entrepreneurship as Social Construction: A Multi-Level Evolutionary Approach." In *Handbook of Entrepreneurial Research*, edited by Zoltan J. Acs and David B. Audretsch, 359–99. Boston: Kluwer.

Alexander, Jeffrey C. 2006. "Cultural Pragmatics: Social Performance between Ritual and Strategy." In *Social Performance: Symbolic Action, Cultural Pragmatics, and Ritual*, edited by Jeffrey C. Alexander, Berhard Giesen, and Jason L. Mast, 29–90. Cambridge: Cambridge University Press.

2011. *Performance and Power*. Cambridge: Polity.

Alexander, Thomas M. 1987. *John Dewey's Theory of Art, Experience, and Nature*. Albany: State University of New York Press.

Alford, John R., Carolyn L. Funk, and John R. Hibbing. 2005. "Are Political Orientations Genetically Transmitted?" *American Political Science Review* 99 (2): 153–67.

Alford, John R., and John R. Hibbing. 2004. "The Origin of Politics: An Evolutionary Theory of Political Behavior." *Perspectives on Politics* 2 (4): 707–23.

Allen, Bentley. 2018. *Scientific Cosmology and International Orders*. Cambridge: Cambridge University Press.

Alter, Karen J., and Sophie Meunier. 2006. "Nested and Overlapping Regimes in the Transatlantic Banana Trade Dispute." *Journal of European Public Policy* 13 (3): 362–82.

2009. "The Politics of International Regime Complexity." *Perspectives on Politics* 7 (1): 13–24.

Amin, Ash. 2002. "Spatialities of Globalisation." *Environment and Planning A* 34 (3): 385–99.

Amin, Ash, and Patrick Cohendet. 2004. *Architectures of Knowledge: Firms, Capabilities, and Communities*. Oxford: Oxford University Press.

Anderson, Benedict. 2003. *Imagined Communities: Reflections on the Origin and Spread of Nationalism*. London: Verso Books.

Anderson, Elizabeth. 2006. "The Epistemology of Democracy." *Episteme* 3 (1–2): 8–22.

2014. "Dewey's Moral Philosophy." In *The Stanford Encyclopedia of Philosophy*, edited by Edward N. Zalta. Metaphysics Research Lab, Stanford University. Available at https://plato.stanford.edu/entries/dewey-moral/.

Ansell, Christopher K. 2011. *Pragmatist Democracy: Evolutionary Learning as Public Philosophy*. New York: Oxford University Press.

Archer, John. 1988. *The Behavioural Biology of Aggression*. New York: Cambridge University Press.

Archer, Margaret S. 1982. "Morphogenesis versus Structuration: On Combining Structure and Action." *British Journal of Sociology* 33 (4): 455–83.

1988. *Culture and Agency: The Place of Culture in Social Theory*. Cambridge: Cambridge University Press.

1995. *Realist Social Theory: The Morphogenetic Approach*. Cambridge: Cambridge University Press.

1998. "Realism and Morphogenesis." In *Critical Realism: Essential Readings*, edited by Margaret Archer, Roy Bhaskar, Andrew Collier, Tony Lawson, and Alan Norrie, 356–82. New York: Routledge.

2000. *Being Human: The Problem of Agency*. Cambridge: Cambridge University Press.

2007. *Making Our Way through the World: Human Reflexivity and Social Mobility*. Cambridge: Cambridge University Press.

Arendt, Hannah. 1958. *The Human Condition*. Chicago, IL: University of Chicago Press.

1965. *On Revolution*. New York: Viking.

1967. "Truth and Politics." *The New Yorker*, February 25.

1970. *On Violence*. Orlando, FL: Houghton Mifflin Harcourt.

1973. *The Origins of Totalitarianism*. Orlando, FL: Houghton Mifflin Harcourt.

Aristotle. 1984. *The Complete Works of Aristotle*, vols. I and II, edited by J. Barnes. Princeton, NJ: Princeton University Press.

2000. *Nicomachean Ethics*, translated by Roger Crisp. Cambridge: Cambridge University Press.

Arnbak, Axel, and Nico A. N. M. van Eijk. 2012. "Certificate Authority Collapse: Regulating Systemic Vulnerabilities in the HTTPS Value Chain." Available at https://papers.ssrn.com/sol3/papers.cfm?abstract_id=2031409.

Arthur, W. Brian. 1994. "Inductive Reasoning and Bounded Rationality." *The American Economic Review* 84 (2): 406–11.

1995. "Complexity in Economic and Financial Markets: Behind the Physical Institutions and Technologies of the Marketplace Lie the Beliefs and Expectations of Real Human Beings." *Complexity* 1 (1): 20–25.

1999. "Complexity and the Economy." *Science* 284 (5411): 107–9.

Augier, Mie, and Michael Prietula. 2007. "Historical Roots of the 'A Behavioral Theory of the Firm' Model at GSIA." *Organization Science* 18 (3): 507–22.

Austin, J. L. 1962. *How to Do Things with Words*. Oxford: Clarendon.

Axelrod, Robert. 1984. *The Evolution of Cooperation*. New York: Basic Books.

1986. "An Evolutionary Approach to Norms." *American Political Science Review* 80 (4): 1095–111.

1997. *The Complexity of Cooperation: Agent-Based Models of Competition and Collaboration*. Princeton, NJ: Princeton University Press.

Axelrod, Robert, and Michael D. Cohen. 2000. *Harnessing Complexity: Organizational Implications of a Scientific Frontier*. New York: Basic Books.

Ba, Alice, and Matthew J. Hoffmann, eds. 2005. *Contending Perspectives on Global Governance: Coherence and Contestation*. New York: Routledge.

Baert, Patrick. 1998. *Social Theory in the Twentieth Century*. New York: New York University Press.

Bailey, D., and L. De Propis. 2004. "A Bridge Too Phare? EU Pre-Accession Aid and Capacity-Building in the Candidate Countries." *JCMS: Journal of Common Market Studies* 42 (1): 77–98.

Baldwin, David A. 2013. "Power and International Relations." In *Handbook of International Relations*, edited by Walter Carlsnaes, Thomas Risse, and Beth A. Simmons, 273–98. London: Sage.

Baldwin, James Mark. 1895. "Consciousness and Evolution." *Science* 2: 219–23.

1897a. *Social and Ethical Interpretations in Mental Development: A Study in Social Psychology*. New York: Macmillan.

1897b. "Organic Selection." *Nature* 55.

1902. *Dictionary of Philosophy and Psychology*, vol. 2. New York: Macmillan.

1903. *Development and Evolution*. New York: Macmillan.

1906. *Thought and Things: A Study of Development and Meaning of Thought or Genetic Logic*. New York: Arno Press.

1909. *Darwin and the Humanities*. Baltimore: Review Publishing Company.

Ball, Kirstie, and Laureen Snider, eds. 2013. *The Surveillance-Industrial Complex: A Political Economy of Surveillance*. New York: Routledge.

Balzacq, Thierry. 2009. "The Frontiers of Governance: Understanding the External Dimension of EU Justice and Home Affairs." In *The External*

Dimension of EU Justice and Home Affairs: Governance, Neighbours, Security, edited by Thierry Balzacq, 1–34. New York: Palgrave Macmillan.

Bandura, Albert. 1986. *Social Foundations of Thought and Action: A Social Cognitive Theory*. Englewood Cliffs, NJ: Prentice-Hall.

2001. "Social Cognitive Theory: An Agentic Perspective." *Annual Review of Psychology* 52 (1): 1–26.

Barab, Sasha A., and Thomas Duffy. 2000. "From Practice Fields to Communities of Practice." In *The Foundations of Learning Environments*, edited by David Jonassen and Susan Land, 25–55. Mahwah, NJ: Lawrence Erlbaum Associates.

Barber, Tony. 2014. "Remembering the Fall of the Berlin Wall." *Financial Times*, November 2.

Barnes, Barry. 1995. *The Elements of Social Theory*. Princeton, NJ: Princeton University Press.

2001. "Practice as Collective Action." In *The Practice Turn in Contemporary Theory*, edited by Theodore R. Schatzki, Karin Knorr Cetina, and Eike Von Savigny, 17–28. New York: Routledge.

Barnett, Michael. 1998. *Dialogues in Arab Politics: Negotiations in Regional Order*. New York: Columbia University Press.

2009. "Evolution without Progress? Humanitarianism in a World of Hurt." *International Organization* 63 (4): 621–63.

2010. *The International Humanitarian Order*. New York: Routledge.

2011. *Empire of Humanity: A History of Humanitarianism*. Ithaca, NY: Cornell University Press.

Barnett, Michael, and Janice Stein. 2017. "Pragmatism, Meaning, and Suffering: Evolutionary Callings and Exhaustions." Paper presented at the conference "A Celebration of Emanuel Adler's Scholarship and Career." Munk School of Global Affairs, University of Toronto, May 12.

Barnett, Michael, and Raymond Duvall. 2005. "Power in International Politics." *International Organization* 59 (1): 39–75.

Bartley, W. W. 1987. "Philosophy of Biology versus Philosophy of Physics." In *Evolutionary Epistemology, Rationality, and the Sociology of Knowledge*, edited by Gerard Radnitzky and W. W. Bartley III, 5–46. La Salle, IL: Open Court.

Bateson, William. 1894. *Materials for the Study of Variation*. London: Macmillan.

Baumer, Franklin L. 1977. *Modern European Thought: Continuity and Change in Ideas, 1600–1950*. New York: Macmillan.

Beck, Ulrich. 2006. *Cosmopolitan Vision*. Cambridge: Polity.

2007. "Beyond Class and Nation: Reframing Social Inequalities in a Globalizing World." *British Journal of Sociology* 58 (4): 679–705.

2013. *German Europe*, translated by Rodney Livingstone. Cambridge: Polity.

Beckert, Jens. 2010. "How Do Fields Change? The Interrelations of Institutions, Networks, and Cognition in the Dynamics of Markets." *Organization Studies* 31 (5): 605–27.

Beinhocker, Eric D. 2007. *The Origin of Wealth: The Radical Remaking of Economics and What It Means for Business and Society*. Cambridge, MA: Harvard Business School Press.

Beitz, Charles R. 1979. *Political Theory and International Relations*. Princeton, NJ: Princeton University Press.

2009. *The Idea of Human Rights*. Oxford: Oxford University Press

Benjamin, Walter. 1977. "Die Aufgabe Des Übersetzers." In *Illuminationen: Ausgewählte Schriften*, 50–62. Frankfurt am Main: Suhrkamp.

Bennett, Colin J. 1988. "Different Processes, One Result: The Convergence of Data Protection Policy in Europe and the United States." *Governance* 1: 162–83.

1991. "What Is Policy Convergence and What Causes It?" *British Journal of Political Science* 21 (2): 215–33.

Berger, Peter, and Thomas Luckmann. 1966. *The Social Construction of Reality: A Treatise in the Sociology of Knowledge*. New York: Anchor.

Bergson, Henri. 1910. *Time and Free Will: An Essay on the Immediate Data of Consciousness*, translated by F. L. Pogson. London: George Allen and Unwin.

1998 [1911]. *Creative Evolution*, translated by Arthur Mitchell. New York: Dover.

Berkeley, George. 1975. *Philosophical Works: Including the Works on Vision*, edited by M. R. Ayers. London: Dent.

Berman, Sheri. 1998. *The Social Democratic Moment: Ideas and Politics in the Making of Interwar Europe*. Cambridge, MA: Harvard University Press.

2006. *The Primacy of Politics: Social Democracy and the Making of Europe's Twentieth Century*. New York: Cambridge University Press.

Bernstein, Richard J. 1971. *Praxis and Action: Contemporary Philosophy of Human Activity*. Philadelphia: University of Pennsylvania Press.

2018. *Why Read Hannah Arendt Now*. Cambridge: Polity.

Bernstein, Richard J., ed. 1985. *Habermas and Modernity*. Cambridge, MA: MIT Press.

Bernstein, Steven. 2001. *The Compromise of Liberal Environmentalism*. New York: Columbia University Press.

Bernstein, Steven, and Hamish van der Ven. 2017. "Best Practices in Global Governance." *Review of International Studies* 43 (3): 534–56.

Beyerchen, Alan D. 1997. "Clausewitz, Nonlinearity, and the Importance of Imagery." In *Complexity, Global Politics, and National Security*, edited by David S. Alberts and Thomas J. Czerwinski, 70–77. Washington, DC: National Defense University Press.

Bhaskar, Roy. 1997. "On the Ontological Status of Ideas." *Journal for the Theory of Social Behaviour* 27 (2–3): 139–47.

1998. *The Possibility of Naturalism: A Philosophical Critique of the Contemporary Human Sciences*. Oxford: Routledge.

Bially Mattern, Janice. 2001. "The Power Politics of Identity." *European Journal of International Relations* 7 (3): 349–97.

2011. "A Practice Theory of Emotion for International Relations." In *International Practices*, edited by Emanuel Adler and Vincent Pouliot, 63–86. Cambridge: Cambridge University Press.

Bicchi, Federica. 2006. "'Our Size Fits All': Normative Power Europe and the Mediterranean." *Journal of European Public Policy* 13 (2): 286–303.

2014. "Information Exchanges, Diplomatic Networks and the Construction of European Knowledge in European Union Foreign Policy." *Cooperation and Conflict* 49 (2): 239–59.

Biggart, Nicole Woolsey, and Thomas D. Beamish. 2003. "The Economic Sociology of Conventions: Habit, Custom, Practice, and Routine in Market Order." *Annual Review of Sociology* 29: 443–64.

Bigo, Didier. 2013. "Security." In *Bourdieu in International Relations: Rethinking Key Concepts in IR*, edited by Rebecca Adler-Nissen, 114–30. New York: Routledge.

Bilge, Leyla, and Tudor Dumitras. 2012. "Before We Knew It: An Empirical Study of Zero-Day Attacks in the Real World." In *Proceedings of the 2012 ACM Conference on Computer and Communications Security*, 833–44. New York: Association for Computing Machinery.

Binder, Sarah. 2015. "The Politics of Centralizing Power in the Fed." *Monkey Cage* blog. *Washington Post*, March 10.

Binder, Sarah, and Mark Spindel. 2013. "Monetary Politics: Origins of the Federal Reserve." *Studies in American Political Development* 27 (1): 1–13.

Blackmore, Susan. 1999. *The Meme Machine*. Oxford: Oxford University Press.

Bloor, David. 2001. "Wittgenstein and the Priority of Practice." In *The Practice Turn in Contemporary Theory*, edited by Theodore R. Schatzki, Karin Knorr Cetina, and Eike Von Savigny, 95–106. New York: Routledge.

Blumberg, Phillip I. 1986. "Limited Liability and Corporate Groups." *Journal of Corporation Law* 11 (4): 573–631.

Blumer, Herbert. 1986. *Symbolic Interactionism: Perspective and Method*. Berkeley: University of California Press

Blyth, Mark. 2002. *Great Transformations: Economic Ideas and Institutional Change in the Twentieth Century*. Cambridge: Cambridge University Press.

2006. "Great Punctuations: Prediction, Randomness, and the Evolution of Comparative Political Science." *American Political Science Review* 100 (4): 493–98.

2011. "Ideas, Uncertainty, and Evolution." In *Ideas and Politics in Social Science Research*, edited by Daniel Béland and Robert Henry Cox, 83–104. New York: Oxford University Press.

Blyth, Mark, Geoffrey M. Hodgson, Orion Lewis, Sven Steinmo, et al. 2011. "Introduction to the Special Issue on the Evolution of Institutions." *Journal of Institutional Economics* 7 (3): 299–315.

Bockman, Johanna, and Gil Eyal. 2002. "Eastern Europe as a Laboratory for Economic Knowledge: The Transnational Roots of Neoliberalism." *American Journal of Sociology* 108 (2): 310–52.

Bohman, James. 2014. "Jürgen Habermas." In *Stanford Encyclopedia of Philosophy*, edited by Edward N. Zalta. Available at https://plato.stanford.edu/entries/habermas/.

Boltanski, Luc. 2011. *On Critique: A Sociology of Emancipation*. Cambridge: Polity.

2012. *Love and Justice as Competences: Three Essays on the Sociology of Action*. Cambridge: Polity.

Boltanski, Luc, and E. Chiapello. 2006. *The New Spirit of Capitalism*. London: Verso.

Boltanski, Luc, and Laurent Thévenot. 2000. "The Reality of Moral Expectations: A Sociology of Situated Judgement." *Philosophical Explorations* 3 (3): 208–31.

2006. *On Justification: Economies of Worth*. Princeton, NJ: Princeton University Press.

Bolton, Robert. 1975. "Plato's Distinction between Being and Becoming." *Review of Metaphysics* 29 (1): 66–95.

Börzel, Tanya A., ed. 2006. *The Disparity of European Integration: Revisiting Neofunctionalism in Honour of Ernst B. Haas*. New York: Routledge.

2007. "Venus Approaching Mars? The European Union as an Emerging Civilian World Power." Paper presented at European Union Studies Association (EUSA) Conference, May 17–19.

2009. *The European Union and the Diffusion of Ideas*. KFG Working Paper, Freie University, Berlin.

2012a. "From Europeanisation to Diffusion: Introduction." *West European Politics* 35 (1): 1–19.

2012b. "When Europeanisation Meets Diffusion: Exploring New Territory." *West European Politics* 35 (1): 192–207.

2013. "Comparative Regionalism: European Integration and Beyond." In *Handbook of International Relations*, edited by Walter Carlsnaes, Thomas Risse, and Beth A. Simmons, 502–30. London: Sage.

Börzel, Tanja A., and Vera van Hüllen. 2015. "Towards a Global Script? Governance Transfer by Regional Organizations." In *Governance Transfer by Regional Organizations*, edited by Tanja A. Börzel and Vera van Hüllen, 3–21. New York: Palgrave Macmillan.

Boulding, Kenneth E. 1978. *Ecodynamics: A New Theory of Societal Evolution*. Beverly Hills, CA: Sage

Bourdieu, Pierre. 1973. "Cultural Reproduction and Social Reproduction." In *Knowledge, Education and Cultural Change*, edited by Richard Brown, 71–112. London: Tavistock.

1977. *Outline of a Theory of Practice*, translated by Richard Nice. Cambridge: Cambridge University Press.

1990. *The Logic of Practices*. Cambridge: Polity Press.

1996. "Cultural Reproduction and Social Reproduction." In *Knowledge, Education and Cultural Change*, edited by Richard Brown, 71–112. London: Routledge.

2000. *Pascalian Meditations*. Stanford, CA: Stanford University Press.

Bourdieu, Pierre, and Loïc Wacquant. 1992. *An Invitation to Reflexive Sociology*. Chicago, IL: University of Chicago Press.

Bouris, Dimitry, and Tobias Schumacher. 2016. *The Revised European Neighbourhood Policy: Continuity and Change in EU Foreign Policy*. London: Palgrave Macmillan.

Boyd, Robert, and John Richerson. 1985. *Culture and the Evolutionary Process*. Chicago, IL: University of Chicago Press.

2005. "Culture, Adaptation." In *The Innate Mind*, vol. 2: *Culture and Cognition*, edited by Peter Carruthers, Stephen Laurence, and Stephen Stich, 23–38. New York: Oxford University Press.

Brachthäuser, Christine. 2011. "Explaining Global Governance: A Complexity Perspective." *Cambridge Review of International Affairs* 24 (2): 221–44.

Bradie, Michael, and William Harms. 2012. "Evolutionary Epistemology." In *Stanford Encyclopedia of Philosophy*, edited by Edward N. Zalta. Available at http://stanford.library.usyd.edu.au/archives/win2015/entries/epistemology-evolutionary/.

Brake, David. 2014. *Sharing Our Lives Online: Risks and Exposure in Social Media*. New York: Palgrave Macmillan.

Branch, Jordan. 2011. "Mapping the Sovereign State: Technology, Authority, and Systemic Change." *International Organization* 65 (1): 1–36.

Brand, Fridolin Simon, and Kurt Jax. 2007. "Focusing the Meaning(s) of Resilience: Resilience as a Descriptive Concept and a Boundary Object." *Ecology and Society* 12 (1): 23.

Bratman, Michael E. 2014. *Shared Agency: A Planning Theory of Acting Together*. New York: Oxford University Press.

Brenner, Susan. 2007. "The Council of Europe's Convention on Cybercrime." In *Cybercrime: Digital Cops in a Networked Environment*, edited by Jack Balkin, James Grimmelmann, Eddan Katz, Nimrod Kozlovski, Shlomit Wagman, and Tal Zarsky, 268–85. New York: New York University Press.

Brey, Philip. 2014. "The Physical and Social Reality of Virtual Worlds." In *The Oxford Handbook of Virtuality*, edited by Mark Grimshaw, 43–53. New York: Oxford University Press.

Brown, Chris. 1992. *International Relations Theory: New Normative Approaches*. New York: Columbia University Press.

2010. *Practical Judgment in International Political Theory: Selected Essays*. London: Routledge.

Brown, John Seely, and Paul Duguid. 1991. "Organizational Learning and Communities-of-Practice: Toward a Unified View of Working, Learning, and Innovation." *Organization Science* 2 (1): 40–57.

2000. *The Social Life of Information*. Cambridge, MA: Harvard Business Press.

2001. "Knowledge and Organization: A Social-Practice Perspective." *Organization Science* 12 (2): 198–213.

Browning, Don S. 1980. *Pluralism and Personality: William James and Some Contemporary Cultures of Psychology*. London: Associated University Presses.

Brubaker, Rogers. 1996. *Nationalism Reframed: Nationhood and the National Question in the New Europe*. Cambridge: Cambridge University Press.

Brunnée, Jutta, and Stephen J. Toope. 2010. *Legitimacy and Legality in International Law: An Interactional Account*. Cambridge: Cambridge University Press.

2011a. "Interactional International Law and the Practice of Legality." In *International Practices*, edited by Emanuel Adler and Vincent Pouliot, 108–36. Cambridge: Cambridge University Press.

2011b. "Interactional International Law: An Introduction." *International Theory* 3 (2): 307–18.

Bryant, William D. 2015. *International Conflict and Cyberspace Superiority: Theory and Practice*. New York: Routledge.

Büger, Christian. 2014. "Boundary Concepts and the Interaction of Communities of Practice: Cases from the Security-Development Nexus, Political Concepts." Working Paper Series. Cardiff.

Büger, Christian, and Frank Gadinger. 2014. *International Practice Theory: New Perspectives*. Basingstoke: Palgrave.

2015. "The Play of International Practice." *International Studies Quarterly* 59 (3): 449–60.

Bukovansky, Mlada. 2002. *Legitimacy and Power Politics: The American and French Revolutions in International Political Culture*. Princeton, NJ: Princeton University Press.

Bull, Hedley. 1977. *The Anarchical Society: A Study of Order in World Society*. New York: Columbia University Press.

Burch, Robert. 2014. "Charles Sanders Peirce." In *Stanford Encyclopedia of Philosopy*, edited by Edward N. Zalta. Available at http://stanford.library.usyd.edu.au/archives/spr2016/entries/peirce/.

Burns, Tom R., and Thomas Dietz. 1992. "Cultural Evolution: Social Rule Systems, Selection and Human Agency." *International Sociology* 7 (3): 259–83.

Busch, Per-Olof, and Helge Jörgens. 2005a. "International Patterns of Environmental Policy Change and Convergence." *European Parliament* 15 (2): 80–101.

2005b. "The International Sources of Policy Convergence: Explaining the Spread of Environmental Policy Innovations." *Journal of European Public Policy* 12 (5): 860–84.

Buss, David. 2016. *Evolutionary Psychology: The New Science of the Mind*. New York: Routledge.

Butler, Judith. 1990. *Gender Trouble and the Subversion of Identity*. New York: Routledge.

1997. *Excitable Speech: A Politics of the Performance*. New York: Routledge.

Buzan, Barry. 2004. *From International to World Society? English School Theory and the Social Structure of Globalisation*. Cambridge: Cambridge University Press.

2005. "Not Hanging Separately: Responses to Dunne and Adler." *Millennium: Journal of International Studies* 34 (1): 183–94.

Buzan, Barry, and R. J. Barry Jones. 1981. *Change and the Study of International Relations: The Evaded Dimension*. New York: St. Martin's Press.

Buzan, Barry, and George Lawson. 2013. "The Global Transformation: The Nineteenth Century and the Making of Modern International Relations." *International Studies Quarterly* 57 (3): 620–34.

2015. *The Global Transformation: History, Modernity and the Making of International Relations*. Cambridge: Cambridge University Press.

Buzan, Barry, and Ole Waever. 2003. *Regions and Powers: The Structure of International Security*. Cambridge: Cambridge University Press.

Byrne, David. 1998. *Complexity Theory and the Social Sciences*. New York: Routledge.

2005. "Complexity, Configurations and Cases." *Theory, Culture and Society* 22 (5): 95–111.

Cabantous, Laure, and Jean-Pascal Gond. 2011. "Rational Decision Making as Performative Praxis: Explaining Rationality's Eternel Retour." *Organization Science* 22 (3): 573–86.

Callon, Michel. 1981. "Pour une Sociologie des Controverses Technologiques." *Fundamenta Scientiae* 2 (3/4): 381–99.

1986. "Some Elements of a Sociology of Translation: Domestication of the Scallops and the Fishermen of Saint Brieuc Bay." In *Power, Action, and Belief: A New Sociology of Knowledge? Sociological Review Monograph*, edited by John Law, 196–233. London: Routledge and Kegan Paul.

2007. "What Does It Mean to Say That Economics Is Performative?" In *Do Economists Make Markets? On the Performativity of Economics*, edited by Donald MacKenzie, Fabian Muniesa, and Lucia Siu, 311–57. Princeton, NJ: Princeton University Press.

Campbell, Donald T. 1960. "Blind Variation and Selective Retention in Creative Thought as in Other Knowledge Processes." *Psychological Review* 67 (6): 380–400.

1965. "Variation and Selective Retention in Socio-Cultural Evolution." In *Social Change in Developing Areas: A Reinterpretation of Evolutionary Theory*, edited by Herbert R. Barringer, George I. Blanksten, and Raymond W. Mack, 26–27. Cambridge, MA: Schenkman.

1974a. "Evolutionary Epistemology." In *The Philosophy of Karl Popper*, edited by Paul A. Schlipp, 413–63. LaSalle, IL: Open Court.

1974b. "Unjustified Variation and Selective Retention in Scientific Discovery." In *Studies in the Philosophy of Biology*, edited by Francisco J. Ayala and Theodosius Dobzhansky, 139–61. London: Macmillan.

1987. "Selection Theory and the Sociology of Scientific Validity." In *Evolutionary Epistemology*, edited by W. Callebaut and R. Pinxten. Dordrecht: Springer.

Campbell-Kelly, Martin, and Daniel D. Garcia-Swartz. 2013. "The History of the Internet: The Missing Narratives." *Journal of Information Technology* 28 (1): 18–33.

Caporaso, James A. 2007. "The Promises and Pitfalls of an Endogenous Theory of Institutional Change: A Comment." *West European Politics* 30 (2): 392–404.

Carlsnaes, Walter. 1992. "The Agency-Structure Problem in Foreign Policy Analysis." *International Studies Quarterly* 36 (3): 245–70.

Carroll, Archie B. 2015. "Corporate Social Responsibility: The Centerpiece of Competing and Complementary Frameworks." *Organizational Dynamics* 44 (2): 87–96.

Carroll, Archie B., and Kareem M. Shabana. 2010. "The Business Case for Corporate Social Responsibility: A Review of Concepts, Research and Practice." *International Journal of Management Reviews* 12 (1): 85–105.

Carruthers, Bruce. 1996. *City of Capital: Politics and Markets in the English Financial Revolution.* Princeton, NJ: Princeton University Press.

Castells, Manuel. 2002. *The Internet Galaxy: Reflections on the Internet, Business, and Society*. Oxford: Oxford University Press.

Caygill, Howard. 1999. "Non-Epistemic Chance: Karl Popper's Ontology." *Tekhnema* Fall. Available at tekhnema.free.fr/5Caygill.html.

Cederman, Lars-Erik. 1994. "Emergent Polarity: Analyzing State-Formation and Power Politics." *International Studies Quarterly* 38 (4): 501–33.

1997. *Emergent Actors in World Politics: How States and Nations Develop and Dissolve*. Princeton, NJ: Princeton University Press.

Cederman, Lars-Erik, and Kristian Skrede Gleditsch. 2004. "Conquest and Regime Change: An Evolutionary Model of the Spread of Democracy and Peace." *International Studies Quarterly* 48 (3): 603–29.

Chancellor, Edward. 1999. *Devil Take the Hindmost: A History of Financial Speculation*. New York: Farrar and Giroux.

Chandler, Alfred Dupont. 1960. "Development, Diversification, and Decentralization." In *Postwar Economic Trends in the United States*, edited by R. E. Freeman, 237–88. New York: Harper and Brothers.

1990. *Strategy and Structure: Chapters in the History of the Industrial Enterprise*. Cambridge, MA: MIT Press.

1992. "What Is a Firm? A Historical Perspective." *European Economic Review* 36 (2–3): 483–92.

Charney, Evan, and William English. 2013. "Genopolitics and the Science of Genetics." *American Political Science Review* 107 (2): 382–95.

Checkel, Jeffrey T. 2001. "Why Comply? Social Learning and European Identity Change." *International Organization* 55 (3): 553–58.

2005. "International Institutions and Socialization in Europe: Introduction and Framework." *International Organization* 59 (4): 801–26.

Chernoff, Fred. 2009. "Defending Foundations for International Relations Theory." *International Theory* 1 (3): 466–77.

Chia, Robert. 1995. "From Modern to Postmodern Organizational Analysis." *Organization Studies* 16 (4): 579–604.

1996. "The Problem of Reflexivity in Organizational Research: Towards a Postmodern Science of Organization." *Organization* 31 (1): 31–59.

1997. "Essai: Thirty Years on: From Organizational Structures to the Organization of Thought." *Organization Studies* 18 (4): 685–707.

1999. "A 'Rhizomic' Model of Organizational Change and Transformation: Perspective from a Metaphysics of Change." *British Journal of Management* 10 (3): 209–27.

2002. "Essai: Time, Duration and Simultaneity; Rethinking Process and Change in Organizational Analysis." *Organization Studies* 23 (6): 863–70.

Chia, Robert, and Brad MacKay. 2007. "Post-Processual Challenges for the Emerging Strategy-as-Practice Perspective: Discovering Strategy in the Logic of Practice." *Human Relations* 60 (1): 217–42.

Choucri, Nazli. 2012. *Cyberpolitics in International Relations*. Cambridge, MA: MIT Press.

Ciccotello, Conrad S. 2014. "The State of the Public Corporation: Not So Much an Eclipse as an Evolution." *Journal of Applied Corporate Finance* 26 (4): 8–21.

Clark, Andy, and David Chalmers. 1998. "The Extended Mind." *Analysis* 58 (1): 7–19.

Clark, David. 2010. "Characterizing Cyberspace: Past, Present and Future." *MIT CSAIL* 1: 2016–28.

Clemens, Elisabeth S., and James M. Cook. 1999. "Politics and Institutionalism: Explaining Durability and Change." *Annual Review of Sociology* 25: 441–66.

Clough, Jonathan. 2012. "The Council of Europe Convention on Cybercrime: Defining 'Crime' in a Digital World." *Criminal Law Forum* 23 (4): 363–91.

2014. "A World of Difference: The Budapest Convention on Cybercrime and the Challenges of Harmonisation." *Monash University Law Review* 40 (3): 698–736.

Coe, Neil M., and Timothy G. Brunell. 2003. "'Spatializing' Knowledge Communities: Towards a Conceptualization of Transnational Innovation Networks." *Global Networks* 3 (4): 437–56.

Cohen, Harlan G. 2015. "International Precedent and the Practice of International Law." In *Negotiating State and Non-State Law: The Challenge of Global and Local Legal Pluralism*, edited by Michael A. Helfand, 268–89. New York: Cambridge University Press.

Cohen, I. Bernard. 1993. "Analogy, Homology and Metaphors in the Interactions between Natural Sciences and the Social Sciences, Especially Economics." In *Non-Natural Social Science: Reflecting on the Enterprise of More Heat than Light*, edited by Neil de Marchi, 7–44. Durham, NC: Duke University Press.

1994. "An Analysis of Interactions between the Natural Sciences and the Social Sciences." In *The Natural Sciences and the Social Sciences*, edited by I. Bernard Cohen, 1–100. Springer.

Cohen, Ira. 1987. "Structuration Theory and Social Praxis." In *Social Theory Today*, edited by Anthony Giddens and Jonathan H. Turner, 273–308. Stanford, CA: Stanford University Press.

Cohen, Jean L. 2012. *Globalization and Sovereignty: Rethinking Legality, Legitimacy, and Constitutionalism*. Cambridge: Cambridge University Press.

Colapietro, Vincent. 2009. "A Revised Portrait of Human Agency: A Critical Engagement with Hans Joas's Creative Appropriation of the Pragmatic Approach." *European Journal of Pragmatism and American Philosophy* 1 (1): 1–24.

Collier, Ruth Berins, and David Collier. 1991. *Shaping the Political Arena: Critical Junctures, the Labor Movement, and Regime Dyamics in Latin America*. Princeton, NJ: Princeton University Press.

Collins, H. M. 2001. "What Is Tacit Knowledge?" In *The Practice Turn in Contemporary Theory*, edited by Theodore R. Schatzki, Karin Knorr Cetina, and Eike Von Savigny, 107–19. New York: Routledge.

Comte, Auguste. 2009 [1853]. *The Positive Philosophy of Auguste Comte*. Cambridge: Cambridge University Press.

Connolly, William. 2011. *A World of Becoming*. Durham, NC: Duke University Press.

Cook, S. D. N., and John Seely Brown. 1999. "Bridging Epistemologies: The Generative Dance between Organizational Knowledge and Organizational Knowing." *Organization Science* 10 (4): 381–400.

Cook, S. D. Noam, and Hendrik Wagenaar. 2012. "Navigating the Eternally Unfolding Present: Toward an Epistemology of Practice." *American Review of Public Administration* 42 (1): 3–38.

Cooper, Michael J., Huseyin Gulen, and Alexei V. Ovtchinnikov. 2010. "Corporate Political Contributions and Stock Returns." *Journal of Finance* 65 (2): 687–724.

Cosmides, Leda, and John Tooby. 1987. "From Evolution to Behavior: Evolutionary Psychology as the Missing Link." In *The Latest on the Best: Essays on Evolution and Optimality*, edited by John Dupre, 277–306. Cambridge, MA: MIT Press.

Cosmides, Leda, John Tooby, and Jerome H. Barkow. 1992. "Introduction: Evolutionary Psychology and Conceptual Integration." In *The Adapted Mind: Evolutionary Psychology and the Generation of Culture*, edited by Jerome H. Barkow, Leda Cosmides, and John Tooby, 3–15. New York: Oxford University Press.

Cowles, Maria Green, James A. Caporaso, and Thomas Risse-Kappen. 2001. *Transforming Europe: Europeanization and Domestic Change*. Ithaca, NY: Cornell University Press.

Cox, Andrew. 2005. "What Are Communities of Practice? A Comparative Review of Four Seminal Works." *Journal of Information Science* 31 (6): 527–40.

Cox, Robert W. 1986. "Production, Power, and World Order: Social Forces in the Making of History." In *Neorealism and Its Critics*, edited by Robert O. Keohane, 204–54. New York: Columbia University Press.

Cox, Robert W., and Timothy J. Sinclair. 1996. *Approaches to World Order*. New York: Cambridge University Press.

Crawford, Beverly. 1991. "Toward a Theory of Progress in International Relations." In *Progress in Postwar International Relations*, edited by Emanuel Adler and Beverly Crawford, 438–68. Berkeley: University of California Press.

Crawford, Neta. 2002. *Argument and Change in World Politics: Ethics, Decolonization, and Humanitarian Intervention*. Cambridge: Cambridge University Press.

Cudworth, Erika, and Stephen Hobden. 2011. *Posthuman International Relations: Complexity, Ecologism and Global Politics*. London: Zed Books.

2012. "The Foundations of Complexity, the Complexity of Foundations." *Philosophy and the Social Sciences* 42 (2): 163–87.

2013. "Complexity, Ecologism, and Posthuman Politics." *Review of International Studies* 39 (3): 643–64.

Czempiel, Ernst-Otto, and James N. Rosenau. 1989. *Global Changes and Theoretical Challenges: Approaches to World Politics for the 1990s*. New York: Free Press.

Dalton, Benjamin. 2004. "Creativity, Habit, and the Social Products of Creative Action: Revising Joas, Incorporating Bourdieu." *Sociological Theory* 22 (4): 603–22.

David, Paul A. 1985. "Clio and the Economics of QWERTY." *American Economic Review* 77 (2): 332–37.

Dawes, Christopher T., and James H. Fowler. 2009. "Partisanship, Voting, and the Dopamine D2 Receptor Gene." *Journal of Politics* 71 (30): 1157–71.

Dawkins, Richard. 1976. *The Selfish Gene*. Oxford: Oxford University Press.

1983. "Universal Darwinism." In *Evolution from Molecules to Man*, edited by D. S. Bendall, 403–28. Cambridge: Cambridge University Press.

1989. *The Selfish Gene*. New York: Oxford University Press.

1996. *The Blind Watchmaker: Why the Evidence of Evolution Reveals a Universe without Design*. New York: W. W. Norton.

De Chardin, Pierre. 1959. *The Phenomenon of Man*. London: Collins.

De Jaegher, Hanne, Ezequiel Di Paolo, and Shaun Gallagher. 2010. "Can Social Interaction Constitute Social Cognition?" *Trends in Cognitive Sciences* 14 (10): 441–47.

Deeks, Ashley. 2016. "Intelligence Services, Peer Constraints, and the Law." In *Global Intelligence Oversight: Governing Security in the Twenty-First Century*, edited by Zachary K. Goldman and Samuel J. Rascoff, 3–36. New York: Oxford University Press.

Deibert, Ronald. 2012. "Growing Dark Side of Cyberspace (. . . and What to Do about It)." *Penn State Journal of Law and International Affairs* 1 (20): 260–74.

2013. *Black Code: Inside the Battle for Cyberspace*. Toronto: Signal.

2015. "The Geopolitics of Cyberspace after Snowden." *Current History* 114 (768): 9–15.

Deibert, Ronald, John Palfrey, Rafal Rohozinski, and Jonathan Zittrain, eds. 2010. *Access Controlled: The Shaping of Power, Rights, and Rule in Cyberspace*. Cambridge, MA: MIT Press.

Deibert, Ronald J., and Masashi Crete-Nishihata. 2012. "Global Governance and the Spread of Cyberspace Controls." *Global Governance: A Review of Multilateralism and International Organizations* 18 (3): 339–61.

Deibert, Ronald J., and Rafal Rohozinski. 2010. "Risking Security: Policies and Paradoxes of Cyberspace Security." *International Political Sociology* 4 (1): 15–32.

2012. "Cyclones in Cyberspace: Information Shaping and Denial in the 2008 Russia–Georgia War." *Security Dialogue* 43 (1): 3–24.

DeLanda, Manuel. 2006. *A New Philosophy of Society: Assemblage Theory and Social Complexity*. London: Continuum.

Deleuze, Gilles, and Félix Guattari. 1987. *A Thousand Plateaus: Capitalism and Schizophrenia*. Minneapolis: University of Minnesota Press.

DeNardis, Laura, and Mark Raymond. 2013. "Thinking Clearly about Multistakeholder Internet Governance." Available at https://papers.ssrn.com/sol3/papers.cfm?abstract_id=2354377.

Dennett, Daniel C. 1991. *Consciousness Explained*. Boston: Little, Brown.

1995. *Darwin's Dangerous Idea: Evolution and the Meaning of Life*. New York: Simon and Schuster.

Depew, David J., and Bruce H. Weber. 1985. "Innovation and Tradition in Evolutionary Theory: An Interpretive Afterword." In *Evolution at a Crossroads*, edited by David J. Depew and Bruce H. Weber, 227–60. Chicago, IL: University of Chicago Press.

Deppe, Kristen Diane, Scott F. Stoltenberg, Kevin B. Smith, and John R. Hibbing. 2013. "Candidate Genes and Voter Turnout: Further Evidence on the Role of 5-HTTLPR." *American Political Science Review* 107 (2): 375–81.

Dessler, David. 1989. "What's at Stake in the Agent-Structure Debate?" *International Organization* 43 (3): 441–73.

Deudney, Daniel, and G. John Ikenberry. 1999. "Realism, Structural Liberalism, and the Western Order." In *Unipolar Politics: Realism and State Strategies after the Cold War*, edited by Ethan B. Kapstein and Michael Mastanduno, 105–23. New York: Columbia University Press.

Deutsch, Karl W., et al. 1957. *Political Community and the North Atlantic Area: International Organization in the Light of Historical Experience*. Princeton, NJ: Princeton University Press.

1963. *The Nerves of Government: Models of Political Communication and Control.* New York: Free Press of Glencoe.

Dewey, John. 1916. *Democracy and Education*. New York: Macmillan.

1922. *Human Nature and Conduct*. New York: Henry Holt.

1929. *The Quest for Certainty*. New York: Milton, Balch.

1960 [1929]. *The Quest for Certainty: A Study on the Relation of Knowledge and Action*. New York: G. P. Putnam's Sons.

1983. *John Dewey: The Middle Works, 1899–1924*, edited by Jo Ann Boydston. Carbondale: Southern Illinois University Press.

1988. *The Middle Works of John Dewey*, vol. 12: *1899–1924. 1920: Reconstruction in Philosophy and Essays (Collective Works of John Dewey)*, edited by Jo Ann Boydston. Carbondale: Southern Illinois University Press.

2008. *The Later Works of John Dewey*, vol. 4: *1925–1953. 1929: The Quest for Certainty (Collective Works of John Dewey)*, edited by Jo Ann Boydston. Carbondale: Southern Illinois University Press.

Dewey, John, and Arthur Bentley. 1949. *Knowing and the Known*. Boston: Beacon Press.

Diffie, Whitfield, and Susan Eva Landau. 2007. *Privacy on the Line: The Politics of Wiretapping and Encryption*. Cambridge, MA: MIT Press.

Dietz, Thomas, and Tom R. Burns. 1992. "Human Agency and the Evolutionary Dynamics of Culture." *Acta Sociologica* 35 (3): 187–200.

DiMaggio, Paul J., and Walter W. Powell. 1983. "The Iron Cage Revisited: Institutional Isomorphism and Collective Rationality on Organizational Fields." *American Sociological Review* 48 (2): 147–60.

1991. "Introduction." In *The New Institutionalism in Organizational Analysis*, edited by Paul J. DiMaggio and Walter W. Powell, 1–44. Chicago, IL: University of Chicago Press.

Dobbin, Frank, Beth Simmons, and Geoffrey Garrett. 2007. "The Global Diffusion of Public Policies: Social Construction, Coercion, Competition or Learning?" *Annual Review of Sociology* 33: 449–72.

Dobzhansky, Theodosius Grigorievich. 1955. *Evolution, Genetics, and Man*. New York: John Wiley and Sons.

1962. *Mankind Evolving: The Evolution of the Human Species*. New Haven, CT: Yale University Press.

Dolowitz, David P., and David Marsh. 2000. "Learning from Abroad: The Role of Policy Transfer in Contemporary Policy-Making." *Governance* 13 (1): 5–23.

Donnelly, Jack. 2012. "The Elements of the Structures of International Systems." *International Organization* 66 (4): 609–43.

Dosi, Giovanni. 1988. "Sources, Procedures, and Microeconomic Effects of Innovation." *Journal of Economic Literature* 26 (3): 1120–71.

Douglas, Mary. 1986. *How Institutions Think*. Syracuse, NY: Syracuse University Press.

Drezner, Daniel W. 2001. "Globalization and Policy Convergence." *International Studies Review* 3 (1): 53–78.

Drieschova, Alena. 2016. "Change of International Orders: Empire, Balance of Power, and Liberal Governance." PhD dissertation, University of Toronto.

2017. "Peirce's Semeiotics: A Methodology for Bridging the Material-Ideational Divide in IR Scholarship." *International Theory* 9 (1): 33–66.

Duguid, Paul. 2005. "'The Art of Knowing': Social and Tacit Dimensions of Knowledge and the Limits of the Community of Practice." *Information Society* 21 (2): 109–18.

Dumouchel, Joelle. 2016. "Regulating International Finance: The Genesis and Transformation of Central Bank Practices." PhD dissertation, University of Toronto.

Dunbar, Robin I. M. 2007. "Evolution and the Social Sciences." *History of the Human Sciences* 20 (2): 29–50.

Dunne, Tim. 1998. *Inventing International Society: A History of the English School*. London: Palgrave Macmillan.

2005. "International Society and World Society: How Does It All Hang Together?" *Millennium: Journal of International Studies* 35 (1): 157–70.

Dunne, Tim, Trine Flockhart, and Marjo Koivisto. 2013. "Introduction: Liberal World Order." In *Liberal World Orders*, edited by Tim Dunne and Trine Flockhart, 1–22. Oxford: Oxford University Press.

Durham, William H. 1991. *Coevolution: Genes, Culture, and Human Diversity*. Stanford, CA: Stanford University Press.

Durkheim, Emile. 1902. *Moral Education*, translated by Everett K. Wilson and Herman Schnurer. New York: Free Press.

1915. *The Elementary Forms of the Religious Life*. London: George Allen and Unwin.

1938. *The Rules of Sociological Method*. New York: Free Press.

1993. *Ethics and the Sociology of Morals*. Amherst, NY: Prometheus Books.

2014 [1893]. *The Division of Labor in Society*. New York: Free Press.

Eckstein, Harry. 1991. *Regarding Politics: Essays on Political Theory, Stability, and Change*. Berkeley: University of California Press.

Edelman, Gerald M. 1987. *Neural Darwinism: The Theory of Neuronal Group Selection*. New York: Basic Books.

Edsall, Thomas B. 2017. "Democracy Can Plant the Seeds of Its Own Destruction." *New York Times*, October 19.

Efinger, Manfred, and Michael Zürn. 1990. "Explaining Conflict Management in East-West Relations: A Quantitative Test of Problem-Structural Typologies." In *International Regimes in East-West Politics*, edited by Volker Rittberger, 64–89. London: Pinter.

Eisenstadt, Shmuel Noah. 2000. "Multiple Modernities." *Daedalus* 129 (1): 1–29.

Eldredge, Niles, and S. J. Gould. 1972. "Punctuated Equilibria: An Alternative to Phyletic Gradualism." In *Models in Paleobiology*, edited by Thomas J. M. Schopf, 82–115. San Francisco: Freeman Cooper.

El-Hani, Charbel Niño, and Sami Pihlström. 2002. "Emergence Theories and Pragmatic Realism." *Essays in Philosophy* 3 (2): article 3. Available at https://commons.pacificu.edu/cgi/viewcontent.cgi?article=1061&context=eip.

Elias, Norbert. 1956. "Problems of Involvement and Detachment." *British Journal of Sociology* 7 (3): 226–52.

1978. *What Is Sociology?* New York: Columbia University Press.

1991. *The Symbol Theory*. London: Sage.

2000. *The Civilizing Process: Sociogenetic and Psychogenetic Investigations*. Oxford: Blackwell.

2001. *The Society of Individuals*. London: Continuum.

Elkjaer, Bente, and Barbara Simpson. 2006. "Towards a Pragmatic Theory of Creative Practice." Paper presented at the Second Organization Studies Summer Workshop, Return to Practice: Understanding Organization as It Happens, Mykonos, Greece, June 15–16.

Elliott, Euel, and L. Douglas Kiel. 1997. "Nonlinear Dynamics, Complexity, and Public Policy: Use, Misuse, and Applicability." In *Chaos, Complexity, and Sociology: Myths, Models, and Theories*, edited by Raymond A. Eve, Sara Horsfall, and Mary E. Lee, 64–78. Hauppauge, NY: Nova Science.

Elsenbroich, Corinna, and Nigel Gilbert. 2014. "We-Intentionality." In *Modelling Norms*, 185–97. New York: Springer.

Elster, Jon. 1982. "The Case for Methodological Individualism." *Theory and Society* 11: 453–82.

1983. *Explaining Technical Change: A Case Study in the Philosophy of Science*. Cambridge: Cambridge University Press.

1989a. *Nuts and Bolts for the Social Sciences*. Cambridge: Cambridge University Press.

1989b. "Social Norms and Economic Theory." *Journal of Economic Perspectives* 3 (4): 99–117.

1989c. *The Cement of Society: A Study of Social Order*. New York: Cambridge University Press.

Emirbayer, Mustafa. 1997. "Manifesto for a Relational Sociology." *American Journal of Sociology* 103 (2): 281–317.

Emirbayer, Mustafa, and Chad Alan Goldberg. 2005. "Pragmatism, Bourdieu, and Collective Emotions in Contentious Politics." *Theory and Society* 34 (5–6): 469–518.

Emirbayer, Mustafa, and Victoria Johnson. 2008. "Bourdieu and Organizational Analysis." *Theory and Society* 37 (1): 1–44.

Emirbayer, Mustafa, and Ann Mische. 1998. "What Is Agency?" *American Journal of Sociology* 103 (4): 962–1023.

Enderlein, Hendrik, Sonja Wälti, and Michael Zürn, eds. 2010. *Handbook on Multi-Level Governance*. Northampton, MA: Edward Elgar.

Engel, Andreas K., Alexander Maye, Martin Kurthen, and Peter König. 2013. "Where's the Action? The Pragmatic Turn in Cognitive Science." *Trends in Cognitive Sciences* 17 (5): 202–9.

Eppink, Derk Jan. 2007. *Life of a European Mandarin: Inside the Commission*. Tielt, Belgium: Lannoo.

Erskine, Toni, ed. 2003. *Can Institutions Have Responsibilities? Collective Moral Agency and International Relations*. Basingstoke: Palgrave Macmillan.

2008. *Embedded Cosmopolitanism: Duties to Strangers and Enemies in a World of Dislocated Communities*. New York: Oxford University Press.

Estlund, David. 2008. *Democratic Authority: A Philosophical Framework*. Oxford: Oxford University Press.

Esty, Daniel C., and Michael E. Porter. 1998. "Industrial Ecology and Competitiveness." *Journal of Industrial Ecology* 2 (1): 35–43.

Evangelista, Matthew. 1999. *Unarmed Forces: The Transnational Movement to End the Cold War*. Ithaca, NY: Cornell University Press.

Eweje, Gabriel. 2006. "Environmental Costs and Responsibilities Resulting from Oil Exploitation in Developing Countries: The Case of the Niger Delta of Nigeria." *Journal of Business Ethics* 69 (1): 27–56.

Ezrahi, Yaron. 2012. *Imagined Democracies: Necessary Political Fictions*. New York: Cambridge University Press.

Fagerberg, Jan. 2003. "Schumpeter and the Revival of Evolutionary Economics: An Appraisal of the Literature." *Journal of Evolutionary Economics* 13 (2): 125–59.

Fama, Eugene F., and Michael C. Jensen. 1983. "Separation of Ownership and Control." *Journal of Law and Economics* 26 (2): 301–25.

Feather, Norman T. 1982. "Human Values and the Prediction of Actions: An Expectancy-Valence Analysis." In *Expectations and Actions*, 263–89. Hillsdale, NJ: Lawrence Erlbaum.

Ferguson, Niall. 2010. "Complexity and Collapse: Empires on the Edge of Chaos." *Foreign Affairs* 89: 1–18.

Fernbach, Philip, and Steven Sloman. 2017. "Why We Believe Obvious Untruths." *New York Times*, March 2.

Fincham, Robin, and Timothy Clark. 2009. "Introduction: Can We Bridge the Rigour-Relevance Gap?" *Journal of Management Studies* 46 (3): 510–15.

Findlay, J. N. 2013. *Hegel: A Re-Examination*. New York: Routledge.

Finnemore, Martha. 1996. "Norms, Culture, and World Politics: Insights from Sociology's Institutionalism." *International Organization* 50 (2): 325–47.

Finnemore, Martha, and Kathryn Sikkink. 1998. "International Norm Dynamics and Political Change." *International Organization* 52 (4): 887–917.

Fioretos, Orfeo. 2011. "Historical Institutionalism in International Relations." *International Organization* 65 (2): 367–99.

Fioretos, Orfeo, Tulia G. Falletti, and Adam Sheingate. 2016. "Historical Institutionalism in Political Science." In *The Oxford Handbook of Historical Institutionalism*, edited by Orfeo Fioretos, Tulia G. Falletti, and Adam Sheingate, 3–30. Oxford: Oxford University Press.

Fioretos, Orfeo, Tulia G. Falletti, and Adam Sheingate, eds. 2016. *The Oxford Handbook of Historical Institutionalism*. Oxford: Oxford University Press.

Fish, Stanley. 2010. "Pragmatism's Gift." *New York Times*, March 15.

Fiske, Susan T., and Shelley E. Taylor. 2013. *Social Cognition: From Brains to Culture*. London: Sage.

Fleck, Ludwik. 1979. *Genesis and Development of a Scientific Fact*. Chicago, IL: University of Chicago Press.

Fligstein, Neil. 1990. *The Transformation of Corporate Control*. Cambridge, MA: Harvard University Press.

Fligstein, Neil, and Doug McAdam. 2011. "Toward a General Theory of Strategic Action Fields." *Sociological Theory* 29 (1): 1–26.

2012. *A Theory of Fields*. Oxford: Oxford University Press.

Florini, Ann. 1996. "The Evolution of International Norms." *International Studies Quarterly* 40 (3): 363–89.

Forcese, Craig. 2015. "Law, Logarithms, and Liberties: Legal Issues Arising from CSE's Metadata Collection Initiatives." In *Privacy, and Surveillance in Canada in the Post-Snowden Era*, edited by Michael A. Geist, 127–62. Ottawa: University of Ottawa Press.

Foucault, Michel. 1970. *The Order of Things*. New York: Pantheon Books.

1972. *Archeology of Knowledge*. New York: Pantheon.

1977. *Discipline and Punish*. New York: Pantheon Books.

1984. *The Foucault Reader*. New York: Pantheon Books.

Fowler, James H., and Christopher T. Dawes. 2008. "Two Genes Predict Voter Turnout." *Journal of Politics* 70 (3): 579–94.

2013. "In Defense of Genopolitics." *American Political Science Review* 107 (2): 362–74.

Fox, Stephen. 2000. "Communities of Practice, Foucault and Actor-Network Theory." *Journal of Management Studies* 37 (6): 853–67.

Frega, Roberto. 2012. "The Practice-Based Approach to Normativity of Frederick L. Will." *Transcripts of the Charles S. Peirce Society* 48 (4): 483–511.

2017. "Pragmatism and Democracy in a Global World." *Review of International Studies* 43 (4): 720–41.

Friedman, Gerald. 2005. Review of Kathleen Thelen "How Institutions Evolve: The Political Economy of Skills in Germany, Britain, the United States, and Japan." *Industrial and Labor Relations Review* 59 (1): 170–72.

Friedman, Milton.1970. "The Social Responsibility of Business Is to Increase Its Profits." *New York Times Magazine*, September 13, 122–26. Available at umich.edu/~thecore/doc/Friedman.pdf.

Frost, Mervyn. 1996. *Ethics in International Relations: A Constitutive Theory*. Cambridge: Cambridge University Press.

2003. "Constitutive Theory and Moral Accountability: Individuals, Institutions, and Dispersed Practices." In *Can Institutions Have Responsibilities? Collective Moral Agency and International Relations*, edited by Toni Erskine, 84–99. London: Palgrave.

2009a. "Ethical Competence in International Relations." *Ethics and International Affairs* 23 (2): 91–100.

2009b. *Global Ethics: Anarchy, Freedom and International Relations*. London: Palgrave.

Frost, Mervyn, and Silviya Lechner. 2016a. "Understanding International Practices from the Internal Point of View." *International Political Theory* 12 (3): 299–319.

2016b. "Two Concepts of International Practice: Aristotelian *Praxis* or Wittgensteinian *Language-Games*?" *Review of International Studies* 42 (2): 334–50.

Fuchs, Stephan. 1992. *The Professional Quest for Truth: A Social Theory of Science and Knowledge.* Albany: SUNY Press.

Fukuyama, Francis. 1989. "The End of History?" *National Interest* 16: 3–18.

Fuller, Lon L. 1969. *The Morality of Law.* New Haven, CT: Yale University Press.

Gadinger, Frank. 2017. "The Normativity of International Practices." Centre for Global Cooperation Research, University of Duisburg-Essen.

Garfinkel, Alan. 1984. *Forms of Explanation: Rethinking the Questions in Social Theory.* New Haven, CT: Yale University Press.

Gartzke, Erik, and Jon R. Lindsay. 2017. "Thermonuclear Cyberwar." *Journal of Cybersecurity* 3 (1): 37–48.

Gat, Azar. 2008. *War in Human Civilization.* Oxford: Oxford University Press.

2009. "So Why Do People Fight? Evolutionary Theory and the Causes of War." *European Journal of International Relations* 15 (4): 571–99.

Geels, Frank W., and Johan Schot. 2010. "The Dynamics of Transitions: A Socio-Technical Perspective." In *Transitions to Sustainable Development: New Directions in the Study of Long-Term Transformative Change,* edited by John Grin, Jan Rotmans, and Johan Schot, 11–104. New York: Routledge.

Geer, Daniel E. 2007. "The Physics of Digital Law: Searching for Counterinuitive Analogies." In *Cybercrime: Digital Cops in a Networked Environment,* edited by Jack Balkin, James Grimmelmann, Eddan Katz, Nimrod Kozlovski, Shlomit Wagman, and Tal Zarsky, 13–36. New York: NYU Press.

Geertz, Clifford. 1973. *The Interpretation of Cultures: Selected Essays.* New York: Basic Books.

Gelderblom, Oscar, and Joost Jonker. 2004. "Completing a Financial Revolution: The Finance of the Dutch East India Trade and the Rise of the Amsterdam Capital Market, 1595–1612." *Journal of Economic History* 64 (3): 641–72.

Gertler, Brie. 2017. "Self-Knowledge." In *The Stanford Encyclopedia of Philosophy,* edited by Edward N. Zalta. Metaphysics Research Lab, Stanford University. Available at https://plato.stanford.edu/archives/fall2017/entries/self-knowledge/.

Geyer, Robert. 2003. "Beyond the Third Way: The Science of Complexity and the Politics of Choice." *British Journal of Politics and International Relations* 5 (2): 237–57.

Gheciu, Alexandra. 2005. "Security Institutions as Agents of Socialization? NATO and the 'New Europe.'" *International Organization* 59 (4): 973–1012.

Gherardi, Silvia. 2008. "Situated Knowledge and Situated Action: What Do Practice-Based Studies Promise?" In *The Sage Handbook of New Approaches in Management and Organization,* edited by Daved Barry and Hans Hansen, 516–25. London: Sage.

2009. "Communities of Practice or Practices of a Community?" In *Handbook of Management Learning, Education and Development,* edited by Steven J. Armstrong and Cynthia V. Fukami, 514–30. London: Sage.

Gherardi, Silvia, Davide Nicolini, and Francesca Odella. 1998. "Toward a Social Understanding of How People Learn in Organizations the Notion of Situated Curriculum." *Management Learning* 29 (3): 273–97.

Gibbs, Raymond W. 2001. "Intentions as Emergent Products of Social Interactions." In *Intentions and Intentionality: Foundations of Social Cognition*, edited by Bertram F. Malle, Louis J. Moses, and Dare A. Baldwin, 105–22. Cambridge, MA: MIT Press.

Giddens, Anthony. 1984. *The Constitution of Society: Outline of a Theory of Structuration*. Berkeley: University of California Press.

1986. "Action, Subjectivity, and the Constitution of Meaning." *Social Research* 53 (3): 529–45.

Gilady, Lilach, and Matthew J. Hoffmann. 2013. "Darwin's Finches or Lamarck's Giraffe: Does International Relations Get Evolution Wrong?" *International Studies Review* 15 (3): 307–27.

Gilardi, Fabrizio. 2005. "The Institutional Foundations of Regulatory Capitalism: The Diffusion of Independent Regulatory Agencies in Western Europe." *Annals of the American Academy of Political and Social Science* 598 (1): 84–101.

Gilbert, Margaret. 1992. *On Social Facts*. Princeton, NJ: Princeton University Press.

2014. *Joint Commitment: How We Make the Social World*. Oxford: Oxford University Press.

Gillman, Max, and Tim Eade. 1995. "The Development of the Corporation in England, with Emphasis on Limited Liability." *International Journal of Social Economics* 22 (4): 20–32.

Gilpin, Robert. 1981. *War and Change in World Politics*. Princeton, NJ: Princeton University Press.

Gladwell, Malcolm. 2002. *The Tipping Point: How Little Things Can Make a Big Difference*. Boston: Little Brown.

Gleditsch, Kristian Skrede, and Michael D. Ward. 2006. "Diffusion and the International Context of Democratization." *International Organization* 60 (4): 911–33.

Gleick, James. 1988. *Choas: Making a New Science*. New York: Viking-Penguin.

Glen, Carol M. 2014. "Internet Governance: Territorializing Cyberspace?" *Politics and Policy* 42 (5): 635–57.

Goddard, Stacie E. 2009. "Brokering Change: Networks and Entrepreneurs in International Politics." *International Theory* 1 (2): 249–81.

Goffman, Erving. 1956. *The Presentation of the Self in Everyday Life*. New York: Doubleday.

1963. *Behavior in Public Place*. Glencoe: Free Press.

1974. *Frame Analysis: An Essay on the Organization of Experience*. New York: Harper Colophon.

1983. "The Interaction Order: American Sociological Association, 1982 Presidential Address." *American Sociological Review* 48 (1): 1–17.

Goldman, Alvin, and Thomas Blanchard. 2016. "Social Epistemology." In *The Stanford Encyclopedia of Philosophy*, edited by Edward N. Zalta. Metaphysics Research Lab, Stanford University. Available at https://plato.stanford.edu/archives/win2016/entries/epistemology-social/.

Goldsmith, Jack L., and Tim Wu. 2006. *Who Controls the Internet? Illusions of a Borderless World*. New York: Oxford University Press.

Gontier, Nathalie. 2006. "Evolutionary Epistemology and the Origin and Evolution of Language: Taking Symbiogenesis Seriously." In *Evolutionary Epistemology, Language and Culture: A Non-Adaptationist, Systems Theoretical Approach*, edited by Nathalie Gontier, Jean Paul van Bendegem, and Diederek Aerts, 195–226. Rotterdam: Springer.

Goodwin, Barbara. 1978. *Social Science and Utopia*. Brighton: Harvester Press.

Gould, Stephen Jay. 2002. *The Structure of Evolutionary Theory*. Cambridge, MA: Harvard University Press.

Gould, Stephen Jay, and Niles Eldredge. 1977. "Punctuated Equilibria: The Tempo and Mode of Evolution Reconsidered." *Paleobiology* 3 (2): 115–51.

Gould, Stephen Jay, and Richard C. Lewontin. 1979. "The Spandrels of San Marco and the Panglossian Paradigm: A Critique of the Adaptationist Programme." *Proceedings of the Royal Society of London B: Biological Sciences* 205 (1161): 581–98.

Grabbe, Heather. 2002. "Stabilizing the East While Keeping Out the Easterners: Internal and External Security Logics in Conflict." In *Migration and the Externalities of European Integration*, edited by Sandra Lavenex and Emek M. Uçarer, 91–104. Lanham, MD: Lexington Books.

2014. "Six Lessons of Enlargement Ten Years On: The EU's Transformative Power in Retrospect and Prospect." *JCMS: Journal of Common Market Studies* 52 (S1): 40–56.

Granovetter, Mark S. 1973. "The Strength of Weak Ties." *American Journal of Sociology* 78 (6): 1360–80.

1978. "Threshold Models of Collective Behavior." *American Journal of Sociology* 83 (6): 1420–43.

"The Great Chain of Being Sure about Things." *The Economist*, October 31.

Greenhouse, Linda. 2016. "The Facts Win Out on Abortion." *New York Times*, June 29.

Greenwald, Glenn. 2014. *No Place to Hide: Edward Snowden, the NSA, and the US Surveillance State*. Toronto: Signal.

Greif, Avner, and David Laitin. 2003. "How Do Self-Enforcing Institutions Endogenously Change?" Unpublished manuscript, Stanford University.

2004. "A Theory of Endogenous Institutional Change." *American Political Science Review* 98 (4): 633–52.

Grodzins, Morton. 1957. "Metropolitan Segregation." *Scientific American* 197 (4): 33–41.

Gronow, Antti. 2011. *From Habits to Social Structures: Pragmatism and Contemporary Social Theory*. Frankfurt am Main: Peter Lang.

Gross, Neil. 2009. "A Pragmatist Theory of Social Mechanisms." *American Sociological Review* 74 (3): 358–79.

Gunitsky, Seva. 2013. "Complexity and Theories of Change in International Politics." *International Theory* 5 (1): 35–63.

2017. *Aftershocks: Great Powers and Domestic Reforms in the Twentieth Century*. Princeton, NJ: Princeton University Press.

Guzzini, Stefano. 2000. "A Reconstruction of Constructivism in International Relations." *European Journal of International Relations* 6 (2): 147–82.

2010. "Imposing Coherence: The Central Role of Practice in Friedrich Kratochwil's Theorising of Politics, International Relations and Science." *Journal of International Relations and Development* 13 (3): 301–22.

2016. "International Political Sociology, or: The Social Ontology and Power Politics of Process." In *Routledge Handbook of International Political Sociology*, edited by Xavier Guillaume and Pinar Bilgin, 368–77. New York: Routledge.

Haack, Susan. 2006. *Pragmatism, Old and New: Selected Writings*. Amherst, NY: Prometheus Books.

Haack, Susan, and Konstantin Kolenda. 1977. "Two Fallibilists in Search of the Truth." *Proceedings of the Aristotelian Society* 51: 63–104.

Haas, Ernst B. 1964. *Beyond the Nation-State*. Stanford, CA: Stanford University Press.

1980. "Why Collaborate? Issue-Linkage and International Regimes." *World Politics* 32 (3): 357–405.

1982. "Words Can Hurt You; Or, Who Said What to Whom about Regimes." *International Organization* 36 (2): 207–43.

1983. "Regime Decay: Conflict Management and International Organizations, 1945–1981." *International Organization* 37 (2): 189–256.

1984. "What Is Progress in the Study of International Organization?" Mimeo. Published in Japanese in *Kokusai Seiji*: 11–46.

1986. "What Is Nationalism and Why Should We Study It." *International Organization* 40 (3): 707–44.

1990. *When Knowledge Is Power: Three Models of Change in International Organizations*. Berkeley: University of California Press.

1997. *Nationalism, Liberalism, and Progress*, vol. 1: *The Rise and Decline of Nationalism*. Ithaca, NY: Cornell University Press.

2000. *Nationalism, Liberalism, and Progress*, vol. 2: *The Dismal Fate of New Nations*. Ithaca, NY: Cornell University Press.

Haas, Peter M. 1989. "Do Regimes Matter? Epistemic Communities and Mediterranean Pollution Control." *International Organization* 43 (3): 377–403.

1992a. "Introduction: Epistemic Communities and International Policy Coordination." *International Organization* 46 (1): 1–34.

1992b. "Banning Chlorofluorocarbons: Epistemic Community Efforts to Protect Stratospheric Ozone." *International Organization* 46 (1): 187–224.

Haas, Peter M., and Ernst B. Haas. 2002. "Pragmatic Constructivism and the Study of International Institutions." *Millennium* 31 (3): 573–601.

Habermas, Jürgen. 1984. *The Theory of Communicative Action*, vol. 1. Boston: Beacon Press.

1987. *The Theory of Communicative Action*, vol. 2: *The Critique of Functionalist Reason*. Boston: Beacon Press.

1989. *The Structural Transformation of the Public Sphere: An Inquiry into a Category of Bourgeois Society*, translated by Thomas Burger. Cambridge, MA: MIT Press.

1990. *Moral Consciousness and Community Action*. Cambridge: Polity Press.

1992. "Further Reflections on the Public Sphere." In *Habermas and the Public Sphere*, edited by Craig J. Calhoun, 421–61. Cambridge, MA: MIT Press.

1996. *Between Facts and Norms: Contributions to a Discourse Theory of Law and Democracy*. Cambridge, MA: MIT Press.

Hacking, Ian. 1983. *Representing and Intervening: Introductory Topics in the Philosophy of Natural Science*. Cambridge: Cambridge University Press.

1999. *The Social Construction of What?* Cambridge, MA: Harvard University Press.

Haeckel, Ernst Heinrich Philipp August. 1905. *The Wonders of Life: A Popular Study of Biological Philosophy*. New York: Harper.

Haken, Hermann. 1990. "Synergetics as a Tool for the Conceptualization and Mathematization of Cognition and Behaviour: How Far Can We Go?" In *Synergetics of Cognition*, edited by Hermann Haken and Michael Stadler, 2–31. Berlin: Springer.

Hall, John R., Laura Grindstaff, and Ming-Cheng Lo, eds. 2010. *Handbook of Cultural Sociology*. London: Routledge.

Hall, Peter A., ed. 1989. *The Political Power of Economic Ideas*. Princeton, NJ: Princeton University Press.

Hall, Peter A., 1993. "Policy Paradigms, Social Learning, and the State: The Case of Economic Policymaking in Britain." *Comparative Politics* 25 (3): 275–96.

2003. "Aligning Ontology and Methodology in Comparative Research." In *Comparative Historical Analysis in the Social Sciences*, edited by James Mahoney and Dietrich Rueschemeyer, 373–406. New York: Cambridge University Press.

Hall, Peter A., and David Soskice. 2001. "An Introduction to Varieties of Capitalism." In *Varieties of Capitalism: The Institutional Foundations of Comparative Advantage*, edited by Peter A. Hall and David Soskice, 1–68. Oxford: Oxford University Press.

Hall, Rodney Bruce. 1999. *National Collective Identity: Social Constructs and International Systems*. New York: Columbia University Press.

2008. *Central Banking as Global Governance*. Cambridge: Polity Press.

2017. "Deontic Power, Authority, and Governance in International Politics." *International Politics* 1–27.

Halpern, Paul, Michael Trebilcock, and Stuart Turnbull. 1980. "An Economic Analysis of Limited Liability in Corporation Law." *University of Toronto Law Journal* 30 (2): 117–50.

Hamilton, W. D. 1964. "The Genetical Evolution of Social Behaviour. I." *Journal of Theoretical Biology* 7 (1):1–16.

Hancock, Emily. 2007. "CALEA: Does One Size Still Fit All?" In *Cybercrime: Digital Cops in a Networked Environment*, edited by Jack Balkin, James Grimmelmann, Eddan Katz, Nimrod Kozlovski, Shlomit Wagman, and Tal Zarsky, 184–206. New York: New York University Press.

Hannan, Michael T. and John Freeman. 1984. "Structural Inertia and Organizational Change." *American Sociological Review* 49 (2): 149–64.

1989. *Organization Ecology*. Cambridge, MA: Harvard University Press.

Harari, Yuval Noah. 2016. *Homo Deus: A Brief History of Tomorrow*. Toronto: Penguin Random House.

Harré, Rom. 1993. *Social Reality*. Oxford: Blackwell.

Harré, Rom, and Grant Gillett. 1994. *The Discursive Mind*. Thousand Oaks, CA: Sage.

Harrison, Neil H., ed. 2006. *Complexity in World Politics: Concepts and Methods of a New Paradigm*. Albany: SUNY Press.

Hasenclever, Andreas, Peter Mayer, and Volker Rittberger. 1996. "Interests, Power, Knowledge: The Study of International Regimes." *Mershon International Studies Review* 40 (2): 177–228.

Haukkala, Hiski. 2011. "The European Union as a Regional Normative Hegemon: The Case of European Neighbourhood Policy." In *Normative Power Europe: Empirical and Theoretical Perspectives*, edited by Richard G. Whitman, 45–64. Basingstoke: Palgrave Macmillan.

Hausman, Carl R. 1993. *Charles S. Peirce's Evolutionary Philosophy*. Cambridge: Cambridge University Press.

2002. "Charles Peirce's Evolutionary Realism as a Process Philosophy." *Transactions of the Charles S. Peirce Society* 38 (1–2): 13–27.

Hay, Colin. 1996. "Narrating Crisis: The Discursive Construction of 'The Winter of Discontent.'" *Sociology* 30 (2): 253–77.

Hayden, Michael V. 2016. *Playing to the Edge: American Intelligence in the Age of Terror*. New York: Penguin.

Hayek, Friedrich August. 1948. *Individualism and Economic Order*. Chicago, IL: University of Chicago Press.

1973. *Law, Legislation and Liberty: A New Statement of the Liberal Principles of Justice and Political Economy*. London: Routledge and Kegan Paul.

1979. *The Counter-Revolution of Science*. New York: Free Press.

1989. "The Fatal Conceit: The Errors of Socialism." In *The Collected Works of F. A. Hayek*, vol.1. edited by W. W. Bartley II. Chicago, IL: University of Chicago Press.

Healey, Jason, ed. 2013. *A Fierce Domain: Conflict in Cyberspace, 1986 to 2012*. Vienna, VA: Cyber Conflict Studies Association.

Hegel, Georg Wilhelm Friedrich. 1977. *The Phenomenology of Spirit*. Oxford: Clarendon Press.

2007. *Hegel's Philosophy of Mind*. Oxford: Clarendon.

Heidegger, Martin. 1962. *Being and Time*, translated by John Macquarrie and Edward Robinson. New York: Harper and Row.

1971. *Poetry, Language, Thought*, translated by Albert Hofstadter. New York: Harper and Row.

Hellmann, Gunther. 2009. "Beliefs as Rules for Action: Pragmatism as a Theory of Thought and Action." *International Studies Review* 11 (3): 638–62.

Helmreich, Stefan. 1998. *Silicon Second Nature: Culturing Artificial Life in a Digital World*. Berkeley: University of California Press.

Henrich, Joseph. 2016. *The Secret of Our Success: Domesticating Our Species and Making Us Smarter*. Princeton, NJ: Princeton University Press.

Herrera, Geoffrey. 2007. "Cyberspace and Sovereignty: Thoughts on Physical Space and Digital Space." In *Power and Security in the Information Age: Investigating the Role of the State in Cyberspace*, edited by Myriam Dunn Cavelty, Victor Mauer, and Sai Felicia Krishna-Hensel, 67–94. Burlington, VT: Ashgate.

Herrmann, Esther, Josep Call, María Victoria Hernàndez-Lloreda, Brian Hare, and Michael Tomasello. 2007. "Humans Have Evolved Specialized Skills of Social Cognition: The Cultural Intelligence Hypothesis." *Science* 317 (5843): 1360–66.

Heylighen, Francis. 1992. "Evolution, Selfishness and Cooperation: Selfish Memes and the Evolution of Cooperation." *Journal of Ideas* 2 (4): 70–84.

2009. "Self Organization." Principia Cybernetica Web. Available at http://pespmc1.vub.ac.be/SELFORG.html.

Hildebrand, David L. 2008. *Dewey: A Beginner's Guide*. Oxford: One World Publications.

Hillman, Robert W. 1997. "Limited Liability in Historical Perspective." *Washington and Lee Law Review* 54 (2): 613–27.

Hirsch, Michal Ben-Josef. 2014. "Ideational Change and the Emergence of the International Norm of Truth and Reconciliation Commissions." *European Journal of International Relations* 20 (3): 810–33.

Hobbes, Thomas, and Edwin Curley. 1994. *Leviathan: With Selected Variants from the Latin Edition of 1668*. Indianapolis, IN: Hackett.

Hodgson, Geoffrey Martin. 1993. *Economics and Evolution: Bringing Life Back into Economics*. Ann Arbor, MI: University of Michigan Press.

2006. "What Are Institutions?" *Journal of Economic Issues* 40 (1): 1–25.

2007. "Institutions and Individuals: Interaction and Evolution." *Organization Studies* 28 (1): 95–116.

Hodgson, Geoffrey M., and Thorbjorn Knudsen. 2004. "The Firm as an Interactor: Firms as Vehicles for Habits and Routines." *Journal of Evolutionary Economics* 14 (3): 281–305.

2006a. "Dismantling Lamarckism: Why Descriptions of Socio-Economic Evolution as Lamarckian Are Misleading." *Journal of Evolutionary Economics* (16) 4: 343–66.

2006b. "Why We Need a Generalized Darwinism and Why a Generalized Darwinism Is Not Enough." *Journal of Economic Behavior and Organization* 61 (1): 1–19.

2007. "Evolutionary Theorizing beyond Lamarckism: A Reply to Richard Nelson." *Journal of Evolutionary Economics* 17 (3): 353–59.

2010. *Darwin's Conjecture: The Search for General Principles of Social and Economic Evolution*. Chicago, IL: University of Chicago Press.

Hofferberth, Matthias, and Christian Weber. 2015. "Lost in Translation: A Critique of Constructivist Norm Research." *Journal of International Relations and Development* 18 (1): 75–103.

Hoffmann, Matthew J. 2006. "Beyond Regime Theory: Complex Adaptation and Global Environmental Governance." In *Global Complexity: Agent-Based Models in Global and International Issues*, edited by Neil Harrison, 95–120. Albany: SUNY Press.

2012. *Ozone Depletion and Climate Change: Constructing a Global Response*. Albany: SUNY Press.

Hoffmann, Matthew J., and John Riley. 2002. "The Science of Political Science: Linearity or Complexity in Designing Social Inquiry." *New Political Science* 24 (2): 303–20.

Holland, John H. 1992. "Complex Adaptive Systems." *Daedalus* 121 (1): 17–30.
1995. *Hidden Order: How Adaptation Builds Complexity.* New York: Addison Wesley.
1998. *Emergence: From Chaos to Order.* New York: Addison Wesley.
1999. "Echoing Emergence: Objectives, Rough Definitions, and Speculations for Echo-Class Models." In *Complexity,* 309–42. Cambridge, MA: Perseus Books.
Holling, E. 1976. "Resilience and Stability in Ecosystems." In *Evolution and Consciousness: Human Systems in Transition,* edited by Erich Jantsch and Conrad H. Waddington, 73–92. Reading, MA: Addison-Wesley.
Hollis, Martin, and Steve Smith. 1991. "Beware of Gurus: Structure and Action in International Relations." *Review of International Studies* 17 (4): 393–410.
Holmstrom, Bengt, and Steven N. Kaplan. 2001. "Corporate Governance and Merger Activity in the United States: Making Sense of the 1980s and 1990s." *Journal of Economic Perspectives* 15 (2): 121–44.
Holsti, K. J. 2016. "The Problem of Change in International Relations Theory." In *Kalevi Holsti: A Pioneer in International Relations Theory, Foreign Policy Analysis, History of International Order, and Security Studies,* edited by Hans Günter Mosbach, 37–55. New York: Springer.
Holsti, Ole R., Randolph M. Siverson, and Alexander L. George. 1980. *Change in the International System.* Boulder, CO: Westview Press.
Holzinger, Katharina, and Christoph Knill. 2005. "Causes and Conditions of Cross-National Policy Convergence." *Journal of European Public Policy* 12 (5): 775–96.
Honneth, Axel. 1992. "Integrity and Disrespect: Principles of a Conception of Morality Based on the Theory of Recognition." *Political Theory* 20 (2): 187–201.
1998. "Democracy as Reflexive Cooperation: John Dewey and the Theory of Democracy Today." *Political Theory* 26 (6): 763–83.
2007. "Recognition as Ideology." In *Recognition and Power: Axel Honneth and the Tradition of Critical Social Theory,* edited by Bert Van den Brink and David Owen, 323–47. Cambridge: Cambridge University Press.
Hopf, Ted. 1998. "The Promise of Constructivism in International Relations Theory." *International Security* 23 (1): 171–200.
2002. *Social Construction of International Politics: Identities and Foreign Policies, Moscow, 1955 and 1999.* Ithaca, NY: Cornell University Press.
2010. "The Logic of Habit in International Relations." *European Journal of International Relations* 16 (4): 539–61.
2013. "Common-Sense Constructivism and Hegemony in World Politics." *International Organization* 67 (2): 317–54.
2018. "Change in International Practices." *European Journal of International Relations* 24 (3): 687–711.
Horowitz, Michael C. 2010. "Nonstate Actors and the Diffusion of Innovations: The Case of Suicide Terrorism." *International Organization* 64 (1): 33–64.
Houmansadr, Amir, Thomas J. Riedl, Nikita Borisov, and Andrew C. Singer. 2013. "I Want My Voice to Be Heard: IP over Voice-over-IP for Unobservable Censorship Circumvention." In the Network and Distributed System

Security Symposium (NDSS). Available at www.freehaven.net/anonbib/cache/ndss13-freewave.pdf.

Howard, Philip N. 2015. *Pax Technica: How the Internet of Things May Set Us Free or Lock Us Up*. New Haven, CT: Yale University Press.

Hronešová, Jessie. 2016. "Might Makes Right: War-Related Payments in Bosnia and Herzegovina." *Journal of Intervention and Statebuilding* 10 (3): 339–60.

Hull, David L. 1988. *Science as a Process: An Evolutionary Account of the Social and Conceptual Development of Science*. Chicago, IL: University of Chicago Press.

Hume, David. 1988. *Enquiries Concerning Human Understanding and Concerning the Principle of Morals*, edited by P. H. Nidditch. Oxford: Oxford University Press.

Humphreys, Paul. 1985. "Why Propensities Cannot Be Probabilities." *Philosophical Review* 94 (4): 557–70.

Hurd, Ian. 1999. "Legitimacy and Authority in International Politics." *International Organization* 53 (2): 379–408.

Hurrell, Andrew. 1995. "Explaining the Resurgence of Regionalism in World Politics." *Review of International Studies* 21 (4): 331–58.

2007a. *On Global Order: Power, Values, and the Constitution of International Society*. Oxford: Oxford University Press.

2007b. "One World? Many Worlds? The Place of Regions in the Study of International Society." *International Affairs* 83 (1): 127–46.

2011. "The Theory and Practice of Global Governance: The Worst of All Possible Worlds?" *International Studies Review* 13 (1): 144–54.

Hutcheon, Pat Duffy. 1995. "Popper and Kuhn on the Evolution of Science." *Brock Review* 4 (1–2): 28–37.

Hutchins, Edwin. 1995. *Cognition in the Wild*. Cambridge, MA: MIT Press.

Huxley, Julian. 1942. *Evolution: The Modern Synthesis*. London: George Allen and Unwin.

Ibert, Oliver, and Felix C. Müller. 2015. "Network Dynamics in Constellations of Cultural Differences: Relational Distance in Innovation Processes in Legal Services and Biotechnology." *Research Policy* 44 (1): 181–94.

Ikenberry, G. John. 2001a. *After Victory*. Princeton, NJ: Princeton University Press.

2001b. "American Power and the Empire of Capitalist Democracy." *Review of International Studies* 27 (5): 191–212.

2011. *Liberal Leviathan: The Origins, Crisis, and Transformation of the American International Order*. Princeton, NJ: Princeton University Press.

2016. "The Rise, Character, and Evolution of International Order." In *The Oxford Handbook of Historical Institutionalism*, edited by Orfeo Fioretos, Tulia G. Falletti, and Adam Sheingate, 538–552. Oxford: Oxford University Press.

2017. "The Plot against American Foreign Policy: Can the Liberal Order Survive?" *Foreign Affairs* 96 (2): 2–9.

2018. "The End of Liberal International Order?" *International Affairs* 94 (1): 7–23.

Iser, Mattias. 2013. "Recognition." In *The Stanford Encyclopedia of Philosophy*, edited by Edward N. Zalta. Available at https://plato.stanford.edu/archives/fall2013/entries/recognition/.

Jackson, Patrick Thaddeus. 2010. *The Conduct of Inquiry in International Relations: Philosophy of Science and Its Implications for the Study of World Politics*. New York: Routledge.

Jackson, Patrick Thaddeus, and Daniel H. Nexon. 1999a. "Relations before States: Substance, Process and the Study of World Politics." *European Journal of International Relations* 5 (3): 291–332.

1999b. "Paradigmatic Faults in International-Relations Theory." *International Studies Quarterly* 53 (4): 907–30.

Jacobi, Wade. 2001. "Tutors and Pupils: International Organizations, Central European Elites, and Western Models." *Governance* 14 (2): 169–200.

Jaffe, Adam B., Steven R. Peterson, Paul R. Portney, and Robert N. Stavins. 1995. "Environmental Regulation and the Competitiveness of US Manufacturing: What Does the Evidence Tell Us?" *Journal of Economic Literature* 33 (1): 132–63.

James, William. 1882. "Rationality, Activity and Faith." *Princeton Review* 2: 58–86.

1890. *The Principles of Psychology*, vol. 1. New York: Henry Holt.

1907. "Pragmatism's Conception of Truth." *Journal of Philosophy, Psychology and Scientific Methods* 4 (6): 141–55.

1977 [1909]. *A Pluralistic Universe*. Cambridge, MA: Harvard University Press.

Jansen, Julia. 2005. "Phantasy's Systematic Place in Husserl's Work: On the Condition of Possibility for a Phenomenology of Experience." In *Edmund Husserl: Critical Assessments of Leading Philosophers*, edited by Rudolf Bernet, Donn Welton, and Gina Zavolta, 221–44. New York: Routledge.

Jantsch, Eric. 1975. *Design for Evolution: Self-Organization and Planning in the Life of Human Systems*. New York: George Braziller.

1981. *The Evolutionary Vision: Toward a Unifying Paradigm of Physical, Biological, and Socio-Cultural Evolution*. Boulder, CO: Westview Press.

Jeffrey, Charlie, and Carolyn Rowe. 2014. "Bringing the Territory Back In: Towards a New Understanding of the Regional Dimension of the European Union." In *The Oxford Handbook of the European Union*, edited by Erik Jones, Anand Menon, and Stephen Weatherill, 749–60. Oxford: Oxford University Press.

Jenrich, Joseph. 2016. *The Secret of Our Success: How Culture Is Driving Human Evolution, Domesticating Our Species, and Making Us Smarter*. Princeton, NJ: Princeton University Press.

Jensen, Michael C., and Kevin J. Murphy. 1990. "Performance Pay and Top-Management Incentives." *Journal of Political Economy* 98 (2): 225–64.

Jepperson, R. L. 1991. "Institutions, Institutional Effects, and Institutionalism." In *The New Institutionalism in Organizational Analysis*, edited by Walter Powell and Paul J. DiMaggio, 143–63. Chicago, IL: University of Chicago Press.

Jeppesen, Soeren, and Michael W. Hansen. 2004. "Environmental Upgrading of Third World Enterprises through Linkages to Transnational Corporations: Theoretical Perspectives and Preliminary Evidence." *Business Strategy and the Environment* 13 (4): 261–74.

Jervis, Robert. 1972. "Consistency in Foreign Policy Views." In *Communication in International Politics*, edited by Richard Merritt, 272–94. Urbana, IL: University of Illinois Press.

1997. *System Effects: Complexity in Political and Social Life*. Princeton, NJ: Princeton University Press.

Joas, Hans. 1985. *George Herbert Mead: A Contemporary Re-Examination of His Thought*. Cambridge, MA: MIT Press.

1990a. "Giddens' Critique of Functionalism." In *Anthony Giddens: Consensus and Controversy*, edited by Jon Clark, Celia Modgil, and Sohan Modgil, 91–102. Brighton: Falmer Press.

1990b. "The Creativity of Action and the Intersubjectivity of Reason: Mead's Pragmatism and Social Theory." *Transactions of the Charles S. Peirce Society* 26 (2): 165–94.

1996. *The Creativity of Action*. Cambridge: Polity Press.

Joas, Hans, and Wolfgang Knöbl. 2009. *Social Theory: Twenty Introductory Lectures*. Cambridge: Cambridge University Press.

Johnston, Alastair Iain. 2001. "Treating International Institutions as Social Environments." *International Studies Quarterly* 45(4): 487–515.

2008. *Social States: China in International Relations, 1980–2000*. Princeton, NJ: Princeton University Press.

Jones, Roy E. 1981. "The English School of International Relations: A Case for Closure." *Review of International Studies* 7 (1): 1–13.

Jordana, Jacint, and David Levi-Faur. 2005. "The Diffusion of Regulatory Capitalism in Latin America: Sectoral and National Channels in the Making of a New Order." *Annals of the American Academy of Political and Social Science* 598 (1): 102–24.

Jordana, Jacint, David Levi-Faur, and Fernández Xavier i Marin. 2011. "The Global Diffusion of Regulatory Agencies: Channels of Transfer and Stages of Diffusion." *Comparative Political Studies* 44 (10): 1343–69.

Juusola, Katariina, Kerttu Kettunen, and Kimmo Alajoutsijärvi. 2015. "Accelerating the Americanization of Management Education: Five Responses from Business Schools." *Journal of Management Inquiry* 24 (4): 347–69.

Kahneman, Daniel. 2011. *Thinking, Fast and Slow*. New York: Farrar, Straus, and Giroux.

Kant, Immanuel. 1998. *Critique of Pure Reason*, translated by Paul Guyer and Allen Wood. Cambridge: Cambridge University Press.

Kaplan, Fred. 2016. *Dark Territory: The Secret History of Cyber War*. New York: Simon and Schuster.

Kaplan, Steven N., and Per Strömberg. 2009. "Leveraged Buyouts and Private Equity." *Journal of Economic Perspectives* 23 (1): 121–46.

Karp, David Jason. 2009. "Facts and Values in Politics and Searle's Construction of Social Reality." *Contemporary Political Theory* 8 (2): 152–75.

2013. "The Location of International Practices: What Is Human Rights Practice?" *Review of International Studies* 39 (4): 969–92.

Katzenstein, Peter J. 1989. *Industry and Politics in West Germany: Toward the Third Republic*. Ithaca, NY: Cornell University Press.

1990. "Analyzing Change in International Politics: The New Institutionalism and the Interpretive Approach." Paper presented as a guest lecture at the MPI für Gesellschaftsforschung, Köln, April 5.

Katzenstein, Peter J. ed. 1996. *The Culture of National Security: Norms and Identity in World Politics*. New York: Columbia University Press.

2010. "A World of Plural and Pluralistic Civilizations: Multiple Actors, Traditions, and Practices." In *Civilizations in World Politics: Plural and Pluralist Perspectives*, edited by Peter Katzenstein, 1–40. New York: Routledge.

Katzenstein, Peter J., and Lucia A. Seybert, eds. 2018. *Protean Power: Exploring the Uncertain and Unexpected in World Politics*. Cambridge: Cambridge University Press.

Kauffman, Stuart A. 1993. *The Origins of Order: Self-Organization and Selection in Evolution*. New York: Oxford University Press.

1995. *At Home in the Universe: The Search for the Laws of Self-Organization and Complexity*. New York: Oxford University Press.

Kavalski, Emilian. 2007. "The Fifth Debate and the Emergence of Complex International Relations Theory: Notes on the Application of Complexity Theory to the Study of International Life." *Cambridge Review of International Affairs* 20 (3): 435–54.

2012. "Complexity and Public Policy: A New Approach to Twenty-First Century Politics, Policy and Society – by Robert Geyer and Samir Rihani." *Political Studies Review* 10 (1): 136–37.

Keck, Margeret E., and Kathryn Sikkink. 1998. *Activists beyond Borders*. Ithaca, NY: Cornell University Press.

Kelley, Judith. 2008. "Assessing the Complex Evolution of Norms: The Rise of International Election Monitoring." *International Organization* 62 (2): 221–55.

Keohane, Robert. 1982. "The Demand for International Regimes." *International Organization* 36 (2): 325–55.

1984. *After Hegemony: Cooperation and Discord in the World Political Economy*. Princeton, NJ: Princeton University Press.

1993. "Institutional Theory and the Realist Challenge after the Cold War." In *Neorealism and Neoliberalism: The Contemporary Debate*, edited by David A. Baldwin, 269–300. New York: Columbia University Press.

Kessler, Amalia D. 2003. "Limited Liability in Context: Lessons from the French Origins of the American Limited Partnership." *Journal of Legal Studies* 32 (2): 511–48.

Kessler, Oliver, and Benjamin Herborth. 2013. "Recognition and the Constitution of Social Order." *International Theory* 5 (1): 155–60.

Kessler, Oliver, and Friedrich Kratochwil. 2012. "Systems Theory beyond Explaining and Understanding." In *New Systems Theories of World Politics*, edited by Mathias Albert, Lars-Erik Cederman, and Alexander Wendt, 23–43. New York: Palgrave Macmillan.

Khurana, Rakesh, and J. C. Spender. 2012. "Herbert A. Simon on What Ails Business Schools: More than 'a Problem in Organizational Design.'" *Journal of Management Studies* 49 (3): 619–39.

Kilpinen, Erkki. 2008. "Pragmatism as a Philosophy of Action." Paper presented at the First Nordic Pragmatism Conference, Helsinki, Finland, June 2–4.

King, Rachael. 2017. "US Invests $258 Million in Supercomputing Race with China." *Wall Street Journal*, June 15.

Kleinrock, Leonard. 2010. "An Early History of the Internet." *IEEE Communications Magazine* 48 (8): n.p.

Knafo, Samuel. 2016. "Bourdieu and the Dead End of Reflexivity: On the Impossible Task of Locating the Subject." *Review of International Studies* 42 (1): 25–47.

Knight, Will. 2017. "AI Fight Club Could Help Save Us from a Future of Super-Smart Cyberattacks." *MIT Technology Review*, July 20.

Knorr Cetina, Karin. 1999. *Epistemic Cultures: How Scientists Make Sense*. Cambridge, MA: Harvard University Press.

2001. "Objectual Practice." In *The Practice Turn in Contemporary Theory*, edited by Theodore R. Schatzki, Karin Knorr Cetina, and Eike Von Savigny, 175–88. London: Routledge.

2005. "Complex Global Microstructures: The New Terrorist Societies." *Theory, Culture and Society* 22 (5): 213–34.

Knorr Cetina, Karin, and Urs Bruegger. 2002. "Global Microstructures: The Virtual Societies of Financial Markets." *American Journal of Sociology* 107 (4): 905–50.

Kondratiev, N. D., and W. F. Stolper 1935. "The Long Waves in Economic Life." *Review of Economic Statistics* 17 (6): 105–15.

Kornprobst, Markus. 2014. "From Political Judgements to Public Justifications (and Vice Versa): How Communities Generate Reasons upon Which to Act." *European Journal of International Relations* 20 (1): 192–216.

Korsgaard, Christine M. 1996. *The Sources of Normativity*. New York: Cambridge University Press.

2003. "The Dependence of Value on Humanity." In *The Practice of Value* by Joseph Raz, edited by R. Jay Wallace, 63–85. New York: Oxford University Press.

Koschut, Simon. 2014. "Emotional (Security) Communities: The Significance of Emotion Norms in Inter-Allied Conflict Management." *Review of International Studies* 40 (3): 533–58.

Kostman, James. 1987. "Aristotle's Definition of Change." *History of Philosophy Quarterly* 4 (1): 3–16.

Krasner, Stephen D. 1982. "Structural Causes and Regime Consequences: Regimes as Intervening Variables." *International Organization* 36 (2): 185–205.

1983. *International Regimes*. Ithaca, NY: Cornell University Press.

1984. "Approaches to the State: Alternative Conceptions and Historical Dynamics." *Comparative Politics* 16 (2): 223–46.

Kratochwil, Friedrich. 1989. *Rules, Norms, and Decisions: On the Conditions of Practical and Legal Reasoning in International Relations and Domestic Affairs*. Cambridge: Cambridge University Press.

2007. "Of False Promises and Good Bets: A Plea for a Pragmatic Approach to Theory Building (the Tartu Lecture)." *Journal of International Relations and Development* 10 (1): 1–15.

2011. "Making Sense of 'International Practices.'" In *International Practices*, edited by Emanuel Adler and Vincent Pouliot, 36–60. New York: Cambridge University Press.

Kratochwil, Friedrich, and John Gerard Ruggie. 1986. "A State of the Art on an Art of the State." *International Organization* 40 (4): 753–75.

Krauss, Elizabeth M. 1998. *The Metaphysics of Experience: A Companion to Whitehead's Process and Reality*. New York: Fordham University Press.

Krippendorff, Klaus. 1986. "Dissipative Structure." *Principia Cybernetica*. Available at http://pespmc1.vub.ac.be/ASC/DISSIP_STRUC.html.

Krueger, Joel. 2011. "Extended Cognition and the Space of Social Interaction." *Consciousness and Cognition* 20 (3): 643–57.

Kugler, Jacek, and Abramo F. K. Organski. 1989. "The Power Transition: A Retrospective and Prospective Evaluation." In *Handbook of War Studies*, edited by Manus I. Midlarsky, 171–94. Boston: Unwin Hyman.

Kuhn, Thomas S. 1970. *The Structure of Scientific Revolutions*. Chicago, IL: University of Chicago Press.

Kuklick, Bruce. 1977. *The Rise of American Philosophy: Cambridge, Massachusetts, 1860–1930*. New Haven, CT: Yale University Press.

Kupchan, Charles A. 2012. "The Democratic Malaise: Globalization and the Threat to the West." *Foreign Affairs*, January/February: 62–67.

Kupchan, Charles A., and Peter L. Trubowitz. 2013. "American Statecraft in an Era of Domestic Polarisation." In *After Liberalism? The Future of Liberalism in International Relations*, edited by Rebekka Friedman, Kevork Oksanian, and Ramon Pacheco Pardo, 117–44. London: Palgrave Macmillan.

Kustermans, Jorg. 2016. "Parsing the Practice Turn: Practice, Practical Knowledge, Practices." *Millennium: Journal of International Studies* 44 (2): 175–96.

Kuyper, Jonathan W. 2014. "Global Democratization and International Regime Complexity." *European Journal of International Relations* 20 (3): 620–46.

La Porte, Todd R. 1975. "Organized Social Complexity: Explication of a Concept." In *Organized Social Complexity: Challenge to Politics and Policy*, edited by Todd R. La Porte, 3–39. Princeton, NJ: Princeton University Press.

Lachmann, Niels. 2010. "NATO-CSDP-EU Relations: Sketching the Map of a Community of Practice." Notes de Recherche du CEPSI 34. Centre for Internatonal Peace and Security Studies, McGill University and University of Montreal.

n.d. "Communities of Practice and the Dynamics of Relations among International Governmental Organizations." Available at www.academia.edu/2267599/Communities_of_practice_and_the_dynamics_of_relations_between_international_governmental_organizations.

Laclau, Ernesto, and Chantal Mouffe. 1985. *Hegemony and Socialist Strategy*. London: Verso.

Lakatos, Imre. 1978. *The Methodology of Scientific Research Programmes*. Cambridge: Cambridge University Press.

Lake, David A. 2009. *Hierarchy in International Relations*. Ithaca, NY: Cornell University Press.

2011. "Why 'isms' Are Evil: Theory, Epistemology, and Academic Sects as Impediments to Understanding and Progress." *International Studies Quarterly* 55 (2): 465–80.

Lamarck, Jean-Baptiste. 1815–22. *Histoire Naturelle des Animaux sans Vertèbres*. Paris: Verdière.

Lane, David, and Robert Maxfield. 1996. "Strategy under Complexity: Fostering Generative Relationships." *Long Range Planning* 29 (2): 215–31.

1997. "Forsight, Complexity and Strategy." In *The Economy as a Complex, Evolving System*, edited by W. Bryan Arthur, Steven Durlauf, and David Lane, 169–98. Reading, MA: Addison-Wesley.

Lapid, Yosef. 2001. "Identities, Borders, Orders: Nudging International Relations Theory in a New Direction." In *Identities, Borders, International Relations: Rethinking International Relations Theory*, edited by Albert Mathias, David Jacobson, and Yosef Lapid, 1–20. Minneapolis: University of Minnesota Press.

Larson, Edward John. 2004. *Evolution: The Remarkable History of a Scientific Theory*. New York: Random House Digital.

Lasswell, Harold D. 1936. *Politics: Who Gets What, When, How*. New York: Whittlesey House.

Latour, Bruno. 1987. *Science in Action: How to Follow Scientists and Engineers through Society*. Cambridge, MA: Harvard University Press.

1993. *We Have Never Been Modern*. Cambridge, MA: Harvester Wheatsheaf.

1999. *Pandora's Hope: Essays on the Reality of Science Studies*. Cambridge, MA: Harvard University Press.

2005. *Reassembling the Social: An Introduction to Actor-Network Theory*. Oxford: Oxford University Press.

Latour, Bruno, and Steve Woolgar. 1986. *Laboratory Life: The Construction of Scientific Knowledge*. Princeton, NJ: Princeton University Press.

Lave, Jean, and Etienne Wenger. 1991. *Situated Learning: Legitimate Peripheral Participation*. New York: Cambridge University Press.

Law, John. 1992. "Notes on the Theory of the Actor-Network: Ordering, Strategy, and Heterogeneity." *Systems Practice* 5 (4): 379–93.

Lee, Amanda. 2017. "China Sets Out Road Map to Lead World in Artificial Intelligence by 2030." *South China Morning Post*, July 21.

Legro, Jeffrey W. 1997. "Which Norms Matter? Revisiting the 'Failure' of Internationalism." *International Organization* 51 (1): 31–63.

2000. "The Transformation of Policy Ideas." *American Journal of Political Science* 44 (3): 419–32.

Lemke, Jay L. 1997. "Cognition, Context, and Learning: A Social Semiotic Perspective." In *Situated Cognition: Social, Semiotic, and Psychological Perspectives*, edited by David Kirshner and James A. Whitson, 37–56. Mahwah, NJ: Lawrence Erlbaum Associates.

Lemley, Mark A., and Lawrence Lessig. 2000. "The End of End-to-End: Preserving the Architecture of the Internet in the Broadband Era." *UCLA Law Review* 48: 925–99.

Lentzos, Filippa, and Nikolas Rose. 2009. "Governing Insecurity: Contingency Planning, Protection, Resilience." *Economy and Society* 38 (2): 230–54.

Levi, Margaret. 1997. "A Model, a Method, and a Map: Rational Choice in Comparative and Historical Analysis." In *Comparative Politics: Rationality, Culture, and Structure,* edited by Mark Irving Lichbach and Alan S. Zuckerman, 19–41. New York: Cambridge University Press.

Levine, Donald N., ed. 1971. *Georg Simmel on Individuality and Social Forms.* Chicago, IL: University of Chicago Press.

Levit, Georgy S., Uwe Hossfeld, and Ulrich Witt. 2011. "Can Darwinism Be 'Generalized' and of What Use Would This Be?" *Journal of Evolutionary Economics* 21 (4): 545–62.

Levitsky, Steven, and Daniel Ziblatt. 2018. *How Democracies Die.* New York: Crown.

Levitt, Barbara, and James G. March. 1988. "Organizational Learning." *Annual Review of Sociology* 14: 319–40.

Levy, Steven. 1994. "Battle of the Clipper Chip." *New York Times,* June 12.

Lewis, Orion A., and Sven Steinmo. 2012. "How Institutions Evolve: Evolutionary Theory and Institutional Change." *Polity* 44 (3): 314–39.

Lewis, Paul G. 2014. *Central Europe since 1945.* New York: Routledge.

Lewontin, Richard C. 1982. "Organism and Environment." In *Learning, Development, and Culture,* edited by H. C. Plotkin, 151–70. New York: Wiley.

Lieberman, Robert C. 2002. "Ideas, Institutions, and Political Order: Explaining Political Change." *American Political Science Review* 96 (4): 697–712.

Lindgreen, Adam, and Valérie Swaen. 2010. "Corporate Social Responsibility." *International Journal of Management Reviews* 12 (1): 1–7.

Lindsay, Jon R. 2015. "Introduction – China and Cybersecurity: Controversy and Context." In *China and Cybersecurity: Espionage, Strategy, and Politics in the Digital Domain,* edited by Jon R. Lindsay, Tai Ming Cheung, and Derek S. Reveron, 1–28. New York: Oxford University Press.

Linklater, Andrew. 1998. *The Transformation of Political Community: Ethical Foundations of the Post-Westphalian Era.* Columbia: University of South Carolina Press.

2010. "Global Civilizing Processes and the Ambiguities of Human Interconnectedness." *European Journal of International Relations* 16 (2): 155–78.

2011. *The Problem of Harm in International Politics.* Cambridge: Cambridge University Press.

2017. *Violence and Civilization in the State System.* Cambridge: Cambridge University Press.

Lipson, Michael. 2001. "Organizational Fields and International Regimes." Working Paper 03, series 1. Christopher H. Browne Center for International Politics, University of Pennsylvania.

List, Christian, and Lauren Valentini. 2016. "The Methodology of Political Theory." In *The Oxford Handbook of Philosophical Methodology,* edited by Herman Cappelen, Tamar Szabo Gendler, and John Hawthorne, 525–53. Oxford: Oxford University Press.

Litfin, Karen. 1994. *Ozone Discourses: Science and Politics in Global Environmental Cooperation.* New York: Columbia University Press.

Locke, John. 2009. *An Essay Concerning Human Understanding: Complete and Unabridged in One Volume.* Milwaukee: WLC Books.

Lohmann, Susanne. 1994. "The Dynamics of Informational Cascades: The Monday Demonstrations in Leipzig, East Germany, 1989–91." *World Politics* 47 (1): 42–101.

Long, Norman. 1992. "From Paradigm Lost to Paradigm Regained? The Case for an Actor-Oriented Sociology of Development." In *Battlefields of Knowledge: The Interlocking of Theory and Practice in Social Research and Development*, edited by Norman Long and Ann Long, 16–43. London: Routledge.

Lopez, Anthony C., Rose McDermott, and Michael Bang Petersen. 2011. "States in Mind: Evolution, Coalitional Psychology, and International Politics." *International Security* 36 (2): 48–83.

Loyal, Steven, and Stephen Quilley. 2004. "Towards a 'Central Theory': The Scope and Relevance of the Sociology of Norbert Elias." In *The Sociology of Norbert Elias*, edited by Stephen Quilley and Steven Loyal, 1–22. Cambridge: Cambridge University Press.

Luhmann, Niklas. 1978. "Temporalization of Complexity." In *Sociocybernetics*, edited by Felix Geyer and Johannes van der Zouwen, 95–111. Boston: Springer.

1995. *Social Systems*. Stanford, CA: Stanford University Press.

Lustick, Ian S. 2011. "Taking Evolution Seriously: Historical Institutionalism and Evolutionary Theory." *Polity* 43 (2): 179–209.

Lynn, William J. Lynn III. 2010. "Defending a New Domain." *Foreign Affairs* September/October.

Ma, Shu-Yun. 2016. "Taking Evolution Seriously, or Metaphorically? A Review of Interactions between Historical Institutionalism and Darwinian Evolutionary Theory." *Political Studies Review* 14 (2): 223–34.

MacIntyre, Alasdair. 1981. *After Virtue: A Study in Moral Theory*. Notre Dame, IN: University of Notre Dame Press.

Mackenzie, Adrian. 2005. "The Problem of the Attractor: A Singular Generality between Sciences and Social Theory." *Theory, Culture and Society* 22 (5): 45–65.

MacKenzie, Donald. 2008. *An Engine, Not a Camera: How Financial Models Shape Markets*. Cambridge, MA: MIT Press.

MacKenzie, Donald A., Fabian Muniesa, and Lucia Siu. 2007. *Do Economists Make Markets? On the Performativity of Economics*. Princeton, NJ: Princeton University Press.

Macy, Michael W. 1998. "Social Order and Emergent Rationality." In *What Is Social Theory? The Philosophical Debates*, edited by Alan Sica, 219–37. Oxford: Blackwell.

Mahoney, James. 2000. "Path Dependence in Historical Sociology." *Theory and Society* 29 (4): 507–48.

Mahoney, James, and Kathleen Thelen. 2010. "A Theory of Gradual Institutional Change." In *Explaining Institutional Change: Ambiguity, Agency, and Power*, edited by James Mahoney and Kathleen Thelen, 1–37. New York: Cambridge University Press.

Mailath, George J. 1998. "Do People Play Nash Equilibrium? Lessons from Evolutionary Game Theory." *Journal of Economic Literature* 36 (3): 1347–74.

Mallon, Ron, and Stephen P. Stich. 2000. "The Odd Couple: The Compatibility of Social Construction and Evolutionary Psychology." *Philosophy of Science* 67 (1): 133–54.

March, James G., and Johan P. Olsen. 1998. "Institutional Dynamics of International Political Orders." *International Organization* 52 (4): 943–69.

Marcoulatos, Iordanis. 2003. "John Searle and Pierre Bourdieu: Divergent Perspectives on Intentionality and Social Ontology." *Human Studies* 26 (1): 67–96.

Markell, Patchen. 2003. *Bound by Recognition*. Princeton, NJ: Princeton University Press.

Markley, Oliver W., and Willis W. Harman. 1982. *Changing Images of Man*. Oxford: Pergamon Press.

Martin-Breen, Patrick, and J. Marty Anderies. 2011. "Resilience: A Literature Review." Available at http://opendocs.ids.ac.uk/opendocs/handle/123456789/3692.

Marx, Karl. 1867. *Das Kapital: Kritik Der Politischen Oekonomie*. Hamburg: Meissner.

1888. Frederick Engels, *Ludwig Feuerbach und der Ausgang der Klassischen deutschen Philosophie ... Mit Anhang Karl Marx über Feuerbach von Jahre 1845* [Ludwig Feuerbach and the End of Classical German Philosophy .. With Notes on Feuerbach by Karl Marx 1845]. Berlin: Verlag von J. H. W. Dietz, 69–72.

2000. *Karl Marx: Selected Writings*, edited by David McLellan. New York: Oxford University Press.

Marx, Karl, and Friedrich Engels. 1967. *The Communist Manifesto* (1848). London: Penguin.

Maslow, Howard A. 1962. *Toward a Psychology of Being*. Princeton, NJ: D. Van Nostrand.

Mathiason, John. 2009. *Internet Governance: The New Frontier of Global Institutions*. New York: Routledge.

Maxfield, Robert. 1997. "Complexity and Organizational Management." In *Complexity, Global Politics, and National Security*, edited by David S. Alberts and Thomas J. Czerwinski, 78–98. Washington, DC: National Defense University Press.

Mayr, Ernst. 1963. *Animal Species and Evolution*. Cambridge, MA: Belknap.

2001. *What Evolution Is*. New York: Basic Books.

McCormick, John. 2010. *Europeanism*. New York: Oxford University Press.

McCourt, David M. 2016. "Practice Theory and Relationalism as the New Constructivism." *International Studies Quarterly* 60 (3): 475–85.

McDermott, Rose. 2004. *Political Psychology in International Relations*. Ann Arbor: University of Michigan Press.

McDermott, Rose, James H. Fowler, and Oleg Smirnov. 2008. "On the Evolutionary Origin of Prospect Theory Preferences." *Journal of Politics* 70 (2): 335–50.

McLean, Paul D. 2007. *The Art of the Network: Strategic Interaction and Patronage in Renaissance Florence*. Durham, NC: Duke University Press.

McNamara, Kathleen R. 2015. *The Politics of Everyday Europe: Constructing Authority in the European Union*. Oxford: Oxford University Press.
Mead, George Herbert. 1913. "The Social Self." *Journal of Philosophy, Psychology and Scientific Methods* 10: 374–80.
1932. *The Philosophy of the Present*. LaSalle, IL: Open Court.
1936. *Movements of Thought in the Nineteenth Century*, edited by Merritt H. Moore. Chicago, IL: University of Chicago Press.
1967 [1934]. *Mind, Self and Society from the Standpoint of a Social Behaviorist*. Edited, with introduction, by Charles W. Morris. Chicago: University of Chicago Press.
2015. *Mind, Self, and Society: The Definitive Edition*, edited by Charles W. Morris, annotated by Daniel R. Huebner and Hans Joas. Chicago, IL: University of Chicago Press,
Meadows, Donella H., Dennis L. Meadows, Jorgen Randers, and William W. Behrens III. 1972. *The Limits to Growth: A Report to the Club of Rome*. New York: Universe Books.
Menand, Louis, ed. 1997. *Pragmatism: A Reader*. New York: Vintage.
Menand, Louis, 2001. *The Metaphysical Club*. New York: Macmillan.
Merton, Robert King. 1948. "The Self-Fulfilling Prophecy." *Antioch Review* 8 (2): 193–210.
1968. *Social Theory and Social Structure*. New York: Free Press.
Meseguer, Covadonga. 2009. *Learning, Policy Making, and Market Reforms*. Cambridge: Cambridge University Press.
Mesoudi, Alex. 2011. *Cultural Evolution: How Darwinian Theory Can Explain Human Culture and Synthesize the Social Sciences*. Chicago, IL: University of Chicago Press.
Meyer, John W., and Brian Rowan. 1977. "Institutionalized Organizations: Formal Structure as Myth and Ceremony." *American Journal of Sociology* 83 (2): 340–63.
Meyer, John W., and W. Richard Scott. 1983. "Centralization and the Legitimacy Problems of Local Government." In *Organizational Environments: Ritual and Rationality*, edited by John W. Meyer and W. Richard Scott, 199–215. Beverly Hills, CA: Sage.
Miettinen, Reijo, Sami Paavola, and Pasi Pohjola. 2012. "From Habituality to Change: Contribution of Activity Theory and Pragmatism to Practice Theories." *Journal for the Theory of Social Behaviour* 42 (3): 345–60.
Miller, Richard W. 1975. "Propensity: Popper or Peirce?" *British Journal for the Philosophy of Science* 26 (2): 123–32.
Mingers, John C. 1995. "Information and Meaning: Foundations for an Intersubjective Account." *Information Systems Journal* 5 (4): 285–306.
Misak, Cheryl J. 1999. *Pragmatism*. Supplementary volume of the *Canadian Journal of Philosophy*.
Misak, Cheryl J. ed. 2007. *New Pragmatists*. Oxford: Clarendon.
2013. *The American Pragmatists*. Oxford: Oxford University Press.
Mishra, Pankaj. 2017. *Age of Anger: A History of the Present*. Princeton, NJ: Princeton University Press.

Mitzen, Jennifer. 2013. *Power in Concert: The Nineteenth-Century Origins of Global Governance*. Chicago, IL: University of Chicago Press.

Modelski, George. 1978. "The Long Cycle of Global Politics and the Nation State." *Comparative Studies in Society and History* 20 (2): 214–35.

1990. "Is World Politics Evolutionary Learning?" *International Organization* 44 (1): 1–24.

1996. "Evolutionary Paradigm for Global Politics." *International Studies Quarterly* 40 (3): 321–42.

Modelski, George, and William R. Thompson. 1996. *Leading Sectors and World Powers: The Coevolution of Global Politics and Economics*. Columbia: University of South Carolina Press.

Moravcsik, Andrew. 1997. "Taking Preferences Seriously: A Liberal Theory of International Politics." *International Organization* 51 (4): 513–53.

Morgan, C. Lloyd. 1923. *Emergent Evolution*. New York: Henry Holt.

Morgan, Richards. 2016. "Oversight through Five Eyes: Institutional Convergence and the Structure and Oversight of Intelligence Activities." In *Global Intelligence Oversight: Governing Security in the Twenty-First Century*, edited by Zachary K. Goldman and Samuel Rascoff, 37–70. New York: Oxford University Press.

Morgan, Thomas Hunt. 1903. *Evolution and Adaptation*. New York: Macmillan.

Morgenthau, Hans. 1949. *Politics among Nations: The Struggle for Power and Peace*. New York: Alfred Knopf.

Morrice, David. 2000. "The Liberal Communitarian Debate in Contemporary Political Philosophy and Its Significance for International Relations." *Review of International Studies* 26 (2): 233–51.

Mueller, Milton. 2010. *Networks and States: The Global Politics of Internet Governance*. Cambridge, MA: MIT Press.

Müller, Felix C., and Oliver Ibert. 2014. "Re-(sources) of Innovation: Understanding and Comparing Time-Spatial Innovation Dynamics through the Lens of Communities of Practice." *Geoforum* 65: 338–50.

Mungiu-Pippidi, Alina. 2014. "The Transformative Power of Europe Revisited." *Journal of Democracy* 25 (1): 20–32.

Nakagami, Teruaki. 2003. "Mathematical Formulation of Leibnizian World: A Theory of Individual-Whole, or Interior-Exterior Reflective Systems." *Biosystems* 69 (1): 15–26.

Nakamoto, Satoshi. 2008. "Bitcoin: A Peer-to-Peer Electronic Cash System." Available at https://bitcoin.org/bitcoin.pdf.

Naraniecki, Alexander. 2014. *Returning to Karl Popper: A Reassessment of His Politics and Philosophy*. Amsterdam: Rodopi.

Naurin, Daniel, and Helen Wallace. 2008. *Unveiling the Council of the European Union: Games Governments Play in Brussels*. London: Palgrave Macmillan.

NDR. 2014. "Snowden Interview: Transcript." Available at www.ndr.de/nachrichten/netzwelt/snowden277_page-2.html.

Nelson, Richard R. 1993. *National Innovation Systems: A Comparative Analysis*. New York: Oxford University Press.

2006. "Evolutionary Social Science and Universal Darwinism." *Journal of Evolutionary Economics* 16 (5): 491–510.

2007. "Universal Darwinism and Evolutionary Social Science." *Biology and Philosophy* 22 (1): 73–94.

Nelson, Richard R., and Sidney G. Winter. 1982. "The Schumpeterian Tradeoff Revisited." *American Economic Review* 72 (1): 114–32.

2002. "Evolutionary Theorizing in Economics." *Journal of Economic Perspectives* 16 (2): 23–46.

Nemeth, Charlan J., Bernard Personnaz, Marie Personnaz, and Jack A. Goncalo. 2004. "The Liberating Role of Conflict in Group Creativity: A Study in Two Countries." *European Journal of Social Psychology* 34 (4): 365–74.

Neufeld, Mark A. 1995. *The Restructuring of International Relations Theory*. Cambridge: Cambridge University Press.

Neumann, Iver B. 2002. "Returning Practice to the Linguistic Turn: The Case of Diplomacy." *Millennium Journal of International Studies* 31 (3): 627–51.

Never, Babette. 2012. "Collective Learning through Climate Knowledge Systems: The Case of South Africa." *Politikon: South African Journal of Political Studies* 39 (2): 231–56.

Nexon, Daniel H. 2009. *The Struggle for Power in Early Modern Europe: Religious Conflict, Dynastic Empires, and International Change*. Princeton, NJ: Princeton University Press.

2010. "Relationalism and New Systems Theory." In *New Systems Theories of World Politics*, edited by Mathias Albert, Lars-Erik Cederman, and Alexander Wendt, 99–126. Basingstoke: Palgrave Macmillan.

Nicolaïdis, Kalypso, and Robert Howse. 2002. "'This Is My EUtopia …': Narrative as Power." *JCMS: Journal of Common Market Studies* 40 (4): 767–92.

Nicolini, Davide. 2012. *Practice Theory, Work, and Organization: An Introduction*. Oxford: Oxford University Press.

2013. *How Matter Matters: Objects, Artifacts, and Materiality in Organization Studies*. Oxford: Oxford University Press.

Nicolini, Davide, Silvia Gherardi, and Dvora Yanow. 2003. *Knowing in Organizations: A Practice-Based Approach*. New York: M. E. Sharpe.

Nicolis, Gregoire, and Ilya Prigogine. 1989. *Exploring Complexity: An Introduction*. New York: W. H. Freeman.

Nietzsche, Friedrich. 1968. *The Will to Power*, translated by Walter Kaufmann and R. J. Hollingdale. New York: Vintage.

1969. *On the Genealogy of Morals and Ecce Homo*, translated by Walter Kaufmann. New York: Vintage.

Nissenbaum, Helen. 2007. "Where Computer Security Meets National Security." In *Cybercrime: Digital Cops in a Networked Environment*, edited by Jack Balkin, James Grimmelmann, Eddan Katz, Nimrod Kozlovski, Shlomit Wagman, and Tal Zarsky, 59–86. New York: New York University Press.

Nonaka, Ikujiro. 1994. "A Dynamic Theory of Organizational Knowledge Creation." *Organization Science* 5 (1): 14–37.

Noutcheva, Gergana, ed. 2013. *The EU and Its Neighbours: Values versus Security in European Foreign Policy*. Manchester: Manchester University Press.

Nowacki, Mariusz, Vikram Vijayanm, Yi Zhou, et al. 2008. "RNA Mediated Epigenetic: Programming of a Genome Rearrangement Pathway." *Nature* 451 (7175): 153–58.

Nowotny, Helga. 2005. "The Changing Nature of Public Science." In *The Public Nature of Science under Assault*, edited by Helga Nowotny, Dominique Pestre, Eberhard Schmidt-Assmann, Helmuth Schulze-Fielitz, and Hans-Heinrich Trute, 1–27. New York: Springer.

Nye, Joseph S., Jr. 2014. "Regime Complex for Managing Global Cyber Activities." Global Commission on Internet Governance Paper Series, no. 1. Centre for International Governance Innovation. Available at www.cigionline.org/sites/default/files/gcig_paper_no1.pdf.

Olsen, Johan P. 2002. "The Many Faces of Europeanization." *JCMS: Journal of Common Market Studies* 40 (5): 921–52.

Onuf, Nicholas G. 1989. *World of Our Making: Rules and Rule in Social Theory and International Relations*. Columbia: University of South Carolina Press.

1995. "Levels." *European Journal of International Relations* 1 (1): 35–58.

2013. *Making Sense, Making Worlds: Constructivism in Social Theory and International Relations*. New York: Routledge.

Ortner, Sherry B. 1984. "Theory in Anthropology since the Sixties." *Comparative Studies in Society and History* 26 (1): 126–66.

Padgett, John F. 2014. "History, Evolution, and Social Networks: Do Actors Make Relations or Do Relations Make Actors?" Institute for Advanced Study. Available at www.ias.edu/ideas/2014/padgett-evolution.

Padgett, John F., and Walter W. Powell. 2012. *The Emergence of Organizations and Markets*. Princeton, NJ: Princeton University Press.

Page, Scott E. 2006. "Path Dependence." *Quarterly Journal of Political Science* 1 (1): 87–115.

Papadimitriou, Dimitris, and David Phinnemore. 2004. "Europeanization, Conditionality and Domestic Change: The Twinning Exercise and Administrative Reform in Romania." *JCMS: Journal of Common Market Studies* 42 (3): 619–39.

Parsons, Talcott. 1937. *The Structure of Social Action*. New York: Free Press.

1951. *The Social System*. New York: Free Press.

1971. "Comparative Studies and Evolutionary Change." In *Comparative Methods in Sociology: Essays on Trends and Applications*, edited by I. Vallier, 97–139. Berkeley: University of California Press.

1977. *The Evolution of Societies*. Englewood Cliffs, NJ: Prentice-Hall.

Patterson, Orlando. 2010. "The Mechanisms of Cultural Reproduction: Explaining the Puzzle of Persistence." In *Handbook of Cultural Sociology*, edited by H. J. Grindstaff and M.-C. Lo, 140–52. New York: Routledge.

Peirce, Charles Sanders. 1933. *Collected Papers of Charles Sanders Peirce*. Edited by Charles Hartshorne and Paul Weiss. Cambridge, MA: Harvard University Press.

1965a. *The Collected Papers of Charles Sanders Peirce*. Cambridge, MA: Harvard University Press.

1965b. "The Fixation of Belief." In *Collected Papers of Charles Sanders Peirce*, vol. 5. Cambridge, MA: Harvard University Press.

1965c. "Pragmatism and Pragmaticism." In *Collected Papers of Charles Sanders Peirce*, vols. 5 and 6, edited by C. Hartshorne, P. Weiss, and A. Burks. Cambridge, MA: Belknap Press of Harvard University.

1974. *Charles Sanders Peirce: Contributions to the Nation*. Lubbock: Texas Tech Press.

Penney, Jon. 2016. "Chilling Effects: Online Surveillance and Wikipedia Use." *Berkeley Technology Law Journal* 31 (1): 117–82.

Peterson, Zachary N. J., Mark Gondree, and Robert Beverly. 2011. "A Position Paper on Data Sovereignty: The Importance of Geolocating Data in the Cloud." In *HotCloud*. Available at www.usenix.org/legacy/events/hotcloud11/tech/final_files/Peterson.pdf.

Phillips, Andrew. 2011. *War, Religion, and Empire: The Transformation of International Orders*. Cambridge: Cambridge University Press.

Philpott, Daniel. 2001. *Revolutions in Sovereignty: How Ideas Shaped Modern International Relations*. Princeton, NJ: Princeton University Press.

Phuong, Catherine. 2005. *The International Protection of Internally Displaced Persons*. Cambridge: Cambridge University Press.

Piaget, Jean. 1952. *The Origins of Intelligence in Children*. New York: International University Press.

1954. "Language and Thought from a Genetic Perspective." *Acta Psychologica* 10: 51–60.

Pickering, Andrew. 1992. *Science as Practice and Culture*. Chicago, IL: University of Chicago Press.

Pierce, David. 2016. "How Apple Taught the World to Smartphone." *Wired*, June 12.

Pierson, Paul. 2000. "Not Just What, but When: Timing and Sequence in Political Processes." *Studies in American Political Development* 14 (1): 72–92.

2004. *Politics in Time: History, Institutions, and Social Analysis*. Princeton, NJ: Princeton University Press.

Pihlström, Sami. 2008. "How (Not) to Write the History of Pragmatist Philosophy of Science." *Perspectives on Science* 16 (1): 26–69.

Pinker, Steven. 2011. *The Better Angels of Our Nature*. New York: Viking-Penguin.

2018. *Enlightenment Now: The Case for Reason, Science, Humanism and Progress*. New York: Viking.

Pirsig, Robert M. 1974. *Zen and the Art of Motorcycle Maintenance*. New York: Bantam Books.

1991. *Lila: An Inquiry into Morals*. New York: Bantam.

Plato. 1968. *The Republic*, 2nd edition. Translated with notes and an interpretive essay by Allen Bloom. New York: Basic Books.

Polanyi, Michael. 1966. "The Logic of Tacit Inference." *Philosophy* 41 (155): 1–18.

1983. *The Tacit Dimension*. Gloucester, MA: Peter Smith.

Popolo, Damian. 2011. *A New Science of International Relations: Modernity, Complexity and the Kosovo Conflict*. Farnham: Ashgate.

Popper, Karl R. 1935. *The Logic of Scientific Discovery*. Vienna: Springer.

1959. "The Propensity Interpretation of Probability." *British Journal for the Philosophy of Science* 10 (37): 25–42.

1963. *Conjectures and Refutations*. London: Routledge and Kegan Paul.

1974. "Replies to My Critics." In *The Philosophy of Karl Popper*, vol. 2, edited by Paul A. Schilpp, 961–1197. La Salle, IL: Open Court.

1978. "Natural Selection and the Emergence of Mind." *Dialectica* 32 (3–4): 339–55.

1979. *Truth, Rationality and the Growth of Scientific Knowledge*. Frankfurt am Main: Vittorio Klostermann.

1982a. "The Place of Mind in Nature." In *Mind in Nature*, edited by Richard Q. Elvee, 31–59. San Francisco: Harper and Row.

1982b. *The Open Universe: An Argument for Indeterminism*. Vol. 1 of *Postscript to the Logic of Scientific Discovery*, edited by W. W. Bartley. London: Hutchinson.

1982c. *The Quantum Theory and the Schism in Physics*. London: Hutchison.

1983. *Realism and the Aim of Science*. London: Hutchison.

1987. "Natural Selection and the Emergence of Mind." In *Evolutionary Epistemology, Rationality, and the Sociology of Knowledge*, edited by Gerard Radnitzsky and W. W. Bartley, 139–56. Chicago, IL: Open Court.

1990. *A World of Propensities*. Bristol: Thoemmes.

2002. *The Poverty of Historicism*. London: Routledge and Kegan Paul.

Pouliot, Vincent. 2007. "'Sobjectivism': Toward a Constructivist Methodology." *International Studies Quarterly* 51 (2): 359–84.

2010. *International Security in Practice: The Politics of Russia–NATO Diplomacy*. Cambridge: Cambridge University Press.

2016. *International Pecking Orders: The Politics and Practice of Multilateral Diplomacy*. Cambridge: Cambridge University Press.

2017. "Practice and Normativity." Paper presented at the NIRT Workshop, Hamburg.

Pouliot, Vincent, and Jean-Philippe Thérien. 2015. "The Politics of Inclusion: Changing Patterns in the Governance of International Security." *Review of International Studies* 41 (2): 211–37.

Pouliot, Vincent, and Mérand Frédéric, and. 2013. "Bourdieu's Concepts." In *Bourdieu in International Relations: Rethinking Key Concepts in IR*, edited by Rebecca Adler-Nissen, 22–24. New York: Routledge.

Poutanen, Petro. 2013. "Creativity as Seen through the Complex Systems Perspective." *Interdisciplinary Studies Journal* 2 (3): 207–21.

Powell, Robert. 1991. "Absolute and Relative Gains in International Relations Theory." *American Political Science Review* 85 (4): 1303–20.

Powell, Walter W., and J. A. Calyvas. 2008. "Microfoundations of Institutional Theory." In *The Sage Handbook of Organizational Institutionalism*, edited by Royston Greenwood, Christine Oliver, Kerstin Sahlin, and Roy Suddaby, 276–98. London: Sage.

Powell, Walter W., Douglas R. White, Kenneth W. Koput, and Jason Owen-Smith. 2005. "Network Dynamics and Field Evolution: The Growth of Interorganizational Collaboration in the Life Sciences." *American Journal of Sociology* 110 (4): 1132–205.

Powell, Walter W., and Kurt W. Sandholtz. 2012. "Chance, Nécessité, et Naïveté." In *The Emergence of Organizations and Markets*, edited by John F. Padgett and Walter W. Powell, 379–433. Princeton, NJ: Princeton University Press.

Powell, Walter W., and Paul J. DiMaggio, eds. 1991. *The New Institutionalism in Organizational Analysis*. Chicago, IL: University of Chicago Press.

Power, Michael. 2005. "The Invention of Operational Risk." *Review of International Political Economy* 12 (4): 577–99.

Pratt, Simon Frankel. 2016. "Pragmatism as Ontology, Not (Just) Epistemology: Exploring the Full Horizon of Pragmatism as an Approach to IR Theory." *International Studies Review* 18 (3): 508–27.

Price, Richard. 2008. "Moral Limit and Possibility in World Politics." *International Organization* 62 (2): 191–220.

Prigogine, Ilya. 1980. *From Being to Becoming: Time and Complexity in the Physical Sciences*. San Francisco: W. H. Freeman.

Prigogine, Ilya, and Isabelle Stengers. 1984. *Order Out of Chaos: Man's New Dialogue with Nature*. New York: Bantam.

Putnam, Hilary. 1981. *Reason, Truth and History*. Cambridge: Cambridge University Press.

1983. *Realism and Reason: Philosophical Papers*, vol. 3. Cambridge: Cambridge University Press.

1990. *Realism with a Human Face*. Cambridge, MA: Harvard University Press.

1994. "Sense, Nonsense, and the Senses: An Inquiry into the Powers of the Human Mind." *Journal of Philosophy* 91 (9): 445–517.

1995. *Pragmatism: An Open Question*. Oxford: Blackwell.

Pyetranker, Innokenty. 2015. "An Umbrella in a Hurricane: Cyber Technology and the December 2013 Amendment to the Wassenaar Arrangement." *Northwestern Journal of Technology and Intellectual Property* 13 (2): 153–80.

Quirk, Joel. 2011. *The Anti-Slavery Project: From the Slave Trade to Human Trafficking*. Philadelphia: University of Pennsylvania Press.

Radaelli, Claudio M. 2004. "The Diffusion of Regulatory Impact Analysis: Best Practice or Lesson-Drawing?" *European Journal of Political Research* 43 (5): 723–47.

Ramirez, Francisco O., Yasemin Soysal, and Suzanne Shanahan. 1997. "The Changing Logic of Political Citizenship: Cross-National Acquisition of Women's Suffrage Rights, 1890 to 1990." *American Sociological Review* 62 (5): 735–45.

Rasche, Andreas, and Robert Chia. 2009. "Researching Strategy Practices: A Genealogical Social Theory Perspective." *Organization Studies* 30 (7): 713–34.

Ratner, Steven R. 2001. "Corporations and Human Rights: A Theory of Legal Responsibility." *Yale Law Journal* 111 (3): 443–545.

Raustiala, Kal, and David G. Victor. 2004. "The Regime Complex for Plant Genetic Resources." *International Organization* 58 (2): 277–309.

Rawls, Anne Warfield. 2009. "An Essay on Two Conceptions of Social Order: Constitutive Orders of Action, Objects and Identities vs Aggregated Orders of Individual Action." *Journal of Classical Sociology* 9 (4): 500–520.

2010. "Social Order as Moral Order." In *Handbook of the Sociology of Morality*, edited by S. Hitlin and S. Vaisey, 95–121. New York: Springer.

Rawls, John. 1955. "Two Concepts of Rules." *Philosophical Review* 64 (1): 3–32.

1971. *A Theory of Justice*. Cambridge, MA: Harvard University Press.

1980. "Kantian Constructivism in Moral Theory: The Dewey Lectures." *Journal of Philosophy* 77: 512–72.

Ray, James Lee. 1989. "The Abolition of Slavery and the End of International War." *International Organization* 43 (3): 405–39.

Raymond, Mark. 2011. "Social Change in World Politics: Secondary Rules and Institutional Politics." PhD dissertation, University of Toronto.

Raz, Joseph. 2003. *The Practice of Value*, edited by R. Jay Wallace. New York: Oxford University Press.

Reckwitz, Andreas. 2002. "Toward a Theory of Social Practices: A Development in Culturalist Theorizing." *European Journal of Social Theory* 5 (2): 243–63.

Reinhardt, Forest. 1999. "Market Failure and the Environmental Policies of Firms: Economic Rationales for 'Beyond Compliance' Behavior." *Journal of Industrial Ecology* 3 (1): 9–21.

Renzi, Barbara G., and Napolitano Giulio. 2011. *Evolutionary Analogies: Is the Process of Scientific Change Analogous to the Organic Change?* Newcastle: Cambridge Scholars Publishing.

Rescher, Nicholas. 1996. *Process Metaphysics: An Introduction to Process Philosophy.* Albany: SUNY Press.

2005. "Knowledge of the Truth in Pragmatic Perspective." In *Hilary Putnam: Pragmatism and Realism*, edited by James Conant and Ursula M. Żegleń, 66–79. New York: Routledge.

Resnick, Lauren B. 1991. "Shared Cognition: Thinking as a Social Practice." In *Perspectives on Socially Shared Cognition*, edited by Lauren B. Resnick, John M. Levine, and Stephanie D. Teasley, 1–20. Washington, DC: American Psychological Association.

Resnick, Lauren B., John M. Levine, and Stephanie D. Teasley, eds. 1991. *Perspectives on Socially Shared Cognition*. Washington, DC: American Psychological Association.

Reus-Smit, Christian. 1999. *The Moral Purpose of the State: Culture, Social Identity, and Institutional Rationality in International Relations*. Princeton, NJ: Princeton University Press.

2013a. *Individual Rights and the Making of the International System*. Cambridge: Cambridge University Press.

2013b. "Constructivism." In *Theories of International Relations*, edited by Scott Burchill et al., 217–40. London: Palgrave Macmillan.

2014. "Emotions and the Social." *International Theory* 6 (3): 568–74.

2017. "Cultural Diversity and International Order." *International Organization* 71 (4): 851–85.

2018. *On Cultural Diversity: International Theory in a World of Difference*. Cambridge: Cambridge University Press.

Richards, Robert J. 1987. *Darwin and the Emergence of Evolutionary Theories of Mind and Behavior*. Chicago, IL: University of Chicago Press.

Richardson, John. 2006. "Nietzsche on Time and Becoming." In *A Companion to Nietzsche*, edited by Keith A. Pearson, 208–229. Malden, MA: Wiley-Blackwell.

Richerson, Peter J., and Robert Boyd. 2005. *Not by Genes Alone: How Culture Transformed Human Evolution*. Chicago, IL: University of Chicago Press.

Ridley, Mark. 2015. *The Evolution of Everything: How New Ideas Emerge*. New York: HarperCollins.

Rinaldi, S. M. 1997. "Complexity Theory and Airpower: A New Paradigm for Airpower in the Twenty-First Century." In *Complexity, Global Politics and National Security*, edited by David S. Alberts and Thomas J. Czerwinski, 119–37. Washington, DC: National Defense University Press.

Ringmar, Erik. 2012. "Performing International Systems: Two East-Asian Alternatives to the Westphalian Order." *International Organization* 66 (1): 1–25.

2014. "The Search for Dialogue as a Hindrance to Understanding: Practices as Inter-Paradigmatic Research Program." *International Theory* 6 (1): 1–27.

Risse, Thomas. 2000. "'Let's Argue!' Communicative Action in World Politics." *International Organization* 54 (1): 1–39.

2010. *A Community of Europeans? Transnational Identities and Public Spheres*. Ithaca, NY: Cornell University Press.

Risse-Kappen, Thomas. 1994. "Ideas Do Not Float Freely: Transnational Coalitions, Domestic Structures, and the End of the Cold War." *International Organization* 48 (2): 185–214.

1997. *Cooperation among Democracies: The European Influence on American Foreign Policy*. Princeton, NJ: Princeton University Press.

Ritzer, George. 2010. *Sociological Theory*, 8th ed. New York: McGraw-Hill.

Rogers, Everett M. 1995. "Diffusion of Innovations: Modifications of a Model for Telecommunications." In *Die Diffusion von Innovationen in der Telekommunikation*, edited by Matthias-W. Stoetzer and Alwin Mahler, 25–38. Bad Honnef: Springer.

Rorty, Richard. 2017. "Justice as a Larger Loyalty." In *Pragmatism and Justice*, edited by Susan Dieleman, David Rondel, and Christian Voparil, 21–36. New York: Oxford University Press.

Rosenau, James N. 1968. "Comparative Foreign Policy: Fad, Fantasy, or Field." *International Studies Quarterly* 12 (3): 296–329.

1990. *Turbulence in World Politics: A Theory of Change and Continuity*. Princeton, NJ: Princeton University Press.

1992. "Governance, Order and Change in World Politics." In *Governance without Government: Order and Change in World Politics*, edited by James N. Rosenau and Ernst-Otto Czempiel, 1–29. Cambridge: Cambridge University Press.

1997. *Along the Domestic-Foreign Frontier: Exploring Governance in a Turbulent World*. Cambridge: Cambridge University Press.

2003. *Distant Proximities: Dynamics beyond Globalization*. Princeton, NJ: Princeton University Press.

Rosenau, James N., and Ernst-Otto Czempiel, eds. 1992. *Governance without Government: Order and Change in World Politics*. Cambridge: Cambridge University Press.

Rosenberg, Matthew. 2016. "At Booz Allen, a Vast US Spy Operation, Run for Private Profit." *New York Times*, October 6.

Rosenberg, Nathan. 1982. *Inside the Black Box: Technology and Economics*. Cambridge: Cambridge University Press.

Rottshaefer, William A. 1991. "Some Philosophical Implications of Bandura's Social Cognitive Theory of Human Agency." *American Psychologist* 46 (2): 153–55.

Rouse, Joseph. 1999. "Understanding Scientific Practices: Cultural Studies of Science as a Philosophical Program." Wesleyan University: Division I Faculty Publications 23. Available at https://wesscholar.wesleyan.edu/div1facpubs/23/.

2001. "Two Concepts of Practices." In *The Practice Turn in Contemporary Theory*, edited by Theodore R. Schatzki, Karin Knorr Cetina, and Eike Von Savigny, 189–98. New York: Routledge.

2007. *Practice Theory: Handbook of the Philosophy of Science*, edited by Stephen P. Turner and Mark W. Risjord, 639–81. Amsterdam: Elsevier.

Rousseau, Jean-Jacques. 1920. *The Social Contract and Discourses*. London: J. M. Dent and Sons.

Ruggie, John G. 1978. "Changing Frameworks of International Collective Behavior: On the Complementarity of Contradictory Tendencies." In *Forecasting in International Relations: Theory, Methods, Problems, Prospects*, edited by Nazli Choucri and Thomas W. Robinson, 384–406. San Francisco: Freeman.

1982. "International Regimes, Transactions, and Change: Embedded Liberalism in the Postwar Economic Order." *International Organization* 36 (2): 379–415.

1983. "Continuity and Transformation in the World Polity: Toward a Neorealist Synthesis." *World Politics* 35 (2): 261–85.

1986. "Social Time and International Policy: Conceptualizing Global Population and Resource Issues." In *Persistent Patterns and Emergent Structures in a Waning Century*, edited by Margaret P. Karns, 211–36. New York: Praeger.

1989. "International Structure and International Transformation: Space, Time, and Method." In *Global Changes and Theoretical Challenges: Approaches to World Politics for the 1990s*, edited by Ernst-Otto Czempiel and James N. Rosenau, 21–35. Lexington, MA: Lexington Books.

1993. "Territoriality and Beyond: Problematizing Modernity in International Relations." *International Organization* 47 (1): 139–74.

1998a. *Constructing the World Polity: Essays on International Institutionalization*. New York: Routledge.

1998b. "What Makes the World Hang Together? Neo-Utilitarianism and the Social Constructivist Challenge." *International Organization* 52 (4): 855–85.

2017. "Multinationals as Global Institution: Power, Authority and Relative Autonomy." *Regulation and Governance*. Available at http://onlinelibrary.wiley.com/doi/10.1111/rego.12154/epdf.

Ruggie, John Gerard, Peter J. Katzenstein, Robert O. Keohane, and Philippe C. Schmitter. 2005. "Transformations in World Politics: The Intellectual Contributions of Ernst B. Haas." *Annual Review of Political Science* 8: 271–96.

Runciman, Walter Garrison. 1989. *A Treatise on Social Theory*. Cambridge: Cambridge University Press.

Russell, Andrew L. 2014. *Open Standards and the Digital Age: History, Ideology, and Networks*. Cambridge: Cambridge University Press.

Ryle, Gilbert. 2009. *The Concept of Mind*. New York: Routledge.
Sady, Wojciech. 2016. "Ludwik Fleck." In *The Stanford Encyclopedia of Philosophy*, edited by Edward N. Zalta. Available at https://plato.stanford.edu/entries/fleck/.
Sagan, Carl. 1985. *Cosmos*. New York: Ballantine Books.
Saltzer, Jerome H., David P. Reed, and David D. Clark. 1984. "End-to-End Arguments in System Design." *ACM Transactions on Computer Systems* 2 (4): 277–88.
Sanger, David E. 2013. *Confront and Conceal: Obama's Secret Wars and Surprising Use of American Power*, updated ed. New York: Broadway Books.
2015. "Report Finds No Substitute for Mass Data Collection." *New York Times*, January 15.
Sanger, David E., and William J. Broad. 2017. "Trump Inherits a Secret Cyberwar against North Korean Missiles." *New York Times*, March 4.
Saperstein, Alvin. M. 1997. "Complexity, Chaos, and National Security Policy: Metaphors or Tools?" In *Complexity, Global Politics, and National Security*, edited by David S. Alberts and Thomas J. Czerwinski, 44–61. Washington, DC: National Defense University.
Sarotte, Mary Elise. 2014. *1989: The Struggle to Create Post–Cold War Europe*. Princeton, NJ: Princeton University Press.
Sassen, Saskia. 2000. "New Frontiers Facing Urban Sociology at the Millennium." *British Journal of Sociology* 51 (1): 143–60.
Saville, John. 1956. "Sleeping Partnership and Limited Liability, 1850–1856." *Economic History Review* 8 (3): 418–33.
Sawyer, Robert Keith. 2005. *Social Emergence: Societies as Complex Systems*. Cambridge: Cambridge University Press.
Schäfer, Hilmer. 2014. "Demanding Current Issues in Practice Theory." Working Paper presented at "Demading Ideas: Where Theories of Practice Might Go Next," June 18–20, Windermere, UK. Available at www.demand.ac.uk/wp-content/uploads/2014/07/wp7-schaefer.pdf.
Scharpf, Fritz W. 1997. "Introduction: The Problem-Solving Capacity of Multi-Level Governance." *Journal of European Public Policy* 4 (4): 520–38.
Schatzki, Theodore R. 1996. *Social Practices: A Wittgensteinian Approach to Human Activity and the Social*. Cambridge: Cambridge University Press.
2001a. "Practice Minded Orders." In *The Practice Turn in Contemporary Theory*, edited by Theodore R. Schatzki, Karin Knorr Cetina, and Eike Von Savigny, 42–55. New York: Routledge.
2001b. "Introduction: Practice Theory." In *The Practice Turn in Contemporary Theory*, edited by Theodore R. Schatzki, Karin Knorr Cetina, and Eike Von Savigny, 1–14. New York: Routledge.
2002. *The Site of the Social: A Philosophical Exploration of the Constitution of Social Life and Change*. University Park: Pennsylvania State University Press.
2005. "Peripheral Vision: The Sites of Organizations." *Organizational Studies* 26 (3): 465–84.
2006. "On Organizations as They Happen." *Organization Studies* 27 (12): 1863–73.
Schatzki, Theodore R., Karin Knorr Cetina, and Eike Von Savigny, eds. 2001. *The Practice Turn in Contemporary Theory*. New York: Routledge.

Schelling, Thomas C. 1969. "Models of Segregation." *American Economic Review* 59 (2): 488–93.

1971. "Dynamic Models of Segregation." *Journal of Mathematical Sociology* 1 (2): 143–86.

Schilpp, Paul Arthur. 1974. *The Philosophy of Karl Popper*. La Salle, IL: Open Court.

Schimmelfennig, Frank, and Ulrich Sedelmeier. 2005. *The Europeanization of Central and Eastern Europe*. Ithaca, NY: Cornell University Press.

Schlosser, Markus. 2015. "Agency." In *Stanford Encyclopedia of Philosophy*, edited by Edward N. Zalta. Available at https://plato.stanford.edu/entries/agency/.

Schluchter, Wolfgang. 1981. *The Rise of Western Rationalism: Max Weber's Developmental History*. Berkeley: University of California Press.

Schmidt, Sebastian. 2014. "Foreign Military Presence and the Changing Practice of Sovereignty: A Pragmatist Explanation of Norm Change." *American Political Science Review* 108 (4): 817–29.

Schmitt, John S. 1997. "Command and (Out of) Control: The Military Implications of Complexity Theory." In *Complexity, Global Politics and National Security*, edited by David S. Alberts and Thomas J. Czerwinski, 99–111. Washington, DC: National Defense University Press.

Schmitt, Michael M. 2013. *Tallinn Manual on the International Law Applicable to Cyber Warfare*. New York: Cambridge University Press.

Schneier, Bruce. 2015. *Data and Goliath: The Hidden Battles to Capture Your Data and Control Your World*. New York: W. W. Norton.

Schoon, Ingrid. 2006. *Risk and Resilience: Adaptations in Changing Times*. Cambridge: Cambridge University Press.

Schotel, Bas. 2013. *On the Right of Exclusion: Law, Ethics and Immigration Policy*. New York: Routledge.

Schumpeter, Joseph. 1934. *Capitalism, Socialism, and Democracy*. New York: Harper and Row.

Schutz, Alfred. 1991. *On Phenomenology and Social Relations*. Chicago, IL: University of Chicago Press.

Scott, W. Richard. 1987. "The Adolescence of Institutional Theory." *Administrative Science Quarterly* 32 (4): 493–511.

1995. *Institutions and Organizations*. Thousand Oaks, CA: Sage.

Searle, John R. 1983. *Intentionality: An Essay in the Philosophy of Mind*. Cambridge: Cambridge University Press.

1995. *The Construction of Social Reality*. New York: Simon and Schuster.

1998. *Mind, Language and Society: Philosophy in the Real World*. Cambridge: Cambridge University Press.

2003. *Rationality in Action*. Cambridge, MA: MIT Press.

2010. *Making the Social World: The Structure of Human Civilization*. New York: Oxford University Press.

Seibt, Johanna. 2017. "Process Philosophy." In *The Stanford Encyclopedia of Philosophy*, edited by Edward N. Zalta. Available at https://plato.stanford.edu/entries/process-philosophy/.

Sending, Ole J., and Iver B. Neumann. 2011. "Banking on Power: How Some Practices in an International Organization Anchor Others." In *International*

Practices, edited by Emanuel Adler and Vincent Pouliot, 231–54. Cambridge: Cambridge University Press.

Sewell, William H. Jr. 2005. *Logics of History: Social Theory and Social Transformation*. Chicago, IL: University of Chicago Press.

Seybert, Lucia A., and Peter J. Katzenstein. 2018. "Protean Power and Control Power: Conceptual Analysis." In *Protean Power: Exploring the Uncertain and Unexpected in World Politics*, edited by Peter J. Katzenstein and Lucia A. Seybert, 3–26. Cambridge: Cambridge University Press.

Shapcott, Richard. 2001. *Justice, Community and Dialogue in International Relations*. Cambridge: Cambridge University Press.

Shelef, Nadav G. 2010. *Evolving Nationalism: Homeland, Identity, and Religion in Israel, 1925–2005*. Ithaca, NY: Cornell University Press.

Shettleworth, Sara J. 2004. "Book Review: *Evolution and Learning: The Baldwin Effect Reconsidered*." *Evolutionary Psychology* 2 (1): 105–7.

Shiller, Robert J. 2003. "From Efficient Markets Theory to Behavioral Finance." *Journal of Economic Perspectives* 17 (1): 83–104.

Shleifer, Andrei, and Robert W. Vishny. 1997. "A Survey of Corporate Governance." *Journal of Finance* 52 (2): 737–83.

Shotter, John. 1983. "'Duality of Structure' and 'Intentionality' in an Ecological Psychology." *Journal for the Theory of Social Behaviour* 13 (1): 19–44.

1995. "In Conversation Joint Action, Shared Intentionality and Ethics." *Theory and Psychology* 5 (1): 49–73.

Shove, Elizabeth, Mika Pantzar, and Matt Watson. 2012. *The Dynamics of Social Practice: Everyday Life and How It Changes*. London: Sage.

Shusterman, Richard, ed. 1999. *Bourdieu: A Critical Reader*. Oxford: Blackwell Oxford.

Shusterman, Richard, 2008. *Body Consciousness: A Philosophy of Mindfulness and Somaesthetics*. Cambridge: Cambridge University Press.

Siewert, Charles. 2017. "Consciousness and Intentionality." In *The Stanford Encyclopedia of Philosophy*, edited by Edward N. Zalta. Available at https://plato.stanford.edu/archives/spr2017/entries/consciousness-intentionality/.

Sikkink, Kathryn. 2011. *The Justice Cascade: How Human Rights Prosecutions Are Changing World Politics*. New York: W. W. Norton.

Simkin, Colin George Frederick. 1993. *Popper's Views on Natural and Social Science*. Leiden: E. J. Brill.

Simmons, Beth A., and Zachary Elkins. 2004. "The Globalization of Liberalization: Policy Diffusion in the International Political Economy." *American Political Science Review* 98 (1): 171–89.

Simmons, Beth A., Frank Dobbin, and Geoffrey Garrett. 2006. "Introduction: The International Diffusion of Liberalism." *International Organization* 60 (4): 781–810.

Simon, Herbert. 1967. "The Business School: A Problem in Organizational Design." *Journal of Management Studies* 4 (1): 1–16.

Skidmore, David. 1997. *Contested Social Orders and International Politics*. Nashville, TN: Vanderbilt University Press.

Smart, John J. C. 1978. "The Content of Physicalism." *Philosophical Quarterly* 28 (113): 339–41.

Smith, Adam. 1981 [1776]. *An Inquiry into the Nature and Causes of the Wealth of Nations*. 2 vols. Edited by R. H. Campbell, A. S. Skinner, and W. B. Todd. Indianapolis: Liberty Fund.

Smith, Daniel, and John Protevi. 2015. "Gilles Deleuze." In *The Stanford Encyclopedia of Philosophy*, edited by Edward N. Zalta. Available at https://plato.stanford.edu/entries/deleuze/.

Smith, John, and Chris Jenks. 2005. "Complexity, Ecology and the Materiality of Information." *Theory, Culture and Society* 22 (5): 141–63.

Snowden, Edward. 2014. TV Interview in Moscow with German TV Station ARD, January 26. Available at www.ndr.de/nachrichten/netzwelt/snowden277_page-2.html.

Solingen, Etel. 1998. *Regional Orders at Century's Dawn: Global and Domestic Influences on Grand Strategy*. Princeton, NJ: Princeton University Press.

2012. "Of Dominoes and Firewalls: The Domestic, Regional, and Global Politics of International Diffusion." *International Studies Quarterly* 56 (4): 631–44.

Solingen, Etel, and Joshua Malnight. 2016. "Globalization, Domestic Politics, and Regionalism." In *The Oxford Handbook of Comparative Regionalism*, edited by Tanja A. Börzel and Thomas Risse, 64–86. Oxford: Oxford University Press.

Somit, Albert and Steven A. Peterson. 1992. *The Dynamics of Evolution: The Punctuated Equilibrium Debate in the Natural and Social Sciences*. Ithaca, NY: Cornell University Press.

Sørensen, Estrid. 2017. "The Social Order of Facts vs. Truths." *EASST (European Association for the Study of Science and Technology) Review* 36 (1).

Sosa, Ernest. 1993. "Putnam's Pragmatic Realism." *Journal of Philosophy* 90 (12): 605–26.

Spencer, Herbert. 1855. *The Principles of Psychology*. London: Longman, Brown, Green, and Longmans.

1904. *First Principles*. London: Williams and Norgate.

Sperber, Dan. 1996. *Explaining Culture: A Naturalistic Approach*. Oxford: Blackwell.

Spruyt, Hendrik. 1994. "Institutional Selection in International Relations: State Anarchy as Order." *International Organization* 48 (4): 527–57.

1998. "Historical Sociology and Systems Theory in International Relations." *Review of International Political Economy* 5 (2): 340–53.

2001. "The Supply and Demand of Governance in Standard-Setting: Insights from the Past." *Journal of European Public Policy* 8 (3): 371–91.

Starkey, Ken, Armand Hatchuel, and Sue Tempest. 2004. "Rethinking the Business School." *Journal of Management Studies* 41 (8): 1521–31.

Starr, Harvey. 1991. "Democratic Dominoes: Diffusion Approaches to the Spread of Democracy in the International System." *Journal of Conflict Resolution* 35 (2): 356–81.

Stein, Janice Gross. 2011. "Background Knowledge in the Foreground: Conversations about Competent Practice in 'Sacred Space.'" In *International Practices*, edited by Emanuel Adler and Vincent Pouliot, 87–107. Cambridge: Cambridge University Press.

Steinmo, Sven. 2010. *The Evolution of Modern States: Sweden, Japan, and the United States*. Cambridge: Cambridge University Press.

Steinmo, Sven, Kathleen Thelen, and Frank Longstreth, eds. 1992. *Structuring Politics: Historical Institutionalism in Comparative Analysis*. Cambridge: Cambridge University Press.

Sterling-Folker, Jennifer. 2001. "Evolutionary Tendencies in Realist and Liberal IR Theory." In *Evolutionary Interpretations of World Politics*, edited by William R. Thompson, 62–109. New York: Routledge.

2006. "Lamarckian with a Vengeance: Human Nature and American International Relations Theory." *Journal of International Relations and Development* 9 (3): 227–46.

Stevens, Tim. 2017. "Cyberweapons: An Emerging Global Governance Architecture." *Palgrave Communications* 3.

Stiennon, Richard. 2015. "A Short History of Cyber Warfare." In *Cyber Warfare: A Multidisciplinary Analysis*, edited by James A. Green, 7–32. New York: Routledge.

Stinchcombe, Arthur L. 1990. *Information and Organizations*. Berkeley: University of California Press.

Stockton, Paul, and Michele Golabek-Goldman. 2013. "Curbing the Market for Cyber Weapons." *Yale Law and Poicy Review* 32 (1): 239–66.

Stokes, Geoff. 1989. "From Physics to Biology: Rationality in Popper's Conception of Evolutionary Epistemology." In *Issues in Evolutionary Epistemology*, edited by Kai Hahlweg and C. A. Hooker, 488–509. Albany: State University of New York Press.

Stone, Diane. 2000. "Think Tank Transnationalisation and Non-Profit Analysis, Advice and Advocacy." *Global Society* 14 (2): 153–72.

Strang, David. 1991. "Adding Social Structure to Diffusion Models: An Event History Framework." *Sociological Methods and Research* 19 (3): 324–53.

Strange, Susan. 1982. "Cave! Hic Dragones: A Critique of Regime Analysis." *International Organization* 36 (2): 479–96.

Streeck, Wolfgang, and Kathleen Thelen. 2005. *Beyond Continuity: Institutional Change in Advanced Political Economies*. Oxford: Oxford University Press.

Stripple, Johannes. 2007. "The Stuff of International Relations? Process Philosophy as Meta-Theoretical Reflection on Security, Territory and Authority." Paper presented at the sixth Pan-European International Relations Conference in Turin, September 12–15.

Studtmann, Paul. 2017. "Aristotle's Categories." In *The Stanford Encyclopedia of Philosophy*, edited by Edward N. Zalta. Available at https://plato.stanford.edu/archives/fall2017/entries/aristotle-categories/.

Stuurman, Siep. 2017. *The Invention of Humanity: Equality and Cultural Difference in World History*. Cambridge, MA: Harvard University Press.

Suteanu, Cristian. 2005. "Complexity, Science and the Public: The Geography of a New Interpretation." *Theory, Culture and Society* 22 (5): 113–40.

Swidler, Ann. 2001. "What Anchors Cultural Practices." In *The Practice Turn in Contemporary Theory*, edited by Theodore R. Schatzki, Karin Knorr Cetina, and Eike Von Savigny, 74–92. London: Routledge.

Sztompka, Piotr. 1993. *The Sociology of Social Change*. Oxford: Blackwell.

Tang, Shiping. 2010. "Social Evolution of International Politics: From Mearsheimer to Jervis." *European Journal of International Relations* 16 (1): 31–55.

2013. *The Social Evolution of International Politics*. Oxford: Oxford University Press.

Tannenwald, Nina. 2007. *The Nuclear Taboo: The United States and the Non-Use of Nuclear Weapons since 1945*. Cambridge: Cambridge University Press.

Taylor, Charles. 1971. "Interpretation and the Sciences of Man." *Review of Metaphysics* 25 (1): 3–51.

1985. *Human Agency and Language*. Cambridge: Cambridge University Press.

1992. *The Ethics of Authenticity*. Cambridge, MA: Harvard University Press.

2001. *Human Agency and Language: Philosophical Papers I and II*. Cambridge: Cambridge University Press.

2004. *Modern Social Imaginaries*. Durham, NC: Duke University Press.

Teschke, Benno. 1998. "Geopolitical Relations in the European Middle Ages: History and Theory." *International Organization* 52 (2): 325–58.

Thayer, Bradley A. 2004. *Darwin and International Relations: On the Evolutionary Origins of War and Ethnic Conflict*. Lexington: University Press of Kentucky.

Theiner, Georg, Colin Allen, and Robert L. Goldstone. 2010. "Recognizing Group Cognition." *Cognitive Systems Research* 11 (4): 378–95.

Thelen, Kathleen. 1999. "Historical Institutionalism in Comparative Politics." *Annual Review of Political Science* 2 (1): 369–404.

2004. *How Institutions Evolve: The Political Economy of Skills in Germany, Britain, the United States, and Japan*. Cambridge: Cambridge University Press.

Thelen, Kathleen, and Sven Steinmo. 1992. "Historic Institutionalism in Comparative Politics." In *Structuring Politics: Historical Institutionalism in Comparative Analysis*, edited by Sven Steinmo, Kathleen Thelen, and Frank Longstreth, 1–32. Cambridge: Cambridge University Press.

Thévenot, Laurent. 2001. "Pragmatic Regimes Governing the Engagement with the World." In *The Practice Turn in Contemporary Theory*, edited by Theodore R. Schatzki, Karin Knorr Cetina, and Eike Von Savigny, 64–82. London: Routledge.

Thomas, Daniel Charles. 2001. *The Helsinki Effect: International Norms, Human Rights, and the Demise of Communism*. Princeton, NJ: Princeton University Press.

Thompson, Michael T. 1979. *Rubbish Theory: The Creation and Destruction of Value*. Oxford: Oxford University Press.

Thompson, William R., ed. 2001. *Evolutionary Interpretations of World Politics*. New York: Routledge.

Thrift, Nigel. 1999. "The Place of Complexity." *Theory, Culture and Society* 16 (3): 31–69.

Tien, Lee. 2007. "Architectural Regulation and the Evolution of Social Norms." In *Cybercrime: Digital Cops in a Networked Environment*, edited by Jack Balkin, James Grimmelmann, Eddan Katz, Nimrod Kozlovski, Shlomit Wagman, and Tal Zarsky, 47–78. New York: New York University Press.

Tilly, Charles. 1984. *Big Structures, Large Processes, Huge Comparisons*. New York: Russell Sage Foundation.

Tilly, Charles, and Robert E. Goodin. 2006. "It Depends." In *The Oxford Handbook of Contextual Political Analysis*, edited by Robert Goodin and Charles Tilly, 3–32. New York: Oxford University Press.

Toffler, Alvin. 1984. "Science and Change." Preface to *Order Out of Chaos: Man's New Dialogue with Nature*, by Ilya Prigogine and Isabelle Stengers. New York: Bantam.

Tolbert, P. S., and Lynne G. Zucker. 1996. "Institutional Sources of Change in the Formal Structure of Organizations: Diffusion of Civil Service Reform, 1880–1935." In *The Handbook of Organization Studies*, edited by Stewart Clegg, Cynthia Hardy, and Walter Nord, 175–90. Thousand Oaks, CA: Sage.

Tomasello, Michael. 2009. *The Cultural Origins of Human Cognition*. Cambridge, MA: Harvard University Press.

Tomasello, Michael, Malinda Carpenter, Josep Call, Tanya Behne, and Henrike Moll. 2005. "Understanding and Sharing Intentions: The Origins of Cultural Cognition." *Behavioral and Brain Sciences* 28 (5): 675–91.

Tomasello, Michael, Ann Cale Kruger, and Hilary Horn Ratner. 1993. "Cultural Learning." *Behavioral and Brain Sciences* 16 (3): 495–511.

Tömmel, Ingeborg. 2013. "The New Neighborhood Policy of the EU: An Appropriate Response to the Arab Spring?" *Democracy and Security* 9 (1–2): 19–39.

Toulmin, Stephen. 1972. *Human Understanding: The Collective Use and Evolution of Concepts*. Oxford: Clarendon.

1977. *Human Understanding: The Collective Use and Evolution of Concepts – International Edition*. Princeton, NJ: Princeton University Press.

1982. "The Genealogy of Consciousness." In *Explaining Human Behavior: Consciousness, Human Action and Social Structure*, edited by Paul F. Second, 53–70. London: Sage.

Traverso, Enzo. 2016. *Fire and Blood: The European Civil War, 1914–1945*. London: Verso.

Trivers, Robert L. 1971. "The Evolution of Reciprocal Altruism." *Quarterly Review of Biology* 46: 35–57.

Tuomela, Raimo. 2007. *The Philosophy of Sociality: The Shared Point of View*. New York: Oxford University Press.

Turner, John D. 2009. "'The Last Acre and Sixpence': Views on Bank Liability Regimes in Nineteenth-Century Britain." *Financial History Review* 16 (2): 111–27.

Turner, Stephen. 1994. *The Social Theory of Practices: Tradition, Tacit Knowledge and Practice*. London: Routledge.

2001. "Throwing Out the Tacit Rule Book: Learning and Practices." In *The Practice Turn in Contemporary Theory*, edited by Theodore R. Schatzki, Karin Knorr Cetina, and Eike Von Savigny, 120–30. New York: Routledge.

Turner, Victor Witter. 1974. *Dramas, Fields, and Metaphors: Symbolic Action in Human Society*. Ithaca, NY: Cornell University Press.

UN General Assembly. 1948. *Universal Declaration of Human Rights* (217 [III] A). Paris.

Urry, John. 2003. *Global Complexity*. Cambridge: Polity.

2004. "Small Worlds and the New 'Social Physics.'" *Global Networks* 4 (2): 109–30.

2005. "The Complexity Turn." *Theory Culture and Society* 22 (5): 2–14.

Van Creveld, Martin. 1999. *The Rise and Decline of the State*. New York: Cambridge University Press.

Van Gennep, Arnold. 1961. *The Rites of Passage*, translated by Monika B. Vizedom and Gabrielle L. Caffee. Chicago, IL: Chicago University Press.

Van Krieken, Robert. 1998. *Norbert Elias*. London: Routledge.

Vance, Cyrus R. Jr., François Molins, Adrian Leppard, and Javier Zaragoza. 2015. "When Phone Encryption Blocks Justice." *New York Times*, August 11.

Veblen, Thorstein B. 1919. *The Place of Science in Modern Civilization and Other Essays*. New York: Huebsch.

Vogel, Ronald J. 1977. "The Effects of Taxation on the Differential Efficiency of Nonprofit Health Insurance." *Economic Inquiry* 15: 605–9.

Vogelsang, Ingo, and Benjamin M. Compaine, eds. 2000. *The Internet Upheaval: Raising Questions, Seeking Answers in Communications Policy*. Cambridge, MA: MIT Press.

Vygotsky, Lev Semenovich. 1962. *Language and Thought*. Cambridge, MA: MIT Press.

1978. *Mind in Society: The Development of Higher Psychological Processes*. Cambridge, MA: Harvard University Press.

Waddington, Conrad Hal. 1977. *Tools for Thought: How to Understand and Apply the Latest Scientific Techniques of Problem Solving*. New York: Basic Books.

Walby, Sylvia. 2009. *Globalization and Inequalities: Complexity and Contested Modernities*. London: Sage.

Waldrop, M. Mitchell. 1992. *Complexity: The Emerging Science at the Edge of Chaos*. New York: Simon and Schuster.

Walker, Rob B. J. 1987. "Realism, Change, and International Political Theory." *International Studies Quarterly* 31 (1): 65–86.

1993. *Inside/Outside: International Relations as Political Theory*. New York: Cambridge University Press.

Walklate, Sandra, Gabe Mythen, and Ross McGarry. 2012. "States of Resilience and the Resilient State." *Current Issues in Criminal Justice* 24 (2): 185–204.

Walklate, Sandra, Ross McGarry, and Gabe Mythen. 2014. "Searching for Resilience: A Conceptual Excavation." *Armed Forces and Society* 40 (3): 408–27.

Wallace, Claire. 2002. "Opening and Closing Borders: Migration and Mobility in East-Central Europe." *Journal of Ethnic and Migration Studies* 28 (4): 603–25.

Wallerstein, Immanuel Maurice. 1974. *The Modern World System: Capitalist Agriculture and the Origins of the European World Economy in the Seventeenth Century*. New York: Academic Press.

2004. *World-Systems Analysis: An Introduction*. Durham, NC: Duke University Press.

Walter, Swen. 2014. "Situated Cognition: A Field Guide to Some Open Conceptual and Ontological Issues." *Review of Philosophy and Psychology* 5 (2): 241–63.

Waltz, Kenneth N. 1979. *Theory of International Politics*. New York: McGraw-Hill.

Walzer, Michael. 1983. *Spheres of Justice: A Defense of Pluralism and Justice*. New York: Basic.

1990. "The Communitarian Critique of Liberalism." *Political Theory* 18 (1): 6–23.

2017. "Discovering What's Already There." *The Nation*, April 6.

Way, Lucan A. 2005. "Authoritarian State Building and the Sources of Regime Competitiveness in the Fourth Wave: The Cases of Belarus, Moldova, Russia, and Ukraine." *World Politics* 57 (2): 231–61.

Weber, Max. 1930. *The Protestant Ethic and the Spirit of Capitalism*. London: G. Allen & Unwin.

1958. "The Three Types of Legitimate Rule (Translated by Hans Gerth)." *Berkeley Publications in Society and Institutions* 4 (1).

Weingast, Barry R. 2002. "Rational Choice Institutionalism." In *Political Science: The State of the Discipline*, edited by Ira Katznelson and Helen V. Milner, 660–92. New York: W. W. Norton.

2016. "Persistent Inefficiency: Adam Smith's Theory of Slavery and Its Abolition in Western Europe." Available at https://papers.ssrn.com/sol3/papers.cfm?abstract_id=2635917.

Weldes, Jutta. 1999. "The Cultural Production of Crises: US Identity and Missiles in Cuba." In *Cultures of Insecurity: States, Communities, and the Production of Danger*, edited by Jutta Weldes, Mark Laffey, Hugh Gusterson, and Raymon Duvall, 35–62. Minneapolis: University of Minnesota Press.

Wendt, Alexander. 1987. "The Agent-Structure Problem in International Relations Theory." *International Organization* 41 (3): 335–70.

1995. "Constructing International Politics." *International Security* 20 (1): 71–81.

1999. *Social Theory of International Politics*. Cambridge: Cambridge University Press.

2003. "Why a World State Is Inevitable." *European Journal of International Relations* 9 (4): 491–542.

2015. *Quantum Mind and Social Science: Unifying Physical and Social Ontology*. Cambridge: Cambridge University Press.

Wenger, Etienne. 1998a. *Communities of Practice: Learning, Meaning, and Identity*. Cambridge: Cambridge University Press.

1998b. "Communities of Practice: Learning as a Social System." *Systems Thinker* 9 (5): 1–5.

2002. "Communities of Practice." In *Encyclopedia of the Social Sciences*, vol. 1.5, Article 5. Amsterdam: Elsevier Science.

2010. "Communities of Practice and Social Learning Systems: The Career of a Concept." In *Social Learning Systems and Communities of Practice*, edited by Chris Blackmore, 179–98. London: Springer.

Wenger, Etienne, Richard McDermott, and William M. Snyder. 2002. *Cultivating Communities of Practice: A Guide to Managing Knowledge*. Boston: Harvard Business School Press.

Wenger-Trayner, Etienne, Mark Fenton-O'Creevy, Steven Hutchison, and Beverly Wenger-Trayner, eds. 2015. *Learning in Landscapes of Practice:*

Boundaries, Identity, and Knowledgeability in Practice-Based Learning. New York: Routledge.

Wenzel, Christian Helmut, and Nantou Hsien. 2004. "Where after All Are the Meanings? A Defense of Internalism. Searle versus Putnam." In *Experience and Analysis: Papers of the Twenty-Seventh International Wittgenstein Symposium*, vol. 12, 408–9. Kirchberg am Wechsel: Austrian Wittgenstein Society.

Weyland, Kurt Gerhard. 2004. *Learning from Foreign Models in Latin American Policy Reform*. Baltimore, MD: Johns Hopkins University Press.

2007. "The Political Economy of Market Reform: A Revival of Structuralism?" *Latin American Research Review* 42 (3): 235–50.

2009. "The Diffusion of Revolution: '1848' in Europe and Latin America." *International Organization* 63 (3): 391–423.

2010. "The Diffusion of Regime Contention in European Democratization, 1830–1940." *Comparative Political Studies* 43 (8–9): 1148–76.

Whitehead, Alfred North. 1929. *Process and Reality: An Essay in Cosmology*. Cambridge: Cambridge University Press.

1978. *Process and Reality*, corrected edition, edited by David Ray Griffin and Donald W. Sherburne. New York: Free Press.

Widmaier, Wesley W., Mark Blyth, and Leonard Seabrooke. 2007. "The Social Construction of Wars and Crises as Openings for Change." *International Studies Quarterly* 51 (4): 747–59.

Wiener, Antje. 2014. *A Theory of Contestation*. Heidelberg: Springer.

2018. *Contestation and Constitution of Norms in Global International Relations*. Cambridge: Cambridge University Press.

Wiener, P. P. 1949. *Evolution and the Foundation of Pragmatism*. Cambridge, MA: Harvard University Press.

Wight, Colin. 2006. *Agents, Structures, and International Relations: Politics as Ontology*. New York: Cambridge University Press.

Wight, Martin.1960. "Why Is There No International Theory?" *International Relations* 2 (1): 35–48.

Wilkins, John S. 1995. "Evolutionary Models of Scientific Theory Change." Master's thesis, Department of Philosophy, Monash University.

Will, Frederick L. 1997. *Pragmatism and Realism*. Lanham, MD: Rowman and Littlefield.

Williams, Eric. 1944. *Capitalism and Slavery*. Chapel Hill: University of North Carolina Press.

Williams, G. C. 1966. *Adaptation and Natural Selection*. Princeton, NJ: Princeton University Press.

Wilson, David S. 2005. "Evolutionary Social Constructivism." In *The Literary Animal: Evolution and the Nature of Narrative*, edited by Jonathan Gottschall and David Sloan Wilson, 20–37. Chicago, IL: Northwestern University Press.

Wilson, Edward. 1975. *Sociobiology: The New Synthesis*. Cambridge, MA: Harvard University Press.

Wilson, Harlan Garnett. 1975. "Complexity as a Theoretical Problem: Wider Perspectives in Political Theory." In *Organized Social Complexity: Challenge to Politics and Policy*, edited by Todd R. La Porte, 281–331. Princeton, NJ: Princeton University Press.

1978. "Complexity as a Theoretical Problem." PhD dissertation, University of California, Berkeley.

Wilson, Robert A. 2001. "Group-Level Cognition." *Philosophy of Science* 68 (S3): S262–S273.

Witt, Ulrich. 1993. "Evolutionary Economics: Some Principles." In *Evolution in Markets and Institutions*, edited by Ulrich Witt, 1–16. Heidelberg: Physica-Verlag Heidelberg.

Wittgenstein, Ludwig. 1953. *Philosophical Investigations.* Oxford: Blackwell.

Wruck, Karen H. 2008. "Private Equity, Corporate Governance, and the Reinvention of the Market for Corporate Control." *Journal of Applied Corporate Finance* 20 (3): 8–21.

Wuthnow, Robert. 1989. *Communities of Discourse: Ideology and Social Structure in the Reformation, the Enlightenment, and European Socialism.* Cambridge, MA: Harvard University Press.

Young, H. Peyton. 1993. "An Evolutionary Model of Bargaining." *Journal of Economic Theory* 59 (1): 145–68.

Young, Oran R. 1982. "Regime Dynamics: The Rise and Fall of International Regimes." *International Organization* 36 (2): 277–97.

1989. "Science and Social Institutions: Lessons for International Resource Regimes." In *International Resource Management: The Role of Science and Politics*, edited by Steinar Andresen and Willy Østreng, 7–24. London: Belhaven Press.

Zakaria, Fareed. 1997. "The Rise of Illiberal Democracy." *Foreign Affairs* 76 (6): 22–43.

Żegleń, Urszula M. 2002. "Introduction." In *Hilary Putnam: Pragmatism and Realism*, edited by James Conant and Urszula Żegleń, 1–6. New York: Routledge.

Zetter, Kim. 2016. "NSA Hacker Chief Explains How to Keep Him Out of Your System." *Wired*, January 28.

Ziman, John. 2000. "Evolutionary Models for Technological Change." In *Technological Innovation as an Evolutionary Process*, edited by John Ziman, 3–12. Cambridge: Cambridge University Press.

Zimmer, Carl. 2001. *Evolution: The Triumph of an Idea.* New York: Harper Collins.

Zucker, Lynne G. 1977. "The Role of Institutionalization in Cultural Persistence." *American Sociological Review* 42 (5): 726–43.

1987. "Institutional Theories of Organization." *Annual Review of Sociology* 13: 443–64.

Zürn, Michael. 2010. "Global Governance as Multi-Level Governance." In *Handbook on Multi-Level Governance*, edited by Henrik Enderlein, Sonja Wälti, and Michael Zürn, 80–102. Northampton, MA: Edward Elgar.

2018. *A Theory of Global Governance: Authority, Legitimacy, and Contestation.* Oxford: Oxford University Press.

Zürn, Michael, Martin Binder, and Matthias Ecker-Ehrhardt. 2012. "International Authority and Its Politicization." *International Theory* 4 (1): 69–106.

Index

Abbott, Andrew, 56, 60–61
abolition, 270
abortion, 123
accountability, 238
acknowledgment, 279–81
acquired characteristics' inheritance, 80–81
action
  communicative action, 62–63
  creativity of, 119
  Joas on, 222–23
  Joas on creative social action, 223
  pragmatism theory of action, 118–19
  recursive action, 109–15
  social action, 117, 119–21
  strategic action fields, 113, 161
action-network theory (ANT), 61, 109–10
adaptation, 261–62
Adger, W. Neil, 262
Adler-Nissen, Rebecca, 303
Advanced Research Projects Agency (ARPA), 221
Advanced Research Projects Agency Network (ARPANET), 16–17, 147, 176, 182–83, 199–200, 221–22
agency, 60, 76, 159
  attributes of, 208–10
  cognitive evolution theory, agential social foundations of, 212–13
  collective, 20, 209
  construction of, 167–68
  evolution of, 216
  social orders and, 123
  structure-agency, 34–35, 197
agential processual social mechanisms, 4, 29–30, 198–99, 212–13
  change and, 199
  communities of practice and, 202
  judgment and, 204–5
  reflexivity and, 204–5
  resilience and, 199
AI. *See* Artificial Intelligence
Aldrich, Howard E., 97–98
Alexander, Jeffrey, 18–19, 111–12
  performative power and, 27, 177–78
alignment, 203, 224–25
Altair 8800, 17
Amazon, 177
American pragmatism, 2, 38, 51–52, 118–22, 287
Amin, Ash, 248
Amsterdam Treaty of 2005, 191–92
anchoring practices, 124, 127–30, 146, 180, 239–40
  background knowledge and, 154
  deontic power and, 140
  of EU, 155
  global, 153
  of legal personality, 175
  of liberal internationalism, 154
  of nuclear weapons, 139–40
  performative power and, 140
Ancien Regime, 147
Anglo-American Five Eyes intelligence community, 174, 227
Ansell, Christopher, 293
ANT. *See* action-network theory
anti-liberal backlash, 154–55
appeal to autonomy, 276–77
Apple, 187
Arab Spring, 242
Archer, Margaret, 216–17
Arendt, Hannah, 277, 290
Aristotle, 49–50, 53, 69
ARPA. *See* Advanced Research Projects Agency
ARPANET. *See* Advanced Research Projects Agency Network
Arthur, Brian, 98, 102
Artificial Intelligence (AI), 240
ASEAN. *See* Association of South East Asian Nations
assemblage theory, 124–25
Association of South East Asian Nations (ASEAN), 228

Austin, John, 64
authority, 235–36
autonomy, 214
awakening of consciousness, 165, 222
Axelrod, Robert, 162

background knowledge, 15, 18–20, 26, 301
  anchoring practices and, 154
  background scientific knowledge, 298
  cognitive evolution theory and, 110–11
  communities of practice and, 24–25,165, 167–68
  creativity and, 223
  deontic power and, 171, 236
  disruptive, 229
  embedded in routines, 31
  generation of, 30–31
  habitus and, 70–71
  intersubjective background knowledge, 21, 45–46, 212
  new fields of, 183
  normative changes in, 220
  practices and, 19
  recursive reproduction of, 217–18
  reflection on, 29–30
  scientific, 175
  Searle and, 111
  selective retention of, 167
  shared, 235
  in state of non-equilibrium, 47
  transformation of, 28
  values and norms and, 200–1
  World 3 and, 74
balance of practices, 23, 124, 175–76, 239, 241, 298
Baldwin, James M., 88, 90–91, 207, 253
Barab, Sasha A., 112
Baran, Paul, 221–22
Barber, Tony, 194
Barnes, Barry, 126
BBS. *See* bulletin board systems
Beck, Ulrich, 242
becoming ontology, 8, 38–39, 64, 69
  from being to becoming, 48–63
  evolutionary theory and, 51
  Heraclitus on, 45
  social orders and, 124
  ways of becoming, 63
being ontology, 45, 48–63
Beitz, Charles, 273–75
Bentley, Arthur, 52–53
Berger, Peter, 256
Bergson, Henri, 53
Berners-Lee, Tim, 233
better practices, 5–6, 130–31, 133, 150–51, 278–79
  common humanity and, 267, 270–72
  normative theoretical exploration of, 275–83
Bhaskar, Roy, 216–17
Binder, Martin, 236
Bitcoin, 177, 192
Blackmore, Susan, 101
Blanchard, Thomas, 292
blind variation, 94–95
Bloor, David, 129
Blumer, Herbert, 53
Bockman, Johanna, 234–35
Boltanski, Luc, 206
Booz Allen Hamilton, 249
Born, Max, 69
Boulding, Kenneth, 85–86
boundary encounters, 225–26
boundary objects, 114–15
boundary practices, 225–26
bounded progress, 2, 5–6, 266–68
  common humanity and, 284–85
  in cyberspace, 283
  in IR, 269
  normative theoretical exploration of, 275–83
Bourdieu, Pierre, 18, 38–39, 56–57, 254
  pragmatism and, 121–22
  on social structure and social action, 120–21
Boyd, Robert, 84, 100
Brexit, 158, 178, 187, 245
brokering, 226
Brunnée, Jutta, 244
Büger, Christian, 303
Bukovansky, Mlada, 161
bulletin board systems (BBS), 17
business education, 185–86, 221
business firms, 98
Butler, Judith, 111
Buzan, Barry, 158–59

CALEA. *See* Communications Assistance for Law Enforcement Act
Callon, Michael, 111, 226
Campbell, Donald, 38, 91–92, 94–95, 219
Campbell's general model of evolutionary change, 1–2, 38, 82, 164, 219
Campbell's rule, 82
capital, 120–21
capitalism, 172–73
Caporaso, James A., 140
Carlsnaes, Walter, 216
Carroll, Archie B., 132

Cartesian ontology, 254
Cassirer, Ernst, 60
causality, 302–3
cause-effect collective understandings, 184–85
Cederman, Lars-Erik, 162
Cerf, Vinton, 199
change, 41, 191, 235–42. *See also* international orders' change, theories of
 agential processual social mechanisms and, 199
 constant, 105
 corporate social order, endogenous change in, 183–84
 in deontic power, 181–82
 dialectical change, 156
 distributional change, 156
 dynamic theories of, 9–10
 endogenous change, 183–84
 ethical change, 284
 evolutionary epistemology, model of evolutionary associated with, 1–2
 incremental, 183–84
 interactive change, 156
 international, 64–65
 nonlinear, 38, 102–3, 105–6
 observed, 48–49
 practice-driven changes, 4
 through reflexivity, 215
 in social orders, 47
 stability and, 36–37, 39
 transformative change, 156
Chia, Robert, 59–60
CitizenFour (2014), 200
The Civilizing Process (Elias), 59
Clapper, James, 178
Clemens, Elisabeth S., 256–57
Clinton, Bill, 184
Clipper Chip, 184
coercive power, 67
cognition, 53, 115. *See also* social cognition
 in communities of practice, 29
 Fleck on, 38, 82
 social cognition, evolutionary approach to, 35–36
 as social condition, 2, 19, 24–25
 in social transactions, 116
cognitive evolution, 2, 47, 95, 155, 208, 295
 collective learning and, 7, 165
 communities of practice and, 166
 complexity theory and, 190–97
 creative variation and, 30–31
 key processes associated with, 4
 master mechanism for, 27
 preferential selective survival and, 15
 samurai crab and, 14
 social power and, 207
 synchronic understanding of, 30
cognitive evolution theory, 9, 18, 24–32, 38, 164, 219, 295–96
 agential social foundations of, 212–13
 assemblage theory and, 124–25
 background knowledge and, 110–11
 building blocks of, 63
 claims of, 4–5
 collective agency and, 209
 communities of practice and, 3
 complementarity between evolution and complexity, 103–4
 deontic power and, 3, 27, 265
 edifice of, 302–3
 epistemic practical authority and, 3, 27
 evolutionary constructivism and, 34–35
 evolutionary epistemology and, 77
 functionalism and, 217
 international social orders and, 6–7
 IR theory and, 8, 41
 normative theoretical claims of, 40–41
 performative power and, 177–78
 practices and, 140
 seven moves of, 18–19
 social cognition and, 116–17
 social power and, 284
 sociocultural evolution and, 8
 structural units of, 81
cognitive progress, 286–87
cognitive psychology, 2
cognitive punches, 161–62
Cohen, Jean, 152
Colapietro, Vincent, 222
collective agency, 20, 209
collective consciousness, 221
collective identity, 159–61
collective intentionality, 20, 73, 132, 210
 deontic power and, 236
 social reality and, 175
collective learning, 256–57, 302
 cognitive evolution and, 7, 165
 collective-social learning, 168
 by communities of practice, 169
 contestation and, 47, 168, 177, 184, 283–85
 deontic power and, 177
 endogenous collective learning and, 4
collective meanings, 9–10, 221
colonization, 15
commenda system, 147
Commission on Security and Cooperation in Europe (CSCE), 232–33, 244–45

common humanity, 5–6, 40–41, 73, 130–31, 133, 266–76
acknowledgment of, 279–80
better practices and, 267, 270–72
bounded progress and, 284–85
collective knowledge of, 281–82
evolved consciousness of, 278
threats to, 290–91
common-sense reality, 6, 41, 267, 290–91
Communications Assistance for Law Enforcement Act (CALEA), 177, 209
communicative action, 62–63
Communist social order, 195
communitarianism, 5, 74, 266, 268
communitarian ethics, 272–75
internationalist, 14–15
communities of practice, 2, 112–13, 122, 144, 198–99, 301
agential processual social mechanisms and, 202
as analytical constructs, 20–21
background knowledge and, 24–25, 165, 167–68
boundaries of, 247
cognition in, 29
cognitive evolution and, 166
cognitive evolution theory and, 3
collective learning by, 169
constellations of, 27–44, 114–15, 172–73, 247
as containers of practices, 119–20
contestation between, 23–24, 184, 223, 300
corporate social order and, 7–8
creative variation and, 220, 224–26
deontic power and, 187
differential selection in and among, 166
emergent processes within, 147
endogenous collective learning and, 4
epistemic practical authority of, 21, 127–28
in EU, 170
in Europe, 230
horizontal and vertical spread of, 242–52
horizontal expansion of, 31
induction into, 251
institutions and, 165–66
legitimacy of, 185
liberal-internationalist practices and, 6–7
material power and, 175–76
mutual engagement in, 38
performative power and, 187
propensity and contingency and, 23
replication and, 26
replication of practices of, 217
social orders and, 28, 123–24
in state of non-equilibrium, 47
transactions within, 29
vertical replication and, 31
Wenger and, 18, 20
Wenger and Lave and, 202–3
community, 88–89
complex adaptive systems, 98
complexity theory, 38, 45
cognitive evolution and, 190–97
concepts of, 51
evolutionary epistemology and, 102–8
computer networking, 16
computer science, 28
consensus theory of truth, 33
constitutional pluralism, 152
constitutive rules, 129
constitutive values and norms, 127–30
construction of social facts, 47
constructivism, 63–65, 249–50, 299. *See also* evolutionary constructivism
constructivist epistemology, 74–75
constructivist evolutionary theory of social ordering, 25
consumers, 24
contestation, 114, 180–81
contingency, 23, 112, 178–79, 276
Convention on Cybercrime, 209
Cook, James M., 256–57
cooperative-security practices, 248, 250
Copenhagen Criteria, 205, 241, 245
corporate fitness, 98–99
corporate practices, 26, 128–29, 246, 282
corporate social order, 145
communities of practice and, 7–8
corporate practices, 128–29
corporation-oriented relations of production, 243
cyberspace and, 17–18
endogenous change in, 183–84
evolution of, 104
financial economics and, 229
modern form of corporation, 28, 146–47, 172–73
multinational corporations, 189–90
spread of form of corporation, 18
transnational, 23
Corporate Social Responsibility (CSR), 24, 132, 148
content and purpose of, 227
emergence of, 146
cosmopolitanism, 5, 152, 266, 268, 272–75
Cox, Robert, 157
Crawford, Neta, 64

creative variation, 4, 146, 220
  birth of new social orders and, 226–33
  cognitive evolution and, 30–31
  communities of practice and, 220, 224–26
  selective retention and, 30, 102, 219
creativity, 2, 88–89, 110, 203–9
  of action, 119
  background knowledge and, 223
  instability and, 223
  Joas on creative social action, 223
  selection processes and, 89
  sudden jumps in, 95
Crimea, 230–31
crypto-currencies, 177, 208–9
CSCE. *See* Commission on Security and Cooperation in Europe
CSR. *See* Corporate Social Responsibility
cultural learning, 81
cultural objects, 66
culture, 36
cyberspace, 16, 132, 177, 185, 246, 296
  bounded progress in, 283
  contested, 23, 188
  continually fluctuating cyberspace order, 127–28
  corporate social order and, 17–18
  cyberattacks, 139–40, 240
  cybercrime, 128–29, 209
  cybersecurity practices, 172
  evolution of, 42
  expansiveness of, 203
  global spread of, 17
  horizontal expansion of across, 31
  open architecture of, 176, 182
  origins of, 221–22
  pervasiveness of, 201, 251
  subordinate practices of, 128
  zero-day vulnerabilities, 212

Darwin, Charles, 51, 78–79
Dawkins, Richard, 80, 100–1
de Chardin, Teilhard, 85–86
De Jaegher, Hanne, 115
Defense Communications Agency, 16–17
deliberative democracy, 268–69
demagoguery, 291
democracy, 6, 22, 154–55, 300
  deliberative democracy, 268–69
  democratization, 241
  Dewey on, 293–94
  illiberal democracies, 293
  practical democracy, 268–69, 290–94
  promotion of, 228
  threats to democratic social order, 40–41
Democritus, 48–49
Dennett, Daniel, 162
deontic power, 27, 30, 67, 239, 265, 270–71, 298
  anchoring practices and, 140
  background knowledge and, 171, 236
  changes in, 181–82
  collective intentionality and, 236
  collective learning and, 177
  communities of practice and, 187
  endogenous processes and, 237
  legal practices and, 244
  reciprocity and, 237
Department of Defense, U.S., 16–17
Descartes, René, 50
descent, 181
descriptive inference, 25
determinism, 52, 85–86, 111–12, 155
Dewey, John, 29–30, 38, 40–41, 51–52, 272–73
  on democracy, 293–94
  evolutionary epistemology and, 87–88
  on practices, 118–19
  on transactions, 52–53, 126–27
Di Paolo, Ezequiel, 115
diffusion, 258–59
DiMaggio, Paul J., 256–57, 260
disassociation, 5–6, 158, 266, 297
  disassociation-type politics, 22
  dissociation-type social order, 15–16
  interconnectedness and, 153, 269
  no ideal types of, 22
  resurgent, 268
discontinuities, 224–25
discourse ethics, 280
discourse principle, 268–69
discursive spaces, 113
disposition, 208
disruptive practitioners, 228
dissipative structures, 106–7, 241
Dobzhansky, Theodosius, 79
domains of knowledge, 20
Douglas, Mary, 253–54
Drieschova, Alena, 303
Duffy, Thomas, 112
Durham, W. H., 82
Durkheim, Emile, 85
dynamic density, 139
dynamic quality, 279

Eastern European countries, 237
eBay, 177
Ecker-Ehrhardt, Matthias, 236
Eckstein, Harry, 265
e-commerce, 177
economic globalization, 282

economic power, 141–42
economics, 96
EEM. *See* evolution of epistemic mechanisms
EET. *See* epistemic evolution of theories
Efficient Market Hypothesis, 170
Einstein, Albert, 51
Eisenhower, Dwight D., 221
Eldredge, Niles, 79–80, 95
Elias, Norbert, 56, 58–59, 286
Elster, Jon, 13–14, 38, 213–18
emergence, 102–3, 162
  of CSR, 146
  of endogenous change, 184
  implications of, 104
  social world and, 104–5
emergent persistence, 235–42
emerging markets, 141–42
Emirbayer, Mustafa, 56, 59–60
emotional attachment, 29, 100, 200
end of history, 267–68
Enderlein, Hendrik, 150
endogenous change, 183–84
endogenous collective learning, 4
endogenous processes, 182, 237
endogenous social interaction processes, 220
engagement, 203, 224–25
Engel, Andreas K., 115
enlargement, 191–92, 245
Enlightenment, 266, 276
ENP. *See* European Neighborhood Policy
environmental practices, 131
environmental social order, 183
epistemic communities, 298–99
epistemic evolution of theories (EET), 77
epistemic practical authority, 3–4, 122, 124, 137, 189–90, 236
  of communities of practice, 21, 127–28
  loss of, 28
  normative appeals and, 250
  performativity and, 237–38
  practices and, 27–44
  selective retention and, 4, 27
  of social orders, 23
epistemic practical recognition, 3
epistemic practical reproduction, 234
epistemic practical selective retention, 234–35
epistemic-practical-authority selection dynamics, 235–42
epistemological insecurity, 6, 40–41, 290
  consequences of, 291–92
  fake news and, 292–93
  post-truth and, 291, 293
  scientific knowledge and, 292
epistemological security, 290–94
equilibrium, 32, 95
Erskine, Toni, 274
ethical normativity, 266–67, 270–75
ethics, 85–86
  communitarian ethics, 272–75
  cosmopolitan ethics, 272–75
  discourse ethics, 280
  ethical change, 284
  ethical standards, 268
  practices and, 40–41
  pragmatist ethics, 272–75
EU. *See* European Union
Europe, 73, 148–49. *See also* postwar European social order
  colonization, 15
  communities of practice in, 230
  European monetary union, 239–40
  European practices and background knowledge, 15
  European refugees' social order, 23–24
  nationalism in, 154
  novel practices in, 16
  transformative aspirations of, 211–12
  Western Europe, 18
European Community, 248
European Neighborhood Policy (ENP), 211–12, 228
European Union (EU), 224, 245, 262–64, 296
  anchoring practices of, 155
  candidate countries for accession, 169
  Cold War and, 31
  communities of practice in, 170
  contestation in, 186–87
  creation of, 14–15
  democratization, 241
  Eastern European countries in, 237
  economic crisis in, 15–16
  European Parliament, 179
  Europeanization, 140, 204
  innovation in, 232
  institutions of, 133, 140, 174–75
  processes of enlargement of, 128–29
  treaties in, 28–29
Euroskepticism, 178, 230, 232
evolution of epistemic mechanisms (EEM), 77
evolutionary biology, 37
evolutionary constructivism, 32–33, 38–40, 274
  becoming ontological concepts of, 63
  cognitive evolution theory and, 34–35
  evolutionary epistemology and, 77
evolutionary constructivist social theory, 1–2
evolutionary economics, 97–99

evolutionary epistemology, 25–26, 38, 55–56, 219
- Baldwin and, 90–91
- Campbell and, 38, 82, 164
- cognitive evolution theory and, 77
- complexity theory and, 102–8
- Dewey and, 87–88
- epistemic version of, 82
- evolutionary constructivism and, 77
- general model of evolutionary change and, 1–2, 38, 82, 164, 219
- influences on, 86–87
- interdisciplinary nature of, 78
- James and, 89–90
- Mead and, 88–89
- model of evolutionary change associated with, 1–2
- naturalist, 81–84
- naturalistic, 99
- Popper and, 92–93
- pragmatic constructivism and, 33–34
- short history of, 84–102
- social constructivism and, 32–33
- sociocultural, 81–84

evolutionary ontology, 38
evolutionary psychology, 99–100
evolutionary social processes, 32–33
evolutionary theory, 78–81, 94
- American pragmatists and, 51–52
- becoming ontology and, 51
- constructivist evolutionary theory of social ordering, 25
- Rescher and, 55–56
- revival in social sciences of, 77–78

evolutionary variants, 219
Executive Order 13010 on Critical Infrastructure Protection (Clinton), 184
exogenous crises, 194–95, 257
expectations, 198
external realism, 65
external shocks, 187
externalism, 116–17
Eyal, Gil, 234–35

Facebook, 139–40, 182
fake news, 292–93
Farage, Nigel, 178
Federal Bureau of Investigation (FBI), 187
Fernbach, Philip, 242–43
Fichte, Johann, 50
fields, 41–42, 56–57, 120–21
- Bourdieu and, 57, 120–22, 206
- practice theory and, 121
- strategic action fields, 113, 161

fields of practices, 3
- emergent, 190
- international social orders as, 142
- social orders and, 122, 126, 144

financial economics, 229
financial markets, 170
Finnemore, Martha, 256
First International Conference on Computer Communications, 199, 221–22
Fleck, Ludwik, 29, 38, 74, 82, 115–16
- thought collective and, 29, 74, 115–16, 202

Fligstein, Neil, 98–99, 113, 256–57
fluctuations, 190–92, 219, 262
- continuous, 223
- order through, 1, 234
- stability and permanent fluctuations, 25–26

Ford Foundation, 221
foresight capacities, 207
Foucault, Michel, 61–63
Frega, Roberto, 271–72, 293
Friedman, Milton, 24
Front National, 178
Frost, Mervyn, 274–75
Fuller, Lon, 244
functionalism, 213, 217

Gadinger, Frank, 303
Galilei, Galileo, 50
Gallagher, Shaun, 115
game theory, 172–81, 260
Geertz, Clifford, 111
generalized Darwinism, 259–60
generative relationships, 196, 221
genopolitics, 100
German idealists, 50–51
German reunification, 205
Giddens, Anthony, 42, 213–18
Gilbert, Margaret, 73
global governance, 150–55
global order, 138, 141–42, 151–55
global warming, 123, 183
- climate change social order, 183
- scientific knowledge on, 231

Goffman, Erving, 56–58, 73, 111, 126–27, 201
golden rule, 5, 280–81, 283
Goldman, Alvin, 292
good life, 274
Google, 139–40
Gould, Stephen Jay, 79–80, 91, 95
Grabbe, Heather, 149
Great Depression, 169

Great Firewall of China, 246
Grexit crisis, 238, 245
Gross, Neil, 121

Haas, Ernst, 33–34, 163, 286–90
Haas, Peter, 33–34, 163
Habermas, Jürgen, 61–63, 268–69, 271
habits, 87–88, 109–10, 120, 205–6
habitus, 70–71, 109, 120–21, 204–5
  Bourdieu and, 18, 56–57, 73, 109–11, 120–21, 254
hacking, 17, 145, 221
Hall, Peter A., 161
harm conventions, 285
Hegel, Georg, 50, 280
Heidegger, Martin, 49–50, 113
Heike clan of samurai, 13–14
Heisenberg, Werner, 69
Helsinki Final Act 1975, 194, 196, 232–34
Heraclitus, 45, 48–49, 57–58, 67
Herrmann, Esther, 37
hierarchy, 112
Hirsch, Michal Ben-Josef, 226–27
historical institutionalism, 163, 257–58, 260–61
history, 64
Hitler, Adolf, 134, 196
Hodgson, Geoffrey M., 98
homeorhesis, 179, 217, 261–64
homeostasis, 261–62
Honneth, Axel, 273, 280, 293–94
Hopf, Ted, 64
horizons of possibilities, 112–13
horizontal accountability, 113, 173–74
horizontal power, 174
horizontal replication, 31, 242–43
horizontal systems of rule, 5–6, 22–23, 40–41, 130–31, 133, 155, 269, 281, 284, 292
Howse, Robert, 232
Hull, David, 80, 96
human intention, 13–14
human rights, 210, 222, 282
human welfare, 286
humanist realism, 5, 269, 283–90
Hume, David, 73
Hungary, 15–16, 179
Hurrell, Andrew, 152
Huxley, Julian, 79

ICANN. *See* Internet Corporation for Assigned Names and Numbers
ICTs. *See* information and communications technologies
identification-shaping processes, 4
IGCs. *See* Intergovernmental Conferences
IGE. *See* International Group of Experts
Ikenberry, G. John, 157–58, 163, 296
illiberal democracies, 293
imagination, 203, 224–25
immanence, 47
increasing returns theories, 98
indeterminacy, 201
individual learning, 170
inequality practices, 140–41
informality, 22, 27–44, 58
information and communications technologies (ICTs), 209
Information Processing Techniques Office (IPTO), 221
innovation, 30–31, 241
  in EU, 232
  selective retention of, 31
  social innovation, 221
instability, 223–25
institutional evolution, 255–61
institutions, 26, 96–97, 151, 255–56
  communities of practice and, 165–66
  EU institutions, 133, 140, 174–75
  historical institutionalism, 163
  informal, 58
  institutional decay, 159–60
  institutional facts, 72
  institutional power, 157
  institutionalized rules, 215
  mediating institutions, 140
  selective retention, institutionalization and, 252–55
  social institutions, 252
integration, 126
intelligibility, 113
intention, 207–8
interactions/transactions, 126–27
interactive learning, 34
interactive negotiation, 223–24
interconnectedness, 5–6, 148, 266, 281, 297
  disassociation and, 153, 269
  horizontal accountability and, 173–74
  increase of, 288
  interactions/transactions and, 126–27
  interconnectedness-type politics, 22
  no ideal types of, 22
  in postwar European social order, 22–23
interdependence, 126
Intergovernmental Conferences (IGCs), 224
international diffusion, 258
International Group of Experts (IGE), 145
international order, 296
  emergent character of, 150
  liberal international order, 40–41, 124

international order (cont.)
multilevel international orders, 6–7
traditional concepts of, 24
international orders' change, theories of
distributional, 156–58
evolutionary, 156, 162–64
friction, 156, 160–62
transformative, 156, 158–60
international pecking orders, 138
international regimes, 6–7, 41, 137–38, 142–50
International Relations (IR)
bounded progress in, 269
cognitive evolution theory and, 8, 41
constructivism, 36
constructivist theories of adaptation and learning in, 37
evolutionary theories of, 162
Haas, E., on progress in, 286–90
"practice turn" in, 9, 64–65
scholars of, 1, 137–38
social theory, IR discipline and, 1
theorists of, 298
international social orders, 1, 23, 146–47, 197
cognitive evolution theory and, 6–7
epistemic differentiation among, 139
evolution of, 28
as fields of practice, 142
as landscapes, 137
multilevel global governance and, 152–53
multiple, 139, 141, 151–55
normative content of, 148
progressive, 290–94
internationalist communitarianism, 14–15
Internet Corporation for Assigned Names and Numbers (ICANN), 239
Internet of Things (IoT), 240
Internet Service Providers (ISPs), 182–83
interorganizational relations, 172
intersubjectivity, 57, 72, 110, 193
intersubjective background knowledge, 21, 45–46, 212
intersubjective cognitive thresholds, 179, 188, 234
intersubjective collective understandings, 73
intersubjective knowledge, 165–66
intersubjective legitimacy, 148
intersubjective social structures, 112
The Invention of Common Humanity (Stuurman), 277–78
IoT. *See* Internet of Things
IPTO. *See* Information Processing Techniques Office
IR. *See* International Relations
ISPs. *See* Internet Service Providers
Israel, 240
issue areas, 146

Jackson, Patrick Thaddeus, 59–60, 72, 74
James, William, 38, 51–52, 89–90, 119
Jantsch, Erich, 85–86
Joas, Hans, 2, 62, 116, 219–20
on action, 222–23
on creative social action, 223
Johnson, Boris, 178
Johnson, Victoria, 56
Joint Stock Companies Act of 1862, 147
judgment, 29–30, 204–5, 214
justice, 272
justification processes, 4–5, 29–30

Kant, Immanuel, 50, 268–69, 277
Katzenstein, Peter, 4, 223
Kauffman, Stuart, 103
Keohane, Robert, 149
Kerry, John, 230–31
Kessler, Oliver, 147–48
Khurana, Rakesh, 232
Knöbl, Wolfgang, 62
Knorr Cetina, Karin, 230
knowing, 202–3
Knudsen, Thorbjorn, 98
König, Peter, 115
Korsgaard, Christine, 266–67, 276–77
Krasner, Stephen, 142, 255–56
Kratochwil, Friedrich, 64, 142–44
Krauss, Elizabeth, 54
Kruger, Ann Cale, 192
Kuhn, Thomas, 91–93
Kurthen, Martin, 115

Lakatos, Imre, 92
Lamarck, Jean-Baptiste, 78, 80–81, 83–84
landscapes, 122, 137
Lane, David, 196
Lapid, Yosef, 49, 59–60
Latour, Bruno, 16, 109–10
Lave, Jean, 2, 202
Law, John, 61
Lawson, George, 158–59
LBO. *See* Leveraged Buyout
Le Pen, Marine, 178, 263
learning processes, 29–30
legal personality, 175
legal practices, 244
Legro, Jeffrey, 64
Leibnitz, Gottfried W., 50
levels, 151–53

Leveraged Buyout (LBO), 229
Levine, Donald, 62
Lewis, Orion A., 100, 259, 261
Lewontin, Richard, 91
liberalism
  anti-liberal backlash, 154–55
  communities of practice, liberal-internationalist practices and, 6–7
  liberal evolutionary theories, 33
  liberal international order, 40–41, 124
  liberal internationalism, 6–7
    anchoring practices of, 154
  liberal nationalism, 14–15, 287, 289–90
  neoliberalism, 234–35
Lieberman, Robert, 160–61
like-mindedness, 20
liminality, 3, 179
Linklater, Andrew, 274, 285–86
Linux, 192, 203–9
Lipson, Michael, 143
Lisbon Treaty, 28–29, 179
Litfin, Karen, 64
Locke, John, 279
longevity, 242–52
Lopez, Anthony C., 99
Luckman, Thomas, 256
Luhmann, Niklas, 61–63, 185
Lustick, Ian S., 259–61

Maastricht treaty, 262
MacIntyre, Alasdair, 131
Macron, Emmanuel, 178, 188–89, 263
Mahoney, James, 257
Malthus, T. R., 78
Markell, Patchen, 280
Martin, Harold III, 249
Marx, Karl, 60, 85–86
Marxist thinking, 85–86
material power, 125–26, 148, 157, 260
  community of practice and, 175–76
  of US, 158, 228–29
  weakening of, 157
materialism, 32–33
Maxfield, Robert, 196
Maye, Alexander, 115
Mayr, Ernst, 79, 96–97
McAdam, Doug, 113, 256–57
McDermott, Rose, 99
Mead, George Herbert, 34, 38, 51–52
  evolutionary epistemology and, 88–89
  Symbolic Interactionism and, 53
means of production, 85–86
mediating institutions, 140
memes, 100–1
Mendel, Gregor, 79
mercantilism, 22, 231
Merkel, Angela, 67, 238, 263
metaphysics, 48
  Aristotelian metaphysics, 49–50
  Peirce and, 52
  process metaphysics, 54–55
  substance metaphysics, 48–49
meta-stability, 3, 36–37, 47, 78
  epistemic meta-stable conditions, 291
  propensity for, 264
  of social orders, 191
microsociology, 57–58
Middle East crisis, 194–95
mild realism, 271–72
military power, 141–42
Modelski, George, 35
moderate realism, 68
modern synthesis, 79–81
Morgan, Conway Lloyd, 51–52, 85
morphogenesis theory, 216
MOSAIC, 17
multilevel global governance, 6–7, 21, 138, 150–53
multilevel international orders, 6–7
multinational corporations, 28, 189–90
multiple modernities, 154–55
multiplicity of social orders, 19
mutations, 94
mutual engagement, 20

Nakagami, Teruaki, 204–5
Nakamoto, Satoshi, 177
National Security Agency (NSA), 177, 184, 227
national security communities, 17
nationalism, 6–7, 239
  authoritarian-populist, 22
  in Europe, 154
  liberal, 14–15, 287, 289–90
  populist nationalism, 15–16
  in US, 154
NATO. *See* North Atlantic Treaty Organization
natural evolution, 162–63
natural selection, 78–81, 91, 165
  artificial, 82–83
  contingency and, 84
naturalization, 254
nature, 36
Nelson, Richard R., 97–98
Nemeth, Charlan J., 224
neoliberalism, 234–35
Netscape, 17
Network Working Group (NWG), 199
networks, 41–42, 113

Neufeld, Mark, 274
new institutionalism, 256, 260
Newton, Isaac, 50
Nexon, Daniel H., 59–60, 160, 303
Nicolaïdis, Kalypso, 232
Nicolini, Davide, 131, 271
Nietzsche, Friedrich, 50–51, 73, 180–81
non-equilibrium, 47, 51, 106
nonlinearity, 193
  nonlinear change, 38, 102–3, 105–6
  nonlinear interactions, 195
normativity, 270–72, 303. *See also* ethical normativity
  background knowledge, normative changes in, 220
  better practices, normative theoretical exploration of, 275–83
  bounded progress, normative theoretical exploration of, 275–83
  cognitive evolution theory, normative theoretical claims of, 40–41
  epistemic practical authority, normative appeals and, 250
  international social orders, normative content of, 148
  Korsgaard on, 276–77
  normative content, 130–34
  normative power, 239
  normative practices, 128, 132
  normative structures, 126
  normative theorizing, 2
North Atlantic Treaty Organization (NATO), 244–45, 248, 250
NSA. *See* National Security Agency
NSDD-145 (presidential directive), 17
nuclear weapons, 139–40
  nuclear arms control, 131, 172–73, 196
  nuclear-deterrence theory, 71
NWG. *See* Network Working Group

Olsen, Johan P., 140
On Distributed Communications (Baran), 221–22
Onuf, Nicholas, 64
open-source communities, 17, 176–77, 192
  hacking and, 221
  resilience of, 192–93
operating systems, 154
Operation Orchard (Israel), 240
operational risk, 229–30
Orbán, Viktor, 245
organic growth, 84
Organization for Security and Co-operation in Europe (OSCE), 248
organizational analysis, 59–60
organizational routines, 97–98
organizations, 26
OSCE. *See* Organization for Security and Co-operation in Europe

packet switching, 16, 28
Padgett, John, 37
paradigms, 93
Parmenides, 45, 48–49
Parsons, Talcott, 86
path-dependence theories, 98
Patterson, Orlando, 222, 234, 246–47
Peirce, Charles, 38, 51–52, 69, 86–87
performative power, 3, 18–19, 30, 111–12, 265, 270–71, 298
  anchoring practices and, 140
  cognitive evolution theory and, 177–78
  communities of practice and, 187
  contingent nature of, 27
performativity, 111, 178–79, 201, 211, 237–38
personal computers, 17
personal shareholder liability, 147
Petersen, Michael Bang, 99
The Phenomenology of Spirit (Hegel), 280
Phillips, Andrew, 159–60
Philpott, Daniel, 161
physical and social environments, 240–41
physical objects, 66
physical reality, 65
Pihlström, Sami, 46
Pinker, Steven, 134
Pirsig, Robert, 279
Planck, Max, 51
Plato, 49, 69
Poland, 15–16
policy-makers, 171
politics, 21–23, 166–95, 270–71, 299–300
  of competence, 30
  evolutionary theoretical understandings of, 33
  political authority, 159
  political context, 244–45
  political orders, 122
  political problems, 165
polities, 26, 189
Popper, Karl, 38, 48–50, 63, 68–71, 92–93
populism, 154, 230, 297
positive feedback, 3
positivism, 32–33, 41–42
Postel, Jon, 182–83, 199
postmodern theory, 38–40
post-structural theory, 38–40
post-truth, 41, 289–90, 293–94

postwar European social order, 7, 14–15, 167
  interconnectedness in, 22–23
  novel integrative practices and, 28–29
potentialities, 53
Pouliot, Vincent, 33, 97, 126–27, 138, 303
Powell, Walter W., 256–57, 260
power stratification, 112
power transitions, 156–57
practical democracy, 268–69, 290–94
practical knowledge, 46
practical life, 222
practical meaning fixation, 3–4
practical rationality, 211
practical reason, 198–99
practice matters, 19, 117
practice rules, 144
practice theory, 62, 109
  fields and, 121
  philosophical roots of, 118
practices, 26, 41–42, 109–10. *See also* anchoring practices; better practices
  background knowledge and, 19
  better practices, 150–51
  boundary practices, 225–26
  cognitive evolution theory and, 140
  communities of practice, replication of practices of, 217
  communities of practice as containers of practices, 119–20
  cooperative-security practices, 248, 250
  corporate practices, 26, 128–29, 246, 282
  cybercriminal practices, 128–29
  cybersecurity practices, 172
  Dewey on, 118–19
  environmental practices, 131
  epistemic practical authority and, 27–44
  epistemological dimension of, 19–20
  ethical normativity and, 270–75
  ethics and, 40–41
  global terrorist practices, 230
  habits and, 110
  inequality practices, 140–41
  learning and, 19
  legal practices, 244
  new fields of, 183
  normative practices, 128, 132
  novel or transformed, 27
  practical knowledge and, 46
  practice-driven changes, 4
  primacy of, 118–19
  recursive action and, 109–15
  selective retention of, 28–29, 129–30, 167
  social orders, practice-based conception of, 122–27
  social orders and, 127–28
  social orders as configurations of, 22
  in state of non-equilibrium, 47
  subordinate epistemic practices, 128
  Swidler and, 127
  technology and, 123
pragmatic constructivism, 33–34
pragmatic realism, 39, 71–76
pragmatism, 41–42, 116. *See also* American pragmatism
  Aristotle and, 49–50
  Bourdieu and, 121–22
  early pragmatists, 107
  pragmatist ethics, 272–75
  pragmatist "fallibility," 92
  pragmatist psychologists, 91–92
  social cognition and, 115–16
  theory of action of, 118–19
Prigogine, Ilya, 51, 106–7, 234
primitivism, 84
private equity firms, 172–73
Process and Reality (Whitehead), 53–54
Process Metaphysics (Rescher), 54–55
process philosophy, 45, 54–56, 75
process-oriented ontology, 25–26, 39
processual informal capacity, 27–44
propensities, 23, 47, 223, 266
  for meta-stability, 264
  as objective processes, 69
  world of, 70
propensity theory, 45–46, 49–50, 63, 68–71
  Popper and, 69
protean power, 223
psychogenesis, 59
psychological explanations, 217–18
punctuated equilibrium, 95, 257
Putin, Vladimir, 230–31
Putnam, Hilary, 39, 71–72

Al Qaeda, 230
quantum theory, 51, 68

ratchet effect, 192
rational choice institutionalism, 255–56, 260
rational choice theories, 39, 214–15
rational-choice explanations, 13–14
Ratner, Hilary Horn, 192
Raustiala, Kal, 142–43
Rawls, Anne, 133
reach, 242–52
reactionary right, 268
Reagan, Ronald, 17
realism, 276–77
realist evolutionary theories, 33
reality, competing understandings of, 160–61
reciprocal mutual engagement, 221

reciprocity, 133, 174–75, 237, 280–81
recognition, 3, 280
recursive action, 109–15
reflective endorsement, 276–77
reflexivity, 29–30, 117, 119, 198–99, 206–7
  agential processual social mechanisms and, 204–5
  change through, 215
  habits and, 205–6
  reflexive reification, 253
regime complexes, 143–44
regional orders, 137–39
regionalism, 152
regularities, 126, 235–42
reification, 114, 170
relational realism, 63
relational sociology, 59–60
relativism, 41–42
repertoire of communal resources, 20
replication, 26, 165–66
  communities of practice, replication of practices of, 217
  communities of practice and, 26
  horizontal, 31, 242–43
  vertical, 31, 242–43, 250–51
Rescher, Nicholas, 49, 52–53
  evolutionary theory and, 55–56
  process philosophy and, 54–55, 75
resilience, 3, 188–89, 192–93
  agential processual social mechanisms and, 199
  of open-source communities, 192–93
  selective retention and, 261–64
Reus-Smit, Christian, 64, 143–44, 159, 161
Richards, Robert, 94–95
Richardson, John, 50–51
Richerson, John, 84, 100
risk management, 230
Ritzer, George, 61–62
Roberts, Lawrence, 221–22
The Rome Declaration, 186–87, 205
Rorty, Richard, 273, 293
Rouse, Joseph, 132
Ruggie, John Gerard, 8, 142–44, 154, 159
rule of law, 154–55

Sagan, Carl, 13
samurai crab, 13–14, 46
San Bernardino, California, terrorist attack in, 187
Santa Fe Institute, 102–8
Sarotte, Mary Alise, 194
Schatzki, Theodore R., 74, 122, 126, 131, 183–84, 208
Schelling, Friedrich, 50
Schrödinger, Erwin, 69
Schumpeter, Joseph, 97
scientific knowledge, 231, 289–90
  background scientific knowledge, 298
  consensual, 286, 289
  epistemological insecurity and, 292
scientific realism, 36
scientific revolutions, 93
Searle, John, 18, 45, 63–64, 73, 236
  background knowledge and, 111
  on construction of social reality, 65–68
  deontic power and, 67, 297
  on intention, 207–8
  world-to-mind direction of fit, 30, 207–8, 212–13
Second Law of Thermodynamics, 106
security communities, 203
selection processes
  communities of practice, differential selection in and among, 166
  creativity and, 89
  epistemic-practical-authority selection dynamics, 235–42
  Richards on, 95
  social reality, construction of, and, 37
selective retention, 4, 30, 36, 89–90, 94–95, 167
  of background knowledge, 167
  creative variation and, 30, 102, 219
  epistemic practical authority and, 4, 27
  epistemic practical selective retention, 234–35
  homeorrhesis and, 261–64
  of innovation, 31
  institutionalization and, 252–55
  of practices, 28–29, 129–30, 167
  resilience and, 261–64
  of social orders, 25
  in space and time, 217
self-awareness, 206–7
self-determination, 232
self-organization, 105
self-organizing collectivities, 2
Seybert, Lucia, 4, 223
Shapcott, Richard, 274
shareholders, 7–8, 24, 147
Simmel, Georg, 60–63
Simon, Herbert, 206
site ontology, 74
slavery, 270
Sloman, Steven, 242–43
Smith, Adam, 270
Snowden, Edward, 200, 228, 249
Snowden disclosures, 178, 182–83, 185
social action, 117, 119–21

social cognition, 2
  cognitive evolution theory and, 116–17
  evolutionary approach to, 35–36
  pragmatism and, 115–16
social constructivism, 32–33, 45
social creation, 4
social Darwinism, 85
social dissonance, 161
social engagement, 52
social entities, 45
social facts, 65–66, 68
social figurations, 113
social heredity, 90–91
social innovation, 221
social institutions, 252
social orders, 74–75, 117, 144. *See also* international social orders
  agency and, 123
  agential processual social mechanisms and, 29–30
  becoming ontology and, 124
  change in, 47
  classic meanings of, 22
  communities of practice and, 28, 123–24
  as configurations of practices, 22
  constructivist evolutionary theory of social ordering, 25
  creative variation, birth of new social orders and, 226–33
  in decline, 166
  epistemic practical authority of, 23
  evolution of, 26, 29–30, 185
  fields of practices and, 122, 126, 144
  merits associated with concept of, 125–27
  meta-stability of, 191
  normative content of, 130–34
  politics and, 21
  practice-based conception of, 122–27
  practices and, 127–28
  resilience of, 188–89
  selective retention of, 25
  stability of, 191
  in state of non-equilibrium, 47
  transformation of, 103
social power, 125, 165, 187, 235–36
  coercive forms of, 160–61
  cognitive evolution and, 207
  cognitive evolution theory and, 284
  horizontal accountability and, 173
  manifestation of, 176
social practices, 32
social quantum theory, 39
social reality, 37, 57, 74–75, 125, 277
  collective intentionality and, 175
  interactive understanding of, 37
  organization and management of, 173
  Searle on construction of social reality, 65–68
Social Science History Association, 61
social selection, 91
social structures, 120–21, 216
social world, 62, 102–5
sociality, 89
socialization, 203
socially constituted knowledge, 32
sociobiology, 91
sociocultural evolution, 8
sociology, 56, 84
  microsociology, 57–58
  relational sociology, 59–60
solidarism, 152
Solingen, Etel, 158
sovereignty, 156
Spencer, Herbert, 84–85
Sperber, Dan, 101, 246
Spruyt, Hendrik, 35, 158
stability, 1, 29, 126. *See also* meta-stability
  change and, 36–37, 39
  permanent fluctuations and, 25–26
  of social orders, 191
static quality, 279
status function, 66–67
Stein, Janice, 205–6
Steinmo, Sven, 100, 259, 261
Sterling-Folker, Jennifer, 162
Stokes, Geoff, 92–93
Strange, Susan, 142–43
strategic action fields, 113, 161
strategic interaction, 171
Streeck, Wolfgang, 258
structural makeup, 26
structural social mechanisms and processes, 181–90
structuralism, 62
structuration theory, 42, 213, 215–16
structure-agency, 34–35, 197
Stuurman, Siep, 277–78
Stuxnet attack, 240
subordinate epistemic practices, 128
surveillance-industrial complex, 247
survival of the fittest, 85–86, 165
Swidler, Ann, 109–15, 127, 129
symbolic interactionism, 53
Syrian refugee crisis, 23, 194–95, 245

Tallinn Manual Process, 145, 247
Taylor, Charles, 73, 126, 131–32, 279–80
Taylor, Robert, 221–22
TCP. *See* Transmission Control Protocol
technocratic competences, 190

technology, 4, 96
  impact of, 240
  practices and, 123
territoriality, 156
terrorism, 187, 226, 230
Thelen, Kathleen, 258
Thérien, Jean-Philippe, 33, 97
thresholds, 193–94, 205
  intersubjective cognitive thresholds, 179, 188, 234
Tilly, Charles, 61–63
Toffler, Alvin, 106
Tolbert, P. S., 256
Tomasello, Michael, 192
Toope, Stephen J., 244
Torvalds, Linus, 192, 203–9
Toulmin, Stephen, 38, 91–92, 94, 278
Toynbee, Arnold, 85
transactionalism, 60
transactions, 150
  cognitions in social transactions, 116
  Dewey on, 52–53, 126–27
  interactions/transactions, 126–27
transcendental idealism, 50
transcendental values, 4–5, 266, 268–69
translation, 30–31, 246–47
translation of meanings, 226
Transmission Control Protocol (TCP), 16–17, 241–42, 249
transnational network, 235
transnational polities, 189
transportation, 271
Treaty of Rome, 28–29, 186–87
tribalism, 154
Trump, Donald, 15–16, 158, 175, 228–29, 292, 299–300
  mercantilism and, 231
  NATO and, 250
truth-and-reconciliation committees, 226–27
Tsipras, Alexis, 238
Turner, Victor, 179
Twitter, 182

UK. *See* United Kingdom
UN. *See* United Nations
uniformity, 20
United Kingdom (UK), 148, 188–89
United Nations (UN), 142
  Universal Declaration of Human Rights, 266–77
United States (U.S.), 18, 140–41
  Great Depression, 169
  material power of, 158, 228–29
  nationalism in, 154
Universal Declaration of Human Rights (UN), 266–77
Uruguay, 22
U.S. *See* United States
usury, 147

values and norms, 200–1, 223
Veblen, Thorstein, 96–97
Venezuela, 22
vertical accountability, 113
vertical forms of power, 23
vertical political differentiation, 35
vertical replication, 31, 242–43, 250–51
vertical systems of rule, 5–6, 291
Victor, David G., 142–43
Voice over Internet Protocol (VoIP), 177
voluntarism, 276–77
Vygotsky, Lev, 115–16

Waddington, C. H., 261–62
Waltz, Kenneth, 288, 296
Walzer, Michael, 273–74, 277–78
WarGames (1983), 17
Weber, Max, 57
Weldes, Jutta, 64
Wendt, Alexander, 33–35, 39, 163, 204–5, 296
Wenger, Etienne, 2, 112, 122, 172, 202, 252–53
  communities of practice and, 18, 20
  on horizontal accountability, 173
  on reification, 170
  on socialization, 203
Western Balkans, 245
Whitehead, Alfred North, 53–54
Wight, Martin, 300
Wikipedia, 185
Will, Frederick, 271–72
Williams, G. C., 79
Wilson, E. O., 91
Winter, Sidney G., 97–98
Wittgenstein, Ludwig, 73, 129, 133
World 3, 68–72, 74, 92, 200
World Ordering, 9, 295–300, 302–3
World Wide Web, 17, 31, 182, 233, 249
World Wide Web Consortium, 239
Wuthnow, Robert, 241
Wälti, Sonja, 150

Young, Oran, 143, 149

Zerox PARC, 16–17
Zimblatt, Daniel, 281–82
Zucker, Lynne G., 256
Zürn, Michael, 150, 236

Cambridge Studies in International Relations

132 NUNO P. MONTEIRO *Theory of unipolar politics*

131 JONATHAN D. CAVERLEY *Democratic militarism* Voting, wealth, and war

130 DAVID JASON KARP *Responsibility for human rights* Transnational corporations in imperfect states

129 FRIEDRICH KRATOCHWIL *The status of law in world society* Meditations on the role and rule of law

128 MICHAEL G. FINDLEY, DANIEL L. NIELSON and J. C. SHARMAN *Global shell games* Experiments in transnational relations, crime, and terrorism

127 JORDAN BRANCH *The cartographic state* Maps, territory, and the origins of sovereignty

126 THOMAS RISSE, STEPHEN C. ROPP and KATHRYN SIKKINK *(eds.) The persistent power of human rights* From commitment to compliance

125 K. M. FIERKE *Political self-sacrifice* Agency, body and emotion in international relations

124 STEFANO GUZZINI *The return of geopolitics in Europe?* Social mechanisms and foreign policy identity crises

123 BEAR F. BRAUMOELLER *The great powers and the international system* Systemic theory in empirical perspective

122 JONATHAN JOSEPH *The social in the global* Social theory, governmentality and global politics

121 BRIAN C. RATHBUN *Trust in international cooperation* International security institutions, domestic politics and American multilateralism

120 A. MAURITS VAN DER VEEN *Ideas, interests and foreign aid*

119 EMANUEL ADLER and VINCENT POULIOT *(eds.) International practices*

118 AYŞE ZARAKOL *After defeat* How the East learned to live with the West

117 ANDREW PHILLIPS *War, religion and empire* The transformation of international orders

116 JOSHUA BUSBY *Moral movements and foreign policy*

115 SÉVERINE AUTESSERRE *The trouble with the Congo* Local violence and the failure of international peacebuilding

114 DEBORAH D. AVANT, MARTHA FINNEMORE and SUSAN K. SELL *(eds.) Who governs the globe?*

113 VINCENT POULIOT *International security in practice* The politics of NATO-Russia diplomacy

112 *Columba Peoples Justifying ballistic missile defence* Technology, security and culture

111 PAUL SHARP *Diplomatic theory of international relations*

110 JOHN A. VASQUEZ *The war puzzle revisited*

109 RODNEY BRUCE HALL *Central banking as global governance* Constructing financial credibility

108 MILJA KURKI *Causation in international relations* Reclaiming causal analysis

107 RICHARD M. PRICE *Moral limit and possibility in world politics*

106 EMMA HADDAD *The refugee in international society* Between sovereigns

105 KEN BOOTH *Theory of world security*

104 BENJAMIN MILLER *States, nations and the great powers* The sources of regional war and peace

103 BEATE JAHN *(ed.) Classical theory in international relations*

102 ANDREW LINKLATER and HIDEMI SUGANAMI *The English School of international relations* A contemporary reassessment

101 COLIN WIGHT *Agents, structures and international relations* Politics as ontology

100 MICHAEL C. WILLIAMS *The realist tradition and the limits of international relations*

99 IVAN ARREGUÍN-TOFT *How the weak win wars* A theory of asymmetric conflict

98 MICHAEL BARNETT and RAYMOND DUVALL *(eds.) Power in global governance*

97 YALE H. FERGUSON and RICHARD W. MANSBACH *Remapping global politics* History's revenge and future shock

96 CHRISTIAN REUS-SMIT *(ed.) The politics of international law*

95 BARRY BUZAN *From international to world society?* English School theory and the social structure of globalisation

94 K. J. HOLSTI *Taming the sovereigns* Institutional change in international politics

93 BRUCE CRONIN *Institutions for the common good* International protection regimes in international security

92 PAUL KEAL *European conquest and the rights of indigenous peoples* The moral backwardness of international society

91 BARRY BUZAN and OLE WÑVER *Regions and powers* The structure of international security

90 A. CLAIRE CUTLER *Private power and global authority* Transnational merchant law in the global political economy

89 PATRICK M. MORGAN *Deterrence now*

88 SUSAN SELL *Private power, public law* The globalization of intellectual property rights

87 NINA TANNENWALD *The nuclear taboo* The United States and the non-use of nuclear weapons since 5

86 LINDA WEISS *States in the global economy* Bringing domestic institutions back in

85 RODNEY BRUCE HALL and THOMAS J. BIERSTEKER *(eds.) The emergence of private authority in global governance*

84 HEATHER RAE *State identities and the homogenisation of peoples*

83 MAJA ZEHFUSS *Constructivism in international relations* The politics of reality

82 PAUL K. RUTH and TODD ALLEE *The democratic peace and territorial conflict in the twentieth century*

81 NETA C. CRAWFORD *Argument and change in world politics* Ethics, decolonization and humanitarian intervention

80 DOUGLAS LEMKE *Regions of war and peace*

79 RICHARD SHAPCOTT *Justice, community and dialogue in international relations*

78 PHIL STEINBERG *The social construction of the ocean*

77 CHRISTINE SYLVESTER *Feminist international relations* An unfinished journey

76 KENNETH A. SCHULTZ *Democracy and coercive diplomacy*

75 DAVID HOUGHTON *US foreign policy and the Iran hostage crisis*

74 CECILIA ALBIN *Justice and fairness in international negotiation*

73 MARTIN SHAW *Theory of the global state* Globality as an unfinished revolution

72 FRANK C. ZAGARE and D. MARC KILGOUR *Perfect deterrence*

71 ROBERT O´BRIEN, ANNE MARIE GOETZ, JAN AART SCHOLTE and MARC WILLIAMS *Contesting global governance* Multilateral economic institutions and global social movements

70 ROLAND BLEIKER *Popular dissent, human agency and global politics*

69 BILL MCSWEENEY *Security, identity and interests* A sociology of international relations

68 MOLLY COCHRAN *Normative theory in international relations* A pragmatic approach

67 ALEXANDER WENDT *Social theory of international politics*

66 THOMAS RISSE, STEPHEN C. ROPP and KATHRYN SIKKINK *(eds.) The power of human rights* International norms and domestic change

65 DANIEL W. DREZNER *The sanctions paradox* Economic statecraft and international relations

64 VIVA ONA BARTKUS *The dynamic of secession*

63 JOHN A. VASQUEZ *The power of power politics* From classical realism to neotraditionalism

62 EMANUEL ADLER and MICHAEL BARNETT *(eds.) Security communities*

61 CHARLES JONES *E. H. Carr and international relations* A duty to lie

60 JEFFREY W. KNOPF *Domestic society and international cooperation* The impact of protest on US arms control policy

59 NICHOLAS GREENWOOD ONUF *The republican legacy in international thought*

58 DANIEL S. GELLER and J. DAVID SINGER *Nations at war* A scientific study of international conflict

57 RANDALL D. GERMAIN *The international organization of credit* States and global finance in the world economy

56 N. PIERS LUDLOW *Dealing with Britain* The Six and the first UK application to the EEC

55 ANDREAS HASENCLEVER, PETER MAYER and VOLKER RITTBERGER *Theories of international regimes*

54 MIRANDA A. SCHREURS and ELIZABETH C. ECONOMY *(eds.) The internationalization of environmental protection*

53 JAMES N. ROSENAU *Along the domestic-foreign frontier* Exploring governance in a turbulent world

52 JOHN M. HOBSON *The wealth of states* A comparative sociology of international economic and political change

51 KALEVI J. HOLSTI *The state, war, and the state of war*

50 CHRISTOPHER CLAPHAM *Africa and the international system* The politics of state survival

49 SUSAN STRANGE *The retreat of the state* The diffusion of power in the world economy

48 WILLIAM I. ROBINSON *Promoting polyarchy* Globalization, US intervention, and hegemony

47 ROGER SPEGELE *Political realism in international theory*

46 THOMAS J. BIERSTEKER and CYNTHIA WEBER *(eds.) State sovereignty as social construct*

45 MERVYN FROST *Ethics in international relations* A constitutive theory

44 MARK W. ZACHER with BRENT A. SUTTON *Governing global networks* International regimes for transportation and communications

43 MARK NEUFELD *The restructuring of international relations theory*

42 THOMAS RISSE-KAPPEN *(ed.) Bringing transnational relations back in* Non-state actors, domestic structures and international institutions

41 HAYWARD R. ALKER *Rediscoveries and reformulations* Humanistic methodologies for international studies

40 ROBERT W. COX with TIMOTHY J. SINCLAIR *Approaches to world order*

39 JENS BARTELSON *A genealogy of sovereignty*

38 MARK RUPERT *Producing hegemony* The politics of mass production and American global power

37 CYNTHIA WEBER *Simulating sovereignty* Intervention, the state and symbolic exchange

36 GARY GOERTZ *Contexts of international politics*

35 JAMES L. RICHARDSON *Crisis diplomacy* The Great Powers since the mid-nineteenth century

34 BRADLEY S. KLEIN *Strategic studies and world order* The global politics of deterrence

33 T. V. PAUL *Asymmetric conflicts* War initiation by weaker powers

32 CHRISTINE SYLVESTER *Feminist theory and international relations in a postmodern era*

31 PETER J. SCHRAEDER *US foreign policy toward Africa* Incrementalism, crisis and change

30 GRAHAM SPINARDI *From Polaris to Trident* The development of US Fleet Ballistic Missile technology

29 DAVID A. WELCH *Justice and the genesis of war*

28 RUSSELL J. LENG *Interstate crisis behavior, 1816–1980* Realism versus reciprocity

27 JOHN A. VASQUEZ *The war puzzle*

26 STEPHEN GILL *(ed.) Gramsci, historical materialism and international relations*

25 MIKE BOWKER and ROBIN BROWN *(eds.) From cold war to collapse* Theory and world politics in the 1980s

24 R. B. J. WALKER *Inside/outside* International relations as political theory

23 EDWARD REISS *The strategic defense initiative*

22 KEITH KRAUSE *Arms and the state* Patterns of military production and trade

21 ROGER BUCKLEY *US-Japan alliance diplomacy 1945–1990*

20 JAMES N. ROSENAU and ERNST-OTTO CZEMPIEL *(eds.) Governance without government* Order and change in world politics

19 MICHAEL NICHOLSON *Rationality and the analysis of international conflict*

18 JOHN STOPFORD and SUSAN STRANGE *Rival states, rival firms* Competition for world market shares

17 TERRY NARDIN and DAVID R. MAPEL *(eds.) Traditions of international ethics*

16 CHARLES F. DORAN *Systems in crisis* New imperatives of high politics at century's end

15 DEON GELDENHUYS *Isolated states* A comparative analysis

14 KALEVI J. HOLSTI *Peace and war* Armed conflicts and international order 1648–1989

13 SAKI DOCKRILL *Britain's policy for West German rearmament 1950–1955*

12 ROBERT H. JACKSON *Quasi-states* Sovereignty, international relations and the third world

11 JAMES BARBER and JOHN BARRATT *South Africa's foreign policy* The search for status and security 1945–1988

10 JAMES MAYALL *Nationalism and international society*

9 WILLIAM BLOOM *Personal identity, national identity and international relations*

8 ZEEV MAOZ *National choices and international processes*

7 IAN CLARK *The hierarchy of states* Reform and resistance in the international order

6 HIDEMI SUGANAMI *The domestic analogy and world order proposals*

5 STEPHEN GILL *American hegemony and the Trilateral Commission*

4 MICHAEL C. PUGH *The ANZUS crisis, nuclear visiting and deterrence*

3 MICHAEL NICHOLSON *Formal theories in international relations*

2 FRIEDRICH V. KRATOCHWIL *Rules, norms, and decisions* On the conditions of practical and legal reasoning in international relations and domestic affairs

1 MYLES L. C. ROBERTSON *Soviet policy towards Japan* An analysis of trends in the 1970s and 1980s